W9-ASG-063

THE VICTORY GARDEN LANDSCAPE GUIDE

PRINCIPAL PHOTOGRAPHY
DAVID M. STONE
LITTLE, BROWN
AND COMPANY
BOSTON TORONTO

BY

THOMAS WIRTH

WITH THE ASSISTANCE OF

JAY HOWLAND

To the memory of my maternal grandmother, Louise Schwab Schaller, who nurtured my roots at a very early age

Copyright © 1984 by WGBH Educational Foundation and Thomas Wirth

All rights reserved. No part of this book may be reproduced in any form or by any electronic or mechanical means including information storage and retrieval systems without permission in writing from the publisher, except by a reviewer who may quote brief passages in a review.

Published simultaneously in Canada by Little, Brown & Company (Canada) Limited

WAK

Printed in the United States of America

Library of Congress Cataloging in Publication Data

Wirth, Thomas.
The victory garden landscape guide.

Includes index.
1. Landscape gardening. I. Howland, Jay. II. Title.
SB472.W59 1984 635.9 83-24919
ISBN 0-316-94845-4
ISBN 0-316-94846-2 (pbk.)

635.9
W799v

ACKNOWLEDGMENTS

I am greatly indebted to Russell Morash — originator, producer, and director of the PBS "Victory Garden" series. Russ provides the stimuli and atmosphere needed to bring out the best in those around him, and by example sets the highest standards of artistry and do-it-yourselfism. Jay Howland put forth a tremendous effort as writer in the preparation of this book, and I am certain it would never have been completed without her. Jay transformed my nearly illegible scribbles and sketches into logical order and readable English, always capturing the essence of what I was trying to say. William D. Phillips, senior editor at Little, Brown, was an uncompromising and enthusiastic supporter during the growth of the book. His acute sense of purpose kept everyone in focus and made us all feel good about hard work. Bill passed the baton to Laura Fillmore during the concluding phase, and it was she who gave the content a much-needed final pruning and reordering. Jack Foley of the WGBH design department is responsible for the design of the book. He masterminded the format to incorporate artfully a voluminous mass of information, photographs, and drawings. David Stone took most of the wonderful photographs — and became less terrified of knocking on strange doors as time progressed. And Marianne Orlando added her fine hand to produce the expert illustrations.

Many of my professional friends at Sasaki Associates provided receptive ears and responsive suggestions. Joe Hibbard was particularly helpful during the early stages, and Paul Gardescu urged simplicity and the concept of landscape as space — ideas I hope I have succeeded in communicating. Mas Kinoshita, my mentor for nearly a decade, whose holistic approach to design is contagious, is present in many places in this book. My friends at universities, arboretums, and nurseries across the country, too many to mention, have been most generous teachers over the years. I did call on Wayne Mezitt of Weston Nurseries in Hopkinton, Massachusetts, and William Flemmer III of Princeton Nurseries in Princeton, New Jersey, to review preliminary plant lists, and I am grateful for their many suggestions.

I cannot omit all the people at Little, Brown, from Mike Mattil, the tireless copy editor, to Peter Carr, who was in charge of manufacturing the book. Or Don Cutler of the Sterling Lord Agency, literary agent for WGBH, with whom I had long discussions early on about the original outline for *The Victory Garden Landscape Guide*. This book has also benefited indirectly from the generosity of George J. Ball, Incorporated, and of Public Television stations, who together sponsor the "Victory Garden" television series.

And finally, a tribute to my family: Helene, my wife, who has labored to keep the larder full while I was writing, and our five children. Each has good reason to feel that this book is partly theirs, too.

29494

CONTENTS

INTRODUCTION

The "Victory Garden" series first aired on public television back in 1975. Originally titled "Crockett's Victory Garden," it began as a show dedicated to growing vegetables. Its setting was a garden in Boston, Massachusetts, right outside the studios of WGBH-TV. Its heart and soul was Jim Crockett, an inspiring gardener and a man much loved by all who were lucky enough to know him — whether in person or through the television series. His knowledgeable successor as host is Bob Thompson, and with Bob at the helm "The Victory Garden" is going strong, watched by millions of viewers every growing season.

Over the years the show has broadened its scope to embrace everything from houseplants to flowers to greenhouse culture to landscaping, in addition to the garden vegetables that were the foundation for the whole thing. And four books have grown out of the series: *Crockett's Victory Garden*, *Crockett's Indoor Garden*, *Crockett's Flower Garden*, and *Crockett's Tool Shed.*

In many ways this book follows the lead of the volumes that preceded it. Like both the books and the show, *The Victory Garden Landscape Guide* responds to Americans' enthusiasm for gardening and their fascination with the natural environment. And as Jim Crockett's and Bob Thompson's involvement grew out of their respective personal backgrounds, I have come to the "Victory Garden" show and to this book from a lifetime of working in the landscape both as a professional and for my own pleasure.

Growing up in rural Pennsylvania, I started gardening with my grandmother in a patch all my own at the age of six. At an early age I also started observing and enjoying the structure of the landscape. There was an old stone tower on a hill in a nearby state park, and I often climbed up and looked out over rolling fields of different crops, contoured ribbons of green and gold, dotted with stone farmhouses and barns. I loved the sight. I was an active 4-H club member, too, and each summer we would travel to the state university for vegetable-judging contests. One of these was held, coincidentally, at the landscape architecture department; and I'll never forget that day. I was totally distracted from the vegetables by the terrific drawings and photographs on display. Then and there I decided that a landscape architect was what I wanted to be, that the built environment fascinated me as much as the natural one.

I spent four and a half years studying horticulture and landscape design at Rutgers University, and two studying landscape architecture at the University of Michigan. Meanwhile I worked at jobs ranging from sod farming to landscape contracting to maintaining landscapes at New York World's Fair pavilions, along with several stints in professional offices. All this hands-on experience led to a long-term position as a member of the firm of Sasaki Associates in Watertown, Massachusetts, where I was part of many teams that designed and oversaw the construction of landscaping projects all over the country.

I still do a great deal of building. It was while I was in the midst of turning a huge old 1800 barn into a family home (which now houses five kids, a very busy wife, four cats, and a dog) that WGBH-TV asked me to appear on another television series, called "This Old House." I've designed and supervised several on-camera landscape transformations for that series, and whenever a special landscaping opportunity comes up on "The Victory Garden" I happily step in. On the show we have tackled many of the challenges facing homeowners: small spaces, steep banks, shady areas . . . in fact, this book grew from all the possible situations we felt our audience might encounter in their own landscapes.

This book is for everyone, from the city apartment-dweller to the suburbanite to the owner of wide-open rural spaces. One of my central themes here is that *any* place can benefit from thoughtful planning, well-informed choices of plants and construction materials, and the application of a few imaginative ideas. And you may be surprised — even if all you have is a stoop or a small backyard — at how many good ideas you have once you start learning how to think about landscaping.

As with the other Victory Garden books, the major part of *The Victory Garden Landscape Guide* (Part II, The Landscaping Year) has a calendar format that follows the twelve months of the year. Each month's entries look at aspects of landscape design, plantings, construction, and maintenance that are in keeping with that season. The twelve-month structure, first adopted in *Crockett's Victory Garden*, has proved tremendously helpful in all the Victory Garden books, but especially in the *Landscape Guide*: it breaks a large and complex subject into manageable, accessible areas of interest.

Yet in many ways *The Victory Garden Landscape Guide* departs from the pattern set by its predecessors both in subject matter and in treatment. A landscape is an entire environment for living, very different from a vegetable patch, a flower bed, or a greenhouse. And a landscape matures not over a summer but over a lifetime. Trees, shrubs, vines, and ground covers can be a big job to plant. Some trees and shrubs grow to a huge size, and they can live for dozens or hundreds of years; deciding what to plant becomes a long-term design decision, not a springtime experiment. Besides, most of these plants are fully as important in the landscape in the dead of winter as they are in spring and summer. The same is true of landscape construction: it's large scale, permanent, and a year-round fixture of the place where you live.

The complexity of the subject has called for yet another departure from Victory Garden tradition — Part I of this book. I have not plunged straight into the first month of the landscaping year, as the earlier books did, but have begun instead with an introductory section, Landscaping Essentials, which provides a brief primer on landscape design. Its goals are to open your eyes, stir your imagination, help you answer some important questions, alert you to some pitfalls, and assist you in setting priorities and making workable plans.

Part I is designed to help you see the possibilities of your situation by perceiving the world in landscaping terms and approaching your project (or problem) with an informed attitude. Basic principles and broad guidelines are the subject in Part I. Part II, on the other hand, invites you to roam from month to month, finding the particular items that pertain to your situation. There are assorted "Landscaping Opportunities" to consider: city gardens, the look of your garden in winter, and easy-maintenance landscaping are among them. There are suggestions and plant lists for all purposes and circumstances as well as monthly maintenance tasks and horticultural projects suited to different seasons. I'll introduce you to all kinds of landscape construction challenges — drainage, stairs, walks, and decks — and to the materials you'll use in building.

Being a successor to *Crockett's Victory Garden* and *Crockett's Flower Garden*, this book tries to build on, not duplicate, much of the specific gardening advice those books contained. For instance, while I heartily endorse the making of compost heaps and the use of compost as soil enrichment and/or mulch, I won't repeat here the excellent composting instructions given in *Crockett's Victory Garden*. Rather than reiterating planting and cultivation information that has already been well covered, I'll focus on ways to use plants in the larger setting; and I'll deal primarily with plants that have not appeared in the previous volumes.

As for prescribing solutions to landscape design problems, this book steers clear of ready-made formulas. Throughout the book I'll look at varied settings, present data about construction materials and their uses, and suggest a wide range of plants to meet given needs. I'll introduce you to the landscape's components and offer you the tools and procedural guidelines for forming them into an environment you can enjoy. Perhaps you're interested in putting some container plants on your patio or grouping shrubs to soften the edge of a lawn. Or maybe you want to redesign and rebuild your backyard from the ground up, put in a terrace, establish a hedge, even install an ornamental pool or fountain. You can find ideas for all these situations here. Browse and investigate. The search for solutions is always exciting, and the final achievement yet more so.

Drafting a chapter at my outdoor table in the shade of young red oaks transplanted from nearby woods.

PART I LANDSCAPING ESSENTIALS

Since the beginnings of time, people have yearned to organize and beautify their surroundings. And probably since the beginnings of time (certainly throughout my experience), people have felt some degree of insecurity or anxiety about their ability to do it. Yet in a very fundamental way, it is precisely the people who inhabit a landscape who are best qualified to decide how it could best function, look, and feel.

One of my chief aims is to convince you that you *can* design an improvement to your property — or a whole new landscape — if you go slowly and learn to look around you. The slowness, the process, is as important as the final product. There's no great mystery about shaping your environment, once you grasp the basic principles of design and composition and come to terms with your raw materials: the soil, the climate, the plants and other material you have at hand.

Landscape design is at once fine art, applied art, and natural science. It combines the disciplines and the fascination of all three. A well-conceived and well-made landscape will be beautiful to all the senses (that's fine art); comfortable and functional in its plantings, structures, and spatial arrangements (that's applied art); and energy-efficient, not too demanding of maintenance, and healthily self-sustaining (that's science). Partly because landscaping is a combination of arts and sciences, and partly because it's a large and long-term assignment, it is natural to feel a little timid about it. But every one of us has the instincts required. A landscaping project is eye-opening to do, rewarding when completed. And it is great fun.

Opposite: early-flowering Korean azalea brightens the border planting at the lawn edge, while shadblow blooms in the background.

1 THE ELEMENTS OF DESIGN

Opposite: Landscape masses: (A) Space is well defined by enclosing elements. (B) Space leaks out with removal of background mass. (C) Removing canopy destroys space. (D) Cluttering or overfilling dilutes space.

The terminology of design is really nothing more than a specialized shorthand, a series of code words used to label qualities of objects or spaces. Happily, in landscape design, the objects and the spaces — and their qualities — are all part of everyone's daily experience. So learning the language is no problem.

This chapter is partly an extended glossary, to let you know what I mean when I use any given term, and partly a preview of the applications of these elements of design. I'll often mention issues to bear in mind and questions to ask as you go about designing, redesigning, or modifying your landscape.

The five elements of design are *mass*, *form*, *line*, *texture*, and *color*. A glance out your window will afford you with examples of all five. It will probably also suggest to you why mass, form, and line are the essence of landscape design — and how texture and color reinforce and enrich the effects created by the first three. In a landscape, mass, form, and line are the cake; texture and color are the frosting.

Mass Mass is volume of space, whether occupied or empty. Every object in the landscape has mass: your house, the trees and shrubs and structures around it, everything that rests on or emerges from the ground plane. Empty space has mass too, for the purposes of landscape design, because the volumes of spaces have to be related to the volumes of objects in and around them.

Visualize for a moment a three-story Victorian house set in front of a wooded area, with a huge evergreen hedge to one side, a shrub border on the other, a stone wall across the front of the lot — and a single

The dominant mass is "negative space" defined by the hollow in the ground, the backdrop of greenery, and the overarching tree limbs.

Orlando
A.
B.
C.
D.

Here, the positive volume of the house is the all-important mass. Newly planted trees and shrubs will play bigger roles as they mature.

magnificent sugar maple in the front lawn. The masses of the house and the sugar maple live happily in the mass of space defined by the encircling hedge, shrubbery, woods, and wall. But alter any one of these components and you will significantly alter the spatial relationships of the whole picture. For instance, removing the woods or the evergreen hedge will allow the space around the house to leak out, so to speak, in all directions. Removing the sugar maple will make the house seem overpowering. Filling the space between the house and the tree with other plantings or structures will dilute the power of the composition by breaking up one mass: the mass of space.

Artists speak of positive space (meaning space occupied by tangible objects) and negative space (meaning space occupied by air); and negative space is at least as important as positive. So think of mass as space, and you're on your way to understanding a pivotal element of design.

Masses are obvious and easy to take for granted. The bigger they are, the easier it is to forget all about them; and a common mistake when you're starting out is to get involved prematurely in minor things like selecting shrubs, shopping for furniture, planning details of a fence or a flight of steps. But none of those details will look quite right in the end, if you don't think through the arrangement and balance of your major masses — including spaces — first.

Form Form means shape. We are surrounded by a host of natural and man-made rectangles, squares, circles, ovals, triangles. Consider the natural geometry of the pyramidal growth of a Norway spruce, not to mention the gables of houses or garages. Circles and ovals? Look at the natural egg shapes of cedar trees, the plump forms of rhododendrons, the soft rounded line of a hilltop or knoll, the rough shoulder of a rock outcropping. Rectangles and squares are a little trickier to find in nature, but they abound in the structures people build, from walls to terraces to houses.

The forms I've been mentioning are all geometric and more or less regular; you could plot their outlines mathematically. What about free forms, those flowing irregular shapes that are far more common in nature than the geometric ones? Free forms are a tantalizing subject, because while there has been a great vogue for their use in gardens and landscapes over the last century or two, they're the hardest of all forms to use successfully in landscape design. Done with sophistication and skill, free-form designs can convey a feeling that is marvellously casual, naturalistic, and, well, free. Done without sophistication or skill, they can convey a feeling that is merely confused.

And it's not only free forms that convey feelings. Every kind of form carries with it a collection of associations based on everyday human experience, and those associations arouse age-old emotional responses. (The table here lists a few.) Forms actually affect the way you feel as you live, work, and play in your landscape.

Forms

Form	*Association*	*Emotional connotation*
Circle	Egg, breast, ball, wheel	Soft, quiet, perfect, unbroken
Square	Block, cube	Stable, rigid, fixed, equal
Rectangle	Box, table, house	Narrow, directed, stable
Triangle	Pyramid, spire, knife	Sharp, strong, tense
Free	Amoeba, blob, squiggle	Loose, casual, undefined, imperfect

So plan your landscape forms carefully. Should they be angular? Four-square? Fat and rounded? Lofty and attenuated? A landscape design consisting of a series of rectangles, for instance, will evoke an altogether different complex of emotions from one that employs ovoid or irregular shapes.

When choosing plants for form, take into account the size and the location of the plant. The soft shapes of dwarf white pine or mugho pine or the rounded cushion of a Sargent weeping hemlock are appealing on an intimate scale; the tall spheres and ovals of maples, beeches, or oaks are grander and must be seen from a distance to be appreciated. (Bear in

Below, left: This man-made curvilinear form has a gentle, flowing shape.

Below, right: The naturally rounded form of cutleaf red Japanese maple also conveys a sense of softness and repose.

mind, too, that many roundish trees branch near the ground, their lowest branches even sweeping the earth if allowed to do so. The effect is pleasant but does take up a lot of space.)

Other tree forms include picturesque types like weeping birches or gnarled, contorted pines; the vase or fan shapes of trees whose branches spread up and out, creating arched spaces beneath; and columnar or fastigiate forms that punctuate the landscape with strong verticals like exclamation points.

With each kind of form, think about its effect not only in itself but in relation to surrounding plantings and structures. There will be some forms you can't change, like the shapes of your house or the neighbors' garage or the wooded lot across the street. Plan the forms on your property to complement and harmonize with what exists; to screen it if necessary; and to suit your own personality and taste.

Line Lines not only define edges and direct the eye; they are an important source of excitement and interest in themselves. Some landscape objects are mainly linear, like fences, driveways, walks, tree trunks and branches, boundaries of plantings or lawns, or the horizon. In winter, in the North, the landscape seems to consist mostly of lines — bare twigs, dry grasses, crisp edges of things. In summer the world leafs out; mass and form and color and texture come into their own; and line ceases to dominate.

As with forms, different kinds of line elicit different emotional responses. Straight lines give a feeling of formality, firmness, repose. Jagged lines and sharp angles suggest tension, excitement, stress. Curved lines are more relaxed and picturesque; irregular curves look "natural." A straight driveway is austere and efficient, whereas a slightly curved one is inviting, even mysterious or romantic.

Haphazard or controlled, rigid or swooping, stark or ornate, lines can distract, entertain, calm, or irritate the eye. Before you choose a picket fence, decide whether that zigzag edge is right for you. If you're

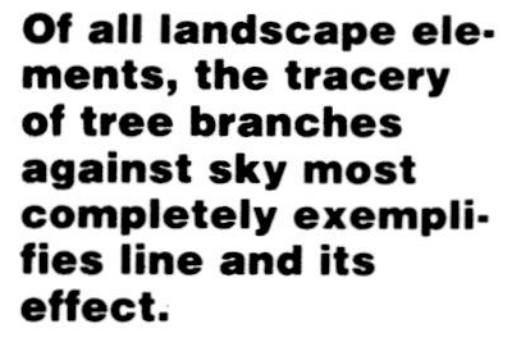

Of all landscape elements, the tracery of tree branches against sky most completely exemplifies line and its effect.

Line applied to man-made structures: strong, crisp lines of wall and pavement echo the architecture and draw the eye to the focal point at the corner of the house.

contemplating adding an S-curve to your drive, visualize how it will go with the lines of the house or the plantings on either side. In a tight site where rectilinear structures prevail, you will generally find it easier to work with square angles and straight lines, or with well-disciplined curves, than with random lines. With more space or in a natural setting, you have more latitude to cultivate free-flowing naturalistic effects.

Texture Visible texture is produced by the play of light and shadow on surfaces. Tangible texture is what you can feel with your hands, your feet, any part of your skin. Texture is perhaps the most sensual element of design, since it appeals to both sight and touch; and yet, like its sister element, color, texture plays only a supporting role in landscaping. It is, for the most part, something to decide on after the large questions of mass, form, and line have been dealt with. Practical considerations (such as slipperiness or tactile comfort) aside for a moment, textures are chiefly of interest for their ability to enhance the major effects you have been working on.

Still, there is much that you can do with texture. A landscape that was completely uniform in texture would be monotonous indeed. Textural variety affords visual relief, drama, even excitement. And since everything in nature, organic and inorganic, has its own texture, achieving this variety is a pleasure. There are countless kinds of grasses in a meadow and ground covers in the woods, and infinite degrees of roughness or smoothness in stone or wood. An herb garden is a perfect example of textural variety. Among the myriad shades of green and the different leaf and stem sizes and shapes, there are dozens of textures, from glossy to velvety to hairy. The textures enrich form, line, and color and create a tapestry of green on green.

Coarse visual textures result from strong contrasts of light and shadow — light washing the topmost surfaces, shadow filling the spaces between — as in a rubblestone wall or the foliage of a large-leaved tree

Pure texture: different particle sizes of washed gravel, boulders, river stones, and exposed-aggregate concrete collect and reflect light in different ways.

like a maple. Coarse textures impart an informal, bold, or rustic feeling. But because they can be uncomfortable to the touch, some coarse landscape textures can also be uneasy to the eye. To many people, rough-textured walks, drives, or seating areas are annoying or even threatening.

Coarse-textured plantings make such a strong statement that they need to be used with discretion. I'd generally recommend using no more than one-third coarse-foliaged trees or shrubs in a residential planting composition. Yet within that limitation, they definitely have a part to play. If you have decided on a shady, wooded corner at the far end of your yard, big-leaved maples or rhododendrons or viburnums (for instance) will add to the bucolic air. You can also use coarse-textured plantings to heighten an impression of perspective, by placing the coarser textures in the foreground and progressively finer ones farther away. Or you can use a single coarse-textured specimen as a focal point.

Texture at work in the landscape: in the Japanese bonsai garden of the National Arboretum, fine foreground textures contrast with the coarser-textured foliage of background plantings.

Fine landscape textures range from uniformly smooth and shiny surfaces to surfaces where there are only minute contrasts between light and shade: a smooth concrete walk, a smoothly finished wooden surface, a fine-leafed shrub like boxwood, a new-mown lawn. They express restraint, refinement, quietude; a neat or even formal feeling. If you want to give an elegant tone to a yard or patio, smooth finishes and fine-textured shrubbery will do the job: plants like small-leaved azaleas, cotoneasters, or spireas.

Finer-textured trees and shrubs often look best planted en masse for maximum impact. This is true, for instance, with birches, willows, spireas, or junipers. Many of these plants naturally tend to grow in clumps, so this is a very logical way to arrange them.

As you think about plant textures for your landscape, don't forget the winter. Evergreens remain the same throughout the year; but the textures of the bare twigs, branches, and trunks of deciduous plants come into their own once the leaves fall. For the most part, you'll find that the texture of the naked plant is closely related to its foliage texture. A Japanese maple's branches and twigs are as fine as its foliage; a red oak, sugar maple, or shagbark hickory has branches as coarse-textured as its leaves.

Color This last of the elements of design is another "secondary" or supporting element, but extremely important both for what it can do and for what it should not do. Used properly, whether as background or

Color, rather than texture, brings this rock garden alive.

as accent, color will enrich the beauty of a landscape. Used improperly, color can be so distracting or abrasive as to ruin an otherwise good design.

If this seems paradoxical, think of photography. A black-and-white photo reveals mass, form, and line, the three linchpins of landscape design. A color photo of the same subject can actually camouflage them. Or think of classical Greek statuary: to people nowadays it is almost distressing to imagine those elegant forms and serene lines decked out in garish pigments, as scholars say they originally were.

The primary colors of landscaping are nature's basic palette: green, brown, and blue. There are the greens and browns of vegetation and soil, and the blue of the sky present everywhere as reflected light. In nature, bright hues are reserved for accent — like the crimson of red-stemmed shrub dogwood or the white of birch bark — and for seasonal fireworks like spring and summer flowers and fall foliage.

Similarly, in a planned landscape the basic colors will be nature's triad of green, brown, and blue; but there's plenty of scope for artistic use of color in year-round accents (whether structures or plantings) and in seasonal displays.

Colors, like forms, lines, and textures, have their own set of emotional associations. Cheerful yellow. Frivolous pink. Businesslike beige. Restful green. Romantic mauve. They also have "temperatures." In an interior, you can warm a room up by painting it peach, or cool it down with blue-gray. Landscape color works the same. You can use pale flowers and bluish foliage to "cool" a hot sunny area, or you can plan for brilliant fall foliage if the autumn is cold where you live. In shady corners, you can plant flowering shrubs or perennials in clear, bright colors. And since cool colors seem to recede and pale colors to enlarge, you can use color to create illusory depth of perspective. A small and crowded garden, for instance, will feel more spacious if pale, cool colors predominate. A feeling of intimacy will result from the use of warmer, more intense colors.

There are a few dos and don'ts to keep in mind when you plan colors for your landscape design. Where flowers are concerned, avoid juxtaposing clashing colors like pink blossoms against red brick masonry, or orange side by side with magenta. And with all landscape plantings — whether leaves, bark, or flowers are the colored element — avoid crowding too many different hues in the same area. Confusion and conflict detract from the beauty of any one color.

White paper birches really sing against a dark-painted house and the dark greens of evergreen shrubs and ground cover.

Compose with autumn foliage color as well as blossom color in mind. Here, white birches, red and yellow maples, and dark green conifers make a beautiful fall triad.

Do consider using large masses of color. For winter effects, think about the soft green of the twigs of a Thurlow willow or the reddish glow of Virginia rose, whose twigs make a dense ground cover. In summer you have the whole palette of flowers and flowering trees and shrubs to work with. Massed blooms of a single color can be magnificent — a bed of pink azaleas, a bank of yellow forsythia. So can a mass of one color next to its complementary color(s), such as blue complemented by oranges and yellows. Or cluster purples, red-violets, and pinks together; or reds, yellow-oranges, and yellows.

To make the most of colored plantings (as with everything else in landscape design), take into account the setting. A contrasting backdrop such as a dark-colored wall or a stand of hemlocks will set off white birches or white flowering dogwoods. For the vivid bark and blooms of an Oriental cherry a light-colored backdrop is better — a white building or an open grassy area. And sunlight has an important impact, whether picking up a haze of golden twigs in wintertime or backlighting the shimmering foliage of beech trees in summer. You can make the light work for you to intensify every chromatic effect.

Mass, form, line, texture, and color. Each element plays a vital part. None can work alone. How effectively you assemble these elements determines how well the overall picture will succeed.

2 PRINCIPLES OF COMPOSITION

To compose means "to put together." Landscape composition puts together plants and all the other elements of a particular scene to make pleasing combinations of masses, forms, lines, textures, and colors. From a visual standpoint, a successful composition is one that brings its different components into harmony and unity. The effect of a well-arranged composition is more than the sum of the effects of the masses, forms, lines, colors, and textures that make it up.

In this chapter I'll try to give you a sense of the underlying principles or rules that make every composition work. I keep these five principles in mind throughout the process of design, and they serve as guidelines or controls for every choice I make. They are *scale, balance, rhythm, emphasis,* and *simplicity.*

Scale Scale means relative size. If something is "out of scale" it's too big or too small for its location and surroundings; if it's "in scale" it is, like the baby bear's chair, just right. Proper scale is absolutely central to landscape design. It is interesting that a concept as easily grasped as scale can also be quite elusive to pin down in practice. It takes a certain amount of experience or training before you feel sure about scale in landscape design: you have to develop an eye for it.

The key to scaling things in the landscape is the human body. This is true because everything that is planted or built in a landscape has to fit the people who will live with it. Human height establishes sight lines — and they in turn decree how high or low a screening hedge or wall should be. Human breadth is the yardstick for the comfortable width of a pathway. Seats, benches, low walls for sitting on, all have to be tailored to the length of human legs. Human paces measure out the proper depth for steps and terraces. The human form determines the dimensions of houses, sheds, and gazebos; and these structures set the scale for the plantings around them.

Foreground elements establish the scale of the vista to Mount Vernon. Without the gate and wall, relative sizes are uncertain.

Bad examples of scale are a lot easier to come up with than good ones. If a picnic table dwarfs a small patio, a giant evergreen overshadows the facade of a house, or a rock garden is lost in the vastness of a formal lawn, an uncomfortable tension results. Very often, when I find myself in a generally pleasant landscape that feels wrong in some undefined way, and I analyze the feeling, I find that what is bothering me is a problem of scale.

Any landscape structure or planting too large or too small for its surroundings is "out of scale" and detracts from the harmony of the composition.

Balance Balance is partly, but not wholly, a matter of scale — because balance has to do not only with the relative sizes of things but with all the other attributes that go to make up their visual "weights" in the landscape. Such attributes include dark versus light colors; massiveness versus delicacy; brightness versus shade; rough textures versus smooth ones; curves versus angles; even noise versus quiet.

What constitutes a well-balanced landscape is partly subjective. For instance, some people are happiest in a very stark, sunny, wide-open environment, while others seek out sheltered grottos of shade and a feeling of great privacy. On the other hand, even an objective outside observer can sense whether the overall composition of a landscape, within its general type, is balanced or unbalanced.

The urge to bring order out of chaos is a deep-seated human instinct, and that's one reason why balance is so important. Also, equilibrium implies a kind of security. It might seem that symmetry would be the easiest route to a balanced landscape composition. After all, if you put two identical weights on a pair of scales, you bring them into balance. Why not just put identical evergreen shrubs on either side of the front door, identical flowering trees at either corner of the lot, and a round pool in the exact middle of the backyard? No, it won't work — at least not with the informal layouts and facades of most American homes. Symmetry is rarely found in the wild landscape, and perhaps for that reason a perfectly symmetrical garden or landscape design has a very strained and

The driveway was moved to this location, where the horizontal mass of the handsome natural rock outcropping will be balanced by the upright mass of spruces planted on the opposite side.

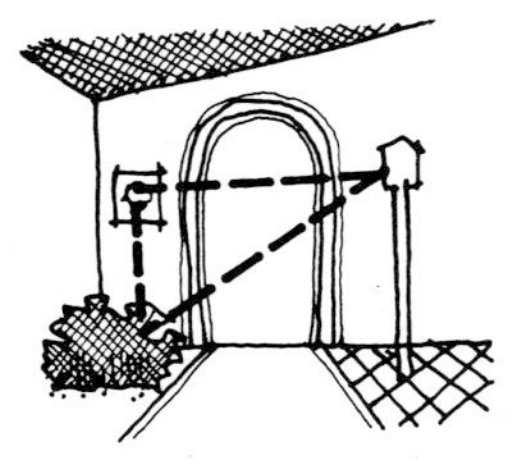

The diagram above and the photo at right show well-balanced composition. The arrangement of flower pot, lamp fixture, and wall sculpture is informal yet carefully planned.

Symmetrical planting at each side of the door is very awkward for this entry approached from one direction. In the second photo, asymmetry in planting and an added step in the landscape make a balanced composition.

stiff feeling, unless it is part of a totally symmetrical larger space. (Symmetry was, of course, the rule in formal gardens from Rome to the Renaissance; but that kind of formality is mostly inappropriate in America today, besides being very demanding and expensive to maintain.) Achieving balance is a more subtle matter, a matter of instinct, experience, and — even for practiced eyes — careful experimentation.

Rhythm Rhythm means the predictably repeated elements in a landscape. A degree of regularity or repetition of masses, forms, lines, textures, and/or colors is necessary to a satisfactory composition. To realize how necessary, think what a hedge would look like if every plant in it were of a separate species. Or imagine a paved walk that combined bricks, paving stones, cobbles, rubblestone, and tiles. Or picture a massed

The key to the effect of this Japanese garden, above, is rhythmic repetition in depth. Gravel mounds and close-clipped yews echo the triangular shapes of the hilltops beyond.

Repetition of form and line: pyramidal branching of weeping hemlock (at left) accompanies the peaked cap of the fence and roof over the gateway. Fence boards and lattice are rhythmic vertical elements.

planting consisting of seventeen different sizes and shapes of trees. Even nature's "massed plantings," otherwise known as woods, are made up of grouped colonies of trees of the same species and similar size.

Excessive repetition can be boring. But there are some things, like pavements, walls, fences, and shrub orders, that really demand a regular, consistent treatment. In a way, rhythm in the landscape has a reassuring effect. The predictable elements in a visual composition, like the predictable patterns in a musical composition, make an expression of unity and completeness.

Emphasis It may be that the single most important factor in a successful composition is the choice and handling of emphasis. Just as a person tries to highlight his or her own best assets, just as a painting must have a central subject or focal point, a landscape should be given a focus or concentration of significance. Emphasis is a way to bring out the latent personality or unique character of a place. Without emphasis, a design can't help but be somewhat bland and characterless.

This is not to say that every family should go overboard and rush out to divert a river into their backyard or construct a monument on their front lawn. Often, giving emphasis to a landscape design is a matter of tact — of gently guiding the eye to the chosen focal point; of allowing an existing feature or quality to assume its natural dominance. The center of emphasis could be an attractively framed doorway, a view of a hill or a pond in the distance, a grand old tree, a charming or interesting piece of sculpture. Emphasis can be developed through bold impact or through subtle enrichment. In a very small garden where the whole thing is treated as a jewel, the garden is its own emphasis. The more sprawling or featureless a landscape, on the other hand, the greater its need for shaping and framing and direction.

Simplicity There are two good reasons why, in landscape design as perhaps nowhere else, "less is more." The first reason is practical:

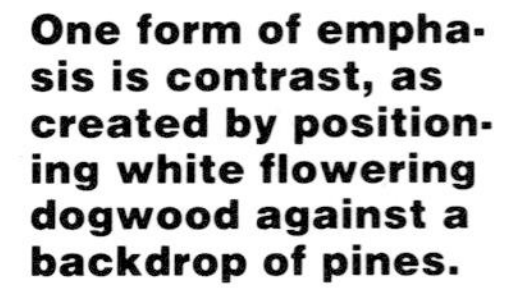

One form of emphasis is contrast, as created by positioning white flowering dogwood against a backdrop of pines.

simplicity saves money, time, and irritating (but hard to undo) mistakes. The second is aesthetic: a simple design is far more likely to work out well than an overly ambitious one.

Even simplicity, of course, can be carried too far. A perfectly flat expanse of green grass is simple, all right, but not much else. Sensitive restraint is the keynote here. A landscape design can achieve an effect of pleasing simplicity by staying away from artificiality or fussy detail; by limiting the variety of different colors, textures, or forms that are used; and by rationing the number of kinds of plants and construction materials. Even within all those constraints, a landscape can be as functional, comfortable, inviting, and richly green or flowery as anyone could wish.

In fact if you think of a landscape you know and enjoy — a landscape you always feel peaceful in — you'll probably discover that it is basically uncomplicated. Maybe there is a nicely settled feeling to the house; maybe the house is framed by one or two big old trees and some reasonably disciplined shrubbery; maybe a sunny side yard is sheltered by a screen of more of the same kind of shrubbery; maybe there is a flower garden behind the house, giving way to woods or an open field with a glimpse of blue distance; maybe a rambling stone wall ties the whole place together. A place like that can be beautifully simple, and simply beautiful.

Simplicity of materials, forms, and lines gives this Bucks County farmhouse landscape great strength and serenity. Note the absence of foundation "landscaping."

As you look at the space around your house and consider ways to refurbish or redesign it, concepts like "balance" and "scale" — basic though they are — may seem rather abstract in relation to the questions you're asking yourself: Where can I clear a level place to sit or play? How do I create a visual boundary for the front lawn, yet still allow sunlight and a sense of openness around the house?

These are really spatial questions. In answering them, you'll move from concepts and principles to more practical structural matters. You'll probably want to spend a lot of time outdoors pacing off distances and envisioning possibilities. Chapter 3 helps you see how to open, enclose, or frame volumes of space in your landscape.

3 THE STRUCTURE OF THE LANDSCAPE

One of the first things many people do to clarify their thoughts when they are planning a space — whether a living room, a vegetable plot, a patio with grouped furniture or container plants, or a roomy front lawn — is to make a rough thumbnail sketch or map of what might go where. This can be a helpful preliminary exercise, but it has one notable limitation for landscape planning: it is two-dimensional. In this chapter I'd like to encourage you to keep thinking about your situation in three-dimensional terms.

A landscape architect tries to form enclosures and openings that relate to each other and to the whole, in much the same way as an architect works out the design of a building. The only real differences (apart from differences of scale and function) have to do with media, since landscape architecture incorporates not only structures but earth and sky, changing climate, and living vegetation.

I'll distill these primary three-dimensional or structural concerns into four terms that are favorites of mine, and that are certainly familiar to everyone: *spaces*, *edges*, *views*, and *entries*.

Spaces Spaces are the "rooms" of the landscape, and it is natural and useful to approach them in ways closely analogous to the ways you'd handle rooms in a house. In a typical residential landscape, whose space is limited, different units are best treated intimately so as to give a sense of charm and fascination. In a more expansive situation you can use space in a grander manner, developing vistas and panoramas (as well as sheltered nooks) much as the great houses of the past used galleries, halls, and ballrooms (as well as cozier spaces). In the smallest situations, such as city gardens or closely circumscribed suburban lots, I'm always looking for ways to enlarge the apparent size of the landscape — perhaps through the placement of plantings or structures; through color or texture; or by exploiting a view of space beyond the legal property line, what I call "borrowed landscape." Your eye takes in all the space it sees, whether that space technically belongs to you or not. Which is another of the delightful facts peculiar to landscape design.

The canopy of pine boughs and walls of surrounding shrubbery form an outdoor living space or "room" whose appeal is enhanced by the placement of furniture.

In any landscape there has to be a hierarchy of spaces: the large and the small, the visual and the utilitarian, all fitting together and supporting one another to make up an attractive and livable whole. Take, for example, a house with a front yard. Consider that yard first as an element of the neighborhood around it. Then look at the yard as the entire space bounded by the house, the street, and the side property lines. Within that, look at the subordinate spaces. There might be the space into which you drive your car; then a walk through a natural pocket of trees and shrubs to the front door; then the area around the front door,

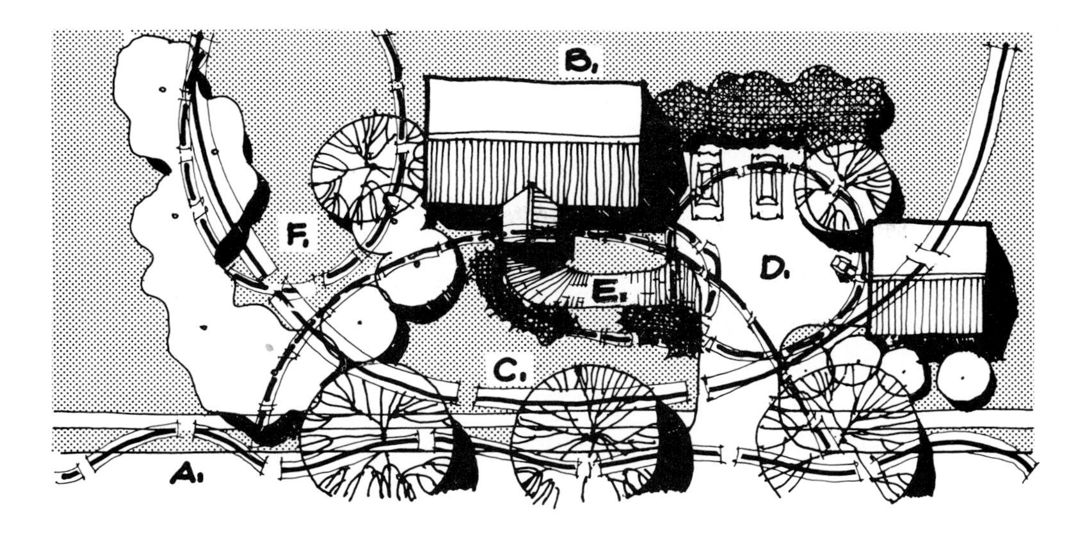

Consider the relationships of spaces with each other and with the setting.

with a recessed entry which is another space in itself. The largest space of all might be primarily of visual "use" — the plantings, ground covers, and lawn between house and street.

The challenge and the excitement of dealing with spaces lie in how you enclose or define them. And they do have to be enclosed or defined. That is a fundamental job of landscape design, just as a job of architecture is to establish the sizes and shapes of rooms within a building.

Edges I use the word "edges" to mean two different things. One group of landscape "edges" are the planes that enclose spaces — the floors, walls, and ceilings of outdoor rooms. The second group are junctions or meeting points where different planes or materials coincide.

Look first at the horizontal plane: the ground. It's tempting to think of the ground plane as flat and more or less neutral. Certainly that's the easiest way to picture it. But by manipulating the topography and texture of the "floor" of the landscape you can achieve some of the most delightful and unexpected effects of all — and often with the least effort or expense. Think of the way you will set apart a small wooded area if you drop the level of the lawn a bit below it. Or imagine the instant effect of seclusion if you recess a sitting area below the grade of the shrubbery that surrounds it.

Vertical edges, the "walls" of the landscape, affect the definition of spaces the most. The sides of the house and other permanent structures are major vertical elements, and there is little you can do to change them. You can, however, soften or screen them if you want. And you should pay attention to their materials and overall style so as to harmonize with them whatever additions you have in mind. Other landscape walls can range from the solid but symbolic (like the low stone wall that stops neither the eye nor anything else) to the transparent but impassable

Well-defined edges of ground and wall planes give this yard a clean, crisp feeling. Large shade trees (and the neighbors' dogwood) provide a "ceiling" for the space.

Transitions are important. Opposite, a Japanese-inspired cobble border affords drainage at the edge of the pavement; a steel edge prevents creep; and a stepping stone adds beauty and comfort.

(like the thorny barberry hedge). Walls can be as picturesque as a grove of birches or as plain as a board fence. Some walls block both view and wind, so as to provide winter shelter; others block the view but let wind breathe through for summer ventilation. Your choice depends on your particular landscape needs.

The topmost ceiling of all landscape spaces is the sky. Yet there are subceilings that can be equally important, either because they contribute to a feeling of privacy and coziness; or because they afford shelter from sun, rain, or snow; or because they are in proportion to a smaller-scaled landscape space. These subceilings include foliage, trellises, or roofs of decks or porches. Some ceilings are dense enough to block out sunlight and the sky altogether. Others let light dapple through all year round. Others cast dense shade in summer but admit sun in winter.

Under my second definition, landscape edges are the boundaries or junctions where two planes or surfaces meet. Where lawn meets shrubbery, where patio pavement meets lawn, where a wall meets the flowers at its foot: all are edges. So are the visual "meetings" of things, like the irregular profile of a tree against the sky or of a group of shrubs against the side of a garage. Walks and pathways are always a big edging challenge, being such strong linear interruptions to the ground plane. The Japanese have always been past masters at careful transitions between structures and the landscape.

When you think about edges and edgings, take into account your general attitude and the character of your place. Some personalities — and some landscapes — go best with soft, undefined edges. Some people prefer things crisp and hard-edged. Some like a lot of ornament and interest in their edges. Here you have to make your own decisions; but as a general rule you will have the best luck if you work for simplicity.

Consistency of materials and style is another important goal. An informal rubblestone wall will look funny abutting a conservative brick house; a tightly sheared boxwood hedge will be out of place bordering an open meadow-style lawn. As always, coordinate edging elements with their surroundings for the most pleasing result.

Views There has long been a dictum among landscaping professionals that views should be pictorial: they should be ideal for photographing or painting. I don't necessarily agree. In fact some of the most satisfying and exciting landscapes I know are almost impossible to photograph — or paint, for that matter. There's an old cartoon that shows two artists looking out their studio window at a stupendously gorgeous sunset over distant rolling hills, one artist saying to the other, "Corny, isn't it?" Like sunsets, many views are more than the sum of their parts. They involve transitory angles of light combined with sound, atmosphere, even smell.

It is true, however, that fine views, particularly when enframed, can be pictorial. When you consider views purely as seen images, you realize how important it is that each view have the elements of a well-

This deck was designed to take advantage of the pleasing outlook and existing vegetation. Surrounding trees make a frame, and a simple low railing allows an uninterrupted view.

composed picture. There should be a background, a middle ground, and a foreground, and well-planned transitions among them. And there should be something — whether planting, structure, or just a certain slant of light — to give a focal point to the composition.

The eye will never tire of looking at beautifully arranged images. For that reason I do recommend that important windows of the house have a considered view, windows being natural frames. Some windows' views will be more important than others, of course. And you should be cautious about getting into heroic measures to frame some far-off vista at the expense of valuable landscape details nearer by. Sometimes the distant view is not worth the compromises you may have to make. In such cases you may actually enjoy the view more if you're obliged to take a short walk to see it.

Speaking of walking, you should also think about the different ways you see views depending on whether you are moving or standing still. You've probably experienced the most extreme example of these differences: your perception of a certain spot when you pass by it in a car, and your changed perception of the same place when you are on foot. If you stop walking and sit down, still other qualities of the view will capture your attention. Duration makes the difference. Japanese gardens recognize and play upon these different ways of seeing through "positions of pause": a pathway may be deliberately made to turn or a pavement to change to a more rubbly texture, which forces you to slow down and look about you.

The effects of light may be the determining factors in the charm — or lack of it — of a given view. If you take a certain sequence of open spaces, trees, and shrubs and look at them in full noon sunlight with the sun behind you, you'll see a rather undifferentiated mass of green. When the sun comes around to the side, it will lend dramatic highlighting to forms and textures, besides casting fine shadows. Backlighting the same scene makes the foliage seem to glow from within with an ethereal quality.

In a small city garden, a raised vantage point gives a delightful view from above. In every kind of setting, keep in mind views from upstairs windows.

Keeping in mind the changing daily patterns of sunlight, you can shape the views around your house to make the most of them. Bright morning sun, for example, is ideal for backlighting foliage near an eastern window or illuminating morning fog or dew rising in a hollow. Views to the north and south are generally best at midmorning and midafternoon, since the sunlight slanting in from the side creates the maximum visual contrast. In early morning and late afternoon, long shadows lie across lawns and pavements at every point of the compass — and the sky itself is full of color and drama. And don't forget the totally different nighttime views you can create with electric light. Done selectively, night lighting outdoors carries the eye beyond the reflective surface of a window and makes for a stunning theatrical effect.

Much of the impact of any view (or any other facet of landscape design, when you come down to it) has to do with the human eye and mind more than with trees, rocks, grass, or even sunlight. I know a wide hillside that slopes down to a bay of the sea, and scattered over the hillside are a dozen houses. Each house has its own view of the water. One view is Olympian: the land and water lie spread out below like a dream, seeming to have almost no connection to the life of the house or its occupants. Another view is pictorial to the nth degree, cherry trees, sumacs, and bayberry framing an enchanting curve of beach and expanse of blue ocean. My own favorite isn't really a big panoramic view at all, but one with great sensual appeal: it's just a peek at the water over some rocks and grasses outside a house that is practically at sea level. Somehow the sound of lapping waves, the feel of the wind, and the smell of salt give this place a special magic.

Entries A landscape is for people, and considering how people move from place to place is crucial to a landscape design. You could almost describe circulation as a series of entries, of moves from outside to inside. In one sense, of course, all landscape spaces are "outside" because they're outdoors. But you really do enter one space from another, even if both are in the open air. It is a psychological fact that moving onto a new turf generates a tiny primitive anxiety in a person. For that reason alone, every entry should be simple, uncluttered, and enticingly designed.

Every gateway, every flight of steps, every place where you round a corner of the house or come to an opening in a hedge or fence is a form of entry. Think of what you can do to make each one enjoyable.

A major part of every landscaping project is to give a pleasurable quality to the sequence of entries involved in approaching and going into a house. At the first entry, the property line, you move from the public domain into the private, often in an automobile. There should be a generous turning radius to let the car move easily from street to drive, and the drive should begin, at least, on a fairly level grade. A driveway of any length should offer some attractive view along the way, such as a glimpse of a garden or the front door of the house.

The next entry occurs when you get out of the car. Space allowing, there should be a clearly defined parking place, ideally with its own landscaping detail. Stepping onto the walk that leads to the front door is another entry, and it calls for a comfortable transition from the pavement of the parking area to the surface of the walk — the transition itself forming a kind of gateway to the space immediately surrounding the house.

An entry with a subtle air of mystery. Grade changes prolong the approach to the house, and a sense of ascending adds to expectation.

All arrival elements are clearly defined: stone gateway with built-in lighting, visitors' parking, and walk leading to the door. (Note hidden residents' parking beyond.)

Finally you come to the house. At the doorway you expect people to use most, you should plan for a stoop or other greeting platform generous enough to let at least two people stand simultaneously, with room for screen or storm doors to open or close at the same time. The doors should be hung so that they can swing all the way open until they're flat against the house wall — not come up short against a railing or other obstacle. If possible, an overhang for inclement weather is a nice detail; so is a bell or knocker that's handy, not concealed behind a locked screen door.

There are many houses where the "back" door is in fact the door that is used by family and friends alike as the main entry into the house. In such cases, these guidelines for planning and landscaping of the path, stoop, and so on apply to the back door — which should also be designed to retain its practical functions as chief access route for groceries, packages, children, or whatever. Meanwhile the front door might be played down, concealed, turned into a window, or allowed to serve simply as access to a terrace or porch.

Here I'm really getting into details of the architecture of the house; but it is important to coordinate these with the design of the landscape. Overhangs, steps, retaining walls, railings, or other landscape construction around the entry to the house should be in keeping with the style and building materials of the house proper. If they aren't, they inevitably look tacked on.

In thinking about landscape composition, and structure, always consider compatibility with — and utilization of — nature's own designs as a basic criterion. After all, nature was creating landscapes long before people got into the business. That beautifully proportioned patio won't get much summer use if it is airless and baking hot (you need to know the sun and wind patterns around your house). That bank of forsythia won't provide the desired splash of springtime yellow if it's overshadowed by trees or buildings (it needs sun for good bloom). Climate, soil, and the natural characteristics and needs of plants are central to both the appearance and the usefulness of your landscape.

4 A NATURAL ORIENTATION

This chapter has to do with some of the basic facts of the science, as opposed to the art, of landscape design: facts about the natural environment.

Unlike our farming forebears of even a couple of generations ago, we Americans tend to take our physical surroundings very much for granted. But the more time you spend working outdoors, the more you will come to marvel at the natural elements that sustain life on this planet. Being close to nature, being able to study it day by day, is one of the things I enjoy most about being a landscape architect. In a sense it's a luxury — which I cherish. Yet it is absolutely crucial that anyone contemplating a landscape design project pay attention to the natural environment and apply its lessons, whether it be on open farmland, in a suburban backyard, or on a city balcony. Ignore nature or try to fight it, and you cannot win. Let nature inspire and guide you, and you cannot go too far wrong.

Using nature to best advantage means orienting your landscape — both organic and inorganic — to the sun, wind, rain, and soil. Energy efficiency will be one important result. Equally important will be the good health of plants and the comfort of people in and around your house.

Climate It is no accident that the weather is one of the commonest topics of everyday discourse. "Where are my sunglasses?" "This humidity really gets me down." "Looks like snow." Climate pervades our lives in more ways than we often realize. It affects our moods, our habitual routines, our attitudes and ambitions, not to mention our specific plans on any given day.

Early colonists and pioneers in this country had no trouble staying in touch with climate. To them, energy-efficient orientation was a matter of common sense combined with age-old skills. In the North, they knew how to back their houses up to shelter (often the barn) and how to

Winter and summer effects of this beech grove are dramatically different. Every landscape plan should allow for seasonal weather changes.

Southerly-facing living areas of this beach house make the most of summer breezes, shade from deciduous trees, and (for winter) the sun's warmth.

turn the faces of their houses to the south or southwest. Winter was the big threat, not just to comfort but to survival. They also knew, however, what a blessing a deciduous shade tree outside the front door could be in summer. In the South, earlier Americans used deep porches and shady groves to keep sun at bay throughout the year.

In a more sophisticated way, but using the identical basic knowledge, Frank Lloyd Wright designed the famous Taliesin West to use climate to advantage. Built of stone in the Arizona desert, Taliesin West is oriented so that winds blow through the structure much of the time. A central water fountain cools the breezes by evaporation — an ancient form of natural air conditioning.

If you orient your indoor and outdoor spaces sensibly and in concert with climate, you can extend the livability of outdoor spaces by several months and improve the quality of life indoors as well. You can have pockets of sun for winter warmth and early spring bloom; cool spots on sultry days; shelter from wind all year long.

The sun The patterns of sunlight and shade on your property have everything to do with what you can grow and where you can grow it. In addition, the sun is the central factor in energy-efficient landscape design. The initial source of all energy on Earth, the sun is the most predictable energy source we have. We know precisely what it will be doing at any given time. It is that reliability that makes the daily path of the sun a major component of every landscaping plan.

The simple diagrams on page 42 illustrate the sunrise-to-sunset patterns as they change from solstice to solstice throughout the northern hemisphere, and the changing angles at which the sunlight strikes the Earth's surface at different seasons. The lessons to be learned here are clear. For warmth in winter, a sensible design will allow the maximum possible amount of sunlight to strike the south-facing walls and windows of the house at that season.

The sun's path changes throughout the year, causing wide variations in the length of day, direction of the sun's rays, and the angle of the sun in the sky.

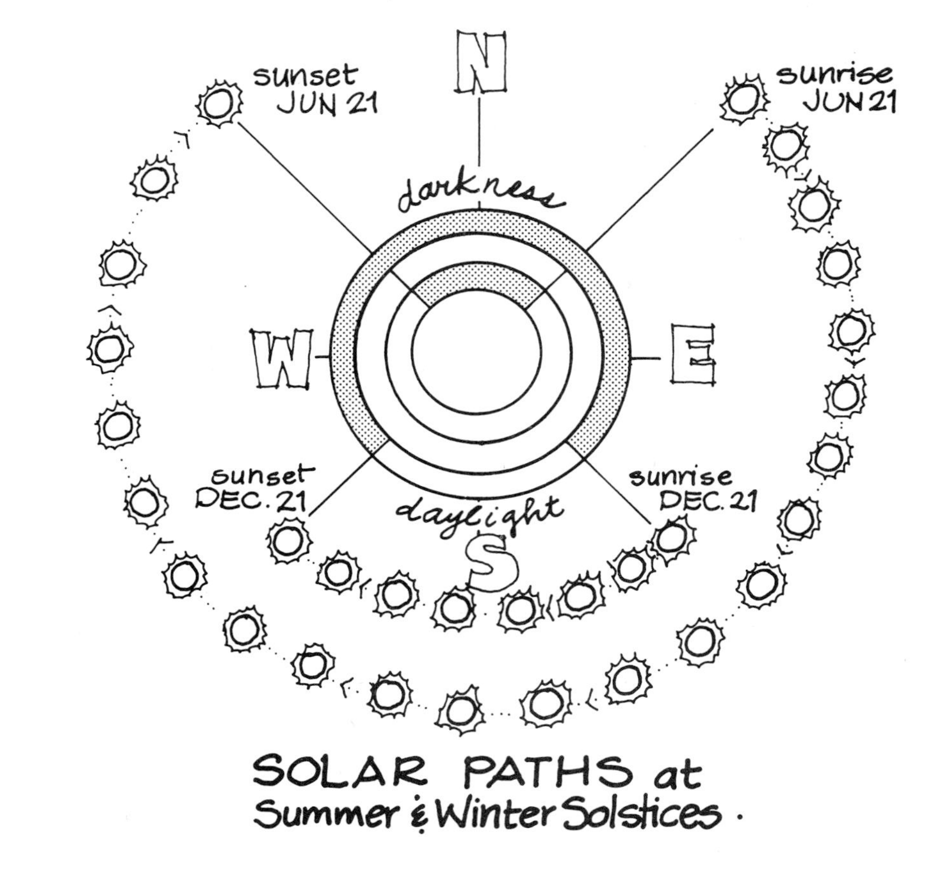

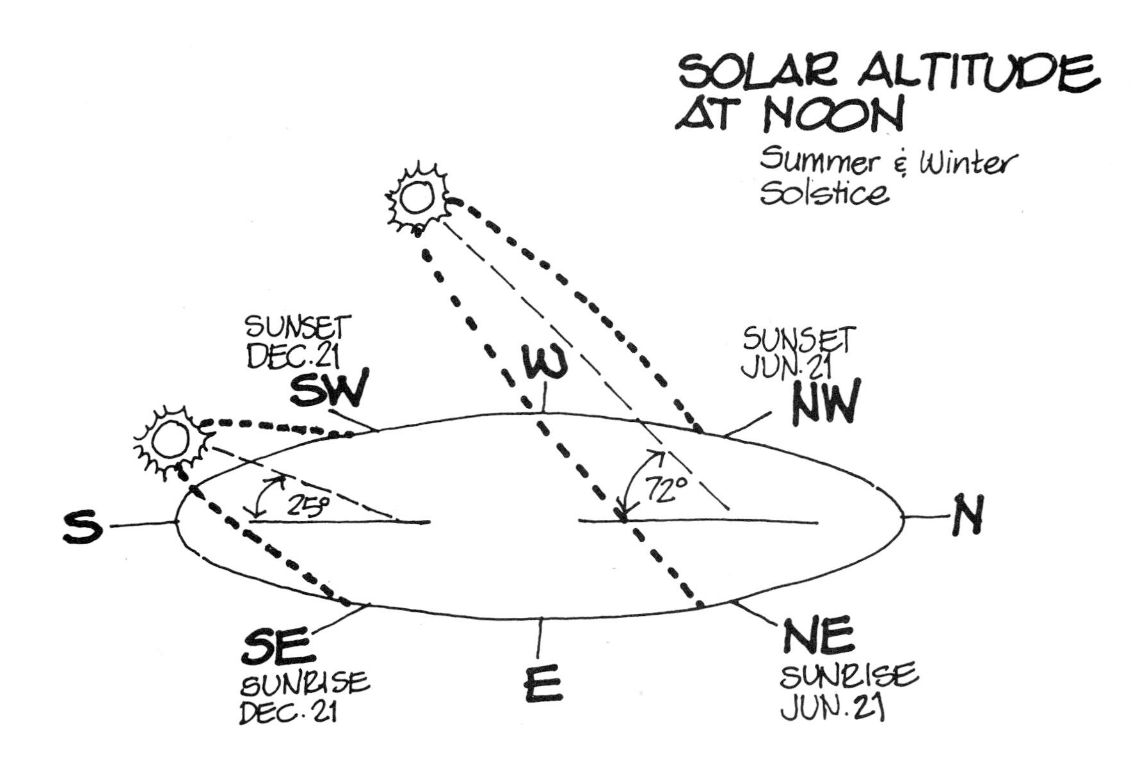

In summer the sun's rays are much closer to the vertical than in winter — so that a fairly narrow overhang or trellis can afford all the protection the south side of a house may need. Windows and walls facing west, where hot afternoon sun slants in, may need a deeper screen or shade. Here's where deciduous foliage can come in. A trellis vine or a shade tree that blocks summer sun will let it come right in once the days are cold again.

Every individual plant has its preferences as to amount and intensity of sunlight. Some shrubs and ground covers are happy in deep day-long shade, while others require at least a dappled sun-shade mixture or sun for part of the day. Some trees and shrubs cannot survive in a place that's both sunny and windy. Many trees and shrubs will tend to lean or reach toward the sun if they are partly shaded, which will affect their form. Keep all these things in mind as you plan; and for specifics of the sunlight needs of any given plant, see the plant descriptions in Part III.

The wind A good deal less predictable than the sun, the wind nevertheless plays an important part in landscape design. You can control or even harness its impact to a degree that may surprise you.

Every section of the United States has its own prevailing winds. In much of the Northeast, for instance, the prevailing fair-weather winds (the winds we're most apt to be outdoors in) are westerlies. In summer they swing around to the southwest, in winter to the northwest. Determine your prevailing wind direction(s) and you can use structures or plantings to create wind channels for evaporational cooling in summer — and windbreaks to reduce winter wind velocities by up to 50 percent. (More on this in the section on energy-efficient landscaping in November.) You can also use your knowledge of wind patterns to assess the ideal or less-than-ideal location for any given plant.

Topography also has an impact on wind and on the temperature of the spaces where you live and garden. Cold air sinks and warm air rises. Masses of cool or warm air, seeking their natural levels, actually create thermal air currents — in other words, wind. Cold air settles in valleys; and because of condensation in cooling moist air, fog pockets in low-lying areas are a familiar phenomenon. So are cooling breezes that flow down the sides of hills or ravines.

These thermal effects of topography may sound as though they'd operate only on a very large scale. But in fact, if your property has any topographical variety, you will find that the varying elevations of your land create their own miniature climates. A friend of mine plants annual flowers in two beds, one next to her house, the other about 80 yards away and 8 feet lower down. Every fall, the lower bed suffers a killing frost days or even weeks earlier than the higher one. Every spring, the earth in the uphill bed thaws out sooner. So if you are seeking a way to cool an area, think about trapping downflowing cool air. If warmth is your goal, blocking the cold air flow is one way to attain it.

Soil Nearly everything we grow and everything we build is in contact with the soil. Interestingly enough, however, the prerequisites for good growing soil and good building soil are very different. Good growing soil would not serve at all well as the base for a wall, a potting shed, a driveway, or a deck. The reasons for this are buried in the structure of soil.

Structure? you may ask. But soil does have structure: it consists of solids and voids. The best growing soil is about half solids (mineral and organic matter) and half voids (air and water). As you walk through a garden, across a meadow, or among the trees of a forest, you're walking on something that is only about half solid.

It is the presence of water and air, which swell and shrink with changes in temperature, that causes soil to rise and fall with the seasons. All that activity can cause cracks in foundation walls, open canyons in paved drives or terraces, or lead to strange tiltings in structures whose underpinnings have unexpectedly settled. If, however, you compress or compact the soil — so as to drive out the air and water — and if in addition you remove or greatly reduce the organic matter, you have the perfect substrate to support a structure or pavement.

Soil for growing Soils are formed during thousands of years of decomposition of underlying bedrock, acted upon by glaciers, air, and water; and by hundreds of years of decomposition of organic materials — that is, plants. It takes millennia for nature to make topsoil, but only a few decades for human activity to sap it of its nutrients and let it waste. This was the unhappy discovery of settlers on the deforested, used-up soils of New England; and of families faced with the Great Plains dust bowl of the 1930s. It was also a discovery of the ancient Greeks and other ancient peoples, who stripped their land and found that it never recovered. Every age seems to have to make the same "discovery" over again.

Most plant growth takes place in topsoil. Large plants' roots penetrate to the underlying subsoil mainly for purposes of extracting water, and for mechanical support. But even big trees' feeder roots seldom go much beyond 1 foot down — as you realize when you see a tree uprooted. There's many a tree native to North America that can thrive with practically no depth of soil at all.

What is this thing called soil, that in such a thin layer nourishes such infinite variety of life? Apart from air and water, the solid components of a good growing soil are about 10 to 20 percent organic matter (decayed plant life) and 80 to 90 percent mineral matter (rocks, sand, silt, clay).

The larger mineral fragments, from sand to rocks, serve mainly as a skeleton or framework. They provide spaces for air, water, silt, and organic matter to fill in — porosity. The smaller mineral fragments are

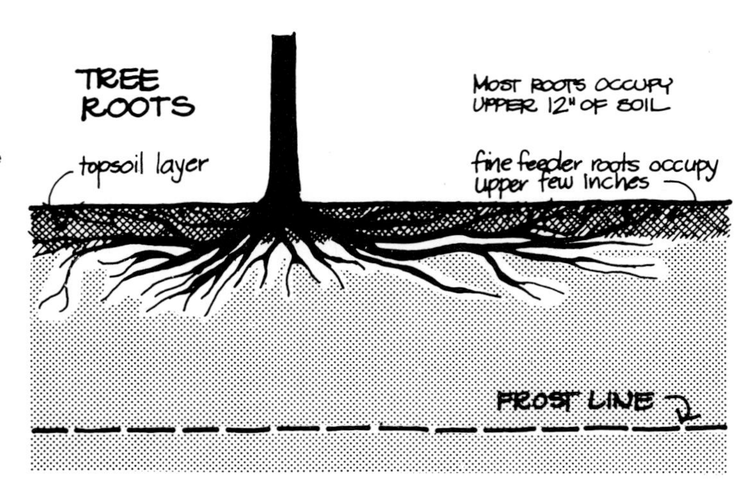

The topmost 12 inches of soil contain the majority of plants' roots. Handle topsoil with care during landscape construction.

silt and clay. They, together with the organic matter, provide the essential nutrients that make plant life possible. Of the "N, P, K" triad in every fertilizer mix, silts and clays are important providers of both P (phosphorus or phosphate) and K (potassium or potash). They also yield calcium, magnesium, iron, and a dozen other nutrients plants need, some of which we probably don't even know about yet.

As for the organic matter, it too has both structural and nutritional roles to play. It holds air and water; it contains many nutrients, most notably the essential fertilizer nitrogen (N); it's also responsible for about half the beneficial chemical reactions that make soil soil. In woods and other wild places, organic matter is kept in its necessary proportion by the constantly renewed supply of decomposing vegetation. Organic matter in soil is rapidly broken down by chemical and bacterial action, however. And in cities and suburbs, the soil-renewing cycle of organic growth and decay often gets interrupted by human activities. That is why it's vital that we keep checking and replenishing the organic content of any soil where we hope to grow anything.

Another aspect of the makeup of soil is its pH value. The pH scale indicates the acidity or alkalinity of soil in numbers from 0 to 14. A pH of 7 means the soil is neutral; higher numbers are alkaline; lower ones are acid. Knowing the soil's pH is important because soil nutrients are most available to a given plant when the soil's degree of acidity is proper for that plant. (I've included plants' specific pH needs in their descriptions in Part III.)

To sum up, the ideal soil for growing things will be a fertile, friable loam made up of half solids and half voids. The solid half will include about 40 percent sand, 40 percent silt, 10 percent clay, and 10 percent organic matter. The other half will be equally divided between air and water. This soil will contain the right amount of air spaces for the circulation of gases; allow water to percolate but hold enough to meet plants' needs; and, of course, provide plants with enough of the essential water-soluble nutrients.

Soil for building Obviously, pavements, foundations, and other rigid construction can't be built directly on topsoil. A firm building base means either well-compacted subsoil or a bed of sand or rock that will absorb the heavings and shrinkings of underlying soil without transmit-

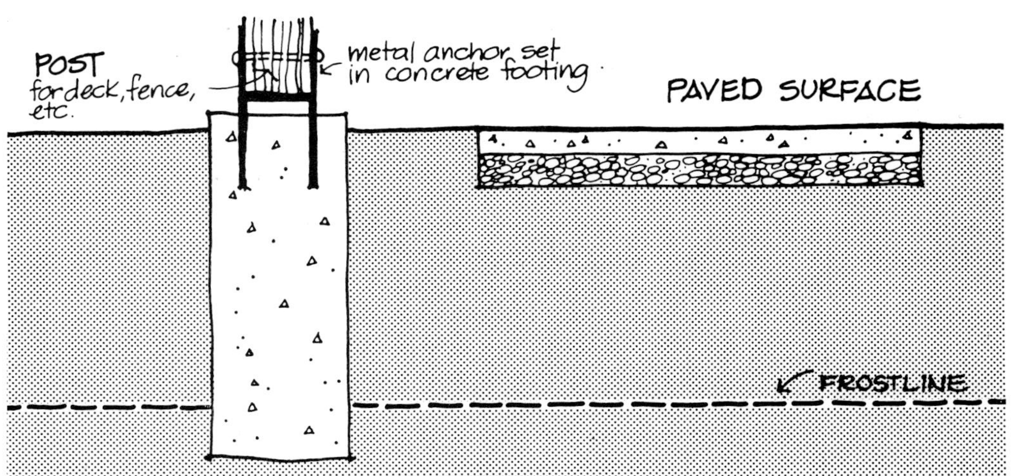

Footings for above-ground landscape structures must extend to solid subsoil below the frost line, while paved areas require only a granular bed to absorb the soil's movement.

ting them to the construction above. Clearly, proper soil for building doesn't just lie around the landscape.

Well-compacted subsoil is what's called for if you are planning major above-the-ground construction such as a deck or gazebo. You have to dig down below frost level, to subsoil that is so hard-packed and so lacking in air and water spaces that — unlike the spongy upper soil — it simply doesn't move around much. There you can rest your footings or foundation, secure in the knowledge that they'll stay where you put them.

For in-the-ground construction like masonry walks or paved patios, you use another approach: digging just deep enough to install a shock-absorbing layer of sand or crushed stone sufficiently coarse and well-drained so that it won't hold water. Everyone has seen the bed of gravel that highway construction crews lay down before they spread the asphalt. A small-scale project works the same.

Drainage There is an old rule of thumb to the effect that of all the rainwater that falls on earth, one-third evaporates; one-third runs off (into storm drains, streams, ponds); and one-third percolates into the soil. Although these proportions can vary hugely according to the locality, the time of year, the type of soil, or a hundred other factors, the point is clear. How well we plan for the drainage of our soil will have a lot to do with how well our soil works for us — whether for growing or for building.

Plants cannot survive in waterlogged soil. They suffocate unless their roots have access to both water and air. And there's another hazard to poorly drained soil: excessive runoff, which leads to erosion. The U.S. loses 4 billion tons of irreplaceable topsoil to erosion by water alone every year. But if you cultivate a porous, well-drained soil and fill it with roots, you don't need to lose an ounce.

Proper drainage is as important to the maintenance of structures as it is to the well-being of plants. Seepage in your cellar, standing water

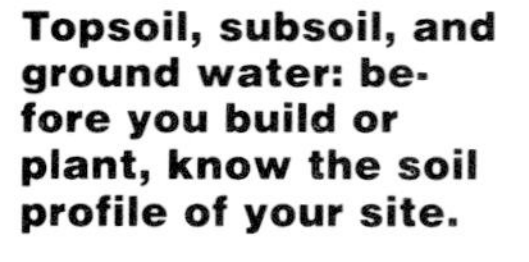

Topsoil, subsoil, and ground water: before you build or plant, know the soil profile of your site.

all over your driveway, puddles in the middle of the terrace — any water where you don't want it is at best a nuisance, at worst a destructive menace. Planning for drainage is fundamental to landscape design, and I'll talk about it in detail in Part II.

Plants and Their Habitats The plants that grow around you are part of the natural environment in more ways than one. They depend for survival on soil, sun, and rain. They also make a big difference to microclimates around a house — by casting shade, blocking noise or wind, absorbing heat, generating oxygen, competing or coexisting with other plantings in their neighborhood. Every growing thing is linked with everything else.

Getting to know plants in their natural state is vital to your success in choosing new plants for your property. Once again, it works far better to cooperate with nature than to try to outsmart it. Be observant; look around you and see how both native and imported plant types in your area have adapted to their natural surroundings. They'll give you many ideas about what might work in your own situation.

Native plants A native plant is so completely adapted to its locale that it is self-sustaining to the point of reproducing itself. Throughout this book, "native" means indigenous, not imported, to North America. Native plants' reproductive capacity makes them essential food suppliers for birds and wildlife. Their seeds — berries, nuts, and fruits — are all highly edible. Also, native plants colonize. A typical native is found in the midst of its relatives, the oldest plants surrounded by their offspring and the offspring in turn surrounded by theirs. The result is often dense growth, providing excellent cover and nesting areas as well as food.

You may have seen the colonizing abilities of native plants at work if you've ever had the opportunity to observe the "plant succession" in an open area or vacant lot that has gone to seed over a number of years. First come low-growing weeds; then taller grasses; then, within a couple of years, young shrubs and the seedlings of trees. Each stage makes possible the one that succeeds it. After fifty years there will be woodland where the open ground used to be.

And there are both rhyme and reason to the ways native plants interact with each other and their setting. Plants, like everything else, have an incredibly subtle and complex system of shared and competing needs, mutual support, and mutual dependency. When they coexist happily in the wild it's no accident; it's the result of a perfect equilibrium having been reached.

Imported plants Throughout history, horticulturists have been fascinated with foreign forms of plant life. In America since colonial times, plant explorers and gardening enthusiasts have introduced thousands of foreign plant species and varieties to this continent.

There are some introduced plants that — though exquisite in many ways — are terribly fussy to maintain. Almost every gardener has (knowingly or not) been exposed to the finicky tastes and fragile health of certain nonnative lawn grasses and flowering shrubs. What with elaborate fertilizing, frequent watering, and periodic applications of pesticides, fungicides, and even herbicides, it's a real chore to keep these invalids going. (Needless to say, you won't find any of these plants listed in the following chapters.)

Ferns and native shrubs are perfectly adapted to life along a streambed in the dappled shade of beeches on ascending slopes.

Many imports, however, thrive here and have contributed immeasurably to our landscaping palette — with their blooms, their foliage, their tolerance of difficult growing conditions, and their resistance to disease. Japanese maple, Oriental cherries, boxwood, Norway spruce . . . the list is endless.

Some imported varieties have become basic staples of the American scene. What would spring be without forsythia and lilacs, or summer without the common orange daylily? Yet none of these old friends is native to this continent.

Other introduced plants have flourished just a little too well. Purple loosestrife, while some people are fond of it, is viewed by many as a mortal threat to wetlands plants and wildlife. Bittersweet, Japanese honeysuckle, multiflora rose, and the notorious kudzu vine are other examples of invaders with a habit of taking over any landscape where they're allowed a foothold. This is not to say that there aren't some equally noxious American natives, with poison ivy heading the list. But the imports have a big advantage: their own natural enemies (pests or blights) often don't follow them to their adopted land, so here they can rampage unchecked.

Plant habitats Whether your local plant community is native, imported, or both, its character will be tied to the kind of soil (acid, sandy, humusy, etc.) and the growing conditions (bright or dark, sheltered or windy, wet or dry) in the area. And these conditions in turn should govern your selection of trees, shrubs, or ground covers for your property.

A million variables go into a plant habitat, but for simplicity's sake I'll choose four broad categories. Almost every plant will be at home in at least one of the following:

- Wet meadow habitats are open and unshaded, often low-lying, with normally damp or even swampy soil.
- Dry meadow habitats, often upland, may have rich or rocky soil; they may be protected or windswept; but they are unshaded and dry most of the time.
- Wet woodland habitats, characteristically shady and damp with humus-rich soil, are often protected from wind by virtue of being both low-lying and wooded.
- Dry woodland habitats are often wooded slopes or plateaus — any places where shade and dry (or at least well-drained) soil conditions predominate most of the year.

Within any one of these categories, the possible subcategories and combined or crossover categories are endless. They'll depend on degree or frequency of wetness; density or constancy of shade; wind direction and velocity; acidity or alkalinity of soil; and so on. A low boggy spot, shaded by big oaks much of the summer and yet well protected from winter winds, will support its own range of plant life. A south-facing gravelly slope, dry much of the year and completely lacking in shade, will foster a completely different pattern of growth.

The important point is that your particular set of circumstances is bound to appeal to a certain set of plants. Stick to them, and you can't help but generate a healthy plant community. And plant health is key to a landscape that is good-looking and readily maintainable.

As you use the plant lists throughout Part II and the detailed descriptions in Part III, you'll find that each description mentions the plant's preferred habitat. With natives, this means the habitats that plants most promptly colonize in the wild in North America; with imports, the habitats they choose in their native Europe or Asia. But many plants are flexible. Moisture-loving plants like red maple, for instance, will survive or even prosper in relatively dry conditions. The reverse does not apply, however: a plant adapted to dryness, like honeysuckle, will usually not endure transplanting into wet conditions. Some plants like gray birch

Another kind of habitat: a thin mantle of soil over and among rock outcroppings supports varied plant life despite dryness and exposure.

and paxistima, which tolerate sterile or rocky soils in the wild, actually prefer good soil and adequate moisture in cultivation. And every plant does best with its own optimum amount of sunlight or shade — although here again, some are more flexible than others.

As you familiarize yourself with your soil, your prevailing winds, the patterns of sunlight around your house, and the kinds of plant life that flourish in your vicinity, you'll learn a lot — and you'll begin to see things in new ways. Seeing is the essence of design, and everything I've been discussing in these chapters is aimed at helping you to see. Chapter 5 continues that effort by taking you outdoors to evaluate, map, and plan.

5 SIZING UP: THE BASE PLAN

I strongly recommend that you make a "base plan" of your place on paper. This educational and constructive first step need not be difficult or expensive; on the contrary, it's usually an eye-opening, exciting, and enjoyable experience.

When you are in the early, pipe-dreaming stages of considering an improvement to your landscape, it's natural to be vague and general. "How about a lovely curving front walk, brick maybe?" "What if we put a cluster of laurels over there and some big viburnums behind them?" "I'd like a tall wood fence here to screen the view of the neighbors' parked car."

If you are serious about going forward, however, it is vital that you come to grips with your site's dimensions, topography, drainage, access routes, sun and shade patterns, and so on. The best way I know to get all the details under control is to go outdoors and measure and make lists, with the goal of producing an annotated map — a base plan.

Making a base plan will give you a boost in many ways. First, planning on paper will force you to see — to assess, make judgments, contemplate alternatives — with more precision and concreteness than any amount of standing around brainstorming. Also, I've found that ideas and solutions begin to speak out for themselves as the paper planning goes on.

Another argument for careful planning is that it's efficient. By the time you have drawn your final sketch and written your final list, you will be in far less danger of making mistakes than if you just plunge in impulsively. At the very least disappointing, mistakes can also be wasteful of time, material, and money. At worst they can actually be destructive. Examples of avoidable mistakes could include planning a pool where ledge is directly below the surface; or planting a deep-rooted tree over a leaching field; or constructing a fence so oriented as to create a tunnel for the prevailing wind. By all means, go ahead and make mistakes; but make them on paper, not in soil or greenery or stone.

The base plan is an elementary diagram or map of your property showing all features of house, grounds, outbuildings, walks, and so on. It will become the foundation for later drawings and elevations (views of things in the vertical plane, like the front facade of a house), if needed. You'll return to the base plan over and over as you tackle problems or indulge in flights of imagination. Using the base plan, you'll be able to make various alternative designs on tracing-paper overlays. So the base plan should be as accurate as you can make it.

Incidentally, there are two possible shortcuts to making the base plan. The first is to transpose onto graph paper (see Equipment, page 52) the plot plan of your property that accompanies the title deed. If you have recently bought the property, putting your hands on the plot plan may be easy. A plot plan usually has been done by a surveyor, which might lead you to assume that it would be one hundred percent accurate. That's not necessarily so, however, especially if yours is very old or if it has been reproduced over and over. Plot plans can also be difficult to use because they tend to be drawn to a very small scale. Nevertheless, a plot plan is often good enough for you to transfer the bare outlines of the house, the property lines, and the driveway (if any) to your base plan.

A second possible shortcut — or a help if you have a really complicated site — can be to hire a surveyor to draw the base plan for you from scratch. Surveyors do get accurate results, which can be essential in some circumstances: for instance, where property lines are in question, or where other structures or features of the landscape could be affected by errors in measurement, or where topography is complex. Against the accuracy you can obtain by having a professional survey done, you have to weigh the fact that surveyors charge a minimum of several hundred dollars a day for the work of the survey crew. On top of that there's the cost of the time it takes the surveyor's office to draw up the plan.

(This last expense — the cost of drafting up the plan based on the surveyor's measurements — may be one corner you can cut. Find out if your surveyor will make you a "field annotated plan." This is just what it sounds like: an accurate but roughly drawn plan, with all information in place but without the refinements of finished drafting.)

For the sake of the argument, let's assume that your situation is not too complicated and you have decided to draw your own base plan. No matter how little experience you have, you can do it. No artistic talent is required. The steps I recommend you take are exactly those I follow myself before I begin preparing a design plan.

Equipment Your first move is a trip to an art or drafting supply store for a few pieces of equipment. Use the following as a checklist.

- Several large (18 by 24 inches) sheets of translucent graph paper, lined at either 8 or 10 squares to the inch so that you can work at scales of either ⅛ inch to the foot or 1/10 inch to the foot. If you're working on only a small piece of land, perhaps a scale of ¼ inch to the foot will be easier to use.
- A piece of plywood, masonite, or heavy-weight Bristol board at least as large as your graph paper, to use as a backup board while you are outdoors making measurements.
- A 12-inch ruler and/or an architect's or engineer's scale — the architect's if you are working at ⅛ inch to the foot, the engineer's if you are working at 1/10 inch to the foot.
- Several HB soft lead pencils, which are somewhat smeary but which give you a dark line.
- A white artgum eraser to clean up mistakes (and the pencil smears).
- A 24-inch roll of tracing paper (sometimes called "flimsy"), which comes in either white or yellow. This paper will be used for later studies, once the base plan is done, but you may as well buy it now.

The only other trip you will have to make is to the hardware store, to obtain:

- A measuring tape; I recommend at least a 50-footer, if not a 100-footer, for more accurate and more efficient measuring.
- A standard 10-foot or 12-foot retractable carpenter's tape. (If you don't mind making successive tapings, you could use this instead of the long tape mentioned above.)
- A hand level or line level for measuring vertical relief (see Vertical Relief, page 55). It's possible that you may have to go to a drafting supply store or blueprint shop for this.

Basic Measurements Clip or tape your graph paper to its backup board, gather up your tape measures, and head outside. A helper is a good idea; but if you don't have anyone to hold the end of the tape for you, use an ice pick, screwdriver, or shish-kabob skewer to anchor the end of the tape to the ground, and you're off. Here is the procedure, step by step.

1. Measure the distance from the center of a wall of the house to the nearest property line. Record these two points on the graph paper. If your paper is ruled to ⅛-inch scale, a 50-foot distance will be 50 spaces, or 6¼ inches. Make sure that you choose points on the paper that will allow enough room in all directions for all the other measurements of house and lot to come. This may involve a little trial and error.

2. Measure carefully all the walls of the house where they meet the ground, and record their dimensions as a series of points on the graph paper, as shown here. Double check all your measurements; there's no hurry, and accuracy now can save a lot of grief later.

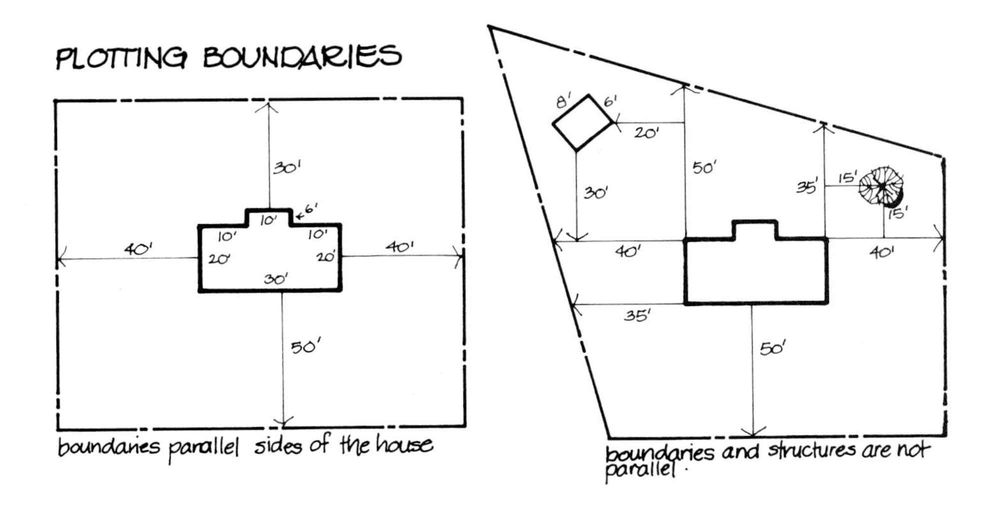

Measuring and plotting property lines is a simple task. Trees, buildings, etc. can be located by means of coordinate offsets as illustrated.

3. Measure the distance from the center point of each remaining house wall to its nearest property line, and record these points. If by any chance you have a perfectly rectangular house situated parallel to the boundaries of a perfectly rectangular property, you are now home free: all you have to do is extend the property lines from the points you've located, and where they intersect are the corners of your lot.

4. In the more common situation, where the walls of the house are far from symmetrical and where the property lines are not parallel to anything at all, even each other, you will need to locate the corners of the lot and measure their distances from each other and from the house in order to arrive at a diagram of the lot. This is where the architect's rule to ⅛-inch scale (or the engineer's to ¹⁄₁₀) can come in handy, for measuring diagonal distances. If you get frustrated pinpointing boundary lines that run at odd angles, try this. Pace out or measure an imaginary line that extends some fixed straight line, such as a house wall, garage wall, or front walk. Mark it with string or tape. Then go back to (say) the corner of the house and mark out another line at right angles to the first. Then pick a series of points along the troublesome boundary; measure the distances between each of these points and the nearest points on the two right-angled lines; and record the measurements. After doing this just a few times, you'll find that you can plot a pretty accurate location for the boundary. You can also use this method for locating objects such as those listed under Other Information, page 54.

5. At this point you may want to go indoors again, to sit down and use your ruler to draw neat lines between the various points you have so conscientiously measured. You will end up with a schematic rendering of the locations, dimensions, and relative positions of your site and your house.

6. Ascertain which direction is north, and turn your paper so that that direction is roughly at either the top or the right-hand side. (This is the convention.) Draw an N with an arrow, and you have established which end of your base plan is up; needless to say, the way you annotate the plan will depend on this.

7. For future reference, make a note of the scale of your plan in some corner of the graph paper — "¼-inch scale," "⅛-inch scale," "¹⁄₁₀-inch scale," or whatever.

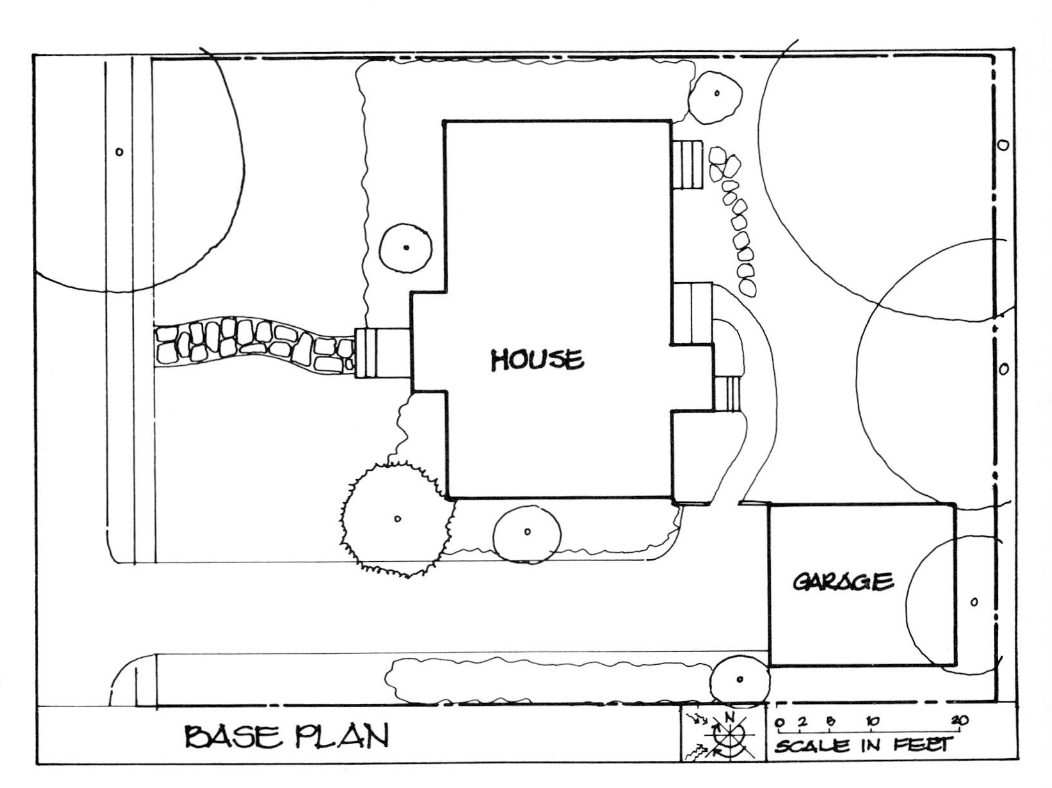

A base plan, clear and uncluttered, shows the edges of all elements that have been measured and located.

Other Information The next move is to decide what other features to include in the base plan. You'll probably want to go outdoors again as you consider these questions. Here is another checklist to guide you; but with this list (unlike the equipment list) I recommend that you pick and choose. Don't get bogged down putting in every little thing at this stage; limit your selections to things that will clearly affect what you are thinking of doing. The base plan is by definition minimal. You can always add details later. Some candidates for inclusion:

- Additional details of the house itself
  - General layout of ground-floor rooms
  - Roof overhangs
  - Windows and doors
  - Downspouts
  - Water spigots
  - Oil fill pipe
  - Meter locations
  - Window wells
  - Doorsteps
- Driveway
- Walks
- Terraces
- Outlines of existing gardens, shrubbery masses, flower beds
- Walls or fences
- Significant shrubs or trees
- Utilities: gas, water, sewer, or septic lines; telephone and electric poles and overhead or underground wires; oil tanks; etc.
- Lampposts and other lighting
- Drainage channels
- Steeply sloping areas

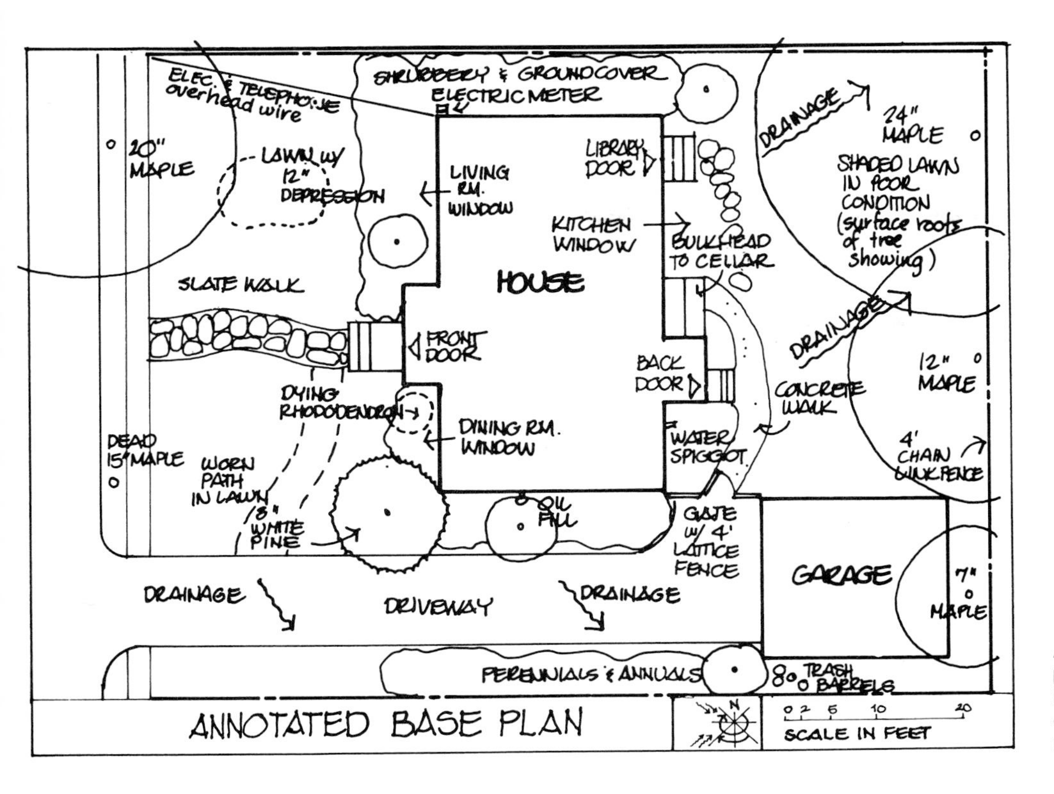

An annotated base plan helps you keep important existing considerations in mind.

- Areas with poor drainage
- Areas with other significance, such as rock outcroppings, old foundations, level areas, etc.

Many of the features listed above can be indicated on your plan simply with a dot and a brief annotation. Do write small, so as not to crowd the plan excessively. Shown here is the plan at this stage; you can see that trees are simply circles (with "deciduous" or "evergreen" noted); walls are heavy lines; pathways and drives are parallel straight or curving lines. Once again, keep it spare and keep it simple, for clarity's sake.

Vertical Relief While you are wandering around with measuring tape in hand, it makes sense to determine the varying elevations of your plot of land — the vertical, as opposed to the horizontal, distances between points. I find that vertical relief often makes a significant difference to my approach to a given landscape, both because of its visual impact and because of functional concerns (how to separate or connect different levels, for example). Very few properties are perfectly flat, but those that are can often be enhanced by the addition of some ups and downs. On the other hand, a plot with drastic variations in vertical relief presents its own set of landscaping challenges (and pleasures).

Here's a very simple way to measure vertical distances. This system uses equipment that you can make and buy at little expense, and it's fine for most residential landscape situations. If, however, you are going to be undertaking complicated grading or construction, or if your site is very large or very difficult topographically, you may want even greater precision than this method can give you. In that case you can rent a surveyor's level or transit. Or, of course, you can get a surveyor to do the job for you.

1. Make a measuring stick 10 to 12 feet long. You can use a two-by-four, a piece of lattice, or any piece of lumber that's long enough and not too unwieldly. If it is not light colored, paint it for visibility. Measure it out into 1-inch sections and paint the foot numbers — 1, 2, 3, etc. — as large and black as possible. Or if you prefer meters and decimeters, use them. You are now ready to use your hand level (the final item in the equipment list on page 52) to start measuring.

2. First, a word about the level. Either a hand level or a line level will do; but I find the hand level a little easier and more flexible to work with, so the instructions that follow are geared to it. A line level consists of a spirit level with hooks by which you attach it to a line that has been stretched between two points at different elevations. This necessitates a firm anchor at point A to keep the line taut while you hold the other end at point B. A hand level, however, you just carry around with you. It has a built-in telescope. You stand at one elevation, adjust the position of the instrument until it is level, and see instantly what the difference in elevation is between where you are standing and where the measuring stick is propped.

3. Choose a low point against which you will measure all succeeding points. Commonly this is the lowest point of your property. Prop your measuring stick upright in a convenient and visible spot, or get a helper to hold it for you. Looking at the stick through the hand level, make a note of the exact height of your eye — 60 inches, for an easy example.

4. Take with you the hand level and perhaps a pad and pencil for noting measurements. Walk to the first higher point that you wish to locate. Since your eye has to be on a plane no higher than the highest mark on the measuring stick, the rise can't be more than 5 feet or so. For greater heights, see step 8 below.

5. Sight through the hand level at the measuring stick. The height you see, minus your original eye-level height, will give the difference in elevation at the point where you're standing. For instance, if your level is aimed at the 94-inch mark, but your eye level on the stick was 60

Although it is helpful to have someone hold the measuring stick, you can also prop it against a tree or building.

inches, you are standing at a spot 34 inches higher than the place where you propped the stick.

6. Repeat steps 4 and 5 until you have located all the different elevations you want to.

7. Now for registering your measurements on the base plan. Call the low point zero, and record all measurements of higher points (such as +24″ or +40″). Important elevations to note are those where a change in grade may call for landscaping work — such as a spot that may need a retaining wall, steps, terracing, or antierosion planting.

8. If there are differences in elevation greater than five feet, you'll need to "back sight." To do this, take the first measurement as outlined in steps 4 through 6 and jot down your results. Repeat the measuring procedure, but use the previously established high point as the new location for your measuring stick; I recommend that you get a helper to follow along after you with the measuring stick. Do this as many times as you need to get to the highest spot you want to locate, each time making a note of the vertical rise you have measured. Finally, add up your accumulated figures, and you have the total difference between the original low point and the final high point. This last number, the total, is the one you enter in the appropriate place on the base plan.

9. There is one kind of circumstance where I often find I can do nicely without the measuring stick. When I'm figuring out the various elevations of a terrain that slopes up and away from the side of a house, I use chalk, charcoal, or tape to mark intervals all the way up the side of the house. The marking operation involves a ladder, needless to say. Then I establish my eye level and walk up the slope, level in hand. It's easy to ascertain the various elevations by taking sights on the marked scale on the side of the house and subtracting my eye-level height from the height I see. I'll go all over the landscape until I've located a good number of different points. A fringe benefit of this system is that you end up relating points in the landscape to the levels of the doors, windows, eaves, porches, or dormers of the house — which is something you ought to do sometime anyway.

Sun and Wind Diagram I spoke in Chapter 4 of the sun and the wind and of some of the ways in which they shape and color our landscapes, our houses, our ways of life. Right at this very basic stage of planning, diagrams of seasonal angles of sun and direction of prevailing winds belong on your base plan. A typical sun diagram and wind arrow are shown here; you can use a compass and a protractor, a drafting compass, or even just a jar lid to make a neat version of a sun diagram in an uncrowded corner of your base plan. It may seem academic as you look at it now, but as you develop your ideas further you'll refer to the sun diagram constantly.

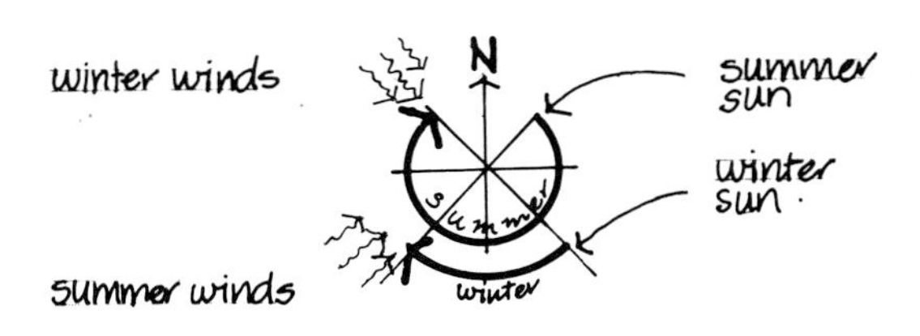

SUN and WIND DIAGRAM.

A simplified version of a sun diagram is accompanied by arrows showing the directions of prevailing summer and winter winds. Put these on a corner of the base plan.

Analysis You are now the proud owner of a base plan. When you are ready to get it printed, go to a blueprint shop (see your Yellow Pages) and get several prints made, the same size as your original plan. Black line prints are my preference, since they look more like the original drawing; but blue line prints work perfectly well too. Now you can write and sketch all over the prints without ruining your original base plan; and that's the object of reproducing the plan: to allow you to think freely and flexibly on paper.

You probably have been thinking in a general way about your landscaping needs and desires, as you went through the routine of preparing the base plan. Now is the moment to get down to cases and start annotating one of the prints. The problems and opportunities you will want to address usually fall into three general categories: your house, your site, and the people involved. The lists below should get you started — but don't feel limited by them. Trust your judgment, your experience, and your imagination.

Site Under the site category, the important things to note at this stage have to do with the existing situation. It isn't yet time to put in specifics of possible future plantings or construction. Do, however, focus on such considerations as the following:

- Views, good and bad; particularly ones you want to emphasize or to screen or block out completely.
- Vegetation that needs attention. This could include trees or shrubs that should be cut back, or even removed, to open up a view or let in more light; or merely areas that call for thinning, pruning, or a cleanup of deadwood and broken limbs.
- Climatic variations, such as areas that are shady, too sunny (in summer), or too windy (in winter). Every site has its microclimates, as you'll already know if you are a gardener; become conscious of these.
- Seasonally wet or dry areas, or other areas with unusual soil conditions.

House As you look at your house, you can be thinking not only about what exists now, but about changes you may want to incorporate into the landscaping plan. Make notes on the plan of such things as:

- Elements of the exterior of the house (forms, angles, textures, colors, building materials) that you may want to duplicate or echo in the landscape, to provide continuity and cohesiveness between the old and the new.
- Alterations to the house that could make for a more attractive and more comfortable relationship between exterior and interior. You may want to think about adding, subtracting, moving, or enlarging windows or doors; or giving rooms more logical uses.

People Again, this category of considerations includes both what is happening now and what you see coming in the future. Some examples:

- Specific uses of parts of the site, such as areas for parking cars, hanging laundry, collecting trash, raising vegetables, entertaining, or engaging in building projects or other hobbies.

- Children's needs. If there's a sandbox or a swing set now, what will you do with that area later on?
- Requirements for pets (doghouse, fenced yard, etc.) if applicable.

Regulations You have almost finished the sizing-up phase of your landscaping project. You've done a lot of careful hands-on work, as well as a lot of daydreaming, introspection, and practical study of what you have to work with and what you want to make of it. Your final move in this first phase is to stand back a bit from the house and the lot that have absorbed your attention so far, and take a look at your plans from a community perspective.

Be sure to do some research into your city's or town's zoning bylaws and building code. Check for any regulations that might affect your plans, particularly those involving setbacks and height restrictions. Watch out for any easements that may have been granted in past years. Read through the rules governing structures, such as fencing, pools, garages, or gazebos; and be aware early on of the requirements you may have to meet. It's generally easy to comply with the rules and regulations, so long as they don't come as a surprise at too late a stage.

Also speak to your neighbors to make sure that they are in sympathy with your plans. I've heard of families who started joyfully building something as apparently harmless as a tree house — only to have the neighbors object and the town planning board force the destruction of the children's leafy hideaway.

If you find that you will need a zoning variance in order to build some structure on your property, your neighbors' cooperation and support can make the difference between victory and defeat. In many cases, an improvement to one piece of property turns out to benefit all adjoining ones and even the whole neighborhood. But even if it doesn't, an atmosphere of friendly communication is important to any project.

This chapter has concentrated on detailed, mechanical procedures involving lots of work with pencils and paper. Now it's time to look up from the graph paper, to stop focusing on what you have and start picturing what you hope to do. Chapter 6 explores the essential qualities of a landscape that is both functional and beautiful.

---

6 DESIGNING YOUR LANDSCAPE

Imagine that your landscape is a series of outdoor rooms. I've already spoken of landscape spaces in architectural terms: "walls," "entries," "ceilings," and so forth. In a very real sense, when you design an exterior space — a landscape — you are doing many of the same kinds of things you do when designing an interior room. You take stock of existing conditions (the size and shape and materials at hand); determine what you'd like to add and subtract; and arrive at a scheme that incorporates spaces, structures, colors, and textures that will suit your taste and serve your purposes.

Every combination of site, house, and family is unique. So I won't attempt here to offer a catalogue of ready-made landscaping styles or prototypes. Not one of them would really fit your needs. Anyway, the delight of designing a landscape lies as much in the process as in the finished product. Very often, a design evolves as you go along. Questions lead to their own answers, problems to their own solutions.

Nevertheless, I can emphasize a few basic precepts about how you go about this process. The first was covered in Chapter 5: make a plan. The second precept: take your time, as much time as possible. Landscaping is a long-term project, and there's no sense in being hasty in the design phase. Spend some time just thinking, looking around you, leafing through gardening magazines, visiting parks and garden centers and other people's houses. You will find that you begin to see landscapes (your own and others) more accurately. You will gradually develop a sensitivity to what pleases you and what might be practical for you — as well as an awareness of what's not your style or is out of your league.

The third golden rule: whenever you make an estimate of a cost, double it. For good measure, also double the time that you allow for any operation to be completed. This realistic word of warning is fundamental to success and happiness in landscape design, especially for the beginner or the do-it-yourself landscaper.

The twin goals of landscape design, as of interior design, are to enhance beauty and to attain a desired level of usefulness, livability, and ease of maintenance. If you had acres and acres to play with, you could consign one area to functional uses and another to visual elegance. But few residential landscapes (or residences) afford that kind of square footage. With space at a premium, your mission is to create a setting that is both a practical living environment and a joy to the eye. Even in very limited space, you can have it all.

I'll focus on the utilitarian aspects of landscape design later in this chapter. For now, however, here are a few guidelines for you in your role as an artist of the beautiful.

Designing for Beauty Ideas and ideals of beauty are as various as people. Once again, I won't try to prescribe, because a landscape that might suit me perfectly might not be your cup of tea. But there are some reliable basic qualities that will improve just about any design.

Back to basics First of all, pay attention to the principles of composition outlined in Chapter 2. Scale, balance, rhythm, emphasis, and simplicity: if your design embodies these five it cannot go far wrong.

Keep in the forefront of your thinking the five elements of design. Masses, forms, and lines make up the basic picture; colors and textures enrich it. Choose them all with an eye to an overall mood or tone that's in keeping with your way of life, the appearance of your house, and your personality.

Appealing to the senses Although I often urge restraint (in the mixing of colors or forms, for instance), when you design with the five senses in mind you can let yourself go. This is one of the particularly exciting things about landscape design. The more senses a landscape appeals to, the better. Sight and touch — the opportunities are obvious and limitless. Hearing — don't discount the importance of the sounds of foliage, water, wind, birds, even the human voice. The sense of smell — at every moment and at every season, you are smelling the world around

A feast for the senses in an English garden: massed shrubs, ground covers, perennials, and herbs are redolent with spring fragrance.

you, however unaware you may be. The fragrance of roses and the heady sweetness of honeysuckle come readily to mind; but the smells of pine trees, newly turned earth, a pile of wet leaves in the fall, or a warm wind are equally important to the nose. The sense of taste might seem minor in connection with the landscape — but don't forget the taste of a blade of grass or of homegrown blueberries, or the way a picnic or even a drink of water outdoors somehow tastes better than it ever does indoors. Even the smallest garden can appeal to all five senses, and it should.

Developing character: the addition of trickling water points up the dramatic beauty of this massive rock outcropping and adds sensory appeal.

Developing character How often we think of or describe someone as having "character," a distinctive quality of personality. To be memorable, a landscape too must possess character, a set of images and associations that identify it and set it apart.

The character of a landscape derives partly from regional climate and geography. It partakes of the nature of local materials, the topography of the land, the native vegetation. And a good landscape design will recognize this. It is as risky for a landscape designer to strive for a lush effect in an open rocky setting, or a desert effect in a woodland, as it is for an architect to create a building without reference to or respect for its surroundings. Neither effort will be successful in the long run. In fact, such strained contrivances look more dated and more absurd with every passing season.

Partly, however, the character of a landscape can be the product of your planning and taste. It can come from your choice of focus or emphasis, such as a notable site feature (a rock ledge or the bank of a stream, for instance) or a particular planting or piece of construction. Or it can come from the success of your composition as a whole: the unique way in which you have put together all the elements that make up your landscape.

Designing for Use Beauty is all very well; but as I have already suggested a number of times, a landscape that is beautiful to the eye can lose all its appeal if it's not fitted to the practical needs of its inhabitants.

Instances of beauty without usefulness aren't hard to come by. I think, for example, of a lawn that looks lush and enticing — but which you sink into up to your ankles if you make the mistake of stepping on it at certain seasons. Or a flight of steps whose treads and/or risers are the wrong dimensions, so that they're uncomfortable or even treacherous to

Fencing and trellis serve two functions, creating a private outdoor living area and at the same time directing visitors to the doorway.

walk on. Or plantings that are too fragile or formal for a young family, or too difficult for an older person to maintain. Or a wall or deck, handsome in itself, that reflects blinding light and baking heat into the windows of the house.

All these are minor errors but irritating ones. They can't help but detract from the charm of the overall landscape — and they are avoidable. Avoiding them was one of the main purposes of the careful assessment and mapping that went on in Chapter 5. And it is a primary goal of the more creative planning that is going on in this section. Devote some imaginative thought to the functions of each area of your landscape: what purpose does the area serve, and can you improve it with different kinds of planting or structures? Consider the ways people will move from one area to another: how could circulation be made more comfortable? And ask yourself how much effort you want to put into maintaining the finished landscape: is freedom from (or ease of) upkeep a high priority? Easy maintenance is a prime consideration for many people, and a very feasible goal.

Function and fit The exercise of making the checklist in Chapter 5 should have left you with a fairly good idea of the kinds of activities you want to engage in on your property. Here's where you start figuring out how and where to modify (or design from scratch) the landscape to fit everything in. Working with a copy of your base plan, reconsider the factors raised in Chapter 4 on natural orientation.

Soil conditions, for example, may have an impact on your ideas about where you put what. Suppose you want to have a paved outdoor sitting area, a small wading pool, and a vegetable plot. If you try to grow vegetables where the old driveway used to run, you'll have to excavate the compact earth and create topsoil where none exists. Put the pool where the rock outcropping just shows at the foot of that tree, and you

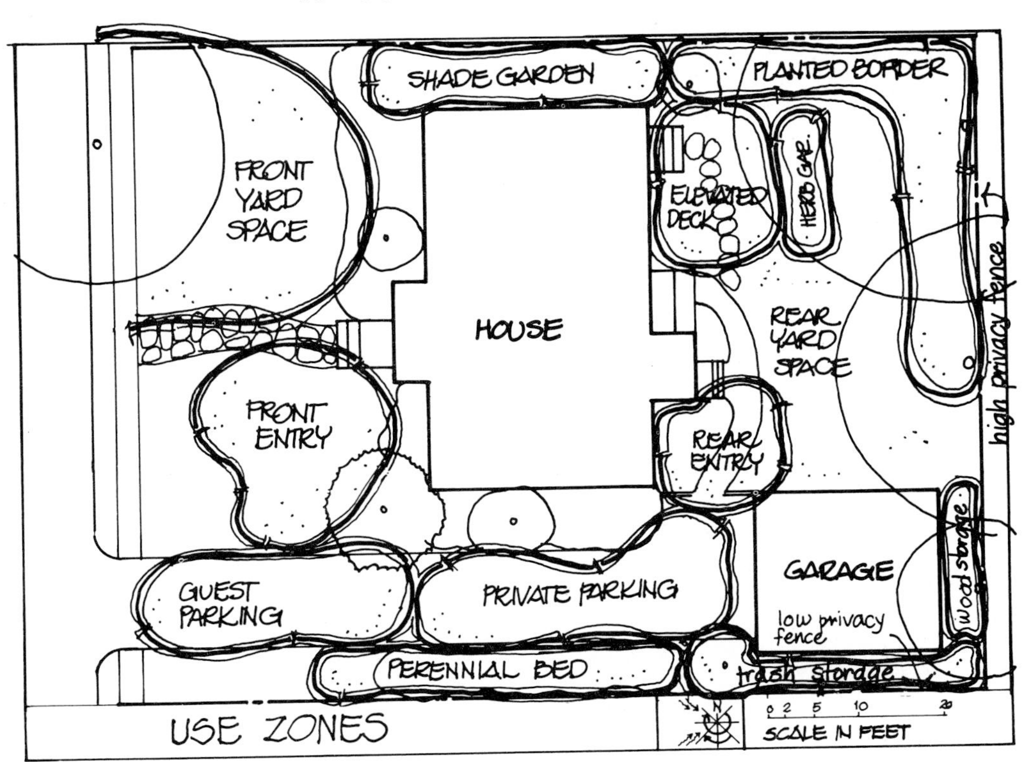

Indicate use zones on a base-plan overlay to clarify the general types of use of different areas.

Two alternative plans for the same site. The final plan selected is shown in the hard-lined sketch on p. 71.

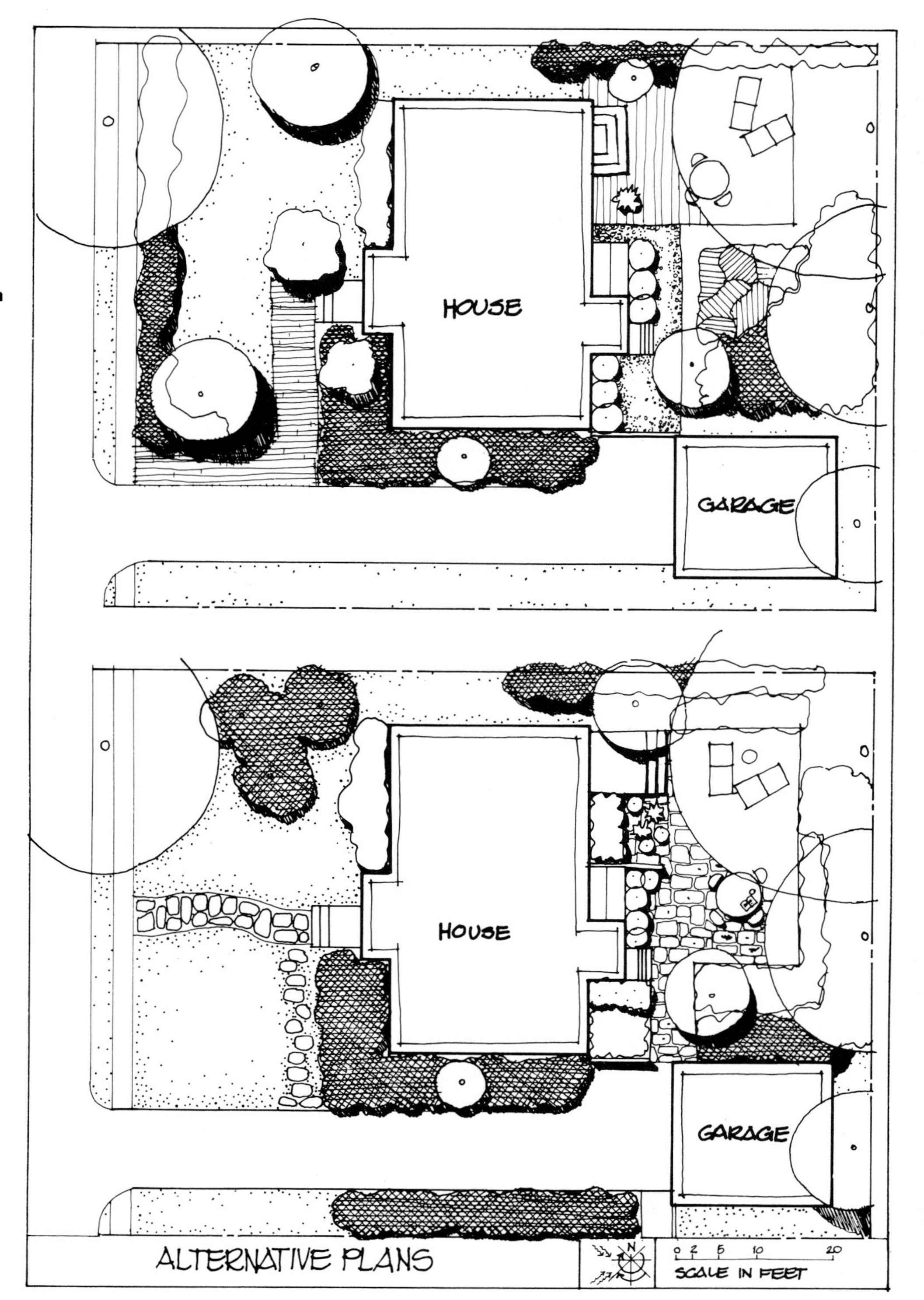

won't just be excavating, you'll be blasting. Pave the corner of the lawn where the grass grows tallest and greenest all summer, and you'll have to dig out all the good loam and replace it with a foot-deep bed of gravel.

Climatic factors, too, will have a lot to do with the livability of outdoor spaces and the uses to which you can put them. A windy passage between house and hedge is great for drying laundry, but terrible for sitting with the morning paper. A hot southern exposure next to the house wall is fine for private sunbathing, but not the place to put a sandbox. A deeply shaded spot is perfect for a bed of pachysandra, but a poor choice for a swimming pool.

There is much you can do with plantings and/or construction to modify the effects of sun and wind: tactics like establishing windbreaks, planting (or cutting down) trees, training vines over trellises, or installing ornamental pools or fountains can create whole new microclimates in different areas around your house. Climatic considerations are basic to every move you make in the landscape — from planting a rhododendron to building a brick wall — and they're discussed in detail in the calendar section.

Sort out the different activities that will take place in your landscape, and consider the best amount and location of space for each one. At the outset, segregate public and private space. You might want to take a crayon or colored pencil in some pale tone and cross-hatch one of the copies of your base plan with different tones to indicate public versus private. Or you could lay a sheet of tracing paper over the base plan and color on that. Then break down those two areas more specifically, into living areas, play areas, service areas, and maybe sites for special purposes such as a garden or swimming pool.

One group of functions that will probably fall under the "private space" heading are the strictly utilitarian. Let's face it, everyone has to store trash somewhere. Or possibly you need a tool shed, or a place to split and store firewood, or a location for a cold frame. Think now about how you might dedicate a certain space to these mundane purposes and screen them from the public view — perhaps even from the patio or the windows of the house. Don't forget, as you plan any such working area, the necessity for getting there with whatever vehicles or machines you'll be using, from boat trailer to wheelbarrow.

Think about all other outdoor activities in the same exhaustive way. How will the living area of the landscape be organized? Is the swimming pool the visual focus as well as the focus of activity (if so, attractive fencing will be a high priority) — or should the pool be tucked away around a corner? Is it important to you to be able to keep an eye on the driveway while you're weeding the vegetable patch? Will the prevailing summer breeze waft the fragrance of barbecuing goodies from your outdoor grille into your own or the neighbors' living room — and if so, how will you or they feel about it?

With unlimited space, of course, there would be no problem allocating areas for activities. The less space you have, the more meticulously you need to plan to make everything dovetail. You may even find that you can't do absolutely everything you'd like. But keep juggling spaces and trying new arrangements. You may be surprised at just how much is possible in a very little space.

While you are thinking conceptually about how these areas of activity are going to fit your site and how they are going to be linked and accessed, you should begin to zero in on some approximate dimensions for them. Allowing ample room for each of the uses you envision may call for some ingenuity. Sometimes, if you're in a space bind, the answer is to position two functional areas so that they can be paired up when necessary, to serve one function or the other. For instance, if you plan to do a lot of outdoor entertaining but can't build a terrace broad enough to accommodate the largest crowd you'd like to invite, then you may be able to double the usable space by placing the terrace next to a grassy lawn and providing easy access from terrace to lawn and vice versa. At the other extreme, if you want your terrace just to fit a breakfast table and two people, you might want to consider a balcony with a railing, which wouldn't impinge on the lawn at all. A driveway and turnaround that are used only by family's and friends' cars can be on the small side; but if the same access route has to serve oil trucks, garbage trucks, and delivery trucks, then you'll need a wider drive and a greater depth or diameter to the turnaround.

Circulation Getting cars and oil trucks in and out of your drive is one form of circulation. But every portion of your landscape has its own requirements for access and egress — and planning for them is part of your job at this stage.

For inspiration you can turn first to the things that please and annoy you (respectively) about the way the movement of people and things around your property works now.

Very often, circulation problems have actually been built into a house and site. A typical case is that of the service doorway which leads to the kitchen and laundry, but which catches the eye of visitors before the front door, so that all visitors come barging right into the kitchen. To obviate this problem, there should be a clearly delineated approach to the front entrance to the house: a route that is fairly direct, visible from the visitor's parked car, and so designed as to say, "Welcome — this is the way in."

Another pet peeve of mine is the drive that leads straight to someone's garage door. As a visitor, you have to park in front of the garage, so that you block access to it, which makes you feel like an intruder. And if the garage door is open it's usually to the owner's embarrassment. The best solution, if at all possible, is to allow for a visitors' parking place separate from the place where the family car is kept. If that's not possible, see what other ingenious means you can develop to steer guests' cars away from the garage and screen its cluttered interior. You might build a curve into the driveway, with shrubbery or a fence to shield the offending garage from view.

And then there are the little things. Has the dog worn a bare spot where he rounds the corner of the house on his way from front door to back? Maybe that's the place for some flagstones or a brick walk. Are you always wishing you could go directly from the living room to the corner of the patio that's warm and sunny even in winter? Maybe a door could be opened up. Does the post office van dig at least one rut in the lawn every spring? Maybe the drive should be wider, or a stone curb be placed along the edge of the grass.

While you are pondering these things, review the checklist you made in Chapter 5. Be sure to provide for access to utilities' meters (for reading), to the septic tank (for cleanouts), to the well or to water or sewer lines (for maintenance). The March Materials and Construction section gives dimensional requirements for walks, steps, and drives. Use

Circulation is especially important around this rambling old house now turned into five condo units. Visitors' parking, service areas, and walkways are carefully planned.

these as a general guide to how much space to allow for these necessary avenues of circulation.

Maintenance Design and installation, exciting though they may be, are the tip of the landscaping iceberg. The rest of it is upkeep: month in, month out, season after season, year after year. Unlike vegetables or annual flowers, landscape plants often outlive the people who planted them. (Many, if not most, trees and shrubs and vines take several years to attain the size and form for which they were chosen in the first place.) And landscape construction materials are by definition engineered to endure years of sun, rain, and ice.

Since these furnishings (as it were) of the landscape will be with you for such a long time, I urge you to decide at the outset how much time you want to spend grooming and cleaning up around them. Minimum maintenance may be your chief priority; or you may enjoy gardening and welcome seasonal chores as a change of pace and an opportunity to be outdoors. Whichever, this is the time to do a little soul-searching and decide on a general approach.

For ease of care, one basic rule is to keep your design simple in every respect. Lay out the lawn — if any — with gently curving edges, no corners or small areas that are fussy to mow. Keep high-maintenance areas like flower beds and vegetable plots few in number, manageable in size, and easy to get at. Steer clear of trees or shrubs that will demand regular pruning or trimming.

For that matter, avoid any plant that will actually create work. Unless you like raking, don't plant a large-leaved deciduous shade tree where it will dump a mountain of leaves on a lawn or terrace every autumn. Keep fruiting trees like cherries or crabapples away from paved areas where their squashed fruit will be a nuisance. And make sure that all plants you select are healthy and well adapted to the use and location you plan for them.

In Part II, the calendar section, every monthly chapter has a

Landscape Tasks entry dedicated to upkeep and maintenance. For those who are more interested in freedom from upkeep, the February chapter talks about planning an easy-maintenance landscape and gives a list of plants that require minimal care.

By now you have come almost full circle, from a crash course in the basics of landscape design, to the production of the base plan and its accompanying checklists, through some conceptual thinking about how you might add to or alter your landscape for both beauty and use, to the part that is the most fun of all — sketching and finally putting into effect the solution.

7 FROM SKETCH TO REALITY

In the preceding chapters I have looked at aspects of landscape design from various angles; and I've tried to encourage you not to make any actual changes in your place until you have thought the project through with great thoroughness. By now, I hope you have done just that. This is the time to settle down in earnest with the base plan and the tracing paper.

Sketching Clip a piece of tracing paper over a clean copy of the base plan and sketch in roughly the various areas and circulation routes you have devised. You will probably want to do this more than once, whether to refine your first thoughts or to try whole different tacks. You may throw out more sketches than you keep. Don't be too compulsive about accuracy or precise dimensions. The idea is to arrive at a design, then pin down the details as needed — much as a fashion designer sketches out a "look" without too much concern for anatomical realism or the exact locations of seams or buttons.

When you have pretty well exhausted your ideas, pick the sketch that you feel will work the best, and start refining it. Check the dimensions of pathways, flights of steps, walls, planting areas; make sure they're going to fit. Think about the kinds of plants, paving, and construction materials you may be using. If you're going to be making any grade changes, review the vertical relief measurements noted on the base plan, and decide whether you will be using masonry retaining walls, wood timbers, sloped banks, or what. And keep looking back at the base plan — to be sure (among other things) that in your enthusiasm you haven't put structures or pavements over septic tanks, utility rights-of-way, town easements, or other hidden pitfalls.

The more details you add, the more jumbled your sketch will look. It's helpful to take some colored pencils or marking pens and color the different surfaces. I make driveways light gray, walks a light tan, decks or terraces the same color as the walks or slightly darker (two layers of the same color), lawns a light green, and planting areas a darker green. Deciduous trees can just be circles with no additional color, so as not to obscure the ground plane. (You may want to fill in the circles that represent evergreens, though, at least if they're the kind of evergreens whose foliage starts right down at ground level.)

At this point the design will begin to look very beautiful and you may be tempted to summon the local brickyard and have the local nursery send over a truckload of shrubs. One more stroke of patience, please — better first to test out your hunches on the ground.

Layout and Mockup Take measurements directly from your scaled drawing and measure out each structure, planting, path, wall, etc. on the ground, using the longest tape measure you have. As you get each measurement correct, mark it somehow so that you can begin to see what the finished product will look like. Let your imagination run riot. Here are a few easy marking ideas:

- Garden hoses are handy for laying out curved bed edges, walkways, or other curved linear elements on the ground plane.
- To lay out perfectly straight lines, use stakes and string.
- If you want to get a bird's eye view of a ground-plane layout, mark the beds, shrubs, etc. with agricultural limestone. Then go up to the top floor of your house and look out the window.
- You can mock up fences or walls with cardboard and stakes; or with blankets draped over string, rope, or wire.
- To locate the tops of things (trees, buildings, porch roofs, and such) and see how they'll affect views and where their shadows will fall, prop up bamboo poles or two-by-fours. I have even on occasion sent up helium-filled balloons on premeasured strings; make sure it is a calm day, though.
- To get a sense of the view and other sight lines from a proposed deck, put yourself on a stepladder at the same height you'd be if you were sitting in a chair on the deck. Now try "standing" on the deck. Repeat several times, moving the ladder to different spots on the imaginary deck.

Some of these gimmicks and acrobatics may sound far-fetched, but you really should do all you can to test out your landscaping plan before you take any steps to make it happen. This on-site visualizing phase is harder than it sounds. Imagine the difference between a bare stage and the same rectangular space with props, scenery, and backdrop in place. The difference in apparent size alone — not to mention the totally changed mood and character — is astounding and often difficult to anticipate. Difficult, but not impossible, and approaching possibility is the object of all this measuring and mocking up.

And again, now, not later, is the time to discover your mistakes. Maybe that fence could be slightly lower, that patio two feet wider, or those steps made into a ramp instead. Replacing plants is a nuisance; relocating or rebuilding construction is an expensive nuisance.

Once you have tested your plan until you feel confident that it is as good as you can make it, a sensible move is to take your final sketch to a garden center or nursery that does construction to get their advice. (Naturally, they may be more lavish with advice if it is clear that you'll be buying materials from them.) Sound them out on the construction materials and details of any decks or terraces, pathways, pools, or other structures you have planned. Get their reactions to the plants you've chosen for various locations and functions. No nurseryman or landscape contractor wants to be party to a disappointing outcome; so there's almost a built-in guarantee they will do all they can to steer you right according to their own best judgment. (I'd certainly expect, however, that after all this planning you would not be too far off the track.)

If your design is simple in concept and modest in scale, you may be able to work straight from your sketch. If, on the other hand, there's

For laying out edges of beds, drives, and walks I often use limestone. Viewing from a distance or from an upstairs window shows how the design will look on the ground.

sophisticated construction, grading, or extensive and elaborate planting involved, you may need to go one further step — to "hard-lining."

Hard-lining To compute needed quantities of construction materials (pipe, lumber, stone, concrete) or to pinpoint relationships like those between flights of steps and the floor grade of a house, you'll need a hard-lined drawing instead of a sketch.

For hard-lining you abandon the tracing paper and go back to transparent graph paper. It's best to use the same scale as that of your base plan (unless you have found that scale unworkable in the long run) so as to avoid a lot of extra mathematics. Using T-square and triangle, make a precise version of the base plan and landscaping design, incorporating all the elements of your working sketch, but neatly, with exact measurements shown.

You may also want to draw one or more elevations (side or front views) or sections (cutaway slices to show foundations, drains, or underpinnings). If you do, you'll have to go outside again to measure or estimate the heights of existing elements — such as your house, a tree, a fence, or a hedge — that you want to represent on the elevation or section. It isn't really hard work to make these drawings, although it is time-consuming. If your design calls for much sophisticated plotting and drafting, however, you may decide that this is one time to consult a professional landscape architect.

Still, I'd encourage you to avoid hard-lining at all, even if you are already working with a landscaping professional, unless the magnitude or complexity of the plan positively demands it. The reason is that hard-lining can stifle imagination and limit flexibility. Just as it is human nature not to want to get rid of something once it's in place, it is human nature to resist changing a hard-lined drawing.

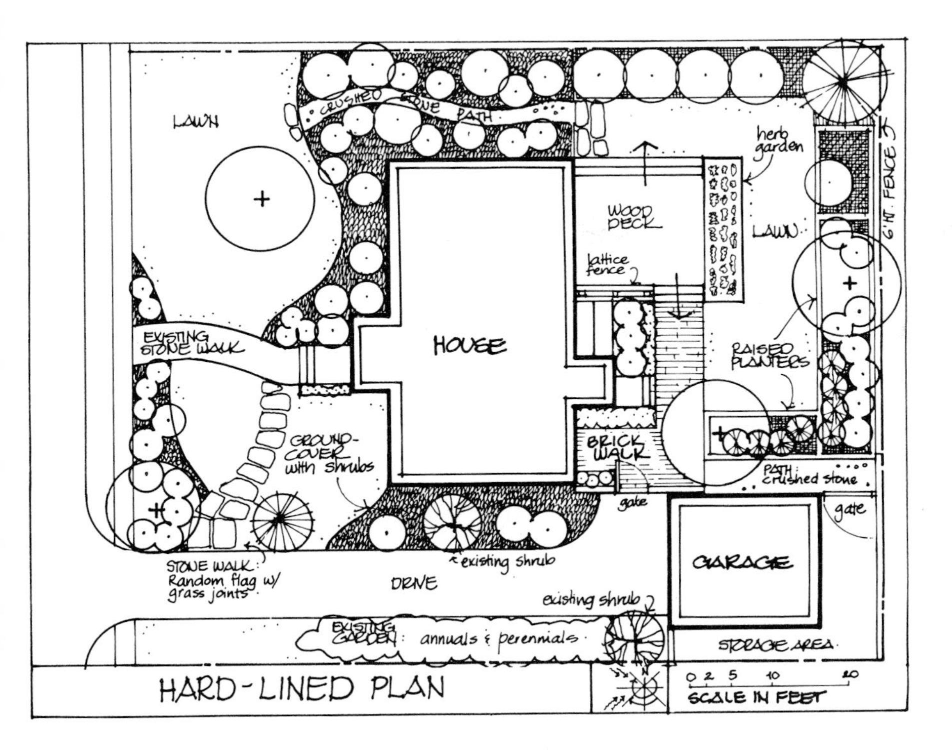

Here, the chosen plan has gone from rough sketch to hard-lined finished drawing.

But in landscaping it is vital that you keep an open mind as you go along. There are always surprises, things you didn't anticipate on paper. Sometimes they are happy surprises, and you find that you end up with a more attractive solution than you thought possible. Sometimes they are unhappy, and you have to have the flexiblity to cope with them. I never design a landscape where the final result matches the paper plan in every detail. And I never tire of making changes and adjustments when I can see there's an improvement to gain.

Into the Ground At last, the fruits of all your careful and creative thought: action! It's time to lay out a schedule, pinpoint costs, and get to work.

Making a schedule In any landscaping job, from the most sweeping transformation to the most minor change, work must progress in sequence — and from the bottom up.

Just like a building, a well-constructed garden almost always has some underpinnings. The schematic drawing here makes the point clear. Is there going to be hard construction, such as a walk, drive, or terrace? Bases must be laid. Will there be a wall, some steps, a deck, or a fence? Footings must be constructed early on. What about drainage — from condition of topsoil to depth of subsoil, from topography to drains, drywells, and gutters? Get the basic groundwork done before anything else. For example, dig trenches for utilities *before* you spread or seed topsoil. Grade soil into the forms and planes desired *before* you put plants into the ground.

Contemplating an adjustment to a landscape plan.

Seasonal considerations also enter in. In the Northeast, for instance, most landscaping work occurs during the six or seven months when the earth is unfrozen and most workable — roughly April through

UNDERGROUND CONSIDERATIONS·

Below-ground preparations often take more time and money than anticipated, yet are critical for quality results in the long run.

October. Whatever area you live in, think ahead realistically about what can be accomplished in the available time. For Hardiness Zones 5 and 6 (see the Zone Map on pages 346–347), a very rough approximation of spring and fall planting seasons might go as follows.

Planting

	Season begins	*Season ends*
Spring Planting		
Lawns	1–15 April	15–30 May
Evergreens	1–15 April	15–30 May
Deciduous plants	1–15 April	15–30 May
Fall Planting		
Lawns	1–15 August	15–30 September
Evergreens	1–15 September	1–15 November
Deciduous plants	1–15 October	15–30 November

(If you're at the northern range of your area, you want to take the later dates for beginning and earlier dates for ending each season; if southern, the opposite: earlier dates for beginning and later dates for ending each season. And if you're in Zone 7 or south, everything can begin and end earlier in spring and later in fall.)

If your project calls for time-consuming construction that runs beyond the spring planting dates, it may be sensible to put off planting until later. Traditionally, fall is the preferred time for planting lawns, and many trees and shrubs — although nurseries now have techniques that allow planting right through the summer. If you're stuck in the fall beyond the dates for seeding a lawn, the solution is usually sod. Consider doing major earth-moving — such as excavating, filling, or otherwise disrupting the site — in the fall. Let the whole project settle in over the winter, then complete and refine it and do the planting in the spring.

Shopping for materials If you are going to undertake your project on your own, you'll be buying your own plants and construction materials; and some exploratory shopping (at least) has to take place before you can firm up your budget. This can be tremendous fun, as well as educational. It's no different from shopping for anything you're unfamiliar with at first. Go through the Yellow Pages, then visit materials yards and nurseries. Find a reputable dealer; ask lots of questions; and buy only when you are satisfied with quality, price, and whatever guarantees are available. Used materials and bargain rates may not really save you money if quality is sacrificed, so go carefully.

Using landscape architects and contractors When to call in a landscape architect, and on what basis? If you find yourself totally unable to decide between different design possibilities, or if you feel technically unequipped to organize or execute the work, a word or two of professional advice can be both helpful and reassuring. It needn't necessarily cost a fortune: most landscape architects offer you the option of a one- or two-hour consultation at a flat hourly rate. A more extensive involvement, of course, is a different matter, with lower hourly rate but lots more hours spent in design, detailing, selecting materials, and supervising construction and planting.

If you decide to hire a contractor to do any phase of the job (or all of it), get him to supply you with samples of the materials he intends to use before starting work; or work out an agreement whereby he'll use materials that you choose and purchase. For instance, if you find a source of stone that's just what you want for a patio or walk, talk with the contractor and make sure he approves of it before you pay for it. The reason it's important to have all these things clear is that contractors' standard operating procedure is to buy materials at a discount (anywhere from 5 to 30 percent), then charge you the full retail price to cover their delivery and handling charges and any guarantees they offer.

If you are undertaking a project that involves several different contractors — say, a mason, an electrician, a driveway contractor, and a carpenter — you can serve as your own general contractor. That is, you hire all the individual contractors yourself and you coordinate their respective efforts. Or you can have a general contractor do this for you. You'll probably pay 10 to 20 percent more for the job as a whole if you use a general contractor, but you'll save any number of headaches.

I am a great believer in having the landscape contractor on a job also serve as the general contractor. Of all the people involved, he is apt to have the best sense of what should happen when; and thus he can ensure a proper meshing of all facets of the project. Be certain he has this capability from previous projects that you have seen or that you know to have been successfully completed.

Budgeting and staging I mentioned earlier how important it is to double every cost estimate at the planning stage. When you start shopping and talking with contractors and so forth, you may actually find that you can't do everything you hope to do all at once. In that event, I'd encourage you to do the work in stages.

The best way to approach staging, I think, is to complete one area at a time — and do a good job of it. That will give you the satisfaction of seeing at least one thing finished before you go on to the next. The alternative — trying to skimp overall, installing mere twigs for plantings,

Staging: only the path, fence, and a few shrubs were installed in the first phase here. Phase 2 will add ground covers and additional planting to extend the blooming through the season.

laying temporary surfaces for pavements — may be necessary in some cases; but it can be very discouraging and trying to the patience. All too often, "good enough just for now" becomes "forever, and never really right."

Be sure of your own priorities. If one thing must precede another, should it be the service area? The public view from the street? The private side terrace? Keep both appearance and practicality in mind.

When you're trying to cut back cost overruns, it's natural to look first at the most expensive items and see if they can wait or somehow be modified. Heavy construction projects like drives, walks, walls, and steps often look like the most obvious candidates for postponement. Yet in some instances, postponing one or more of these jobs for reasons of economy can hamper your enjoyment or use of the site or actually create larger costs later on. An exposed, unstabilized bank or steep unpaved drive, for example, can erode so badly that extensive (and expensive) repair work has to be done before the final planting or paving can be installed. In the long run it may be best to have all these big jobs done in one fell swoop, because you save on equipment costs. Once machines or equipment are on-site it's efficient to keep them in use; besides, remobilizing at a later date always costs extra.

Contracts No matter how small the job may seem, you should always have written contracts with all help, from electricians to general contractors to landscape architects. A signed agreement clarifies everyone's expectations as to service or material to be provided, cost, and date of completion or delivery.

Landscape design and construction does take patience, care, and love — but so does any project that's worth doing. All you really need are some ideas to stir your imagination and some practical guidance to keep your feet on the ground. And so on to Part II, where you should find plenty of both.

PART II THE LANDSCAPING YEAR

The twelve-month structure of Part II has offered me some wonderful opportunities. Many facets of landscaping are indeed seasonal. There are indoor times and outdoor times; planting, pruning, and building times; times for bloom and for fruit and for shade. It's the most natural thing in the world to deal with these subjects in the months appropriate to them.

This calendar format has also, however, presented me with some interesting dilemmas. Many topics simply cannot be restricted to one month or even one season: they're year-round in application. I have made choices, often very personal or arbitrary ones, about where to include what. For instance, I have talked about drives and walks in early spring, a time when it's natural to plan and construct major landscape spaces or to make improvements in anticipation of warmer weather. But paving can be laid in any month from March to October. By the same token, dogwoods crop up all over the place: like many landscape plants they come in many forms and have innumerable useful and ornamental roles to play. That's why I have not detailed the specific characteristics or cultural requirements of individual plants as they appear in the month-by-month chapters here, but have assembled them in Part III. This is a major departure from the other Victory Garden books, but makes good sense in terms of accessibility, I think.

Locating things in Part II is a matter of following the directories. The contents of each month's chapter are listed in the table of contents at the beginning of the book; they're also thumbnailed on the title page of each month; and of course they are exhaustively indexed at the back of the book.

Detailed how-to instructions for all the topics raised in Part II fall under two headings. For inanimate materials and construction projects, I'll introduce each material — its origins, its assets and liabilities, its relative costs, its uses — and show you how I tackle numerous projects from the standpoint of design, utility, and economy. But this isn't a construction manual. There are excellent publications available telling you how to lay a concrete pavement, build a wooden deck, or pipe an artificial water-

Layers of white, pink, and red azalea bloom carpet this woodland floor.

fall. I have listed many of them in Further Reference at the end of this book. Look there if do-it-yourself construction is your interest. Here I'm concerned more with the whys and wherefores than with the how-tos.

For plants, the detailed how-to information can be found in the Part III description of each individual plant. In monthly sections dealing with flowering shrubs, shade trees, ground covers, and so on, I'll generally just remind you to give each plant the kind of soil, amount of sun, and degree of shelter that it likes best.

Nor will I try to write here the ultimate treatise on coping with bugs, viruses, bacteria, fungus diseases, weeds, and other garden nuisances. Both *Crockett's Victory Garden* and *Crockett's Flower Garden* do a good job on many specific ailments and their cures. But the permanent landscape plants I talk about in this book — trees, shrubs, vines, and ground covers — really should be able to endure most of the cyclical pests and blights that come their way. A basically healthy oak tree afflicted with leaf gall (for example) just isn't comparable to a zucchini riddled with borers or a tea rose smothered in powdery mildew. In addition, my overall approach to landscape plants tends toward the Darwinian: I give them an environment suited to their needs, and from there on it's survival of the fittest.

I will, however, indicate in the Landscape Tasks section each month the times of the year when you may want to undertake controls or preventive measures such as dormant oil spraying of fruit trees, fertilizing lawns and beds, or killing poison ivy. For myriad other problems, from Japanese beetles to fire blight, I refer you to the chemical and biological controls available at your garden center or through landscape nurseries or garden centers.

I should mention here that this book carries on the Victory Garden tradition of focusing primarily on the plants, soils, and climate of the region where the Victory Garden is: the Northeast, roughly Zones 5 and 6. The Zone Map on pages 346–347 will enable you to make any necessary adjustments in planting information.

In the interest of breaking the multifarious subject matter of Part II into manageable and findable segments, I've organized each month's material into the following five subject areas.

Landscaping Opportunities This monthly section sets up a seasonal landscape situation or scenario and explores the aspects I've found to be important. Many of these sections offer lists of recommended plants. Some, like the sections on energy-efficient landscaping or on the winter landscape, approach their topics more in terms of general concepts and issues.

Plants for a Purpose Hedging, shading, year-round color or form, ease of care — many Plants for a Purpose sections group plants by their functions. Others represent major, multipurpose horticultural categories, like native plants, broad-leaved evergreens, or small deciduous trees. While these sections are placed in seasonally appropriate months, every plant listed has a part to play all year long.

Every plant mentioned in this book appears in at least one of these Plants for a Purpose lists; many appear on several. Taken all together, the lists make up a complete collection of the trees, shrubs, vines, and ground covers that I recommend most highly for use in our region. But please be aware that I've really had to limit myself. Many personal favorites of mine have had to be excluded because of slow growth, disease problems, or other liabilities. Russian olive, white oak, and black locust are examples.

Materials and Construction Dedicated to the inorganic side of landscaping, these sections introduce the raw materials you'll be working with, and will help you think in terms of design. Sometimes they follow in sequence from month to month. May's section on wood for outdoor construction precedes June's discussion of decks, for instance. In other cases, they're linked to plant-oriented topics covered that month. In November, fences and gates accompany a section on hedges, since all three are useful for screening and protection from wind.

Plants by Design These lists suggest plants purely for visual qualities. In the winter and fall lists I have grouped plants with colorful bark and twigs and interesting bark textures; plants with attractive fruits and with yellow, orange, or red foliage; and plants with notable textures and forms. In March through August I have listed flowering trees and shrubs in order of bloom — so that if your aim is to have at least one plant or group of plants flowering in every month, you can make a selection from these lists.

Two cautions about using the order-of-bloom lists. First, the succession of bloom (what follows what) will be about the same wherever you are — but the absolute dates will vary widely according to your location and the particular nuances of local weather. (Make adjustments according to the Zone Map.) Second, try not to overdo. If you go much beyond one or two varieties in bloom at any one time (unless your place is really huge), your plantings may detract from, rather than complement, each other's beauty.

Landscape Tasks If seasonal projects and annual upkeep are your pleasure, this section should give you plenty to do. It's essentially a checklist, and you are encouraged to pick and choose.

Finally, a word about plant names and the organization of the dozens of plant lists throughout Parts II and III.

In the text, I've used familiar common names of plants. In lists in Part II, the common name comes first, followed by the Latin botanical name. (I have followed *Hortus* as my authority where spellings were in question.) But each list and each section of Part III (where the botanical name precedes the common name) is alphabetical by *botanical* name — because so many plants go by two or more common names that the only firm nomenclatures are the botanical ones. Most plant lists in this book name individual species — as in "weeping birch (*Betula pendula*)." Where I'm talking about a whole genus as a group, however, you'll see entries like "birches (*Betula* spp.)," meaning simply "various species of birch." The abbreviation "spp." stands for "species."

If you're in doubt about where to find any plant, just look in the index. Every plant is thoroughly cross-indexed under all its names.

The calendar year begins with January, and by a happy coincidence that's when many a successful landscaping project also enters the planning stages. It makes a very good month to begin our exploration of the real stuff of landscaping.

JAN

Landscaping Opportunities
The Winter Landscape

Plants for a Purpose
Plantings for Birds and Wildlife

Materials and Construction
Stone and Gravel

Plants by Design
Colorful Bark and Twigs

Landscape Tasks for January

Masses and forms of evergreens in a winter silhouette, dramatized by a squall of snow.

The winter landscape has a profound fascination. Far from dead, it is waiting, full of sleeping life. It abounds with stark contrasts and subtle colors — and often with dramatic lines, forms, and textures. This chapter explores aspects of landscaping appropriate to winter: stratagems for making the most of the latent beauty of the landscape; plantings to provide food and habitats for birds and wildlife; trees and shrubs with colorful bark for bright accents at this time of year. The Materials and Construction section looks at stone and gravel — materials you'd install later, but which you may now want to investigate, price, and contemplate using in projects in the coming months.

Landscaping Opportunities

THE WINTER LANDSCAPE

Most of the year we use our landscape, enjoying it, maintaining it, engaging in various activities outdoors. In the winter we tend to be in physical contact with the landscape far less often. In this season *seeing* becomes the main interaction between us and the landscape, and views from windows take on new importance.

Sleeping Beauty Much to the dismay of my family — and often of the professional gardeners or custodians involved — I enjoy visiting gardens and parks in midwinter. Amid cries of "but there's nothing to see," and "you really should come back in June when the azaleas bloom," I can wander happily among bare boughs and frozen soil. What there is to see is the architecture of the landscape, stripped of the summer's concealing green mantle. It is the undulating form of the land itself; the skeletons of the trees and shrubs growing there; the shapes of manmade structures.

Special winter effect: a dusting of snow emphasizes pattern and line. Snow melts off the warmer surfaces of paving stones and remains in the colder joints between.

Line becomes all-important. The tracery of leafless boughs against the sky; intricate shadow patterns on snow or bare ground; the now visible edges of paths, fences, trellises, walls. Linear elements that were softened by summer growth come into focus now with new clarity.

Light and color have new contexts and new meanings in winter. The rays of winter sunlight strike the earth at a shallower angle, creating longer shadows and lighting objects more from the side than from above. And everyone knows what snow does to a landscape: how it makes the sky seem bluer, and how all those long shadows reflect the sky's deep azure.

Even without snow, winter light unveils new ranges of color: the pinkish tops of long grasses, the purple hue of a hillside covered with second growth, the silvery or red tones of tree trunks we normally assume are brown, or the red-orange glow of shrubs we always think of as green.

Space itself changes (to the eye) in winter. Boundaries and demarcations seem to move. Summer's dense clump of leafy shrubbery or small trees suddenly grows transparent in winter, allowing the view to include a slope, a clearing, or larger trees beyond. A shady planting drops its umbrella of leaves, opening a huge space of sky above. Low-angled the sunlight may be, but in winter there's lots more of it, if you live among deciduous trees.

Even in a newly installed landscape, winter changes are dramatic.

Unlimited Possibilities Learning to see the beauty of the winter landscape is your first step. Thinking about ways to shape it to your taste and needs is the second. Now, while everything is open and exposed, look for projects that can be carried out in milder seasons, for your pleasure in winters to come.

The slanting winter light, for example, is ideal for backlighting dramatic elements in the landscape. You need to make sure that those dramatic elements are positioned properly in relation to your house and the sun. Put a picturesque tree such as a Japanese maple, or a wall or fence with interesting spaces built into it, to the south, southeast, or southwest of your house, and it will be backlit for a good part of the day.

Think about bringing things into silhouette, with or without backlighting. Some silhouettes make themselves, like the graceful curves of birches against a tall hemlock, or the dark forms of smaller evergreens against a pale wall or lawn. Other silhouettes you can create or emphasize through your choice of plantings or by clearing away underbrush or competing growth.

Line, light, and shadow are all-important in this rhythmic winter composition.

This is the season when evergreens really come into their own — yews, cedars, hemlocks, pines, and other conifers large and small; and broad-leaved evergreens like laurels, hollies, or rhododendrons. These were just part of the general greenery a few months ago, but now they take center stage. They establish boundaries, frame views, add blocks of solid form and color; and they play several parts at once. A clump of red cedars, for instance, affords a perfect haven for birds and small animals. In addition, its individual trees are appealing in shape and send dramatic elongated shadows across a grassy or snowy lawn. Besides, the bluish gray-green foliage of the trees is a perfect foil to the grays, browns, or greener greens around it.

(Be cautious with evergreens, though. Too large or too numerous conifers can create a dark and gloomy effect. Above all, never plant a forest tree like a Canadian hemlock or white pine right next to the house: it will rapidly take over the whole landscape.)

You can use the colors, textures, and densities of your plantings to affect visual perspective and the apparent scale of things, particularly in winter. Formal gardens in the classical mode employed rows of shrubbery to give an impression that long allees were receding into the distance. In an informal way and on a humbler scale, you can team conifers and deciduous trees to create vistas with an illusion of depth or distance greater than actually exists. Light-colored (such as autumn olive) or bluish-colored (such as Colorado blue spruce) or fine-textured (such as Thurlow willow) plants, set at the far edge of your field of vision, will help it seem farther away than it really is.

Deciduous trees and shrubs have their own special places in your winter landscape, and the plant lists this month highlight aspects of their seasonal appeal. You can select plants with a view to attracting birds and wildlife from the Plants for a Purpose section. Or think about plants with colored bark or twigs, either as individual accents or in groupings for stronger long-distance effects: this month's Plants by Design list has lots of suggestions. Your job is to achieve the maximum effect with the plantings you choose, and you can do this by arranging them carefully. If you put a beautiful red-stemmed shrub dogwood or gray-barked shadblow against a backdrop of second growth fifty yards from your house, it won't amount to much. But place the same plant northwest of the house and ten feet from a window, and the afternoon sun will illuminate the graceful silvery branches of the shad or set the scarlet branchlets of the dogwood ablaze with color. If you can, group three or five Oriental cherries (for instance) in a well-lit spot, within view of the house and against a light-toned background that will set them off, and they'll really make a statement.

Plants for a Purpose

PLANTINGS FOR BIRDS AND WILDLIFE

Birds are the flowers of our winter landscape; and January is a fine time to watch the birds at their busiest. It is also a good time to think about the kinds of trees and shrubs that can make your garden an appealing place for birds and small wildlife. My emphasis here is not on feeding birds at feeding stations (although that's a fine idea too) but on including a variety of food and water sources, cover, and nesting areas in the design of your landscape itself. As a sampler of the kinds of plants we'll be looking at, one study of the wildlife food value of woody plants listed the ten most important as oak, blackberry, cherry, dogwood, grape, pine, blueberry, maple, sumac, and beech.

Why encourage wildlife around your property? The entertainment value and sheer beauty of birds and chipmunks and rabbits can't be denied (even if you are not a rodent fan). And like everything in nature, all these creatures play roles in the ecosystem. A landscape devoid of any wildlife would indeed be sterile.

Landscaping for Birds and Wildlife The basic needs of wild creatures are little different from our own, and even the smallest garden can meet many of them. They include:

- Food such as seeds, nuts, berries, other fruits, flower nectar, insects, grubs, earthworms, etc.
- Cover, from overhanging eaves to dense evergreens to hollow trees, for refuge from predators as well as shelter from weather.
- Water for drinking and bathing throughout the year.
- Nesting areas with shelter and privacy.

A variety of plantings is important. You are aiming for both a diverse assortment of food sources and a year-round sequence of flowering and fruit bearing. This is not to suggest, however, that you should buy one of every kind of plant birds and animals like and sprinkle them indiscriminately around the landscape. You can easily incorporate a healthy variety of plants for wildlife and still follow good principles of design. If you want to use several kinds of small trees and shrubs, plant them in groups. Limit your single specimens to larger trees, and set them behind or beyond the clustered lower plantings.

Many wild animals, including birds, gravitate to "edges" — spots where two habitats meet, such as lawn and flower beds, shrubbery and taller trees, field and woodlot. By staying around the edge area, a creature can have two habitats in the space of one: forage plus shelter, or nesting plus bathing, for instance. A well-planned landscape will offer some edge territory, and the birds will be pleased.

A bit more of a challenge — and what's most appealing to wildlife — is something as close as possible to a natural habitat. It's not that this is hard to do, but it may not be to your taste or feasible in your particular situation. You need two things: native plants (or naturalized plants that have adapted completely to local conditions) and a certain amount of untidiness.

For the first requirement, the plant list in this section offers all kinds of good candidates that meet the needs of wild creatures. These plants also serve many design requirements, from screening and shade to color, texture, and other ornamental interest. After looking at the list you may want to purchase some nursery-grown plants for your wildlife; or you may find that you already possess quite a few. If there are maples, pines, wild berry bushes, or fruiting vines (for instance) on your land, you can just hold on to them and supplement them with a few well-chosen shrubs, small trees, or ground covers.

Favored customer: birds brings animation and color to the winter landscape.

The second challenge is providing for some messy areas. It has been said that the gardening slob is the birds' best friend. You don't really have to be a slob, but you will have better luck with birds if you can plan for some areas that are not immaculately groomed. Birds and animals love dead trees and rotting logs, tall grasses, brush piles, brier patches, boggy areas, and flowers gone to seed. With a few unkempt spaces such as these, you will keep — or soon acquire — a fine population of wildlife. But if you just don't have the space, you can still achieve many of the effects of wilderness in microcosm, by using hedges, massed plantings, a compost heap, a few thorny or prickly plants, a water source of some sort, and a couple of plants that provide berries or seeds at different seasons. The drawing on page 86 suggests a range of wildlife habitats; compress or expand them according to the space and the flexibility you have.

As you plan your landscape, keep an eye on the habits of the birds and animals that are already there. It is always simpler to keep existing wildlife happy than to attract them to a place where they've never lived before. I think of a neighbor of mine whose property is bounded by a tumbledown low stone wall. The wall used to house a dozen chipmunk families, and we all enjoyed watching them industriously gathering acorns in fall, or basking in the late-afternoon sun in spring, or coming out to view the world after a summer rain. Then my neighbor built a cedar fence all along the southeast side of the wall — and the chipmunks moved out. I don't really know why, although I have a few

Wildlife habitats in an idealized cross-section. Include a sampling of these conditions in a home landscape to attract birds and other wild creatures.

ideas. The wall is much mossier now, and I think it is probably colder and damper all year. Also, the chipmunks may have resented the loss of their 360-degree view from the top of the wall; perhaps they felt threatened by sneak attack. Or perhaps the air currents along and through the wall have been disrupted. Whatever their reasons for leaving, my neighbor misses the chipmunks. As do I.

I do realize that there are those who don't wholeheartedly adore chipmunks — or, for that matter, rabbits or any small rodents. Would-be growers of vegetables, strawberries, or other berries fall into this category. It is worth noting, though, that if supplies of water and wild berries, nuts, and seeds are abundant, birds and animals seem far less inclined to raid the human beings' food supply. This is just one more argument for landscaping with an eye to the needs of birds and wildlife.

Specific Plants for Birds and Wildlife The list here represents my own favorites among the hardy plants that are attractive to birds and wildlife. It includes many native plants and ranges from very large trees down to ground covers. If you can work into your landscape design a selection of these plants, you can expect within a few seasons to have visits from most of the resident birds.

There are countless other possibilities, of course. Your nurseryman may have good suggestions. Or if you're especially interested in attracting particular kinds of birds, your nearest Audubon Society can recommend plantings that will suit the tastes of your favored customers.

Winterberry holds its fruit right through till spring, provender for wild birds and color for a winter landscape.

Another plant for birds is Virginia creeper or woodbine. The vine's dark fruit contrasts with its colorful foliage in the fall.

Plantings for Birds and Wildlife

Large Trees

Red maple (*Acer rubrum*)
American beech (*Fagus grandifolia*)
Red cedar (*Juniperus virginiana*)
White pine (*Pinus strobus*)
Red oak (*Quercus rubra*)
Canadian hemlock (*Tsuga canadensis*)

Small Trees and Tall Shrubs (fruiting in summer; good for keeping wildlife out of crops)

Shadblow, juneberry, or serviceberry (*Amelanchier canadensis*)
Flowering dogwood (*Cornus florida*)
Black or rum cherry (*Prunus serotina*)
Elderberry (*Sambucus canadensis*)

Small Trees and Tall Shrubs (holding fruit into winter)

Washington hawthorn (*Crataegus phaenopyrum*)
Autumn olive (*Elaeagnus umbellata*)
Winterberry (*Ilex verticillata*)
Flowering crabapple (*Malus floribunda*)
Fragrant sumac (*Rhus aromatica*)
Korean mountain ash (*Sorbus alnifolia*)
Arrowwood (*Viburnum dentatum*)
American cranberrybush (*Viburnum trilobum*)

Small to Medium Shrubs

Japanese barberry (*Berberis thunbergii*)
Gray dogwood (*Cornus racemosa*)
Regel privet (*Ligustrum obtusifolium regelianum*)
Tatarian honeysuckle (*Lonicera tatarica*)
Bayberry (*Myrica pensylvanica*)
Highbush blueberry (*Vaccinium corymbosum*)

Ground Covers

Creeping juniper (*Juniperus horizontalis*)
Canada yew (*Taxus canadensis*)
Lowbush blueberry (*Vaccinium angustifolium*)

Vines

Bittersweet (*Celastrus scandens*)
Virginia creeper or woodbine (*Parthenocissus quinquefolia*)
Grapes (*Vitis* spp.)

Detailed information and recommended varieties can be found in Part III.

Materials and Construction

STONE AND GRAVEL

It's still too early in the year to do outdoor construction, for the most part. But that makes this a natural time to lay plans and choose materials for projects to be implemented later.

The longest-lasting material and the material that does most to impart a feeling of permanence to any landscape is stone. That goes both for stone that occurs naturally in the form of outcroppings, rock ledges, or boulders, and for man-made structures. Egyptian tombs and obelisks, Greek statuary and temples, Roman forums and arcades have lasted undamaged for thousands of years. (It took our century's burning of fossil fuels to create the atmospheric pollutants that are now dissolving these ancient works of stone. Even so, their endurance record is pretty good.) Stone's beauty and permanence have made it the material of choice for all sorts of public and monumental construction in every continent, right down to the present. And stone remains the material of choice for many applications today, from pavements, walls, steps, and rock gardens to sculptures, water basins, and light standards.

Stone does have its liabilities as a construction material. It is not notably flexible. In fact it is excruciatingly difficult to work with, from first quarrying through milling, transportation, and installation. Every phase of the handling of stone calls for special equipment and expertise. Therefore it is costly, both in time and in dollars.

Even so, stone has its place. This section deals with the basic facts about stone and gravel and the forms in which they're available to you, the consumer. And it touches upon some of the pleasures and perils of working with stone.

Stone Stone or rock (but in the stone business it's called stone) is bedrock that has been quarried, then cut or milled into any of a multitude of forms and dimensions.

Properties of stone If you think about it, you're probably already aware of many of the natural properties of different kinds of stone,

Huge slabs of granite dwarf quarry workers. The stone will serve many purposes after being cut into dimension stone, flagstones, crushed stone, or stone dust.

Wide variation in texture and color exists within a single kind of stone. Here, granite paving stones surround a larger bluestone slab.

just from living with them. There are the workable, crumbly textured sandstones; the smoothly striated slates; the indestructible, quartz-flecked granite; the waxy, fragile, beautifully streaked marble. The table here shows some of the kinds of stone most often used in landscape construction.

Stone for Landscape Construction

Type	*Relative Cost*	*Texture and hardness*	*Color range*	*Landscape uses*
Granite	Expensive	Coarse crystals to fine graining; very hard	Wide range, from light gray to black, with intermediate greens, reds, and pinks	Blocks, sets, or cobbles for paving, curbs, or steps; flagstones; irregular rubble or cut stone for walls; crushed for aggregate in concrete
Limestone	Moderately expensive	Fine to crystalline; fairly soft	White or light gray to buff	All uses
Sandstone (including bluestone)	Least expensive	Granular, with grains cemented together	Light buff to light brown or brick red to blue-gray	Walls, flagstones, copings, steps
Slate	Least expensive	Fine crystalline	Gray-green, brick red or dark brown, gray	Flagstone, copings, steps, low walls
Marble	Most expensive	Fine granular to coarse crystalline	Highly varied, from white to black, with intermediate greens and pinks	Thresholds, furniture, custom ornamental features, refined paving

Commercial forms Stone is available commercially (see your Yellow Pages under "stone — crushed" and/or "stone — natural") in six forms, which go under the following designations:

- Fieldstone: irregularly shaped pieces of stone, usually weathered, which have been found lying around in open fields. Hence the name.
- Rubble: irregular, rough-textured fragments of quarried stone with at least one "good" face.

Cut rubblestone and fieldstone: different approaches convey different feelings. Cut stone is crisper, more architectural (and costly); fieldstone softer and less formal.

- Dimension stone: pieces cut to given sizes, either left rough or with smoothly ground or polished surfaces.
- Flagstone: flat slabs in asymmetrical shapes, sliced anywhere from 1 to 2 or more inches thick.
- Crushed or broken stone: quarried stone that has been crushed mechanically into sharp-edged fragments anywhere from 1/4 inch to 2 1/2 inches across. Not to be confused with "gravel" — see below.
- Stone dust or powder: mechanically crushed fragments sized less than 1/4 inch across. Again, this is not the same as what's referred to as "gravel."

Gravel In the terminology of the stone business, "gravel" means a material distinct from small broken-up bits of quarried stone. Gravel comes in small pieces naturally, rather than being quarried and crushed by machines. It is formed when bedrock is fractured or eroded by natural forces such as glaciers, rain, rivers, or the sea. Wear and tear further reduce the sizes of the individual pebbles, and the pieces become worn or even rounded at the edges. Gravel may range in size from very small pebbles (but larger than sand) to biggish chunks that look to the uninitiated a lot like rocks.

Commercial Forms Like stone, gravel acquires a terminology when it becomes a consumer product. The classifications of gravel are:

- Pea gravel: the smallest-sized pieces, ranging from 1/4 inch to 1/2 inch across.
- Small graded gravel: pebbles anywhere from 1/2 inch to 3 1/2 inches across.
- Cobbles and boulders: worn or rounded chunks, larger than 3 1/2 inches across.
- Pit or bank-run gravel: ungraded material directly from the gravel pit or "bank," containing everything from sand and small pebbles all the way up to large rocks.
- Crushed gravel: coarse gravel that has been machine-crushed into sizes ranging from 3/8 inch to 2 1/2 inches across.

Designing and Building with Stone and Gravel The thumbnail descriptions of stone and gravel types above suggest pretty clearly the ways you might use them in the landscape. Fieldstone and rubble yield very naturalistic or rustic effects. For walls, pavements, or other structures, you'll get a more smooth and civilized look with dimension stone or flagstone. Crushed stone can be compacted into a solid base for pavements of all kinds, and stone dust is a good setting bed for modular pavers like bricks or granite blocks. Gravel is at home in driveways, parking areas, and many kinds of paving uses; or even as a "stone mulch" around plantings. (See the Materials and Construction sections of March, April, and October.)

A few words of inspiration here — and of caution. Stone is a marvelous material. Wherever circumstances and available funds permit, I try to work stone into my landscape designs. One can achieve a vast spectrum of effects, from gutsy rusticity to great refinement or formality, depending on one's choice of texture, color, and joint patterns. Stone also serves as a most satisfactory way to link a man-made construction to the soil and growing things around it — since stone itself is from and of the earth. It ties the parts of a landscape design together.

But a stone masonry project is not to be undertaken lightly or inadvisedly. This is not just a matter of its relatively high price, which I mentioned above. I have built many things out of stone — fireplaces and walls, slate and bluestone pavings, fieldstone and boulder rock gardens — and every one I have finished only with some pain and anguish. Working with stone really hurts. It's as if you had to match your stubbornness and patience against the obduracy of the stone itself.

Yet if you can manage to finish a piece of work in stone, there's absolutely nothing quite so satisfying. You'll need time, patience, willpower — and, unless you do it all yourself, lots of money. Only you can decide if stone is for you.

Red-stemmed shrub dogwood is one of many plants (listed on next page) whose colorful bark and twigs make striking accents in the winter landscape.

Plants by Design

COLORFUL BARK AND TWIGS

Gray-Barked Trees and Shrubs

Red maple (*Acer rubrum*)
Shadblow, juneberry, or serviceberry (*Amelanchier canadensis*)
Allegheny serviceberry (*Amelanchier laevis*)
Yellowwood (*Cladrastis lutea*)
*Summer-sweet clethra (*Clethra alnifolia*)
*Gray dogwood (*Cornus racemosa*)
*Autumn olive (*Elaeagnus umbellata*)
American beech (*Fagus grandifolia*)
European beech (*Fagus sylvatica*)
Rivers beech (*Fagus sylvatica* 'Riversii')
Tatarian honeysuckle (*Lonicera tatarica*)
Korean mountain ash (*Sorbus alnifolia*)
*European cranberrybush (*Viburnum opulus*)
*American cranberrybush or highbush cranberry (*Viburnum trilobum*)

Green-Barked Trees and Shrubs

*Bronx forsythia (*Forsythia viridissima* 'Bronxensis')
*Kerria (*Kerria japonica*)
Thurlow weeping willow (*Salix elegantissima*)
Sassafras (*Sassafras albidum*)
Japanese pagoda tree (*Sophora japonica*)

Yellow-Barked Trees and Shrubs

*Yellow-twig red-osier dogwood (*Cornus sericea* 'Flaviramea')
Golden weeping willow (*Salix alba tristis*)

Red-Barked Trees and Shrubs

Paperbark maple (*Acer griseum*)
*Japanese maple (*Acer palmatum*)
River birch (*Betula nigra*)
*Siberian dogwood (*Cornus alba* 'Sibirica')
Red-osier dogwood (*Cornus sericea*)
*Flowering dogwood (*Cornus florida*)
Tanyosho pine (*Pinus densiflora* 'Umbraculifera')
Oriental cherry (*Prunus serrulata*)
Meadow rose (*Rosa blanda*)
Virginia rose (*Rosa virginiana*)
Japanese stewartia (*Stewartia pseudocamellia*)
Dwarf European cranberrybush (*Viburnum opulus* 'Nanum')

White-Barked Trees

Paper birch (*Betula papyrifera*)
European birch (*Betula pendula*)
Cutleaf European birch (*Betula pendula* 'Gracilis')

***Indicates a plant whose younger twigs have the desired color, so that regular pruning (to stimulate abundant young growth) is needed for maximum winter color effect.**

Detailed information and recommended varieties can be found in Part III.

LANDSCAPE TASKS FOR JANUARY

Catalogues If you are already on a few mailing lists, you don't need this reminder. If you aren't, let this be your cue to think about your gardening needs for the coming growing season. January is definitely the time to map out your plans and to choose and order what you need from seedsmen's and nurserymen's catalogues.

Salt Salt for melting snow and ice should be used with great discretion. As an alternative, as long as the weather is not too cold, try a light application of commercial fertilizer.

Paperbark maple offers not only rich color but paper-thin peeling strips for textural interest.

The two salts widely available are sodium chloride (effective to 10°F) and the more expensive calcium chloride (effective to −40°F). Often calcium chloride is mixed with sodium chloride to boost its potency. But both salts will damage lawns and many plantings; and they do more insidious and long-lasting damage if they are used where they can percolate through groundwater into wells, streams, or reservoirs. So go easy.

De-icing Brush snow from ornamental evergreens before it can melt (or be rained on) and then freeze, resulting in a heavy load of ice.

Antidesiccants In a mild spell (when the temperature is above freezing for a day or so) you may want to use an antidesiccant spray on needled and broad-leaved evergreens. Rhododendrons, azaleas, laurels, boxwood, yew, pine, and spruce are among the plants that may "winterburn." The sprays coat the leaves or needles with a plastic film; this slows plants' water loss when the ground is frozen, and thus helps prevent winterburn. Particularly for new plantings whose root systems are still getting established, antidesiccants are sometimes a sensible form of insurance for the first two seasons or so.

Vines This leafless season is a good time to cut back overgrown vines, both domestic (English ivy, wisteria, Virginia creeper) and wild (woodbine, wild grape, bittersweet, honeysuckle).

Mulches Use evergreen boughs from Christmas or from pruning to mulch over evergreen perennials, bulb beds, and rock gardens — any of the smaller, more shallow-rooted plants in your garden.

Christmas Trees Another way to recycle Christmas greens: collect a few neighbors' Christmas trees and stack them together into a teepee for the birds. Birds will appreciate both the dense protective foliage and the resulting bare patch of ground underneath (for foraging and scratching).

Rooting Hardwood Cuttings An easy way to propagate many garden plants, and a good project for January, is to make hardwood cuttings. This method works well with the plants listed here, among others.

Buttonbush (*Cephalanthus occidentalis*)
Dogwood (shrub types) (*Cornus* spp.)
Forsythia (*Forsythia* spp.)
Kerria (*Kerria japonica*)
Privet (*Ligustrum* spp.)
Honeysuckle (*Lonicera* spp.)
Mock-orange (*Philadelphus* spp.)
Willow (*Salix* spp.)
Elderberry (*Sambucus canadensis*)
Spirea (*Spiraea* spp.)
Stephanandra (*Stephanandra incisa*)
Coralberry (*Symphoricarpos* spp.)
Persian lilac (*Syringa persica*)
Viburnum (*Viburnum* spp.)

You'll get the best stems for hardwood cuttings if you start a year in advance by pruning the plant back hard in the previous dormant season — to encourage vigorous new growth. These fast-sprouting shoots will be the readiest to send out roots when you make them into cuttings the following fall or winter.

To make the cuttings, cut 6- to 8-inch pencil-thick sections with the top end cut at least an inch above the nearest growth bud. Tie the cuttings into bundles you can grasp comfortably in one hand, and tap the bottoms of the bundles to bring all the bottom ends of the cuttings even with each other. Tie the bundles with wire or cord; label them; and bury them in earth, damp sawdust, or dampened peat moss, to keep them from drying out. Store them for three to four weeks at 50° to 55°F; after that, reduce the temperature to 32° to 40°F so that the tops won't start to grow too soon.

After six to eight weeks of storage, hardwood cuttings can be set in the ground to grow, preferably in full sun, as soon as the ground can be worked.

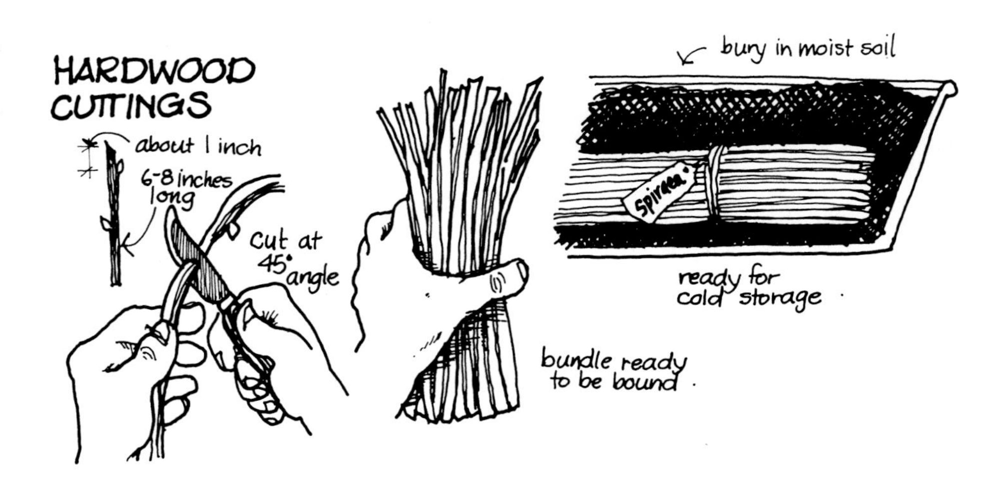

Cutting, bundling, and storing hardwood cuttings: a winter project for new plants in spring.

Rooting Evergreen Cuttings Another, slightly trickier, propagation project for midwinter is rooting cuttings of broad-leaved evergreens and conifers. Some particularly good candidates for rooting at this season are shown below.

Box (*Buxus* spp.)
False cypress (*Chamaecyparis* spp.)
Euonymus (*Euonymus* spp.)
English ivy (*Hedera* spp.)
Holly (*Ilex* spp.)
Juniper (*Juniperus* spp.)
Japanese spurge or pachysandra (*Pachysandra* spp.)
Firethorn (*Pyracantha* spp.)
Yew (*Taxus* spp.)
Arborvitae (*Thuja* spp.)

(Also see June for softwood cuttings to be taken in spring.)

Take cuttings in early morning. Using a sharp knife or a razor blade, make a cut at about a 45-degree angle, and about ¼ inch below a node (where leaf joins stem) if possible. The best cuttings come from the terminal sections of stems, but a long growth can be cut into several sections. The cuttings should be 2 to 6 inches long, depending on how husky the stems and leaves are.

Remove the bottom third of the leaves or needles on each cutting; then immediately dip the base of the stem into rooting hormone and set the cutting into a moist, well-drained rooting medium. (If there will be any delay, store cuttings in a plastic bag in the refrigerator.) They should be inserted to about one-third of their total length in the medium.

For the first week or so, keep the cuttings protected in a glass or plastic container (to hold moist air in) and lightly shaded from direct sunlight. Once roots have formed and grown at least ½ inch long, you can carefully transplant the cuttings to pots for the greenhouse or windowsill, where they can stay until spring.

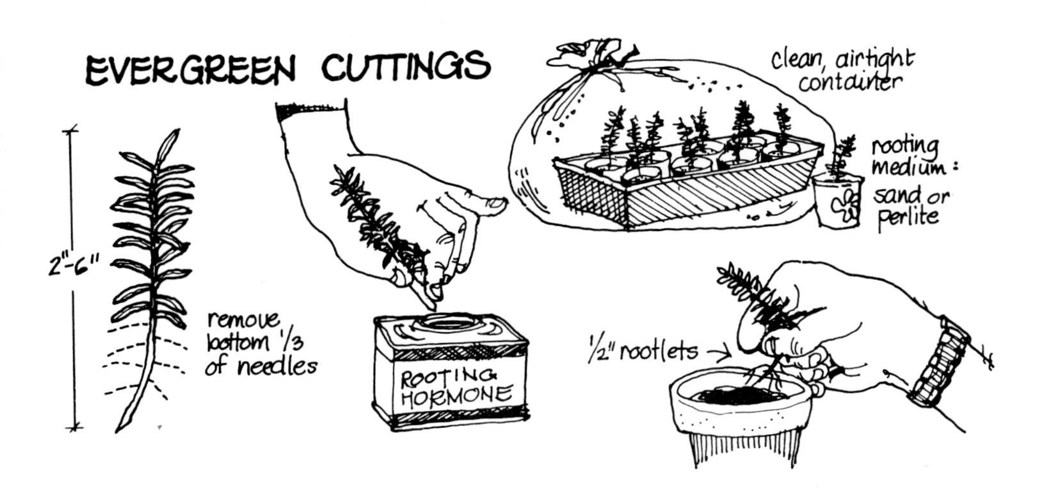

Many evergreen shrubs and trees can also be propagated by cuttings taken now.

FEB

Landscaping Opportunities
Easy-Maintenance Landscaping

Plants for a Purpose
Trees and Shrubs Requiring Minimum Care

Materials and Construction
Concrete and Asphalt

Plants by Design
Textured Bark

Landscape Tasks for February

A colorful variety of evergreen foliage in a dwarf conifer nursery.

Lacebark pine: outer plates peel off to reveal multicolored inner bark layers.

In February the days are lengthening perceptibly but winter has by no means relaxed its grip on the landscape. Much of our appreciating of the outdoors is still being done from indoors, through windows. For close-range viewing, the Plants by Design list this month features interesting bark textures. There are plants with silky or velvety bark (like beeches or yellowwood); plants with "exfoliating" bark that peels off in strips or flakes, often revealing contrasting colors below (like red cedar or lacebark pine); and plants with deeply fissured barks, for a rugged look (like white ash or shagbark hickory).

Indoor activities are already beginning now for vegetable and flower gardeners, whose seeds go into flats starting around Washington's Birthday. But aspirations for the landscape are still primarily restricted to planning. Major paving projects are one excellent subject for early planning; continuing from last month's section on stone, I'll introduce concrete and asphalt here. Another good thing to plan for is ease of — or freedom from — upkeep. (Concrete and asphalt certainly qualify in that department.) And the Landscaping Opportunities and Plants for a Purpose sections this month are devoted to the maintenance-free theme.

Landscaping Opportunities

EASY-MAINTENANCE LANDSCAPING

Every landscape requires some maintenance. How much or how little depends on many different factors. The most significant of these are the kind of landscape you start with (whether intensive or extensive, simple or complex, wild or cultivated); the standards you set for your landscape and yourself; and the kinds of landscape furnishings you use, from plants to inanimate materials.

Many people derive great joy from puttering in the garden, and seek out projects and plantings that will offer creative challenges in the puttering department. But what if your goal is to do as little maintenance as possible? You can reduce to a minimum upkeep time, energy, and expense without sacrificing either the beauty or the well-being of a landscape.

Simplicity of design is central. Obviously, you may not have complete control over the basic nature of your landscape: topography, older plantings, and layout of spaces may have been determined before you moved in. But if you have the luxury of starting from scratch, you can build into your planning the various suggestions listed here and vastly lighten your maintenance burdens in years to come.

Another form of luxury is owning a woodland property. There you can simply let nature happen around you, carving out a few finite open spaces for lawn, vegetable or flower beds, or shrubbery as desired.

A far more typical situation, though, is the moderately open property with a few scattered mature trees and some lawn and planting areas that you're hoping to keep looking respectable with as little effort as possible. Or you may be retaining some sections of an established landscape and redoing others to suit your tastes or your budget of time.

Whatever your circumstances, I can offer the following ideas. Many of my suggestions come under the heading of avoiding tasks to start with by designing with forethought. Beyond that, I'll suggest ways to streamline tasks if you do undertake them.

In this easily maintained yard, planted and paved areas are edged, beds are raised and narrow, and shrubs are selected for minimum care.

Space Planning Make certain that each use you plan for your landscape will happen in the most appropriate part of the site. There's a best place for everything. Making the logical choices can avert a lot of extra effort directed at forcing success, rather than letting it come naturally. Put a parking area in a flat place, a vegetable patch where the soil and sun are best, and so on.

At the initial planning stage, or when redesigning, make high-maintenance areas small. (Obvious though this sounds, it's a precept honored more in the breach than in the observance.)

Group together types of planting that require similar kinds of maintenance — watering, weeding, feeding, pruning, etc.

Avoid planting anything in deep shade, particularly lawn grasses.

Around driveways and walks, leave sufficient unobstructed space to cope with mounds of snow at snow-shoveling time.

Lawns Lay out lawns for ease of mowing. That means no sharp corners where you'll have to stop or turn around, and no nooks or crannies.

Rule out the necessity of hand trimming. Put "mowing edges" alongside all planting beds, structures, and grade changes. Install sand pits around tree-trunks.

Establish gentle grades. Banks with slopes steeper than 1:3 (33 percent) are too hard to mow.

For an instant lawn, use sod rather than seeding. (Keep in mind that this is a more expensive method.)

To eliminate lawn damage (and dirt splashing on foundations or siding), install gravel strips under drip lines of roof edges without gutters.

Although it takes a few years to establish, a no-lawn approach like this bed of evergreen pachysandra totally eliminates lawn maintenance chores.

Trees and Shrubs Use the best possible soil for all growing areas. Again, this may seem obvious, but it's terribly important. Any plant is more trouble-free if it's truly healthy and well-nourished; any plant will behave like an invalid in soil unsuited to its needs.

Select the best-quality disease- and pest-resistant plants available. Look around you to see what types of plants are thriving in your area, and follow the clues they provide. I have avoided listing excessively fussy plants throughout this book; but for a list of notably unfussy ones, see the Plants for a Purpose section this month. Your local nursery is also an invaluable source of local information.

Slow-growing and dwarf varieties will keep pruning to a minimum. Your initial cost will probably be higher, however, because greater numbers of small plants are required to fill a given area; besides, these little gems are expensive, since they take so long to grow in the nursery.

For sturdy growth, space trees and shrubs sufficiently far apart so they'll be exposed to sun and good circulation of air on all sides.

Avoid planting trees that litter — like fruit trees or others known for heavy seed drop — adjacent to paved surfaces. Their fruits tend to get squashed underfoot or their litter accumulates and becomes a nuisance to clean up.

Prune trees for open branching, to let the wind blow through harmlessly and forestall breakage.

Irrigation When planting trees and shrubs, build a mulched reservoir to hold water around each plant. Or group plantings, consolidating them into a single mulched bed.

Space water faucets no less than 100 feet apart, so every area can be reached with 50 feet of hose.

If absolutely necessary (although generally I try to avoid this), take the plunge and install underground irrigation piping. It will free you from dragging hoses and sprinklers around your property day after day.

Flower and Vegetable Beds Make sure the soil is the best and most fertile you can provide.

For the sake of your back, where weeding or other hand work will be needed in a planted bed, consider raising the bed above grade level. Also make sure that every spot in the bed is within reach from the edge — or at least within reach when you've got one foot in the bed.

Use some form of edging to keep grass rhizomes out of beds, and mulch in.

Preventing migration of mulch or granular paving, a steel edge cleanly separates this peastone path from the planting bed.

Vegetable gardens should be either very small or very large. That is, plant them compact, with raised beds and intensive cropping (foliage shades out weeds and no ground lies fallow); or plant them roomy, spaced out sufficiently so that you can use a power tiller or push cultivator for cultivating between rows.

Separate beds of different kinds of plants; keep those with similar cultural needs together.

For flowers, choose perennials over annuals. Perennials bloom for a shorter period each year, but they do it all by themselves. With some planning you can have an assortment of perennials blooming in any given week all summer long.

When you're picking out ground covers, perennials, bulbs, etc., select the varieties that are easiest to care for once established. Eschew those that call for regular or annual digging, dividing, pruning, fertilizing, or pest-control spraying.

Equipment Organize your tools and maintenance equipment in one convenient location, preferably a shed or ell with its own entrance.

Make certain that wheeled vehicles (lawn mowers, grass-seed spreaders, wheelbarrows, leaf carts, etc.) can get around your entire property without having to double back or detour because of steps, walls, steep banks, or narrow passageways.

Keep pavements flush with lawn areas to avoid obstructing lawn mowers or other wheeled vehicles.

Provide electrical outlets in convenient locations for hedge shears and other electric-powered gadgets.

Structures and Furnishings For permanent landscape fixtures, select materials for longevity. Good candidates include stone, concrete, and pressure-treated or naturally rot-resistant woods. Watch out for any material that's going to need to be replaced in a short time. Stay away from woods that will demand painting, varnishing, or staining.

Wherever possible, build in. Walls can incorporate seats; fences and rails can incorporate benches; trellises can take the place of umbrellas; and so on.

Fences can be used rather than shrubbery for privacy. A fence takes a lot less work than a hedge or shrub screen, particularly a hedge or screen that requires regular clipping or pruning. If you want a green wall, you can always plant vines to curtain the fence.

Plants for a Purpose

TREES AND SHRUBS REQUIRING MINIMUM CARE

If your resolve is to plant only trees and shrubs that can virtually be forgotten once established, then the list here is for you. You may have to do without some of the shrubs with the most exciting flowering or fruiting characteristics, or some of the grandest foliage trees; but even so, here is a wide choice of plants that includes good candidates for almost any situation you may have.

My criteria are simple: plants included here are subject to few pests or diseases, and/or tolerant of those that do come along; they call for limited, if any, pruning; they drop minimal quantities of needles or leaves (which is why there are few large deciduous shade trees on the list); they are adaptable to most soils and conditions. And although some of the big evergreens are indeed large, you can obtain smaller sizes and slower growth of these durable favorites if you select compact or dwarf varieties.

You'll notice that native plants are well represented in this list — a testimony to their crusty perseverance once established in compatible surroundings.

In addition to the plants offered here, many of the ground covers and vines that appear in the June Plants for a Purpose section call for very little maintenance once established. Some of them, of course, need more care than others. And some of them — particularly among the vines — are such vigorous growers that they require restraining. But they are a group well worth your attention as you consider low-maintenance plantings for your garden.

Three times I have used the phrase "once established." By that I mean "after fully recovering from transplanting and pursuing vigorous unimpeded growth." To recapitulate once more my familiar theme, it is up to you to provide proper soil and sufficient light; to plant these trees and shrubs with care; and to water them as needed until they get settled. Any plant, no matter how stalwart, has certain minimum requirements for survival. And any plant in a weakened state (whether from transplanting shock or from inadequate basic conditions) is vulnerable to attack by insects and diseases that would not normally bother it.

Katsura tree is one of those plants with minimal insect or disease problems. As shown in autumn here, the foliage remains clean and undamaged throughout the season.

Minimum-Care Trees and Shrubs

Small to Medium Deciduous Trees

Shadblow, juneberry, or serviceberry (*Amelanchier* spp.)
River birch (*Betula nigra*)
European hornbeam (*Carpinus betulus*)
Katsura tree (*Cercidiphyllum japonicum*)
Yellowwood (*Cladrastis lutea*)
Kousa or Japanese dogwood (*Cornus kousa*)
Cornelian cherry dogwood (*Cornus mas*)
Smoke tree (*Cotinus coggygria*)
Washington hawthorn (*Crataegus phaenopyrum*)
Autumn olive (*Elaeagnus umbellata*)
Golden-rain tree (*Koelreuteria paniculata*)
Star magnolia (*Magnolia stellata*)
Crabapples (*Malus* spp.)
Sorrel tree or sourwood (*Oxydendrum arboreum*)
Amur cork tree (*Phellodendron amurense*)
Sassafras (*Sassafras albidum*)
Japanese pagoda tree (*Sophora japonica*)
Japanese stewartia (*Stewartia pseudocamellia*)
Bradford pear (*Pyrus calleryana* 'Bradford')
Fragrant sumac (*Rhus aromatica*)
Korean mountain ash (*Sorbus alnifolia*)
Korean stewartia (*Stewartia koreana*)

Large Deciduous Trees

Red maple (*Acer rubrum*)
Beeches (*Fagus* spp.)
Ginkgo or maidenhair tree (*Ginkgo biloba*)
Thornless honey locust (*Gleditsia triacanthos inermis* and vars.)
Sweet gum tree (*Liquidambar styraciflua*)
Dawn redwood (*Metasequoia glyptostroboides*)
Black gum or black tupelo (*Nyssa sylvatica*)
Zelkova (*Zelkova serrata*)

Deciduous Shrubs

Korean white forsythia (*Abeliophyllum distichum*)
Chokeberries (*Aronia* spp.)

Detailed information and recommended varieties can be found in Part III.

Materials and Construction

CONCRETE AND ASPHALT

Preparing for the active months to come, last month's Materials and Construction section talked about stone and gravel — the most basic and most permanent of landscape construction materials, and strictly natural in origin. Now for some man-made products that share some of the attributes and uses of stone: concrete and asphalt. Both are in fact made partly of stone. Both are, like stone, hard and durable and easy on upkeep. Both work together with (or in place of) stone in paved areas, from walks and drives to patios and terraces. And concrete finds still further uses in nonpaving construction such as steps, walls, planters, and pools.

Almost anywhere you go, you will walk, drive, park, shop, play, or work on asphalt or concrete or both. These materials are so widely used in public places that the response they elicit in many people is a definite ho-hum. Yet there are good reasons for their ubiquitous presence. Besides being durable, they are versatile; they are readily available; and

Minimum-Care Trees and Shrubs *(continued)*

Japanese barberry (*Berberis thunbergii*)
Summer-sweet clethra (*Clethra alnifolia*)
Sweet fern (*Comptonia peregrina*)
Gray dogwood (*Cornus racemosa*)
Red-osier dogwood (*Cornus sericea* vars.)
Fragrant winter hazel (*Corylopsis glabrescens*)
Redvein enkianthus (*Enkianthus campanulatus*)
Winged euonymus (*Euonymus alata* vars.)
Forsythias (*Forsythia* spp.)
Fothergillas or witch alders (*Fothergilla* spp.)
Witch hazels (*Hamamelis* spp.)
Rose-of-Sharon or shrub althea (*Hibiscus syriacus*)
Hydrangeas (*Hydrangea* spp.)
Regel privet (*Ligustrum obtusifolium regelianum*)
Honeysuckles (*Lonicera* spp.)
Bayberry (*Myrica pensylvanica*)
Bush or shrubby cinquefoil (*Potentilla fruticosa*)
Shining sumac (*Rhus copallina*)
Rugosa rose (*Rosa rugosa*)
Spireas (*Spiraea* spp.)
Crispa cutleaf stephanandra (*Stephanandra incisa* 'Crispa')
Coralberries (*Symphoricarpos* spp.)
Viburnums (*Viburnum* spp.)

Evergreen Trees

White fir (*Abies concolor*)
Hinoki false cypress (*Chamaecyparis obtusa* vars.)
Thread false cypress (*Chamaecyparis pisifera* 'Filifera' and vars.)
Norway spruce (*Picea abies* vars.)
Pines (*Pinus* spp.)
Douglas fir (*Pseudotsuga menziesii*)
Umbrella pine (*Sciadopytis verticillata*)
Canadian hemlock (*Tsuga canadensis* vars.)

Evergreen Shrubs

Japanese or boxleaf holly (*Ilex crenata* vars.)
Inkberry (*Ilex glabra*)
Winterberry (*Ilex verticillata*)
Junipers (*Juniperus* spp.)
Canby paxistima (*Paxistima canbyi*)
Rhododendrons (*Rhododendron* spp.)
Yews (*Taxus* spp.)

they are relatively inexpensive, which is often the primary reason for their use.

In designing for your home landscape, however, you have a chance to use concrete and asphalt with far greater care and imagination than are feasible in large-scale public construction. You can take advantage not only of their utilitarian virtues but of their other essential qualities — including, of all things, beauty.

With every plant or construction material I use, I try to think first about the intrinsic nature of the material itself, so I can bring out its full potential. The one thing asphalt and concrete have in common is that each consists of a form of glue binding together loose granular material to make a monolithic mass. That's where the similarity of the two materials ends. Their components and chemistry are completely unrelated. Once hardened, concrete is rigid and rocklike; it can be used for three-dimensional construction as well as for paving. Asphalt, on the other hand, always retains some degree of flexibility.

I won't attempt here to make you an instant concrete or asphalt expert. But I will give you enough basic information to be an informed consumer of both products.

Concrete The three components of concrete have changed very little since the days of the Roman Empire. First, there's cement, now a patented formula called Portland cement. Second, there's the "aggregate" of granular materials the cement binds together: sand and gravel or crushed stone. It is the nature of the gravel in the aggregate that provides much of the color, texture, and specific character of a given concrete mix. Finally, there's water, which sets off a chain of chemical reactions in the cement. These reactions cause the concrete to set within the first 45 minutes or so after pouring; to harden within the first 10 hours; to cure within the first 7 days; and to reach its final maximum strength at the end of 28 days.

The compressive strength (resistance to crushing) of concrete is measured in pounds per square inch, or psi. Concrete formulated for landscape work should range from 2000 to 3500 psi, depending on its intended use.

Buying concrete You can buy concrete in any of three forms. If you're going to need more than 1 cubic yard (27 cubic feet) of concrete, the most prudent way is often to buy it completely mixed and ready to pour. This form is called transit-mix and is delivered in the familiar trucks with the rolling barrels that mix the concrete en route. With transit-mix your big job is to measure your needed quantity correctly, prepare the site carefully, and have all systems go for delivery on the appointed day. Transit-mix company drivers do not have time or flexibility to wait around while you get organized. If they do have to wait, you usually have to pay them extra.

Transit-mix companies generally will not deliver amounts smaller than one cubic yard. For these small jobs, you may decide to buy ready-mix concrete. This is a bagged mixture of all the dry ingredients (cement, sand, and gravel), to which you just add water. Like prepared food mixes, this product saves time but is frequently more expensive than the raw materials if you buy them separately and put them together yourself.

Mixing your own concrete from scratch has its drawbacks (hard work) and its pleasures. In the long run, the advantages are in cost — compared to ready-mix or transit — and in the freedom this method gives you. You can spread the mixing and pouring over several work periods rather than doing it all at once, if you want; and you can experiment and perfect just the texture and color you desire. (More on texture and color under Variations, below.)

To compute how much concrete you are going to need (and therefore, possibly, what form you will buy it in) measure all dimensions of whatever you plan to construct. Use this formula:

$$\frac{\text{width (feet)} \times \text{length (feet)} \times \text{thickness (inches)}}{12} = \text{cubic feet}$$

For instance, suppose you are building a concrete pad 10 feet square and 4 inches thick. That's $10 \times 10 \times 4 = 400 \div 12 = 33\frac{1}{3}$ cubic feet, or somewhat more than 1 cubic yard. If you are working with larger amounts, dividing your cubic-foot amount by 27 will give you the number of cubic yards. Now you can start considering whether to order transit-mix, buy the bagged ready-mix, or mix your own.

Variations on the concrete theme A wonderful variety of colors and textural effects can be given to concrete with a little extra thought and effort. All these variations are ways to liberate concrete from its pallid gray public image.

You've probably seen textured concrete surfaces created by wood or steel floats or brooms. Another standard finish, "exposed aggregate," results when the cement paste is washed and scrubbed away from the uncured concrete to reveal a pebbly layer of aggregate at the surface. Other ways to expose the aggregate include sandblasting, bush hammering, or grinding the concrete. Hammering and grinding are best left to experienced masons; sandblasting you may decide to do yourself with rented equipment.

Exposed aggregate is all the more colorful and appealing if ornamental stones or gravel have been incorporated in it. They can also be embedded in the top layer of concrete after spreading, but it is better to have them mixed right in if you can. If this makes the aggregate just too expensive, some masons pour a base slab of standard concrete, but leave the surface unfinished. Then, at the point when the base is still "green" but its surface water is gone, they make up a mixture with the more fancy aggregate and apply it 1 inch thick.

A particularly nice exposed-aggregate concrete. Pebbles were thoughtfully selected for color and texture and are smooth enough for bare feet to walk on.

Another way to color concrete is with pigments. Pigment can constitute up to 10 percent of the weight of the cement in the mix. For colors other than grays and browns, however — even with white cement — I find that pigmented concrete colors are pretty much limited to pastel tones. If I am looking for a really strong color, I often end up using brick or stone instead, or go to an exposed aggregate with naturally colored gravel to add the color. A pigment, like an ornamental aggregate, can either be mixed in with the concrete or sprinkled on top after pouring. (In this case it's called "shake.") I prefer to mix pigment into the concrete itself, which seems to me to give better durability and greater uniformity of color.

Asphalt Asphalt, certainly one of the least glamorous of landscape construction materials, has a few undeniable virtues. For large, hard-working pavements like drives and turnarounds, it is tough, easy to come by, and relatively cheap. And although its spectrum of colors and textures is narrower than that of concrete, asphalt is still a lot more versatile than you might imagine if your main exposure to it has been on highways and sidewalks.

This sticky blackish substance has an ancient pedigree. As early as 3000 B.C., people in Mesopotamia and the Indus Valley were using asphalt in masonry, street construction, and waterproofing. The Egyptians employed it in mummification. They recognized that it was resilient, waterproof, and permanent; our word *asphalt* comes from the Greek for "safe, secure, and steadfast."

The earliest users of asphalt found it in the form of partly evaporated petroleum deposits, or "lakes." Since 1865, when petroleum drilling began, we've relied on asphalt created as a byproduct of the petroleum refining process. Mixed with sand or stone, it becomes the basic binding ingredient of asphalt paving, and that is its chief role in landscape construction.

How asphalt paving is made Asphalt paving consists of a mixture of about 10 percent asphalt (by weight) with stone aggregate. Both the mixing and the spreading of asphalt are generally jobs for a contractor. Your responsibility is to seek out a reliable contractor who will work with you to achieve the texture and color you want. Particularly if you're hoping for special textures or colors (see below), you should ask to see some successful installations the contractor has done in the past. A good contractor will be pleased to show off his work.

The most common and most commonly recommended mixing procedure involves heating the asphalt and mixing it with the aggregate at a temperature of 275°F in a hot-mix plant. Transported rapidly to the site, this mixture is laid and compacted before it can cool beyond 185°F. With hot mixes, as you can see, a short distance between site and mixing plant is desirable, so it is generally mandatory that your contractor be a local one.

Cold-mix asphalt contractors are fewer and farther between, but when you can find it, cold mix can be less expensive. The problem with cold mix is that it takes many months to reach its final hardness, and in the meantime all traffic has to be kept religiously off it or you end up with dents and scars in the finish. But if you can postpone using your new asphalt for the requisite amount of time, and if you can find a contractor who has good experience using cold-mix asphalt, I recommend considering it for economy's sake.

There's also the old form of asphalt paving called macadam, after the man who invented the process. In macadam the stone is laid and compacted in place, then sprayed with controlled quantities of emulsion or hot asphalt. Then fine aggregates are spread over the whole thing and rolled in to fill the chinks. Time and wear expose the surfaces of the stones, and the resulting colors and textures are very attractive, especially if large stones were used at the beginning. Macadam installation today is a specialty operation, however, and expensive.

Textures All asphalt mixes are put together according to formulas or recipes calling for the specific proportions of various sizes of aggregate that will create the proper texture for the job. The terminology for these mixes varies from place to place; you'll run into names such as "sand mix," "rice mix," "binder," and so on, denoting coarser- and finer-textured formulas. Nomenclature aside, the standard numerical designations in the industry are as follows:

Designation	*Maximum stone size*
2A	1½ inches
3A	1 inch
4A	¾ inch
5A	½ inch
6A	⅜ inch
7A	#4 (± ¼ inch)
8A	#16 (± 1/16 inch)

If a pavement of very fine-textured asphalt is desired (say 7A or 8A), it's common practice to lay a "base course" or "binder course" of coarser mixture such as 3A or 4A, followed by a 1-inch "wearing course" of 7A or 8A. The reason for this is that a full 3-inch thickness of the finest-textured mixture might soften and suffer damage in very hot weather.

Most widely used for walks and drives are types 5A, 6A, or 7A. Ask your contractor what degree of fineness he likes to work with and why, and go take a look at installations of the type he suggests in situations comparable to yours. There's no significant difference in price or durability from one type to another, so your choice is a matter of taste; but contractors sometimes have preferences based on habit or convenience.

Colors Newly laid asphalt paving is always blackish, the color of the asphalt emulsion itself. The eventual color usually comes from the stones in the aggregate: time and traffic wear away the asphalt from the surface of the pavement, and the stones' own color comes through.

This asphalt base layer has coarse-textured stones. In the top layer, the oil mix will slowly wear off and reveal the color and texture of the pebbles.

They are most often gray, so that weathered asphalt is usually gray too. But other colors can be attained. If the aggregate in the mix incorporates white, green, brown, or red stones, these colors will emerge very gradually. (There are some beautiful slate-red roads I know of in Massachusetts and Pennsylvania.) The larger the stones in the aggregate, the greater the amount of surface and the more color will eventually be revealed. That's probably the best and surest route to colored asphalt, but it is slow. Besides, you may have trouble prevailing on an asphalt mix plant to use special colored aggregate for a small batch of mix such as you're apt to need for a residential installation — so don't get your hopes up.

Several possible methods for achieving a colored asphalt surface have been suggested in the literature, although I have yet to meet a contractor who has actually tested them out. One is to roll a layer of crushed stone into the surface of newly laid hot asphalt. Another involves spreading stone dust and cement on hot asphalt before rolling. Another calls for sandblasting the surface of cured asphalt for an instant weathered look.

When you investigate these specialized forms of asphalt installation you'll meet with considerable diversity of regional practice and individual opinion. The secret is to find a reputable specialty contractor who can show you installations that have stood the test of time. You should be prepared for specially mixed or laid paving to cost more than standard paving — although with a little creative prodding you may be able to pay only slightly more than for a quality standard job.

Finally, consider practicality versus eye appeal and make sure that what you're getting is worth the investment. The most decorative surfaces are not necessarily the most practical. Rough textures can be annoying to walk or ride bikes on; light-colored surfaces will show oil and grease stains, and won't heat up to melt ice and snow as fast as dark ones. If a pavement leads right to your front door or is part of the view from some important windows, then a pleasing appearance may be worth a little impracticality — not to mention extra effort and cash. If not, perhaps a well-installed standard black asphalt walk or drive will answer your needs very well.

Peeling bark strips and checkered patches are among the many landscape contributions of mature paper birch. See the list on the next page for other textured barks.

Plants by Design

TEXTURED BARK

Smooth Barks (Silky or Velvety)

Shadblow, juneberry, or serviceberry (*Amelanchier canadensis*)
Allegheny serviceberry (*Amelanchier laevis*)
Gray birch (*Betula populifolia*)
Yellowwood (*Cladrastis lutea*)
American beech (*Fagus grandifolia*)
European beech (*Fagus sylvatica*)
Paperbark cherry (*Prunus serrula*)

Exfoliating Barks (Peeling in Strips or Flakes)

Paperbark maple (*Acer griseum*)
River birch (*Betula nigra*)
Paper birch (*Betula papyrifera*)
Shagbark hickory (*Carya ovata*)
Kousa or Japanese dogwood (*Cornus kousa*)
Red cedar (*Juniperus virginiana*)
Lacebark pine (*Pinus bungeana*)
Japanese stewartia (*Stewartia pseudocamellia*)
American arborvitae (*Thuja occidentalis*)

Coarse or Deeply Fissured Barks

Norway maple (*Acer platanoides*)
Shagbark hickory (*Carya ovata*)
White ash (*Fraxinus americana*)

Detailed information and recommended varieties can be found in Part III.

LANDSCAPE TASKS FOR FEBRUARY

Lawn Furniture and Tool Maintenance Before the first warm spell, get your outdoor furniture and gardening tools in shape. Oil wooden surfaces, or apply preservative if needed; apply rust inhibitors to metal surfaces.

Catalogues Last chance to order new plants and seeds from mail-order suppliers for planting in the coming season.

Bird Feeding Just when the days are lengthening and you can see spring around the corner, the supply of food for birds is at its lowest. Your bird population needs not only seeds but water and grit. In addition, suet helps keep birds warm; but beware of peanut butter or soft fats. Their gluelike consistency can actually be dangerous.

Dormant Oil Spraying Peaches (right now) and apples, pears, and cherries (when their buds show a tip of green) may benefit from a spraying with viscous oil. Harmless to birds and bees, this coats and smothers the egg masses of damaging insects; it can make a big difference to the fruit crop later on.

Antidesiccants Broad-leaved and needled evergreens that have been exposed to strong sun and/or drying winds over the winter may need to be sprayed with an antidesiccant again (see January). Pick a day when the temperature can be expected to stay above freezing.

Tree Guards Roving rodents can kill a fruit tree by girdling it — that is, by chewing off a belt or "girdle" of bark and cambium all the

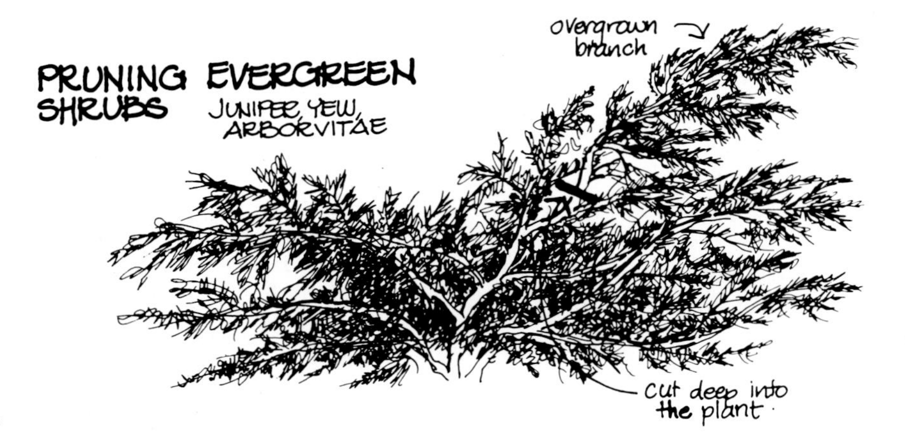

Give evergreen shrubs like juniper, yew, or arborvitae minor trimming now; or cut overgrown shoots back deep into the plant.

way around the trunk, which interrupts the circulation of water and nutrients to the upper trunk and branches. If you've set up tree guards (see November) to protect your trees, check them now and make sure they're intact and doing their job. If not, trample down snow around the bases of the trunks to keep rodents from reaching the tender bark higher up.

Mulches Check mulches over perennials or rock garden plants and replace any that have become dislodged. When and if the soil thaws this month, tamp back into place any small perennial plantings that have been heaved up by frost; then mulch to protect for the duration of the early spring.

Tree Transport If you are planning on removing a large tree or having one installed, either of which is a job for a professional and requires the use of heavy equipment (trucks, cherry pickers, backhoes), this may be the time to do it. Machinery that would plow deep ruts in your lawn during the spring or fall will do far less damage when the ground is frozen solid. Talk to your landscape contractor or tree man, and be certain he's had experience planting big trees in frozen soil.

Dormant Pruning February is the time for dormant pruning of fruit trees, evergreens, and any ornamental trees and shrubs that bloom from the end of June onwards.

Fruit trees Apple, pear, and peach trees benefit from careful pruning now if they are overgrown, with limbs tangling or competing for sun. Consider pruning them if they have damaged limbs; or if heavy lateral limbs are distorting the trees' shapes or weakening their crotches; or if there are vertical shoots springing skywards parallel to the main trunk or leader. Cut any offending branches cleanly, leaving no stumps. Always use clean, sharp shears and saw. As a further hygienic measure, get rid of old dried-up fruits and cut off and burn any cankered growth, to eliminate the canker-causing fungi or bacteria.

Narrow-leaved evergreens including arborvitaes, junipers, and yews may call for one of two kinds of pruning at this season: elimination of dead or unwanted boughs, and trimming of tips for shape or neatness. I don't recommend shearing them into rigid shapes, but merely guiding their growth and keeping their size within bounds, if needed. (Pines, firs, spruces, and hemlocks are best done later on.)

Ornamental trees and shrubs that bloom in late June or after can be pruned now as needed — from minor shaping to drastic surgery of old overgrown limbs or thinning of multiple bushy shoots. These plants form flower buds on this spring's growth, so pruning will only encourage more lavish bloom. Often improved by more or less severe pruning at this season are such shrubs as butterfly bush, rose-of-Sharon, and shrub hydrangeas.

Another group of plants you can prune hard now are kerria and the shrub dogwoods grown mainly for the red or yellow winter color of their young stems. If you cut them back to stumps now, they'll be a mass of color next winter.

Many spireas, even though they bloom in June, do well if their oldest stems and small weak shoots are cut back to the ground now — much like the treatment prescribed for lilacs later on (see May).

Do not, however, do heavy pruning now on early-spring-flowering plants if you want to see any bloom this year. Their buds are already set on last year's stems. These include flowering quince, forsythia, honeysuckle, mock-orange, andromeda or pieris, flowering cherries, azaleas and rhododendrons, some spireas, and lilacs.

There are some small trees that — although they bloom in spring — can be discreetly thinned now for better form or overall size. Cut away sucker growth, overgrown limbs, or branches that rub against each other. You can guide new growth to some extent by cutting back just to a bud that is pointed in the general direction you want the branch to go. Shadblow, redbud, white fringe tree, flowering and Kousa dogwoods, hawthorns, golden-rain tree, magnolias, crabapples, sorrel tree, and mountain ash all can be given this kind of pruning in dormancy.

Other candidates for the most cautious of thinning now are the spring-blooming shrubs and small trees whose fruit has ornamental value. Obviously, if you prune them all over now they won't flower much — and no flowers means no fruit. On the other hand, if you prune all over after they bloom, you'll get the flowers but still no fruit. Therefore, limit pruning to cutting out only the most disorderly or leggy stems or suckers in the dormant season. Among this group: barberries, smoke tree, Cornelian cherry dogwood, gray dogwood, cotoneaster, autumn olive, winged euonymus, shrub honeysuckles, bayberry, firethorn, some shrub roses, snowberry, and viburnums.

MAR

Landscaping Opportunities
The Wild Garden

Plants for a Purpose
Native Plants

Materials and Construction
Drives, Walks, Steps, and Walls

Plants by Design
March Bloomers

Landscape Tasks for March

Early spring sunlight floods through leafless branches, and naturalized squill (scilla) makes a blanket of glorious blue.

Fuzzy harbingers of spring.

This is an exciting month: we're at the beginning of the landscape planting season.

The technical arrival of spring is the vernal equinox on March 21. In much of the Northeast, admittedly, spring may still seem a distant prospect as gusty March winds pile last fall's dead leaves in new and unwelcome places and mud reigns supreme. But even in this climate there are signs that the season is changing. The weather is somewhat milder, all in all. And whenever the clouds lift, this is a beautifully bright time of year — the days are as long as they were in October, but because there are no leaves on the trees there is actually far more light. And the first flowers appear on trees and shrubs: witch hazels, red maples, pussy willows, forsythia.

With the excitement of spring in the air, I'd like to take this month to consider one of my favorite kinds of landscape: the "wild" garden. Native plants, appropriate in wild gardens (and everywhere else), are my topic in Plants for a Purpose. In the Materials and Construction section, I'll look at some uses of stone, concrete, and asphalt: drives, walks, steps, and walls. And the very first flowering trees and shrubs of spring appear in Plants by Design this month, beginning a sequence of bloom that will go on through August.

Landscaping Opportunities
THE WILD GARDEN

There are two ways to create a wild garden. The first is the laissez-faire, let-it-happen method. The second is the management or cultivation method. The two are not necessarily mutually exclusive — although if you carry them to extremes they will produce very different end results.

Under a total laissez-faire approach, all you do is let your land go back to nature. You'll get tall grasses; weeds (burdocks, milkweed); vines (wild morning-glory, wild grape, woodbine); and in a short time, young shrubs (gray dogwood, sweet fern) and the saplings of what will some day be tall trees. The precise species that move in will depend largely on your climatic and soil conditions. If you try this, you may like what you get or you may not. At any rate, in a mere twenty years or so, if the neighbors let you live that long, your back-to-nature corner will be quite a little jungle.

There are not, however, very many residential settings where you would want — or be able — to let the land return to the wild, whole hog. A far more attractive and more feasible approach is a variation on this theme: a modified or partial laissez-faire attitude.

Modified laissez-faire is a convenient and appropriate choice, for instance, for a wooded corner or overgrown edge of your property. You can let the native trees and underbrush take over. Your only mandatory chore is to repel pernicious invaders (such as nettles, poison ivy, or wild grape) that threaten the well-being of your family or your other plantings. Beyond that, you can do as much or as little as you like.

Another possible, though sometimes controversial, candidate for modified laissez-faire is the lawn. Many people find they can live very happily with a meadow instead. For some thoughts on meadows see next month's Plants for a Purpose section on lawns.

Cultivating Your Wild Garden The managed or cultivated wild landscape is only distantly related to the let-it-happen scene. Here we're talking about two things: deliberately concentrating on native plants, and using those plants to enhance or even to create from scratch a "natural" or wild-seeming landscape. Basic to the whole idea, of course, is the goal of capitalizing on the assets of the native plants themselves. The choice of plants and the design of the wild landscape should reinforce each other. And the whole arrangement should be as maintenance-free (as in nature) as possible.

Habitats for native plants As with every planting project, deciding on natives to be kept in or introduced into a wild garden is a matter of matching the plant to the habitat. And as usual, the first step is some thoughtful observation. Consider the soil type and degree of wetness, the exposure to wind and sun, the rainfall and extremes of temperature. Study the plants that are already flourishing in or near the location you have in mind.

Chapter 4 in Part I of this book describes the range of typical plant habitats; and each plant description in Part III indicates that plant's preferred setting. Here are just a few examples of plants you might consider (a lot more are in Plants for a Purpose this month):

Often-used plants for open, low-lying "wet meadow" situations are shadblow, arrowwood, summer-sweet clethra, and of course willows.

Open, upland "dry meadow" habitats attract plants like Washington hawthorn, red cedar, sumac, and black haw.

If yours is a sheltered, shady "wet woodland" site, it is suited to all sorts of large forest trees, from beeches to oaks to shagbark hickory; and shrubs like mountain laurel, elderberry, and drooping leucothoe.

For shady, well-drained "dry woodland" habitats consider trees like red oaks and hemlocks, together with acid-loving shrubs like azaleas, rhododendrons, and highbush blueberries.

Designing a Wilderness Having determined the characteristics of and the plants suited to your wild habitat, you can think about the visual effects you'd like to achieve. In some ways, a pleasing "wild" design has to work like any other kind of design. The principles of scale, balance, rhythm, emphasis, simplicity, and so on apply here as anywhere. As in any composition, you'll need to establish background, middle ground, and foreground. For backdrop, you could use larger conifers or densely branching trees and large shrubs. In the middle ground you might group smaller trees with display interest, such as showy flowers, fruits, or colored branches. The shrubs or trees in the foreground could be planted singly or in small clusters to complete the composition.

In other ways, designing a wild garden presents a special set of challenges and opportunities. Since you're aiming to create (or emphasize) an effect of naturalness, you need to be attentive to the ways plants actually do arrange themselves in the wild. An obvious instance is natives' colonizing habit. You should imitate it, and plan on small colonies of at least 3 or 5 plants.

Always keep in mind, too, that you're shooting for a self-maintaining habitat. So try to anticipate how your wilderness will do after a few years of benign neglect. Will that tree create a thicket of saplings around itself? Will this vine smother the nearby shrubs to death?

The plants in your wild garden should also be adapted to harmonious coexistence with each other. Group them according to their mutual

This man-made "wild" garden, photographed in late summer, brings nature almost into the house. Plantings (many native) surround the small pool at the base of a rock outcropping.

needs (such as acid soil, shade, or moisture) and according to their ability to promote each other's welfare. Under a shade tree whose roots are going to drain the soil of its nutrients, plant a ground cover that likes poor soil — and that can tolerate heavy annual mulchings of fallen leaves. On a steep bank where erosion prevention is a priority, be sure not to give your bank-dwelling plants more (or less) shade than they want.

A simple wild garden design might include the following steps. First, the determination to leave a few large existing native trees in place to form a partial canopy of shade. Second, the choice of "understory" material to be clustered around and under the trees. Third, the addition of a few specimen middle-sized trees or larger shrubs for accent use (spring bloom, fall foliage, textured bark, etc.). And finally, but perhaps most important of all, the establishment of dense ground covers adapted to the setting, to prevent unwanted plants from springing up and to provide food and cover for small wildlife.

One of the joys of the wild garden is that space — or lack of it — is no object. Maybe all you have is a patch about 12 feet square. Right there you have room for a hollowed-out boulder (to hold water) with a clump of gray birch behind it, some low-growing blueberries around it, and a group of red-osier dogwoods at one side. It will be lovely.

Nor is a rural location in any way a requirement. You could have a wild garden on a city rooftop, if it came to that. One of my favorite "wild" gardens is a tiny plot about 30 feet square, in the shadow of Boston's tallest skyscraper. It's planted with several black cherries in the rear, a large group of tall viburnums in the middle, and spreading juniper in the front. In and among the branches birds flute and chirp, in casual disregard of the busy hotel traffic across the street and the construction of another tower less than a hundred feet away.

Plants for a Purpose
NATIVE PLANTS

Native plants are the obvious choice for a "wild" garden, but I'm certainly not advocating that you limit your use of natives to wild-seeming landscapes. Whatever your landscaping need — color, shade, hedging, attractive form, texture, or fruit — a native plant will very often meet it in fine style. Each time I reach the stage of deciding on plant materials for a design (and particularly for a more-or-less "natural" design), I look to natives first; then to "naturalized" imports that perform just as if they belong here.

Interestingly enough, however, the landscape design and horticultural professions of any given geographical region traditionally haven't paid much attention to their native vegetation. The emphasis has usually been on importing, studying, and cultivating "exotic" or "ornamental" plants — plants native to anywhere except the area in question. For that reason (and especially if you live in the Northeast, to which this list is specifically tailored), you may be startled when you read the list of native plants that follows. Like the man in the Moliere play who was enchanted to learn that he was speaking prose every time he opened his mouth, you may be pleased to discover that you're already quite an expert on native plants.

A composition of native broad-leaved and needled evergreens and deciduous trees and shrubs in driveway planting: bayberry, dogwood, spreading juniper, holly, white pine.

Choosing Natives for Landscape Use Native plants, in addition to all their other fine qualities, are practical: often the hardiest and easiest-to-care-for candidates for any given situation. They have adapted over millions of years to coexistence with each other and with their environment. They've developed hereditary defenses against, or tolerance of, many native bugs, weeds, fungi, and diseases.

Why consider nonnatives at all? Well, there are an awful lot of beautiful and useful plants that have been introduced from other parts of the world. I think it's a mistake to be too dogmatic on the question of natives versus nonnatives. Some gardeners do feel that natives should be given total free rein to take over the landscape, with only minimal help or control. Others are willing to help nature to a greater degree, by introducing into their locality native plants that haven't existed there before. Others use natives mixed with nonnatives to achieve just the landscape look they want. And there are plenty of people who don't know or particularly care what's native and what isn't, just so it grows.

I certainly can't dictate what you may want to do. But if you are interested in giving native plants a boost in your landscape, here are a few tips.

Buying Native Plants First, look around you and see what's already growing happily in your immediate neighborhood. Next, decide on how you'll be using natives.

If you're hoping to find native plants through commercial sources, prepare yourself to hunt around a bit — for two reasons. The first is one of attitude. A plant that is native to an area is often perceived by people as a weed; or at best, as just part of the background, nothing to seek out or make a fuss over. The second reason for the spotty availability of native plants in nurseries is that they are often tricky, sometimes virtually impossible, to transplant once they've grown to a decent size. Most of them are no trouble to move when they're tiny. But when you start with a plant that's scarcely more than a seedling, it takes years to achieve the

Above left: nurseries are using containers to make native plants more readily available. Above right: moving large trees is a job for a professional nurseryman such as this expert.

landscape effect you're after. This state of affairs does have its silver lining, however: when you can find them, native plants are often very young and small and therefore inexpensive.

Recently, too, the advent of containerized growing has brought more and bigger natives to the marketplace. Containers, together with the new awareness of and interest in native plants, may make a tremendous difference to the native-plant scene within the next few years. One sign that things are changing is the experience of a friend of mine in New Jersey — who founded his very successful nursery business on nothing other than native plants. Around 1960, he started contracting with local farmers to clean out their drainage ditches. He dug out saplings of native red maple, black gum, and shadblow (among others); trucked them to his place; set them out in nursery rows; nurtured and pruned them carefully; and marketed them as "specimens," which in the nursery trade means plants of the highest quality. It still prospers, marketing native trees as well as nonnatives.

So if you're shopping for native plants, my best advice is to take a list of alternative choices with you, and look around. You may well be lucky. As a jumping-off place, here is a list of my own favorites.

Native red maples grow along highways and make a welcome splash of color in the earliest spring (despite litter around their feet).

Native Plants for Many Landscape Uses

Small Deciduous Trees

Shadblow, juneberry, or serviceberry (*Amelanchier canadensis*)
Redbud (*Cercis canadensis*)
Flowering dogwood (*Cornus florida*)
Washington hawthorn (*Crataegus phaenopyrum*)
Sorrel tree or sourwood (*Oxydendrum arboreum*)
Black haw (*Viburnum prunifolium*)

Medium and Large Deciduous Trees

Red maple (*Acer rubrum*)
Sugar maple (*Acer saccharum*)
River birch (*Betula nigra*)
Shagbark hickory (*Carya ovata*)
Yellowwood (*Cladrastis lutea*)
American beech (*Fagus grandifolia*)
White ash (*Fraxinus americana*)
Thornless honey locust (*Gleditsia triacanthos inermis*)
Sweet gum (*Liquidambar styraciflua*)
Black gum or black tupelo (*Nyssa sylvatica*)
Black cherry or rum cherry (*Prunus serotina*)
Scarlet oak (*Quercus coccinea*)
Sassafras (*Sassafras albidum*)

Deciduous Shrubs

Red chokeberry (*Aronia arbutifolia*)
Summer-sweet clethra (*Clethra alnifolia*)
Sweet fern (*Comptonia peregrina*)
Red-osier dogwood (*Cornus sericea*)
Fothergillas or witch alders (*Fothergilla* spp.)
Witch hazel (*Hamamelis virginiana*)
Bayberry (*Myrica pensylvanica*)
Bush or shrubby cinquefoil (*Potentilla fruticosa*)
Pink pinxter azalea or pinxterbloom (*Rhododendron nudiflorum*)
Rose-shell, early, or honeysuckle azalea (*Rhododendron roseum*)
Swamp azalea (*Rhododendron viscosum*)
Shining sumac (*Rhus copallina*)
Highbush blueberry (*Vaccinium corymbosum*)
Arrowwood (*Viburnum dentatum*)
American cranberrybush or highbush cranberry (*Viburnum trilobum*)

Evergreen Trees

American holly (*Ilex opaca*)
Red cedar (*Juniperus virginiana*)
White pine (*Pinus strobus*)
Canadian hemlock (*Tsuga canadensis*)

Evergreen Shrubs

Inkberry (*Ilex glabra*)
Mountain laurel (*Kalmia latifolia*)
Drooping leucothoe (*Leucothoe fontanesiana*)
Mountain andromeda or pieris (*Pieris floribunda*)
Carolina rhododendron (*Rhododendron carolinianum*)
Catawba rhododendron (*Rhododendron catawbiense*)
Rosebay rhododendron or great laurel (*Rhododendron maximum*)
Canadian yew (*Taxus canadensis*)

Ground Covers

Bearberry (*Arctostaphylos uva-ursi*)
Black chokeberry (*Aronia melanocarpa*)
Bunchberry (*Cornus canadensis*)
Wintergreen (*Gaultheria procumbens*)
Creeping juniper (*Juniperus horizontalis*)
Partridgeberry (*Mitchella repens*)
Canby paxistima (*Paxistima canbyi*)
Lowbush blueberry (*Vaccinium angustifolium*)
Yellowroot (*Xanthorhiza simplicissima*)

Vines

Trumpet vine or common trumpet creeper (*Campsis radicans*)
Bittersweet (*Celastrus scandens*)
Virginia creeper or woodbine (*Parthenocissus quinquefolia*)

Detailed information and recommended varieties can be found in Part III.

Materials and Construction

DRIVES, WALKS, STEPS, AND WALLS

March is not only the beginning of the planting season but the beginning of the season for landscape construction. And whether you are designing a whole new landscape or doing a major or minor overhaul, you are very likely to be altering or adding a drive, a walk, some steps, or a wall. The first three — drives, walks, and steps — are essential components of your landscape's circulation system. Their design and layout, dimensions, and constituent materials will have great impact on the overall feeling and workability of your landscape. Walls are included here because they have a close family relationship to steps. They're made of many of the same materials and in much the same manner as steps, and the two often go together where changes in grade are involved.

Opposite: this door in the wall enframes a curvilinear walkway, making a pleasant and inviting entry.

Every situation demands a unique solution, so I won't attempt to offer blueprints here, just broadly applicable specifications for proper construction and comfortable dimensions. The creativity has to come from you. There's at least some degree of flexibility in all the minimums and maximums and ideal ratios I'll outline here: my guidelines are intended to help you, not stump you.

Drives and Walks I feel strongly about the comfort and safety of people as they arrive at your home (see Chapter 6 in Part I, on design). The entry drive, parking area, front walk, and main entry into the house should be clearly visible and easy to negotiate.

Without a doubt the shortest distance between two points is a straight line, but that does not mean that the ideal walk or drive should be laid out perfectly straight. Even with very little space, there's almost always a more exciting (and often more practical) solution. A drive or walk with a gentle curve or sequence of curves, or a pathway with an

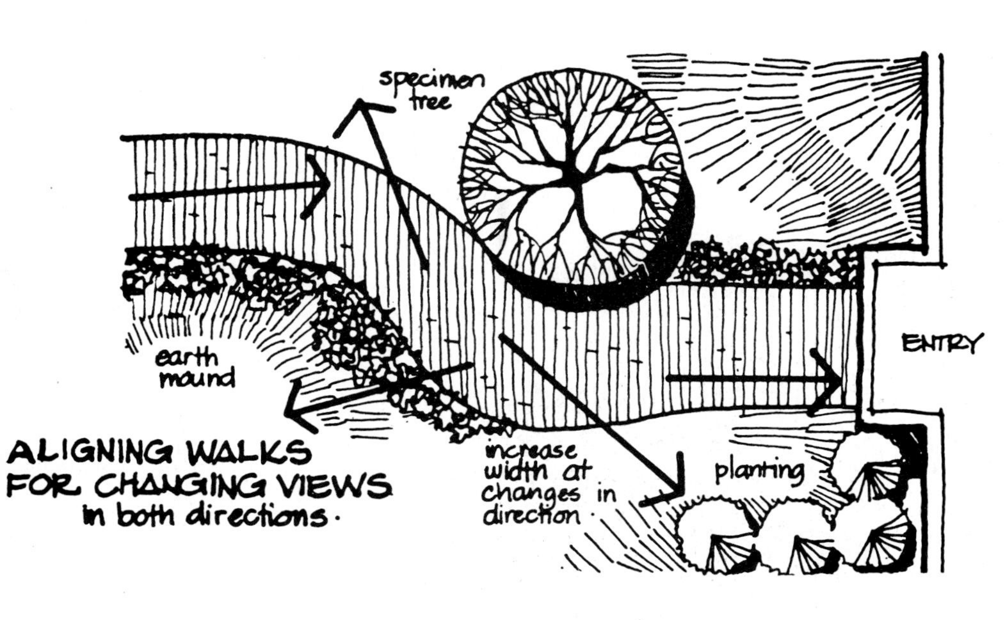

Changing orientations along walks and drives add interest to the views both entering and leaving the house.

Lay out intersecting curves without straight stretches: straight lines spoil the effects of smoothly flowing walks, drives, or planting-bed edges.

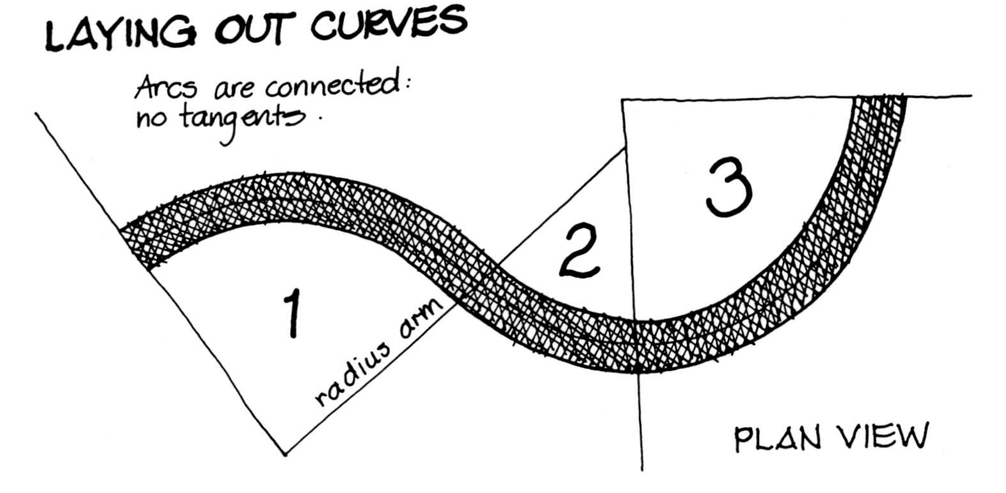

offset or jog part way along can afford a pleasant series of changing views. You can tailor your design to existing views, create new spots of interest with plantings or structures, or open up sightlines by removing old trees or shrubbery. It's exciting to explore the possibilities, and there's usually more than one good option. Keep in mind that with front walks it's reassuring always to have a glimpse of the front door visible along the way — although it certainly doesn't have to be in full view all the time.

As you begin to envision your new or revamped drive or walk, there are some design and structural criteria that you should be aware of.

Curves For visual interest always give sequential curves arcs of different radii. Connecting tangents (straight stretches) should be short or, preferably, nonexistent. For ease of layout, sketch the radius point or center of each curve on the radius arm of the last preceding curve. These rules apply to all curves in the landscape: walks, drives, walls, or edges of plantings or beds.

The one generic drawback of a drive or walk that is curved or offset purely for visual appeal is that it will be longer, will take more time and more materials to build, and therefore will cost more than a straight one. But the smaller the project, the less the difference in cost; and conversely, the larger the project, the greater the gain in interest and satisfaction. Either way, I think it is almost always worth it.

Slopes A practical reason for lengthening a drive or walk by curving it is to reduce the steepness of its slope. On uphill terrain, the more winding a path, the less abrupt its angle of rise.

The ideal slope for a walk is between 1 and 5 percent (see April Materials and Construction on earthwork and drainage). It should never exceed 10 percent — so if the immediate approach to your house is steeper than that, some curving or zigzagging of the walk or use of steps or ramps will be mandatory. As for drives, the optimum grade is 1 to 7 percent; they should never exceed 20 percent, and that only for short distances. Parking areas should not be sloped more than 5 percent, and preferably 2 to 3 percent.

Knowing the total rise of the area in question and the desired percentage of slope for the walk, drive, or parking area, you can easily determine the proper length for the pavement with this formula:

$$S = \frac{R}{D}$$

where

S = slope as a percentage (for instance, 5 percent, or .05)
R = rise in feet and
D = distance in feet.

If you have to join two slopes (one down, one up), allow for a gradual, smooth transition — or vertical curve, as engineers call it — at bottom or top. Avoid sharp intersecting peaks or valleys. Finally, if you're curving a drive or walk so as to ease travel up a grade, avoid tight curves. Snow or ice can turn a narrow curve into a treacherous trap for pedestrians or cars.

Drainage In a landscape where topography is varied and runoff occurs, drives and walks will have a tendency to become drainage reservoirs — and in winter, ice-skating rinks — unless you take steps to drain them properly at or before the time of their construction.

For a flat paved surface running cross-slope, the best approach is to build a catchment uphill to trap rainwater and melting snow, then channel it along the slope parallel to the pavement until it can be directed into a storm drain. Sometimes this isn't possible, and in such cases a second alternative is to angle the paved surface itself slightly downhill, to force water to drain across it and away.

Another solution works well but is expensive: you can "crown" a walk or drive, giving it a smooth convex curve from side to side with the crest running down the middle of the pavement for all of its length. Even in the heaviest rains, there will be a dry spot along the crest of a well-

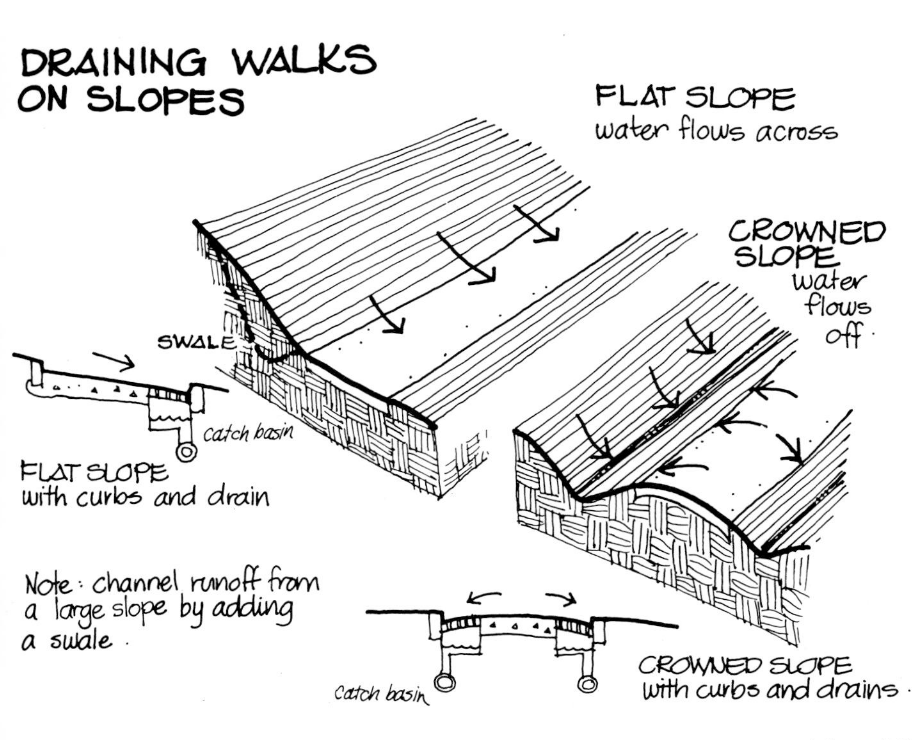

Two approaches to draining pavements are shown here. If runoff is a problem, intercept and channel rainwater uphill of the pavements.

crowned pavement. With good soil drainage, the runoff from a crowned drive can be allowed to percolate by itself; you may need cobbled or graveled gutters at the edges to channel the water, however. A softly crowned drive is handsome, but in view of the complexity and cost of building it I am usually more inclined to settle for a shallow, flat slope that lets water flow off to one side rather than both.

Dimensions Standard dimensions for walks and drives are based upon the dimensions and speed of movement of the people and vehicles (respectively) that are expected to be using them. Comfort, ease, and safety are the common goals.

Walks in gardens or lawns should be at least 3 feet (36 inches) wide; better still, 42, 48, or 54 inches, if the scale of the setting permits, to let two people walk easily side by side. For a flowing, fluid look you can vary the width of a walk along its length or flare it at either end. For an illusion of greater or lesser distance, you can make a walk narrower at one end or the other. Or for comfort at bends or corners, try adding extra latitude, just as a river carves out space for itself at its bends.

Whenever a fence, hedge, or other object beside a path is higher than 2 feet — an average minimum height for the hands of adults walking along swinging their arms — there should be a buffer strip at least 2 feet wide between the object and the path. The buffer strip can be grass, flowers, a ground cover, stones, gravel, you name it. By the same token,

Widen walks at curves, and flare at the ends for ease of transition.

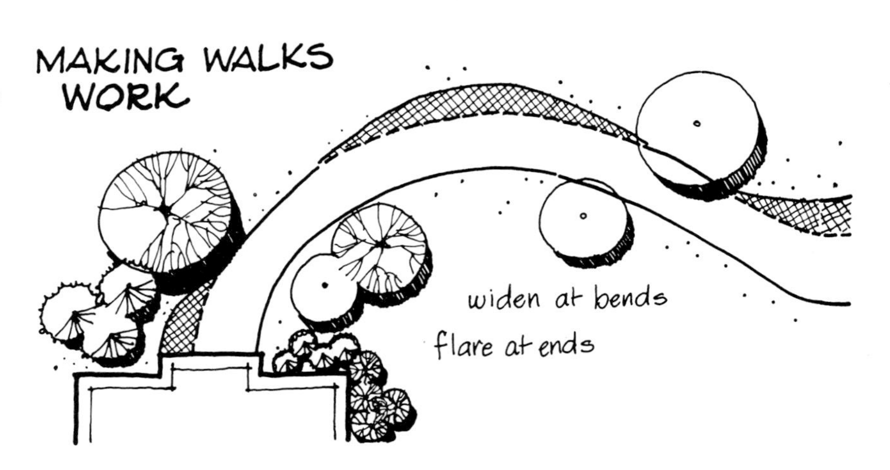

For a comfortable feeling, make a wall next to a walk no higher than 24 inches; or maintain a border strip next to a higher wall.

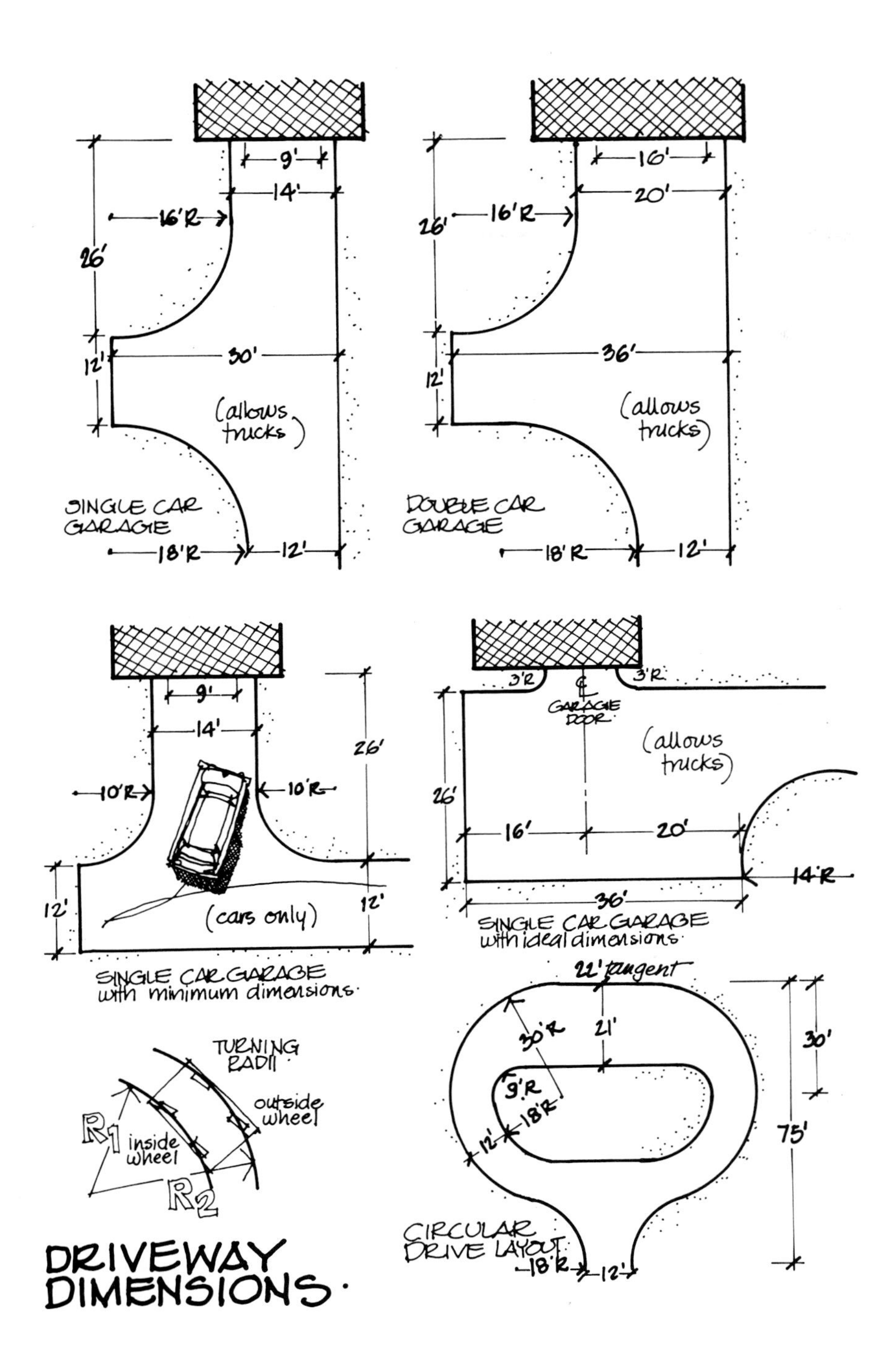

The driveway layouts and dimensions shown give a wide range of options for many different conditions. In the bottom left drawing, R1 = 20 feet and R2 = 30 feet to allow for vans, ambulances, etc.; R1 = 15 feet and R2 = 25 to allow only for a car.

if a wall is to run right along one side of a walkway, its height should be kept to 2 feet or less so that you won't brush your hand against it or feel crowded.

Drives should never be less than 10 feet wide. Preferably they should measure 11 or 12 feet for straight runs or gradual curves, and 12 to 14 feet at corners or sharp curves. Radii for driveways and parking areas are based on the turning radii of the vehicles for which they're designed.

Steps and Walls Both steps and retaining walls signal grade changes, and as such they have major impact where they appear. Free-standing walls are equally important in the landscape because they are so solid and opaque; they define or divide space emphatically.

Since steps and walls are made of building construction materials, they can be closely tied to the house or other structures in style and degree of formality. Or if they're at a distance, they can be very much a part of the garden or open landscape, and appropriately informal or rustic. In any setting and whatever the style, the design and building of steps and walls offer great scope for creativity. There's always a way to make them gracious and attractive, and it is fun to do.

Steps Steps are for people, and must be designed to fit the average comfortable pace. A hundred years ago the great landscape architect Frederick Law Olmsted worked out a formula for the proper relationship of riser height to tread depth, and his rule still stands. It states: $2R + T = 27$, where R = riser height in inches and T = tread depth in inches.

For safe and comfortable outdoor steps and ramps, stay as close as possible to these established guidelines.

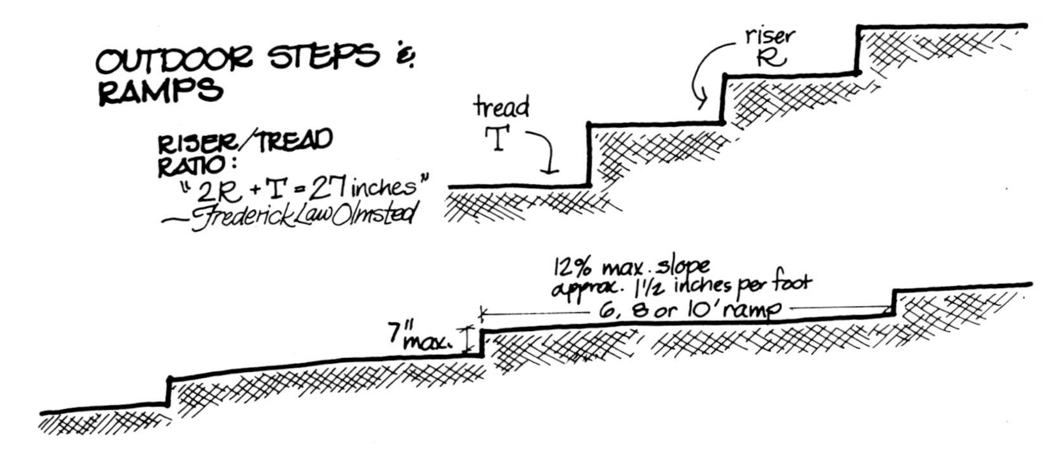

For outdoor steps, risers should be not less than 4 inches or more than 7 inches high. The accompanying tread depths are shown in the table here. I like best to build outdoor steps with risers of 5 to 6 inches, treads of 17 to 15 inches. These proportions are visually satisfying and physically comfortable. You can actually cheat on tread depths by an inch one way or the other, if space or design demands. What you must never do, however, is vary the riser and/or tread dimensions within a single flight of steps. That throws people off balance and constitutes a real safety hazard.

Riser and Tread Dimensions for Outdoor Steps

Risers	*Treads*
4 inches	19 inches
4½	18
5	17
5½	16
6	15
6½	14
7	13

The soft, flowing contour of a fieldstone retaining wall is punctuated by the crisp lines of a flight of granite steps.

Some other guidelines on steps:

- In general, steps should not be narrower than the walks they connect (if any), and preferably not narrower than 42 inches anyway. There are occasional exceptions, such as with a miniature garden path or where there's a space bind.
- Never use just one step — it's a tripper. If you've got only one step's worth of rise, figure out an alternative. You could build a gradual ramp instead; or raise the upper grade or depress the lower grade to use more than one step. Three steps is the desirable minimum, although two is acceptable.
- Always construct the top tread flush with the upper surface, as warning for those about to descend the steps. A change of texture or material — from gravel path to stone step, from brick to bluestone, from bark chips to timbers, or whatever — serves as additional warning.
- For drainage, slope the treads slightly forward. Minimum slant is 1 percent, maximum 2 percent.
- Use a railing on at least one side if you have more than four steps.
- For large grade changes, say more than 5 feet or more than you can handle with 10 risers, you should plan to incorporate landings. Landings allow both visual and physical refreshment. A change in direction in a long flight of stairs is also a good idea, to lessen the daunting impression of a lengthy climb and provide the added attraction of changing views at turning points. To permit one pace between the end of one flight and the beginning of the next, a landing should be at least 4 feet long; to permit two paces, 6 feet.
- A long shallow slope is best negotiated with ramp-steps: a combination of single risers set at even intervals of 6, 8, or 10 feet with intervening ramps angled upwards not more than 12 percent.

Informal ramp-steps: timbers form steps and contain the loose gravel on the sloped ramps.

Walls or steps of pressure-treated timbers are often a feasible do-it-yourself project.

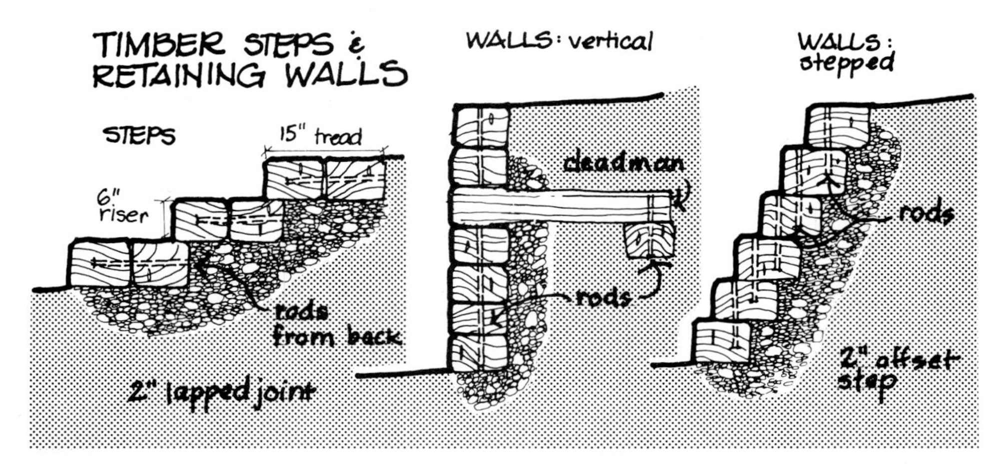

Retaining walls The primary function of a retaining wall is to hold back the soil behind it, permitting an abrupt change in grade without an erosion disaster. A retaining wall can be of any height from 1 foot up; a wall a foot or less in height is called a curb. I always try to engineer things so I can make a retaining wall 18 to 24 inches high that will serve for sitting as well as retaining.

Often, however, it's necessary to hold back more soil than a 2-foot wall can handle, and this is where retaining-wall construction gets tricky. The weight of soil and water and disruptive activities of frost necessitate both strong construction and sophisticated drainage. You have to avoid water buildup behind the wall by providing for water to drain down to and through the base of the wall.

The figures here indicate the kinds of footings and dimensions that will make for sturdy retaining walls constructed of commonly available materials like timber, stone, or brick in a climate where water and frost do their best to knock down whatever you put up.

One of the most elementary forms of retaining wall is a dry-laid stone wall. Its great advantage is that it is automatically self-draining and needs no separate concrete footing: you just dig down and begin laying the stones a foot or so below ground level. If you can find a skilled dry-wall mason to lay one up for you, or if you're patient enough to learn to do it yourself, this can be an attractive and practical way to hold back soil. But if you are contemplating a retaining wall 3 feet or more in height, I do recommend that you at least consult with a stone mason to ensure that you will be using the proper materials and methods. It's too arduous a task not to do it right the first time.

You can also build a mixture of dry-laid and mortared wall, using some mortar within the wall to hold it together. This compromise approach is useful for the less patient or experienced among us and works very well.

It's important to find the right kind of stone for the kind and size of retaining wall you want. Rubblestone or fieldstone will give a rough, informal look. A more formal or architectural appearance is created by cut stone or by stones with naturally flat cleavage planes that fit together neatly — such as slate, some sandstones, or some limestones.

Freestanding walls Freestanding walls lend a sense of solid permanence to a landscape. They define or segregate spaces with absolute finality. Whether formal or informal, unrelated, related, or even connected to buildings, they are almost always very architectural in feeling.

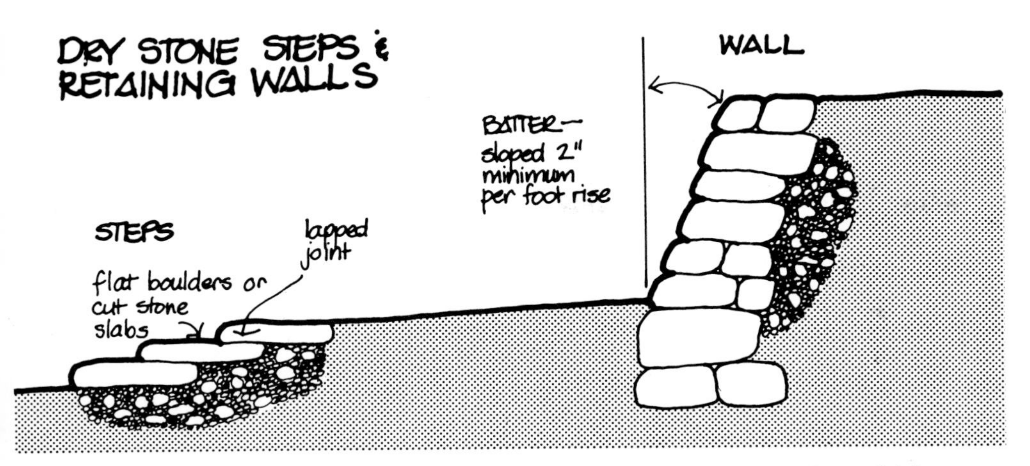

Dry-laid stone steps and retaining walls are other possibilities for the home owner, but entail somewhat more effort and skill.

They are also expensive — particularly tall freestanding walls, which present some specialized architectural and engineering challenges and are really beyond the scope of this discussion.

If you are inclined to build a low seat wall and can afford it, I think it's the way to go. A low masonry wall is the perfect border, never needing trimming, fertilizing, or replacement. It provides attractive built-in seating. And it can afford shelter and privacy, too, if you back it or top it with an open fence or plantings.

In a climate where winter freeze-thaw cycles are a way of life, two all-important precautions must be taken with any freestanding masonry wall. First, always build a solid foundation below frost level. And second, always provide the wall with a water-tight coping along the top, to prevent water from seeping into joints, freezing, and causing the joints to crack. Such a coping can be made of brick, stone, concrete, shingles, or even painted boards; but it is crucial to the durability of the wall.

The construction of walls is not an easy undertaking or one for the total novice. Just moving the materials from place to place — be they bricks, stone, concrete, or concrete block — is a staggering job. Specialized skills are required if you want to achieve a professional-looking product; and you really do, since you're building for posterity. If at all possible, I'd recommend that you find a contractor who will work with you and be guided by you in a spirit of teamwork.

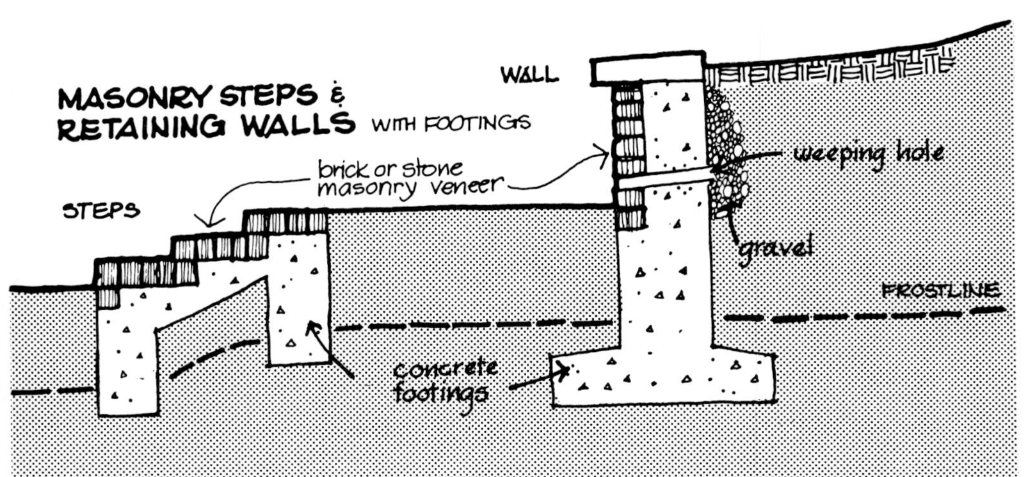

Masonry steps and retaining walls (or freestanding walls) with concrete footings involve greater skill and more time, equipment, and expense.

Plants by Design

MARCH BLOOMERS

For earliest flowering in Zones 5 and 6.

Red maple (*Acer rubrum*)
Cornelian cherry dogwood (*Cornus mas*)
Showy border forsythia (*Forsythia intermedia* 'Spectabilis')
Chinese witch hazel (*Hamamelis mollis*)
Vernal witch hazel (*Hamamelis vernalis*)
Goat willow (*Salix caprea*)

Detailed information and recommended varieties can be found in Part III.

LANDSCAPE TASKS FOR MARCH

Uncoverings Choose an overcast day (to avoid a sudden shock of bright sun) and remove protective winter windscreens from boxwoods or other evergreens around the house. This should be accomplished by the end of the month.

Last Call for Dormant Pruning Even though their buds may no longer be dormant, strictly speaking, you can do some last-minute dormant pruning (see February) of fruit trees and late-flowering shrubs if you haven't done so already. But the sooner the better. And you can still trim shade trees and flowering trees, except dogwood. Dogwood and the early-spring-flowering shrubs — that is, flowering before June — should not be pruned until after they bloom.

Pest Control March is also the last call for dormant oil spraying of apple and pear trees (see February).

Transplanting As soon as the soil becomes workable after frost is gone, you can plant orchard and ornamental trees purchased from a nursery — or transplant your own to different locations. In particular, trees that do not take kindly to fall transplanting should be installed as soon as possible. This means birches, magnolias, dogwoods, and fruit trees. Rhododendrons and azaleas should ideally go into the ground in spring, too. (See September and April Landscape Tasks sections for planting/transplanting details.)

Repair and Rehabilitation Hedges or shrubs that have suffered bad breakage in winter storms should be pruned out, to encourage healing and healthy new growth. Damaged privet, for instance, can be cut back to stumps only a few inches high and it will stage a rapid and abundant resurgence.

In bloom this month, delicate yellow flowers of Cornelian cherry dogwood mark the advent of early spring.

Root-Pruning in Advance If you are planning to move an established tree or shrub from one place to another, I recommend that you root-prune it at least one full growing season (or up to a year) in advance. And this is the month to do it, since active root growth is starting now.

This is a trick many nurseries use with their field-grown (as opposed to container) stock. It's particularly helpful with trees or larger shrubs that are difficult to move, such as oak or magnolia; and with wild-growing natives like flowering dogwood or cherry.

With shrubs and very small trees, just chop the roots with vertical spade-cuts in a circle around the plant. The diameter of the circle should be roughly 10 inches for every 1 inch of diameter of the plant's stem.

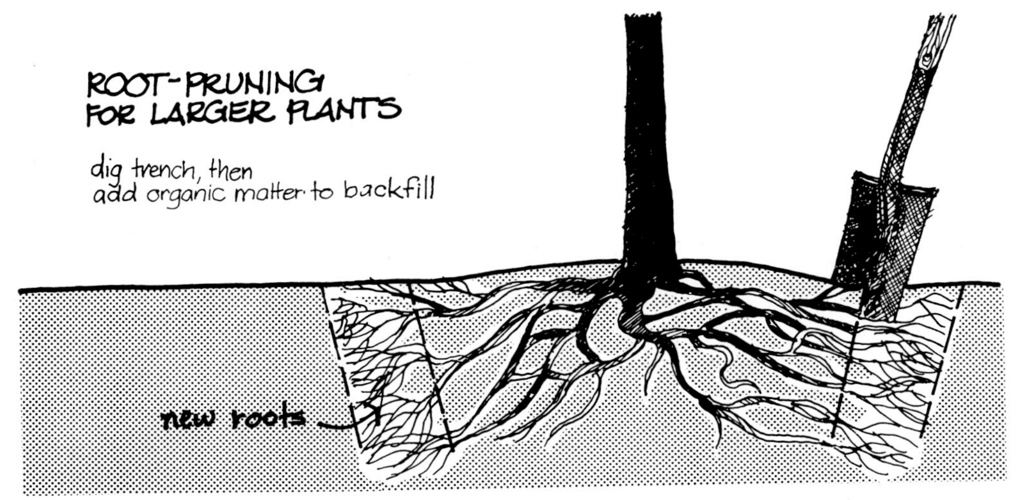

Root-pruning now will concentrate the feeder roots within a limited area. This helps the plant recover from digging and transplanting in the fall or in the following spring.

For larger shrubs and trees, use the same diameter rule but dig down deeper, making a trench all around the plant and cutting each exposed root with sharp clippers. When you backfill the trench, amend the soil with organic matter and fertilizer; and in a dry season, water regularly.

The result of root-pruning will be the development of a dense bundle of new roots close to the base of the stem. When you dig up the tree in the fall (or a year from now), its feeding system will be in place for rapid recovery from transplanting.

Soil Testing Soil acidity, or pH level (see page 45), has a bearing on the success of your landscape — because the wrong pH for a plant, whether too low (acid) or too high (alkaline), will bind up soil nutrients so the plant can't get at them. With the growing season getting under way this month, this is the time to find out whether your soil is right for your chosen plants. Most landscape and garden plants appreciate a slightly acid pH of about 6 to 6.5; but there are many exceptions, such as azaleas and blueberries. The descriptions in Part III should be your guide.

Amounts of Agricultural Limestone to Bring Soil pH to 6.5

	Pounds of limestone per hundred square feet		
pH	*Sandy loam*	*Loam*	*Clay loam*
4.0	11.5	16	23
4.5	9.5	13.5	19.5
5.0	8	10.5	15
5.5	6	8	10.5
6.0	3	4	5.5

Note: Hydrated limestone is more expensive but works more quickly, and you use only three-fourths as much as indicated above.

In general, soils west of the Mississippi tend to be somewhat alkaline; that is why it's such hard work to succeed with azaleas in parts of the Midwest. Western gardeners can and do boost the acidity of their soil by adding agricultural sulfur.

Soils east of the Mississippi tend to be somewhat acid, largely as a result of the leaching effect of thousands of years of water runoff — not to mention the more recent phenomenon of acid rain. Because of both these factors, eastern soils move gradually toward greater acidity as time passes. The addition of limestone will bring the soil back closer to neutral, and a limestone treatment every three to five years is generally advisable.

Before you add limestone or anything else to your soil, however, run a soil test. I recommend sending a soil sample or samples to your state university extension service. They can provide you with not only a pH reading but a nutrient analysis indicating what — if anything — should be done to improve the fertility of your soil. You can also purchase home soil test kits and run the test yourself; but the extension service route is often free for the asking or available at only nominal cost, and I think it gives fuller and more precise information.

With either method, your main job is to get a good soil sample. At several evenly spaced locations in the testing area, take small samples — about a cup each — every 2 inches from the surface to 8 inches down.

Spread all the samples to dry on newspaper in some conveniently out-of-the-way spot. When the soil is completely dried out, mix and pulverize it well, and pack up a sample of no less than a pint for the laboratory.

If your landscape conditions or the uses you plan for your soil vary greatly, then separate samples should be prepared for the different conditions or intended uses. Label the samples and have them tested individually. An example of this kind of circumstance would be a site where part of the land was dry and part very wet. Or a site where part of the land had been pine woods for many years, part open field — but all was intended to be turned into lawn. Or a site where a former lawn was to be converted to part evergreen shrubbery, part perennial bed.

The table here is a quick guide to the correct amounts of limestone to use to modifiy the pH of your soil. The results of your soil test will show you just where you stand on the pH scale, as well as what other improvements you will want to make to tailor each area of soil to the needs of its specific crop.

APR

Landscaping Opportunities
Banks and Slopes

Plants for a Purpose
Lawns and Lawn Grasses

Materials and Construction
Earthwork and Drainage

Plants by Design
April Bloomers

Landscape Tasks for April

Magnolias' blossoms are a billow of white, and their gray bark adds highlights among the muted tones of April woods.

April is an unpredictable month. Sometimes it's showery, sometimes freezing, sometimes too hot too soon. Two things you can usually count on, however: greenery and water. There's a haze of green in woods and shrubberies. And all around you the ground plane is turning green — from hills and fields to playgrounds, parks, and lawns. This seems a good month to think about plantings and configurations for the ground plane: banks and slopes and the plants for them, the handling of soil drainage, and lawns.

Landscaping Opportunities

BANKS AND SLOPES

Steep man-made banks occur inevitably wherever people construct level living spaces in sloping terrain. Cutting into a hillside to level an area for a terrace, for instance, or building up from grade to enlarge a backyard, will disturb topsoil, subsoil, and often even underlying rock. If your landscape includes any such artificially banked areas, this section is for you.

Naturally formed slopes like hillsides, riverbanks, or glacial moraines are usually no problem. Nor should there be any difficulty with topographical variations you add to your place for design purposes, such as a gentle contouring of the lawn or a berm (a ridge with plantings) to baffle traffic noise. Angling such surfaces to forestall erosion is part of correct construction procedure.

But the banks created by the leveling of sloped areas do present a challenge: how to establish plantings or build retaining structures to prevent the big enemy of man-made banks, erosion.

Banks and Erosion Erosion is influenced by a complex of causes that range from chemical to mechanical; but the three central factors are soil quality, type of bank construction, and location.

Soil Every soil has its own "angle of repose": the steepest angle at which that soil can rest without the force of gravity causing its particles to roll downhill. The angle of repose for a moist, heavily organic loam is very different from that of a light, dry, sandy or pebbly soil. The kind of soil a bank consists of will have a lot to do with its ability to stay put.

Construction In terms of origin, there are two kinds of man-made banks: "cut" and "fill." Often, when a slope is terraced to obtain a level area, both kinds of banks are constructed, one above the level, one below. But sometimes you'll be working with just one or the other.

When you cut into a slope, making a *cut bank*, you remove the topsoil and expose the vulnerable subsoil. It's vulnerable because it lacks the organic "glue" and web of plant roots to bind its mineral components together. Under the onslaught of rain and weather, the tendency of exposed subsoil is to run in rivulets downhill. You have surely seen this along fresh highway cuts, if not on your own property.

When you build out from a slope, making a *fill bank*, you have a somewhat different and often more serious erosion problem. No matter how high quality the soil you add on to the existing slope, it has been profoundly disturbed by excavation, transportation, and reinstallation. And the more disturbed soil is, the more swift it is to wash away under the further disruptions of frost, wind, and rain.

Location The tendency of a bank to erode is also partly a function of where it is situated in relation to the rest of the landscape. With a cut bank — whose soil is likely to lack organic matter, fertility, or other redeeming qualities — a dry uphill location is one more hazard to overcome. If there is a large runoff area above the bank in question, whether a cut or a fill bank, you'll face a constant threat of erosion; but at least you'll have a built-in water supply for any plantings you establish to hold the soil in place.

Coping with Banks Once you become bank-conscious, you'll begin noticing all around you the various approaches to the engineering and landscaping of banks. Highway and other construction sites are sources of endless examples, good and bad, even though their scale sets them apart from anything you'll be dealing with in a residential situation.

The first thing to ask yourself about the treatment of any bank is how the bank fits into the overall design of your place. Do you look at it or over it? If a bank is the main view from your living-room windows, you'll want to dedicate considerable care and imagination to making it a thing of beauty (as well as restraining it from disintegrating in the first heavy rain). If it's the boundary strip at the far side of the children's play area, your chief concerns are soil retention and safety. If it's a transitional area between the driveway and the front lawn, perhaps it should be decorative in an unobtrusive way; or perhaps you'll want it to support some screening plantings.

Other than walls, you have two broad groups of materials with which to shape and control your banked areas. Plantings are usually the easiest and least expensive, and you'll probably want to use some plantings even if you introduce other structures too. But you may also have access to terracing helpers in the form of stone or wood.

Stone and wood Stones, large and small, can be great for informal terracing — in part because they're often conveniently present in or around the same bank you're hoping to terrace. You can use a riprap of small, medium, and medium-large stones to enclose earth pockets, which in turn will support shrubs, vines, or ground covers. For boulder terracing, you can move larger rocks into place to create topsoil terraces where shrubbery or grass could be planted.

Or you can use wood: boards, logs, railroad ties, or other heavy timbers, appropriately pressure-treated for rot resistance. Any of these will break the sloping angle of the bank just enough to hold vegetation and keep the soil where you want it.

The ultimate structural retention for a steep bank is, of course, a retaining wall. But since the construction of a wall is as much an architectural or design decision as an engineering one, I discussed and diagrammed retaining walls in last month's Materials and Construction section.

The terms "cut" and "fill" refer to ways banks are created as a result of leveling operations. Boulders, timbers, and plantings aid in stabilizing soil at man-made banks.

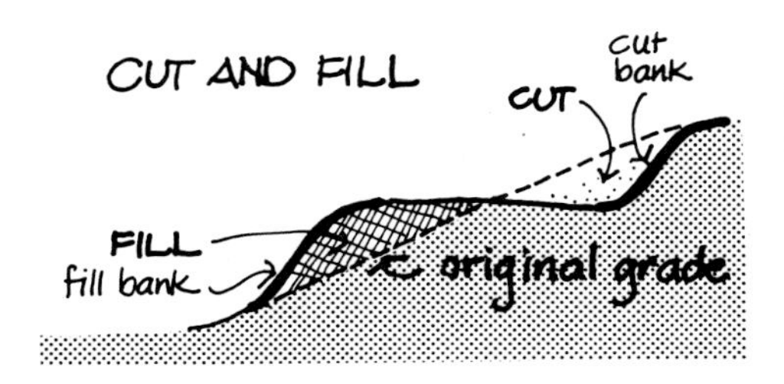

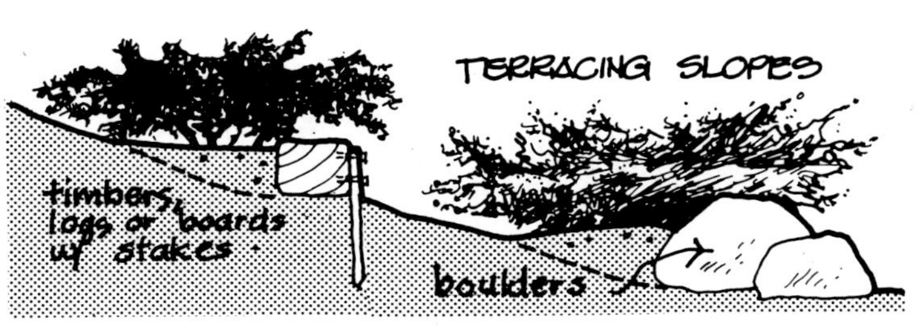

Above left: a six-foot bank is held in place by a combination of evergreen ground covers and boulders nestled into the soil. Above right: cut stone, hand set into the bank, retains soil and forms a clean-edged surface.

Plantings Unless you are privy to some source of free boulders, pressure-treated timbers, or modular stone for retaining walls, the first choice for banks is generally planting. Whether grass, shrub, vine, or ground cover, you are looking for plants that will rapidly develop fibrous root systems to enmesh the soil — as well as anchor the plants themselves. They should also tolerate low soil fertility (especially with cut banks), low moisture, and/or heavy shade or exposure to strong sun, depending on the orientation of the bank.

Because of the tough, fast-growing network of roots they develop, sod-forming or bunch-forming grasses are often the best plants for banks. (If you're planning to mow your grassed bank, however, it must not have a slope greater than 1 foot rise for every 3 feet horizontal distance.) Many varieties are available at nurseries or garden centers. There are good sod-forming mixtures of Kentucky bluegrass and creeping red fescue; or a type known as K-31 fescue, which is so cohesive it is often used in athletic fields. Or if your bank is large enough to handle the tall, tufty, bunch-forming ornamental grasses — many of which grow to be 3 to 5 feet tall — consider native grasses like switchgrass or panicgrass, or handsome imports such as ribbongrass or a South African variety called weeping love grass. All these grasses, besides keeping the earth from eroding, will supply cover for small wildlife and attractive seed heads for dried flower arrangements.

Shrubs and other nongrass plantings for banks should be of kinds that propagate readily from rhizomes or from branches that root spontaneously when they touch the ground. The whole idea is to establish a close-knit, tenacious community of plant life as fast as possible. The following are a few excellent candidates for the job.

Plants for Banks and Slopes

Shrubs and Small Trees

Sweet fern (*Comptonia peregrina*)
Siebold forsythia (*Forsythia suspensa sieboldii*)
Creeping juniper (*Juniperus horizontalis*)
Fragrant sumac (*Rhus aromatica*)
Memorial rose (*Rosa wichuraiana*)
Coralberry or Indian currant (*Symphoricarpos orbiculatus*)
Lowbush blueberry (*Vaccinium angustifolium*)
Yellowroot (*Xanthorhiza simplicissima*)

Vines

Bittersweet (*Celastrus scandens*)
Wintercreeper (*Euonymus fortunei*)
Henry honeysuckle (*Lonicera henryi*)
Hall's honeysuckle (*Lonicera japonica* 'Halliana')

Ground Covers

Bearberry (*Arctostaphylos uva-ursi*)
English ivy (*Hedera helix*)
Japanese spurge or pachysandra (*Pachysandra terminalis*)
Ribbon grass (*Phalaris arundinacea picta*)
Vinca, periwinkle or myrtle (*Vinca minor*)

Detailed information and recommended varieties can be found in Part III.

Hall's honeysuckle grows vigorously on a steep, sunny bank. But don't let it escape its bounds or it will smother everything in sight!

Plants for a Purpose
LAWNS AND LAWN GRASSES

With everything starting to grow and turn green, April is one of the best times to plant, feed, and generally refurbish your lawn. (August/September is also an ideal time to start a lawn.)

Lawn grass, hard-working ground cover for large areas, can also be treated sculpturally as in this landscape composition.

There's no denying the beauty of a clipped green lawn. It finishes off an outdoor space, satisfying the eye's need for a landscape floor that is restful and inviting in texture and color. Lawns have become part of the American vernacular; and although they're not for everyone (I encourage no-lawn solutions for small properties and wooded properties, for instance) they do find a place in a great many settings, even if only in the form of a small green terrace in an otherwise natural or wild landscape.

Lawns also have their utilitarian functions. For one thing, they can be beneficial to their natural environment. They do a superb job of erosion prevention. They contribute massive amounts of organic matter to the soil in the form of clippings and dead roots. (Fifty percent of all grass roots die each year and are replaced with new ones.) And think of the volume of oxygen returned to the air by the constant "breathing" of lawn grasses.

Lawns serve their human proprietors in countless ways as well, undergoing incredible abuse in the process. We're apt to take lawn grasses too much for granted. They go through life tightly crowded, continually pruned, repeatedly crushed; few other plants could endure such treatment.

Yet lawn grasses are plants too, and plants that form a permanent part of almost every home landscape. Because we demand so much from them — in beauty and in hard service — their selection and care call for as much attention as we give any other plant.

What Kind of Lawn Is for You? Before you plant a new lawn or set to work to improve an old one, think about what kind of lawn you really want. The types of grass you plant will depend not only on soil, exposure, and climate but on the effect you want to achieve and the amount of annual upkeep you want to devote to the finished lawn.

Conventional lawn-grass mixtures are blended of assorted grasses such as fescues, bluegrasses, bent grasses, and others, including many nonnatives. The goal of conventional lawn care is to prevent the growth of other types of plants by promoting thick growth of the approved grasses and keeping them short.

Decide at the outset just how fussy you want to be. At one extreme, perhaps nothing less than a showpiece of close-cropped green will satisfy you. If so, you should plant by the book and plan on intensive fertilization, weed and disease control, watering, and spot reseeding.

Or you may be of my general school of thought. For my lawn, I provide excellent soil and I seed or overseed with the best obtainable mix of grass seed for my location. After that, I pretty much let the lawn cope on its own. I mow, but I'm not a heavy waterer or constant weeder.

Possibly you'll find that you can be happy with a rough lawn that is really just a clipped pasture, full of clover and plantains and other visiting vegetation. If so, you can seed on a casual basis, ignore the feeding and watering guidelines offered below, and mow when needed to keep it looking reasonably neat.

Or perhaps you're the type for a meadow rather than a lawn. A meadow is not seeded with conventional lawn grasses. For a meadow, native grasses that reproduce themselves by seeds or rhizomes are permitted to grow relatively long and tufty. And among and between the tufts you will soon have a vast diversity of plant and animal life: clovers; thistles; wildflowers like daisies, goldenrod, buttercups, or Queen Anne's lace; all sorts of small creeping plants and infant shrubs, like wild strawberries, wild roses, and blackberries; and birds and other small creatures attracted by this bounty. If you mow once a year in late fall you can maintain a good stand of wildflowers; or if you prefer a neater summer look, also mow in early summer.

Right now, around my own house, much of the open space is kept as lawn. I am fond of its conventional crisp neatness and its lovely color. Still, the mown lawn is a fairly recent tradition, having begun around the mid-1800s among affluent landowners who were able to pay gardeners to cut the grass by hand. Before gardeners it was grazing animals that fertilized and cropped the grass, and what they produced was far from velvety greensward. Nowadays, few of us can hire gardeners — and still fewer possess grazing animals — and keeping that turf in good repair can be a big job. I am not sure I'd be quite so devoted to my lawn if my children didn't mow it so as to be able to play ball games on it. Once the kids leave home, I just may let some of the lawn-grass carpet grow into a meadow-grass shag.

One good answer to the lawn question is a combination of styles. You might settle for a small area of fine-quality turf right next to the house, where you look at it or use it often, with an expanse of rougher and less demanding grass around the fringes, maybe 10 yards out or so — a kind of adaptation of the golf course "green" and "rough."

Lawn Soils and Slopes For every kind of lawn, good soil is a must. You can't expect miracles from a few grass seeds scattered on infertile subsoil, particularly if the soil is steeply pitched, hard-packed clay, or badly drained. The grass will fail and the soil will either wash away or sprout weeds, or both.

Good lawn soil should be loose, not compacted. It should contain lots of organic matter (peat moss, compost, composted manure, or humus); if it doesn't, spread a layer a couple of inches thick over the top of

Soil preparation is indispensable for lawns (and all other plantings). Piles of loam, manure, and sand are ready to be mixed and spread before seeding, sodding, or planting.

the soil and work it in. The soil's pH should be about 6.5. If it is lower than 6.0, add limestone to raise the pH (see Soil Testing in the March Landscape Tasks).

As for the slope, a lawn should always be graded *away* from the house, at least 2 percent (for drainage). Rarely should it be graded more than 33 percent, or 1:3. A slope of more than 1:3 is too hard to mow. I like to blend a lawn's contours into the existing terrain as much as possible, using broad but subtle bowls (properly drained, of course) and roundish hills. I do this for two reasons. First, the effects of sunlight and shadows — especially in early morning and late afternoon — are far more dramatic on slightly undulating terrain. Second, it's very difficult to create a lawn that is perfectly flat. Rather than trying to obliterate unevenness, it makes sense to exploit it, even accentuate it. Leave the flat planes to decks and patios, and treat the soil in a more sculptural way.

Choosing Lawn Grasses Whether you are seeding from scratch or overseeding or patching an established lawn, the correct choice of lawn grass seeds is crucial to success. See if your garden center has a mix that is recommended for your climate, soil type, exposure (sun or shade), and planned use (from purely ornamental to heavy wear and tear). Some other dos and don'ts:

- Don't use a single variety of a single species of seed. It's too easy for a single infestation of insects (like chinch bugs) or fungi (like snow mold or fusarium blight) to wipe it out.
- Don't use the very fine bent grasses that are intended for putting greens; the care and feeding of these is a job for professional turf-tenders.
- Do read the label on any seed mix carefully. Look for more than one variety of one species, plus at least one other species. Make sure that the seed is fresh, dated the current year. Look for at least 50 percent combined bluegrasses and fine fescues, and not more than 25 percent of the turf-type perennial ryegrasses. Check to see that the germination rate is 80 to 90 percent (or higher) and that "weed" and "crop" seeds add up to less than 1 percent.

The table on page 146 shows in a nutshell the salient characteristics of bluegrasses and fescues, which are the top choices for lawns in the Northeast. It's easy to see why these two types complement each other so well, and why they do such a good job in our climate.

Creeping red fescue, once it is established, can be left unmowed for a "meadow look" and cut just three or four times a year. Tall fescue varieties are the most durable for athletic fields or other areas subject to hard use, but they are very coarse textured. Another grass you may encounter in your label-reading is redtop; but redtop should not constitute more than 10 percent of any mix. It is a short-lived "nurse grass" that germinates in several days, gives a green appearance to an area while the slower varieties are germinating, then disappears as the prime grasses starve it out.

Lawn Grass Care Like all growing plants, lawn grasses respond to attention — but more dramatically than most, because they are so small and their roots are superficial. You've probably seen a lawn turn two shades greener overnight after its fall or spring feeding, or watched a brown dormant lawn miraculously grow green within days following a

Grass Types

Grass species	*Advantages*	*Disadvantages*
Kentucky bluegrass (*Poa pratensis*)	Best all-around color and texture	Dislikes shade Poor in sandy soils Requires abundant moisture Browns out at 80°F (revives with irrigation) Requires 6.0–7.0 pH — more lime applications
Fescues (*Festuca* spp.), including chewings fescue, creeping red fescue	Tolerate sun or shade Tolerate low fertility Will accept 5.5–6.5 pH — fewer lime applications Tolerate drought	Stiff and wiry; do not form superior quality turf

late-summer rainfall. Having provided the right soil and proper drainage, and having seeded your lawn with the right grasses for its location and use, you have three main responsibilities in the maintenance department: mowing, watering, and feeding.

Mowing Turf grasses thrive best when no more than one-third of their total height is removed at a mowing. If you let the grass grow to a straggly 6 inches, then hack it down to 3 inches, you'll remove 50 percent of the grass plants' leaves, which weakens the plants and thus the turf as a whole. The point of this is that your mowing schedule has to adjust itself to grasses' seasonal rhythms of growth. Frequent spring mowings give way to more widely spaced mowings as summer advances — even no mowings at all if you let your lawn go dormant (see Watering, below). Things speed up again in fall, until cold weather brings growth to a halt once more.

As a general rule, I recommend keeping grass cut to a height of not less than 2½ inches. USDA studies have demonstrated that bluegrass cut to 1 inch contains 10 times as many weeds as the same grass cut to 2 inches. The longer grass simply shades out the weeds. The best crabgrass control I know of is to feed the lawn in the fall, then keep it cut to 3 inches in the spring until the germination of crabgrass slows down. When crabgrass no longer threatens, you can lower the blade to 2½ inches.

Watering Most lawn grasses flourish best when they are supplied with the equivalent of at least 1 inch of water per week. If this amount does not come consistently from rainfall, and it rarely does, you can supplement it with a sprinkler or automatic irrigation system.

On the subject of irrigation systems, my general rule is the more manual the better. If a built-in system is truly necessary in your particular circumstances, I recommend that you go to a thoroughly reputable local contractor for advice and installation. But even for a large and demanding lawn, I feel that a preferable solution is to install a few quick-coupling valves at strategic locations and move hoses and sprinklers to where they're needed. My reasoning is that each patch of lawn, with its particular sun, shade, and soil conditions, has its own irrigation needs — as do the trees, shrubs, and other plantings in and around the lawn. An automatic system generally over- or underwaters some of the landscape all of the time. Besides, drainage and runoff are problems; and really good materials, fittings, and hardware for lawn systems are hard to find.

The grass is genuinely wilted and in need of a drink when it turns a light blue-green and visible footprints remain after it's been walked on. At this point a deep soaking is in order. You want the soil to be moist 6 or 8 inches down; this can take several hours with the sprinkler.

After the spring burst of growth is over, it's not harmful to let established, well-rooted lawn grasses go into summer dormancy. The leaves will turn dull-colored or brown, but the crowns will stay alive until cooler weather and fall rains bring forth new green growth.

Feeding Most lawns stay healthiest with one or two feedings per year, 1 pound of nitrogen per 1000 square feet per feeding. For all lawns, September to October is the best time to feed; the next best is April. Your garden center can supply you with good fertilizers and directions for application. I use organic fertilizers like manure, cottonseed meal, or Milorganite (dried sewage sludge) myself, but just so there's plenty of nitrogen your lawn won't care where it comes from.

Finally, keep an eye on your soil's pH or acidity (see Soil Testing in the March Landscape Tasks). If you need to spread lime, fall and early spring are best; but if you don't get around to it in fall, you can apply lime at any time in the winter.

Materials and Construction

EARTHWORK AND DRAINAGE

In Chapter 4 of Part I, I pointed out the differences between soil for growing plants and soil for supporting structures. There's one respect in which plants and structures share the same need, however. They both

Drainage at dripline below eaves: instead of a gutter and downspouts, decorative stones have wood edging and the drain pipe is buried underneath.

require soil that is properly drained. Excess water can suffocate the roots of plants; and when it freezes it will cause the soil and anything constructed on top of it to heave, tip, settle, or crack.

Handling the soil and planning the final configuration of a piece of property so as to provide for satisfactory drainage needn't necessarily be difficult. And yet I find that I run into at least the potential for drainage problems on almost every project in which I'm involved.

The origins of these problems are many. When I am working on rehabilitation of a tired landscape in an older neighborhood, the challenge often boils down to worn-out, badly compacted soil. With a new house, the configuration of the land may have been well enough thought out; but the ravages of excavation, backfilling with poor soil, compaction by heavy machinery, and/or a too-hasty spreading of topsoil have often left an erosive and infertile wasteland.

There are also those instances where land previously considered "marginal" and left undeveloped is now being converted to residential use. Under the pressure of demand for housing in already overpopulated suburbs, house lots are being laid out in former wetlands, on steep slopes, or on top of or adjacent to major masses of bedrock. These sites present a special set of serious problems to contractor, landscape designer, and homeowner alike. Without sophisticated engineering of a kind that's beyond the budget of most developers, many of these lots are just drainage disasters waiting to happen.

So if yours is a new landscape — or an old one ripe for revitalization — you may have drainage on your agenda. Proper drainage is basically a matter of two things: the structure of the soil, and the surface configuration of the land and its pavements.

Handling the Soil Most soils in metropolitan areas have been mapped and identified as to physical characteristics, limitations, and potential uses. Begin by checking with your county cooperative extension or U.S. soil conservation service; they should be able to provide you with soil characteristics for your property.

The right soil profile for drainage The natural "profile" of soil — that is, the positions and thicknesses of its various layers in a natural state — is the ideal you are striving for. The topsoil should be several inches to 1 foot deep, and should be high in humus, fertile, and crumbly or "friable." Below that, the subsoil should be 2 to 3 feet thick and capable of being spaded without superhuman effort. The transition from topsoil to subsoil should be gradual, not abrupt. And the two layers should consist of "compatible" soils: their textures (loamy, sandy, or clayey) should be closely enough related so that water that drains through the topsoil will also be able to percolate through the subsoil.

This profile will allow rainwater to move slowly but steadily down through the upper 3 feet or so of earth, where most growth occurs, before joining the groundwater. And it will keep the groundwater or water table down where it belongs, not too close to the surface.

The wrong soil profile and how to fix it Soil that is too thin or too compacted will let excessive amounts of rainwater run off. A disturbed soil with inadequate organic matter for cohesion may permit percolation at first, but it will rapidly erode and eventually settle into a muddy sump.

The typical new home construction site often combines all these problems. There may be assorted excavations that have been backfilled with construction debris; a layer of subsoil from the basement excavation, now bulldozed over the surface of the landscape; an extremely thin coating of old topsoil right around the house; or possibly some imported topsoil (which may or may not be compatible with the site's subsoil) spread just barely thick enough to support newly seeded grass or a carpet of newly laid sod. And the machines that have accomplished all this will probably have packed the subsoil to a degree where a shovel thrust into the ground meets rocklike resistance 3 inches down.

Certainly not an ideal situation. But time and natural forces will be on your side, and you can do a lot to help. Nature's biggest contribution is the annual series of freeze-thaw cycles, which heave, shatter, ventilate, and loosen compacted soil. Your contribution is to add organic matter — peat moss or compost, at least 3 inches thick before you fork it in — and to fertilize, cultivate, and irrigate where necessary. The purpose of all this is to make it possible to develop a lively community of plant growth. That done, the roots and leaves of the plants will aerate and add compost to the soil mix — and a better-draining profile will result.

You still may find that you have to add topsoil. If so, remember that when soils are excavated they get shaken up and loosened, and their volume increases by almost 25 percent. But once installed, they settle down to their original volume. So order at least 25 percent more cubic footage than you need for the area to be covered.

When adding topsoil, be sure to scratch up the surface of the subsoil so that the two soils will blend somewhat where they meet. This will avert what's known as an "interface" problem, where roots encounter a dramatically alien subsoil and react by stopping dead, just as though they'd met the inside of a pot or container.

For the same reason, if you are replacing topsoil in a pit that was dug for a new plant, backfill the pit with the same soil that was taken out of it (after enriching it with manure and peat moss or compost), rather than dumping in topsoil from a different source.

Surface Configurations Well-constructed and -cultivated soil will permit maximum percolation of rainwater into the subsoil. For the excess water that just won't percolate even in the best of soil, the surface configuration of the land is critical. Practically every surface should have some degree of slope or pitch, however minute, so that it will shed rainwater and allow you to channel it where you want it. That is, away from buildings, off patios, to the edges of grassy lawn areas, across walks, and off driveways.

Water table maintenance One of the goals of good drainage is to keep the soil's water table, or level of groundwater, as stable as possible and at the level to which existing plants and structures are adjusted. In many urban and suburban situations a low water table is a problem. (Large quantities of pavement direct rainfall right into storm drains — and from there into rivers and the sea. The groundwater and the overall structure and quality of the soil suffer as a result.) So avoid funneling all rainwater off your property. Try to find some spot where you can allow water to collect and leach back into the soil. This could be a drywell or "French drain" (a pit filled with gravel); an out-of-the-way corner of a lawn; or a dip in a gravel drive or cobbled walk.

Or you may have the opposite problem, a water table that's elevated seasonally (or permanently) to the point where it will drown the roots of trees or shrubs in your yard. You can handle this in two ways, as

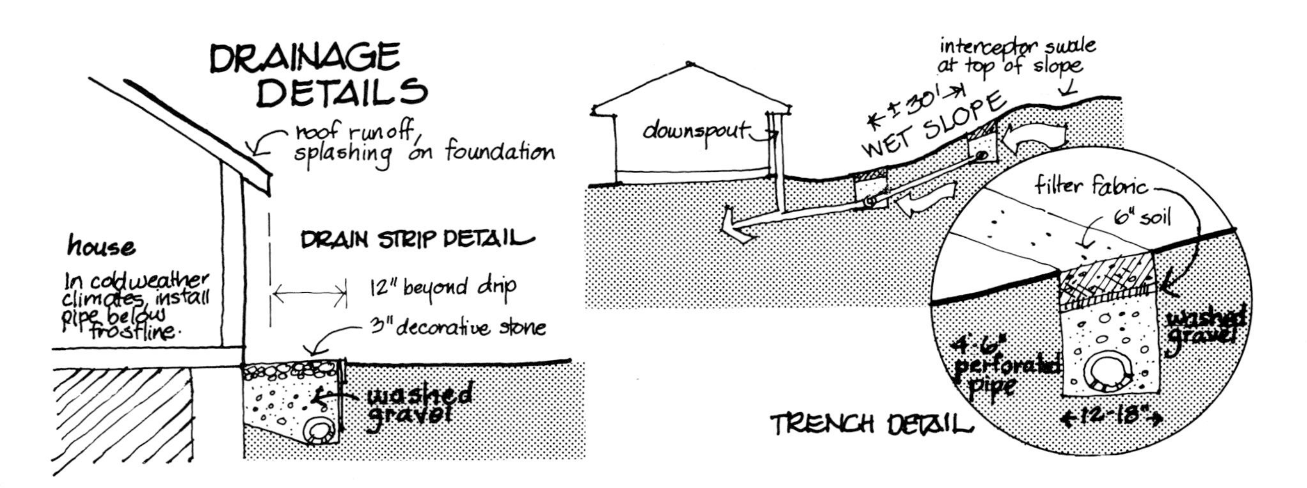

Some ways of handling typical drainage problems right around the house.

shown in the diagrams here: install drain tile to lower the groundwater, or build raised beds to keep the roots of your plants above the water table.

Slopes for landscape surfaces There are some well-established guidelines for the best angles of slope for different kinds of landscape space. These angles are expressed as ratios of rise to distance. An example: a slope that rises 1 foot over a distance of 4 feet is called a 1:4 ("one to four") or 25 percent slope.

Slopes from 10 to 100 percent are normally referred to in terms of ratios, rather than percentages. Slopes from 1 to 10 percent — the most minimal, gentle slopes — are usually expressed in percentages. For instance, a walk that rises 5 feet over a distance of 100 feet has a 5 percent slope.

Slope Ratios and Percentages

Ratio	*Percentage*
1:1	100
1:2	50
1:3	33
1:4	25
1:5	20
1:10	10

The following table, showing the minimum, maximum, and optimum slope angles for landscape surfaces, should come in handy if you're in the position of grading your property (or part of it) from scratch. In that case you may well be able to build in the best possible surface drainage. But if that is not your situation, these figures may offer some helpful clues to the causes of unsatisfactory drainage. Often, correcting a drainage problem is a matter of making only a small adjustment.

Making adjustments in grade can, of course, give rise to a common dilemma: what will the grade change do to an existing tree in its path? If the change is more than a couple of inches, the effects on many trees could be fatal. An established root system is where it is because it gets just the right amounts of water, oxygen, and nutrients from its par-

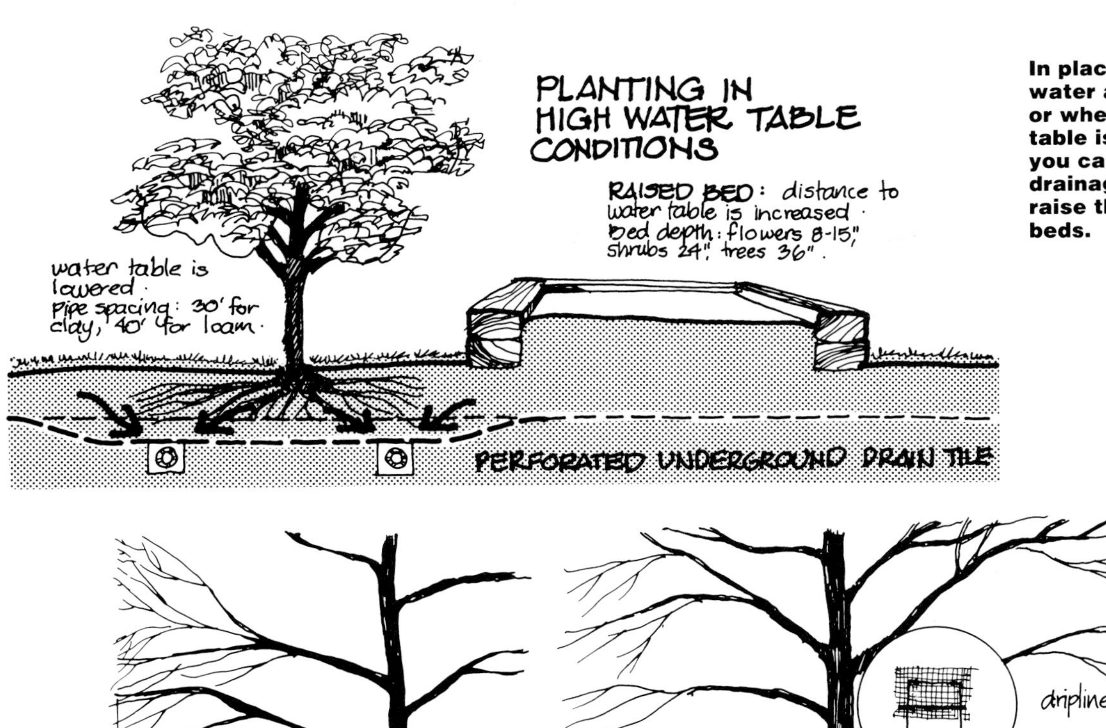

In places where water accumulates or where the water table is too high, you can install drainage tiles or raise the planting beds.

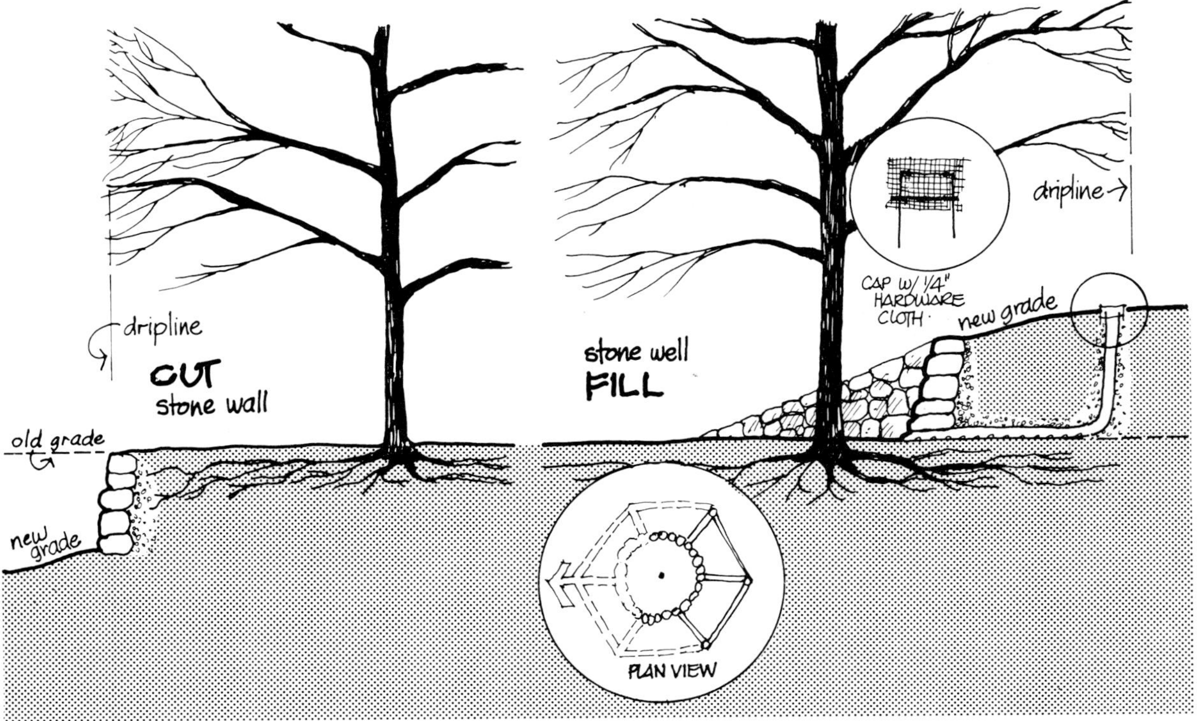

ticular type and depth of soil. Add to — or subtract from — the grade level and you'll alter this whole picture. Not to mention the fact that a quick way to kill any established tree is to pile soil up around, or scrape it away from, the base of its trunk.

Whether filling or cutting away grade around an established tree, the dripline of the tree is a critical dimension. The detail shows a plan view of ventilation pipes if the tree is surrounded by fill on all sides.

Slopes for Landscape Surfaces

Type of surface	*Maximum*	*Minimum*	*Optimum*
Lawns/grass areas	1:4	1%	1½% to 10%
Berms/mounds	2%	.5%	1%
Mowed slopes	1:4	—	1:5
Planted slopes	10%	.5%	3% to 5%
Unmowed banks	Angle of repose	—	1:4

The solution is to make for the plant an island of the same grade it has been used to: a pit or platform of soil, as shown on page 151. This will probably require some retaining structure to support the terrace of higher ground around the tree (if you've lowered the grade) or the higher surrounding level below which the tree's roots are established (if you've raised it). Again, this need not be an expensive or difficult piece of construction, but it is a necessary one if you want to maintain the health of that heirloom tree.

Cascading sprays of Japanese andromeda (pieris) blossoms delight the eye in April.

Plants by Design

APRIL BLOOMERS

Trees

Norway maple (*Acer platanoides*)
Red maple (*Acer rubrum*)
Birches (*Betula* spp.)
Cornelian cherry dogwood (*Cornus mas*)
Magnolias (*Magnolia* spp.)
Sargent cherry (*Prunus sargentii*)
Higan cherry (*Prunus subhirtella*)
Yoshino cherry (*Prunus yedoensis*)

Shrubs

Korean white forsythia (*Abeliophyllum distichum*)
Shadblow, juneberry, or serviceberry (*Amelanchier* spp.)
Littleleaf box (*Buxus microphylla*)
Forsythias (*Forsythia* spp.)
Winter honeysuckle (*Lonicera fragrantissima*)
Mountain andromeda or pieris (*Pieris floribunda*)
Japanese andromeda or pieris (*Pieris japonica*)
Korean azalea (*Rhododendron mucronulatum*)
Bridal-wreath spirea (*Spiraea prunifolia*)

Ground Cover

Vinca, periwinkle, or myrtle (*Vinca minor*)

Detailed information and recommended varieties can be found in Part III.

Forsythia's sunny yellow gives a sense of warmth on a brisk spring day. Pruning back shoots after flowering will improve the form of this particular hedge.

LANDSCAPE TASKS FOR APRIL

Lawn Care April is one of the best times to start a new lawn from seed (see September Landscape Tasks); and if your lawn is ready for seeding now, it's all to the good.

This is also a good month to feed an established lawn with a high-nitrogen fertilizer, both to encourage it as it revives from winter dormancy and to fortify it for the summer ahead (see September Landscape Tasks).

Vine Pruning Prune vines growing on trellises or against the house. With vines around the house, inspect them carefully to make sure they're not invading window frames or working their way under gutters or shingles. Vines will bounce back from fairly heavy cutting, so don't be shy.

Lily Planting April is the month to set out lily-of-the-valley pips, water-lily bulbs, and daylily (*Hemerocallis*) plants.

Spring Planting Tips Fall (see September) is a fine time to plant many trees and shrubs; but if your plant list includes any of the following, get them into the ground now:

Red maple (*Acer rubrum*)
Birch (*Betula* spp.)
Dogwood (*Cornus* spp.)
Cotoneaster (*Cotoneaster* spp.)
Hawthorn (*Crataegus* spp.)
European beech (*Fagus sylvatica*)
English ivy (*Hedera helix*)
Rose-of-Sharon (*Hibiscus syriacus*)
Mountain laurel (*Kalmia latifolia*)
Sweet gum (*Liquidambar styraciflua*)
Tulip tree (*Liriodendron tulipifera*)
Magnolias (*Magnolia* spp.)
Andromeda or pieris (*Pieris* spp.)
Rugosa rose (*Rosa rugosa*)
Azalea and rhododendron (*Rhododendron* spp.)
Yew (*Taxus* spp.)

Many nurseries do manage to install these plants in the fall — very carefully — with considerable success. Many others, however, attempt it only with some rate of failure. In my experience it is best to stay with spring planting of these species.

Heeling in: a temporary measure for holding bareroot plants if circumstances prevent immediate planting.

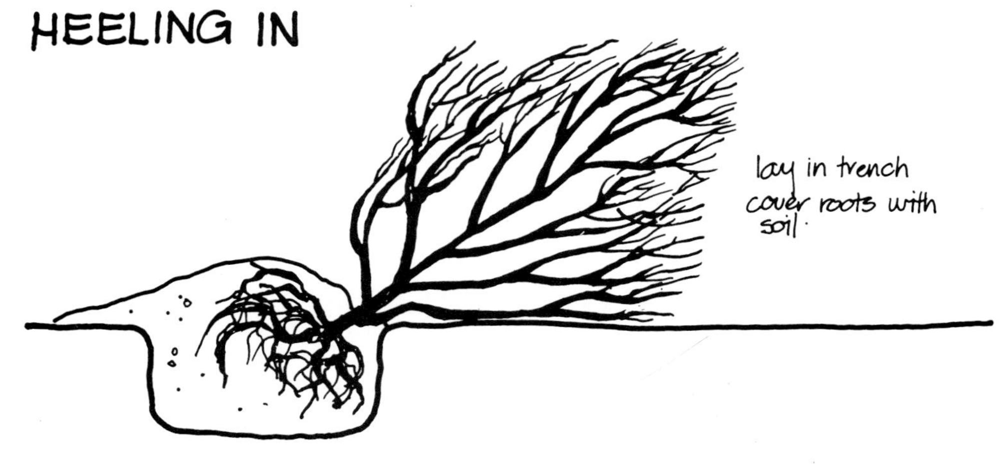

You can find the main rundown of planting procedures in the September Landscape Tasks section. But there are a few special points about spring planting that I'd like to make here.

First, although the soil doesn't have to be warm, it must be workable. It should crumble readily in your hand. Never plant in mud.

Second, if you are planting or transplanting bareroot, it's vital that you prevent the roots from drying out. At this season there can be interruptions before you can get a plant in the ground — sudden snowstorms, frozen or waterlogged soil, and so on. If there's going to be a substantial wait, dig a trench and heel the plant(s) in. That is, lay the roots into the trench so that the stem emerges at an angle to the ground, cover the roots with soil, and water well. For a shorter wait, such as overnight, some gardeners stir up a slurry of soil and water and set the roots in it. My preference is simply to cover the roots with moistened spaghnum moss or burlap and keep the plants out of the sun.

Finally, don't forget your plants once they're in place. If the spring season is dry, water faithfully.

MAY

Landscaping Opportunities
The Fragrant Garden

Plants for a Purpose
Deciduous Shrubs for Seasonal Display

Materials and Construction
Wood

Plants by Design
May Bloomers

Landscape Tasks for May

Fragrance and the hum of honeybees fill the air along this pathway through a flowering crabapple grove.

With the beauty of flowering plants, fresh green foliage unfolding everywhere, and the sounds and scents of spring, May beckons you outdoors to enjoy the landscape. And the long days combined with temperate weather make this also an ideal month to go outdoors and build things. This month I'll focus on some of the loveliest elements of the landscape: fragrant plants; deciduous shrubs (many of them flowering); and wood as a material for structures like decks and trellises to ease and enhance your hours outdoors.

Landscaping Opportunities

THE FRAGRANT GARDEN

Perhaps more than any other single sensory quality, the fragrance of a place leaves an indelible impression in the mind. If you think for a minute about your memories of places, you'll realize that all memories involve smells. "Scents more than sounds or sights make the heartstrings crack," said Rudyard Kipling; and it's true that a scent can call up instantly a complex of memories and emotions.

When you are on vacation or visiting a new spot, you're especially open and awake to your surroundings; and some of your liveliest scent-associations come from these moments. It takes no more than the mingled smells of snow and conifers to lift a mountain lover's spirits. As for me, the scent of Hall's honeysuckle always takes me back to a friend's swimming pool in the Massachusetts woods: in summer the air is filled with sweetness from the honeysuckle vines that curtain the fence around the pool area. I also remember with pleasure the fragrance of silver lindens in the Brooklyn Botanic Garden; the redolence of boxwood in the sun at Mount Vernon; and the heady scent of rugosa roses along the Nantucket shoreline.

But fragrances and their happy associations belong in your workaday life as well. Every house has its own characteristic, unmistakable smell; so should every garden. With a little planning, you can enhance the beauty and the personality of your place through fragrance.

Fragrant sweet alyssum is planted in front of a bed of thyme and sage.

Planning a Fragrant Landscape The ancient Greeks cultivated their best-smelling plants near their windows, and medieval monasteries had beds of fragrant herbs near their infirmaries to soothe and to cure the ill. Essentially, you want to put the fragrant plants within close range of the places where people live, work, and play — maybe even within touching distance. Here are some examples to start you off:

Doors Try putting near doorways plants that will give off scent when people brush their foliage in passing. These could be permanent plantings, or movable. In summer, for instance, I always crowd our back door with large pots of rosemary.

Windows to the south and/or west, where summer breezes will draw through, are wonderful locations for sweet-smelling flowering plants. Ground-floor windows are easy; for second-floor windows use tall shrubs (like mock-orange, elaeagnus, or lilac) or small trees (like crabapple, magnolia, or linden).

Fragrant perennial herbs If you grow these herbs near where you walk or sit outdoors, their aromas are released when you touch them or crush their foliage. Put low-growing thyme among stepping stones;

mint (with a good deep edging to contain it) in a shady spot; lavender in a protected corner. By the way, chives among your roses are handsome in bloom, handy for cooking, and repellent to the roses' insect pests.

Vines Honeysuckle or wisteria or other vines can be trained over arbors or on fences, or on supports around windows or entryways.

Massed shrubs yield a bonus of fragrance by virtue of sheer strength of numbers. Consider borders or screens of fragrant flowering shrubs like summer-sweet, lilac, mock-orange, honeysuckle, or viburnum.

Lilacs, age-old favorites, evoke nostalgia as they saturate the air with delightful scent.

Trees Crabapples, magnolias, or lindens planted in clusters (a minimum of three) are extra-splendid if you can prune their lower branches to allow you to walk or sit under them. They make a bower of bloom that is a feast for the senses, delightfully fragrant and delightful to look at as well.

Evening fragrance adds enchantment to the spring and summer landscape. Plants that continue to perfume the air even in darkness are good choices for areas where you'll be sitting outdoors after sundown, or for south-facing windows that stay open at night. There are many trees and shrubs in this category, and some particularly attractive ones are marked with asterisks in the plant list that follows.

As you select fragrant plants, keep in mind the successive seasons for bloom, and try for a plant or two to highlight each one. Coming with the first thawing of the earth in late winter, witch hazels' blossoms are harbingers of the general reawakening. Magnolias, crabapples, fothergilla, viburnum, and early honeysuckle drench the spring air with fragrance; bulbs like hyacinths and narcissus do their part as well. Lilacs, native and hybrid azaleas, mock-orange, fringe tree, and later honeysuckles usher in the summer. Roses are a world of fragrance unto themselves. Then come lindens and summer-sweet. In fall there's the fragrant foliage of bayberry and sweet fern; and the autumnal blossoms of native witch hazel are the year's last hurrah.

Rugosa or saltspray rose is one of the sweetest-smelling roses and a wonderful shrub for many settings.

Fragrant Plants

Orange-eye butterfly bush (*Buddleia davidii*)
Boxwood (*Buxus* spp.)
*White fringe tree (*Chionanthus virginicus*)
Summer-sweet clethra (*Clethra alnifolia*)
Sweet fern (*Comptonia peregrina*)
Chinese witch hazel (*Hamamelis mollis*)
Common witch hazel (*Hamamelis virginiana*)
*Regel privet (*Ligustrum obtusifolium regelianum*)
Winter honeysuckle (*Lonicera fragrantissima*)
*Hall's honeysuckle (*Lonicera japonica* 'Halliana')
Magnolia (*Magnolia* spp.)
*Crabapple (*Malus* spp.)
Bayberry (*Myrica pensylvanica*)
Mock-orange (*Philadelphus virginalis*)
*Rose-shell azalea, or early or honeysuckle azalea (*Rhododendron roseum*)
Pinxterbloom or pinxter azalea (*Rhododendron nudiflorum*)
Swamp azalea (*Rhododendron viscosum*)
Azalea and rhododendron hybrids (*Rhododendron* spp.)
Roses (*Rosa* spp.)
Sassafras (*Sassafras albidum*)
*Persian lilac (*Syringa persica*)
Common lilac (*Syringa vulgaris*)
*Lindens (*Tilia* spp.)
Korean spice viburnum (*Viburnum carlesii*)
*Japanese wisteria (*Wisteria floribunda*)

*indicates plants fragrant after dark.
Detailed information and recommended varieties can be found in Part III.

Plants for a Purpose
DECIDUOUS SHRUBS FOR SEASONAL DISPLAY

This month, deciduous ornamental shrubs are in their glory. Azaleas, lilacs, viburnums, spireas — they flower in a rainbow of colors and a bright bouquet of fragrances.

Yet flowers are not all that this vast and varied group of plants has to offer. Of all landscape plants, to my mind, deciduous shrubs give you the most for the least. Among them you can find plants that are gorgeous in spring or summer bloom or fall foliage color; plants adapted to every conceivable kind of growing condition, soil, or exposure; plants that resist every pest or disease known to horticulture; plants that grow fast (or slow); plants you can propagate easily without a greenhouse; and even plants that are comparatively cheap.

The sizes, forms, and textures of deciduous shrubs are wonderfully various. As a result, you can use them in many different ways in the landscape. Grow them singly or massed; up close or at a distance; neatly clipped or running wild; as borders, hedges, specimens, or background planting. The individual descriptions in Part III suggest uses for each shrub.

Always think about the nature of a shrub as you decide where and how to use it. Consider not only its likes and dislikes as to soil, sun, moisture, and so on, but its natural ultimate size. All too often an appealing nursery-size plant grows rapidly into a monster 12 to 18 feet tall and equally broad. A shrub like that is not a wise choice for a spot next to a walk or up against a foundation, where it will have to be repressed mercilessly on an annual basis.

If yours is a small property, do investigate small or slow-growing varieties of the shrubs that appeal to you. Breeders are constantly developing new selections with smaller gardens in mind. Some of the plants listed below are naturally small. Others have dwarf cultivars mentioned

Korean white forsythia, not a true forsythia, deserves wider use. Sprays of April blossoms add a dash of white, nice in companionship with its yellow-flowering namesake.

here or elsewhere in this book. Many others, however, are available in dwarf forms if you ask around.

This list of deciduous ornamental shrubs represents a careful culling of my own favorites. There are many, many additional plants that could have been included if I'd had a whole book to devote to the subject. The ones selected here, however, should give you a fine palette of possibilities to meet almost any landscaping need. *Please note* that the size ranges suggested are very variable, according to growing conditions; they're intended only as the most general guide.

Redvein enkianthus: spring flowers (here topped with late-season snow) and fall foliage color are among many assets of this upright shrub or small tree.

Deciduous Ornamental Shrubs

Small Shrubs (up to 5 feet mature height, approximately)

Korean white forsythia (*Abeliophyllum distichum*)

AZALEAS

Korean azalea (*Rhododendron mucronulatum*)

Pinxterbloom or pinxter azalea (*Rhododendron nudiflorum*)

Japanese barberry (*Berberis thunbergii*)

Sweet fern (*Comptonia peregrina*)

Dwarf red-osier dogwood (*Cornus sericea* 'Kelseyi')

Yellow-twig red-osier dogwood (*Cornus sericea* 'Flaviramea')

Cranberry cotoneaster (*Cotoneaster apiculatus*)

Skogsholmen bearberry cotoneaster (*Cotoneaster dammeri* 'Skogsholmen')

Dwarf winged euonymus (*Euonymus alata* 'Compacta')

Bronx forsythia (*Forsythia viridissima* 'Bronxensis')

Dwarf fothergilla or witch alder (*Fothergilla gardenii*)

Annabelle hydrangea (*Hydrangea arborescens* 'Annabelle')

Kerria (*Kerria japonica* 'Pleniflora')

Regel privet (*Ligustrum obtusifolium regelianum*)

Bush or shrubby cinquefoil (*Potentilla fruticosa*)

Fragrant sumac (*Rhus aromatica*)

Rugosa rose (*Rosa rugosa*)

Virginia rose (*Rosa virginiana*)

Anthony Waterer spirea (*Spiraea bumalda* 'Anthony Waterer')

Daphne spirea (*Spiraea japonica* 'Alpina')

Snowmound Nippon spirea (*Spiraea nipponica* 'Snowmound')

Crispa cutleaf stephanandra (*Stephanandra incisa* 'Crispa')

Chenault coralberry (*Symphoricarpos chenaultii*)

Coralberry or Indian currant (*Symphoricarpos orbiculatus*)

Dwarf Korean lilac (*Syringa palibiniana*)

Dwarf European cranberrybush (*Viburnum opulus* 'Nanum')

Yellowroot (*Xanthorhiza simplicissima*)

Medium-Size Shrubs (5 to 10 feet mature height, approximately)

Red chokeberry (*Aronia arbutifolia*)

AZALEAS

Flame azalea (*Rhododendron calendulaceum*)

Exbury hybrid azaleas (*Rhododendron* 'Exbury Hybrids')

Ghent azaleas (*Rhododendron gandavense*)

Jane Abbott hybrid azaleas (*Rhododendron* 'Jane Abbott Hybrids')

Rose-shell, early or honeysuckle azalea (*Rhododendron roseum*)

Royal azalea (*Rhododendron schlippenbachii*)

Pink-shell azalea (*Rhododendron vaseyi*)

Swamp azalea (*Rhododendron viscosum*)

Buttonbush (*Cephalanthus occidentalis*)

Flowering quince (*Chaenomeles speciosa*)

Summer-sweet clethra (*Clethra alnifolia*)

Siberian dogwood (*Cornus alba* 'Sibirica')

Red-osier dogwood (*Cornus sericea*)

Showy border forsythia (*Forsythia intermedia* 'Spectabilis')

Siebold weeping forsythia (*Forsythia suspensa sieboldii*)

Large fothergilla or witch alder (*Fothergilla major*)

Vernal witch hazel (*Hamamelis vernalis*)

Winterberry (*Ilex verticillata*)

Winter honeysuckle (*Lonicera fragrantissima*)

Tatarian honeysuckle (*Lonicera tatarica*)

Bayberry (*Myrica pensylvanica*)

Deciduous Ornamental Shrubs *(continued)*

Virginal mock-orange (*Philadelphus virginalis*)
Beach plum (*Prunus maritima*)
Meadow rose (*Rosa blanda*)
Father Hugo rose (*Rosa hugonis*)
Elderberry or American elder (*Sambucus canadensis*)
Bridal-wreath spirea (*Spiraea prunifolia*)
Vanhoutte spirea (*Spiraea vanhouttei*)
Persian lilac (*Syringa persica*)
Potanin or daphne lilac (*Syringa potaninii*)
Late lilac (*Syringa villosa*)
Highbush blueberry (*Vaccinium corymbosum*)
Burkwood viburnum (*Viburnum burkwoodii*)
Korean spice viburnum (*Viburnum carlesii*)
Linden viburnum (*Viburnum dilatatum*)
European snowball viburnum or guelder-rose (*Viburnum opulus* 'Roseum')
Doublefile viburnum (*Viburnum plicatum tomentosum*)

Large Shrubs (over 10 feet mature height, approximately)

Orange-eye butterfly bush (*Buddleia davidii*)
Cornelian cherry dogwood (*Cornus mas*)
Gray dogwood (*Cornus racemosa*)
Fragrant winter hazel (*Corylopsis glabrescens*)
Autumn olive (*Elaeagnus umbellata*)
Redvein enkianthus (*Enkianthus campanulatus*)
Winged euonymus (*Euonymus alata*)
Chinese witch hazel (*Hamamelis mollis*)
Common witch hazel (*Hamamelis virginiana*)
Rose-of-Sharon or shrub althea (*Hibiscus syriacus*)
Peegee hydrangea (*Hydrangea paniculata* 'Grandiflora')
Spicebush (*Lindera benzoin*)
Amur honeysuckle (*Lonicera maackii*)
Shining sumac (*Rhus copallina*)
Goat willow or French pussy willow (*Salix caprea*)
Chinese lilac (*Syringa chinensis*)
Common lilac (*Syringa vulgaris*)
Arrowwood (*Viburnum dentatum*)
European cranberrybush (*Viburnum opulus*)
Black haw (*Viburnum prunifolium*)
Siebold viburnum (*Viburnum sieboldii*)
American cranberrybush or highbush cranberry (*Viburnum trilobum*)

Detailed information and recommended varieties can be found in Part III.

A May-blooming variety of spirea, an old-fashioned and well-loved flowering shrub.

Materials and Construction
WOOD

Everyone feels at home with wood. From the soft and silvery touch of a weathered shingle, to the warm glow of a hardwood floor, to the comfortable creak of an old rocking chair, the qualities of wood are part of our American experience.

Beyond its familiarity and sensory appeal, wood is a practical and popular choice for a multitude of landscaping uses. It is versatile, workable, relatively economical, and available almost everywhere. You can make anything with wood: decks, steps, or bridges; fences, railings, trellises, or shelters; planters, light standards, edging, or garden furniture.

The more you know about wood — as with any material — the better able you will be to choose and use wood properly. And that's important, because with proper selection and construction, wood will provide years of trouble-free use and pleasure. Used incorrectly — years of trouble. Let's look at wood from three vantages: wood as a raw material, wood as a commercial product, and wood as it enters into design and construction.

Wood in the Raw All wood is divided into two categories: "hardwood" and "softwood." Hardwood comes from deciduous trees, softwood from coniferous trees. Many hardwoods are in fact very soft (such as basswood or balsa); and many softwoods are among the hardest available woods (such as yellow pine or Douglas fir). Whether hardwood or softwood, all woods consist of hollow cellulose tubes (about 70 percent) and of lignin, the adhesive that gives wood its strength or rigidity (about 30 percent).

Hardwoods are rarely used for landscape construction. They are tough to work with; besides that, they tend to split, check, and/or discolor, and they will rot faster outdoors than softwoods will, because of their lower levels of natural preservatives (oils and resins). The exceptions are isolated species such as teak or black locust; and railroad ties, usually made of oak treated with creosote as a preservative.

Wood for outdoor use comes in a wide range of colors, textures, grains, and hardnesses. Here, left to right, are cedar, fir, and redwood.

Softwood Types

Wood	*Hardness/ softness*	*Strength*	*Workability*	*Weathering capability and rot resistance*	*Availability*	*Cost*
Cedars (northern white, western red)	soft; low density	weakest	easy to work but won't hold nails well; paintable	rot resistant; weathers to silver gray	readily available as stringers and fencing	moderately expensive
Cypress	tough; medium density	strong	holds paint well	rot resistant; weathers to black, then gray	hard to find	expensive
Douglas fir (includes Sitka spruce, Engelmann spruce, white fir, etc.)	moderately hard; dense	strong	does not hold paint well; difficult to work; splinters	moderate resistance to rotting (requires preserving and stain)	available as timbers for structure	moderately expensive
Pine (southern yellow)	hard; dense	strongest	shrinks and warps; does not hold paint well, but does stain well; hard to work	treated for resistance to decay; requires stain	widely available	least expensive
Redwood	moderately dense	strong	most versatile; easy to work, paint, and stain	rot resistant; weathers to uniform gray	hard to find in all grades	expensive

The softwoods used in outdoor construction are generally cedar, cypress, Douglas fir, southern yellow pine, and redwood. This table gives a condensed breakdown of these woods' salient natural characteristics, their assets and liabilities, and their relative availability and cost.

Wood in the Lumber Yard When you begin looking for wood for your project, find out first what is conveniently available. Be as flexible as you can as to type of wood, grain, grade, and dimensions of boards, and you'll give yourself a wider selection to choose from. Don't be shy about telling your supplier what you are planning to do and asking for his advice. There are often two or three different (and differently priced) solutions to a given problem. Pick the one that makes sense for you.

Do, however, always use seasoned wood. "Green" wood, being about 50 percent water, is weaker, more likely to warp, and more apt to rot. Seasoned wood is 2½ times stronger. Air-dried wood has a moisture content of 15 percent, which is ideal for outside construction as this is the equilibrium moisture content that is reached naturally out of doors. Kiln-dried wood has the lowest moisture content of all, 7 to 10 percent, and is best used for interior woodwork only. If you do use it for outdoor work, make sure it is well fastened; when it absorbs moisture to attain that 15 percent equilibrium level, it will probably warp.

Standard dimensions are traditionally cited in even inches. As you know if you've ever built anything, however, boards' nominal sizes are not their actual measurements but their measurements before the shrinkage that comes with drying. The table here shows how shrinkage affects measurements; to take an example, a "1 by 8 inch" board is actually ¾ inch by 7¼ inches.

In the lumber business, "boards" are anything under 2 inches thick; "lumber," 2 to 5 inches thick; and "timber," 5 or more inches thick. Standard sizes of boards, lumber, and timber are listed below. Be warned, however, that not all sizes are always available at every lumberyard.

Lumber Dimensions

Nominal	Actual
1 inch	3/4 inch
2	1 1/2
4	3 1/2
6	5 1/2
8	7 1/4
10	9 1/4
12	11 1/4

Standard Dimensions

	Thickness	*Width*	*All available in these lengths*
Boards:	1 inch	2, 3, 4, 5, 6, 8, 10, 12 inches	8 feet
Lumber:	2 inches	2, 3, 4, 6, 8, 10, 12 inches	10 feet
	4 inches	4, 6, 8, 10, 12 inches	12 feet
Timber:	6 inches	6, 8 inches	14 feet
	8 inches	8 inches	16 feet
			18 feet
			20 feet

Grain means the visible pattern on the surfaces of a board, created by the exposure of the tree's growth rings when the saw cuts through the trunk. The most common method of making logs into wood is "plainsawing," where the log is simply sliced into parallel boards from end to end. As the diagram on page 168 suggests, this procedure results in boards whose grains vary from "vertical grain" (or "edge grain") to "flat grain." An older method of sawing logs was "quarter sawing," where the log was sliced so as to produce all vertical-grained boards. You can see from the diagram on page 168 that quarter sawing generates a lot of waste wood and therefore is expensive — and seldom used today for construction lumber. (It is still used with fine hardwoods for furniture, cabinetry, boatbuilding, or other specialized applications.)

The reason for quarter sawing, however, remains valid: vertical-grained boards are subject to minimal distortion, and distortion can be a major hazard in construction projects. Cupping, shrinkage, or diamonding of boards all result from the grain of the boards involved.

The lesson to be learned here is the importance of checking the end graining of all wood you select — provided, of course, that the lumberyard will let you. Choose vertical-grained boards if you can; if you can't, at least be conscious of the grain in each board so that you can position it properly once you start building. Always put the bark side downward when building anything outdoors.

Grades are designations of levels of quality in seasoned softwoods — softwoods other than redwood, that is, which has its own grading system (page 169). Essentially, the top grade is all "clear" (no knotholes), vertical-grained, blemish-free stock. The lowest grade may have holes, bark, or other scars or blemishes, and will be suitable only for the roughest uses (crates, pallets, etc.).

My personal choice for landscape construction is common number 1 or 2, whose defects are not particularly noticeable outdoors. Number 3 is fine for rustic effects.

This drawing shows the three types of wood grain: flat, vertical or edge, and cross grain.

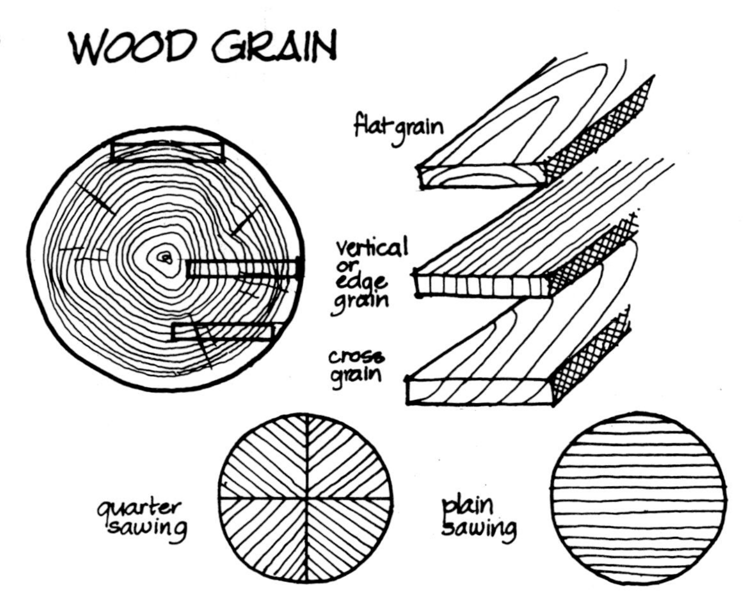

Redwood, usually my first choice for outdoor construction, has its own separate system of grades. Redwood suppliers recommend that heartwood Grade D or sapwood Grades D and E be used outdoors; they refer to these as the "garden grades." You may find, however, that Grade D heartwood, "construction heart," contains too great a mixture of heartwood and sapwood and is too streaky to give you the advantages you seek when you use redwood — namely, even color, consistent weathering, and uniform resistance to rot. Grade C "select" all heart is preferable for finish surfaces and for surfaces exposed to dampness.

Lumber Grades

SELECT: Good appearance for finish; no or small knots

Grade A	(best) — clear	suitable for natural finishes
Grade B	(or "B and better") — blemish-free	
Grade C	small defects	suitable for paint finishes
Grade D	(utility) — knots under ½ inch	

COMMON

No. 1	sound knots	little waste
No. 2	loose knots	
No. 3	larger knots, bark edges	
No. 4, No. 5	poorest	considerable waste

Preservatives are necessary with some woods whose own natural rot resistance isn't adequate for the job they are being asked to do. Every wood preservative is either petroleum based (these include creosote and pentachlorophenol, known as "penta") or water based (compounds of copper, zinc, arsenic, chrome, or chloride). There are any number of different brands and processes utilizing these two families of preservatives, and your lumber supplier should be able to give you informative literature on the particular product and process you are considering.

Do be sure, if you buy preservative-treated wood, that it is pressure treated rather than surface treated. Surface-treated wood has merely been dipped or painted with preservative, which affords at best only the most temporary protection against decay. Surface treatment will weather away; it is useless wherever the wood is in contact with soil, and it's equally useless above ground wherever the wood is not also stained or painted.

Pressure treatment, on the other hand, comes in two degrees, depending on your requirements. For applications above ground, preservative is pressure-pumped into the microscopic interstices between the cells of the wood. For below ground, the cells themselves are permeated with the preservative solution.

A few words of caution if you are working with preservative-treated wood. First, do not use wood treated with a petroleum-based compound for any construction that will come in contact with human skin: these compounds burn (and they also smell, particularly when heated by the sun). This goes for benches, decks, garden furniture of all kinds. Petroleum-based preservatives work well, however, for fences, sills, underpinnings, and stringers.

Second, be aware that cutting or drilling will violate the pressure-treated member by exposing untreated inner portions to air and water and therefore rot. If you do have to cut into treated wood, apply to the cut or drilled surfaces a liberal dose of whatever liquid preservative your supplier recommends. And remember to wear gloves and to avoid breathing in the sawdust. You may want to use a disposable dust mask. Some of the preservative solutions are definitely toxic.

Designing and Building with Wood I've already touched on the important elements in your decisions about what kinds of wood to use: availability and common sense. For special situations where dimensional precision and finished appearance are critical, such as a trellis over a formal patio, the better grades of the best available woods will give you the most satisfactory results. Conversely, the "utility" grades aren't really suitable for much but the roughest or temporary construction work.

For most outdoor construction, redwood is my first choice. It is easy to work with; it lasts practically forever with little care; it always looks attractive, both new and weathered. It is, however, expensive. You can often find an economical alternative in a fir or pressure-treated pine; but bear in mind that both of these woods have to be stained rather than painted. If painting is essential in your situation, you should use cypress or, once again, redwood. It's ironic that the same woods that do best when left to weather naturally are also the ones that take paint the best.

Many of the same elementary rules that apply to landscape design in general also apply to designing with wood. Proper scale, simplicity, and compatibility with existing structures all are important.

Redwood Grades

All Heartwood		*Containing Sapwood*	
Grade A	(clear, all heart, vertical grain)	Grade A	(clear, vertical grain)
B	(clear, all heart)	B	(clear)
C	(select, all heart)	C	(select)
D	(construction heart)*	D	(construction)*
		E	(merchantable)*

*Grades suitable for landscape construction, known as "garden grades."

All-important in wood construction: strong joints where wood members meet.

Wood building tips All the rules for outdoor wood construction share one overriding goal: to keep water out. Any piece of wood that contains or absorbs more than 20 percent moisture will rot sooner or later. Do whatever you can to prevent moisture from coming or staying in contact with wood.

Take special care at joints; use flashing or tarpaper, and don't leave endgrains exposed (they act as wicks for water).

The hardware for outdoor joining and fastening work should always be galvanized or an aluminum alloy. Any metal that will oxidize (rust) will rot the wood directly around it. Rot will allow the fastener to loosen and eventually pull out, and that's the end of that joint.

Avoid putting wood into direct contact with soil. Use concrete footings, beds of stones, or a sand base, if possible.

Ventilate. Space joints instead of butting them; leave an air space wherever a structure meets another structure; use washers with bolts, and so on.

Avoid concave warping of horizontal boards (which will trap water) by laying the boards with the convex side of the grain (the bark side) down. This way, if the boards do warp they will tend to shed rather than accumulate water.

And finally, use standard lumber sizes. It's far easier and cheaper to tailor your construction project to available lengths and widths of lumber than the other way around.

I enjoy working with wood — the activity itself, as well as the finished products. Wood is a very forgiving material. Whatever you build, however, don't be tempted to try shortcuts or substitute inferior types or grades of wood. Stick to approved materials and methods and your wood construction will be a source of lasting pleasure.

A wood deck set on the ground needs a well-drained base.

In bloom in May are spirea (above left) and pink flowering dogwood (above right).

Plants by Design

MAY BLOOMERS

Early May

Sugar maple (*Acer saccharum*)
Flowering quince (*Chaenomeles speciosa*)
Saucer magnolia (*Magnolia soulangiana*)
Japanese flowering crabapple (*Malus floribunda*)
Tea crabapple (*Malus hupehensis*)
Zumi crabapple (*Malus zumi calocarpa*)
Beach plum (*Prunus maritima*)
Oriental cherry (*Prunus serrulata*)
Callery pear (*Pyrus calleryana*)

Mid-May

Horse chestnut (*Aesculus hippocastanum*)
Redbud (*Cercis canadensis*)
Flowering dogwood (*Cornus florida*)
Redvein enkianthus (*Enkianthus campanulatus*)
Large fothergilla (*Fothergilla major*)
Kerria (*Kerria japonica* 'Pleniflora')
Sargent crabapple (*Malus sargentii*)
Carolina rhododendron (*Rhododendron carolinianum*)
Royal azalea (*Rhododendron schlippenbachii*)
Bridal-wreath spirea (*Spiraea prunifolia*)
Common lilac (*Syringa vulgaris*)
Korean spice viburnum (*Viburnum carlesii*)

Late May

Amur honeysuckle (*Lonicera maackii*)
Tatarian honeysuckle (*Lonicera tatarica*)
Bush or shrubby cinquefoil (*Potentilla fruticosa*)
Black or rum cherry (*Prunus serotina*)
Catawba rhododendron (*Rhododendron catawbiense*)
Boule de Neige rhododendron (*Rhododendron catawbiense* 'Boule de Neige')
Ghent azaleas (*Rhododendron gandavense* vars.)
Pinxterbloom or pinxter azalea (*Rhododendron nudiflorum*)
Snowmound Nippon spirea (*Spiraea nipponica* 'Snowmound')
Vanhoutte spirea (*Spiraea vanhouttei*)
Chinese lilac (*Syringa chinensis*)
Persian lilac (*Syringa persica*)
European cranberrybush (*Viburnum opulus*)
Black haw (*Viburnum prunifolium*)
Siebold viburnum (*Viburnum sieboldii*)
Japanese wisteria (*Wisteria floribunda*)

Detailed information and recommended varieties can be found in Part III.

LANDSCAPE TASKS FOR MAY

Garden Visitations This is the best time of year to visit gardens in bloom — not only private gardens but public arboretums, botanical gardens, and parks, as well as commercial nurseries. You can visit just for pleasure; or you can take notes and photos of plants you particularly like, then look them up in this book to see how and where they might fit into your own landscape design.

Spent Flower Removal Now and throughout June, pinch off or cut off the spent blooms of lilacs, rhododendrons, and mountain laurel. This may sound like a nuisance, but it doesn't take that much time and it will definitely boost flower production in the following year. The reason is that throughout the summer the shrub will put its energies into forming new flower buds rather than ripening seeds where the old flowers bloomed. Besides, this pinching is often all you need to do by way of "pruning" to keep rhododendrons, azaleas, and mountain laurel neat and compact.

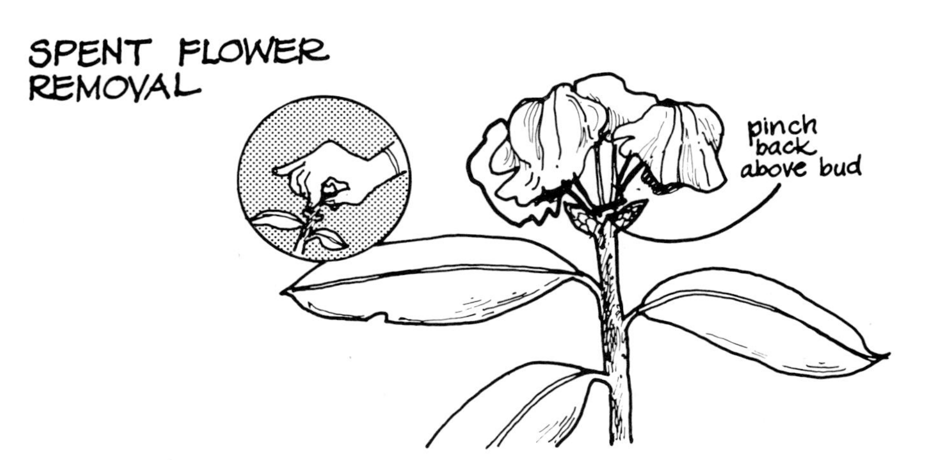

Removing spent blooms from rhododendrons, laurels, and lilacs helps insure better flowering next year.

Cutting and Pruning The dormant pruning season (see January and February) is long past. Now and next month are the time to prune plants that have finished blooming so that their postpruning growth can include formation of new flower buds for next spring — and to prune evergreens that are putting out new bright green growth. Every family of trees and shrubs has its own timetable for pruning.

Cherries and magnolias should be cut back this month after their blossoms fall, but only very sparingly. Both these plants recover slowly from pruning, and extremely slowly from severe pruning.

Spireas and lilacs in flowering hedges will stay in good condition if you cut them back quite strongly after they finish flowering. A good approach to lilacs is to cut down all of the small shoots or suckers every year; to trim back the longer young growth (for shape) every year; and to cut at least one-third of the largest, oldest stems to the ground every two or three years. Spireas can be pruned even more drastically: remove most of their oldest stems every spring to encourage sturdy new growth.

Needled evergreens such as yew, hemlock, pine, and arborvitae are eligible for trimming and shaping now. Snip off the tips of the soft

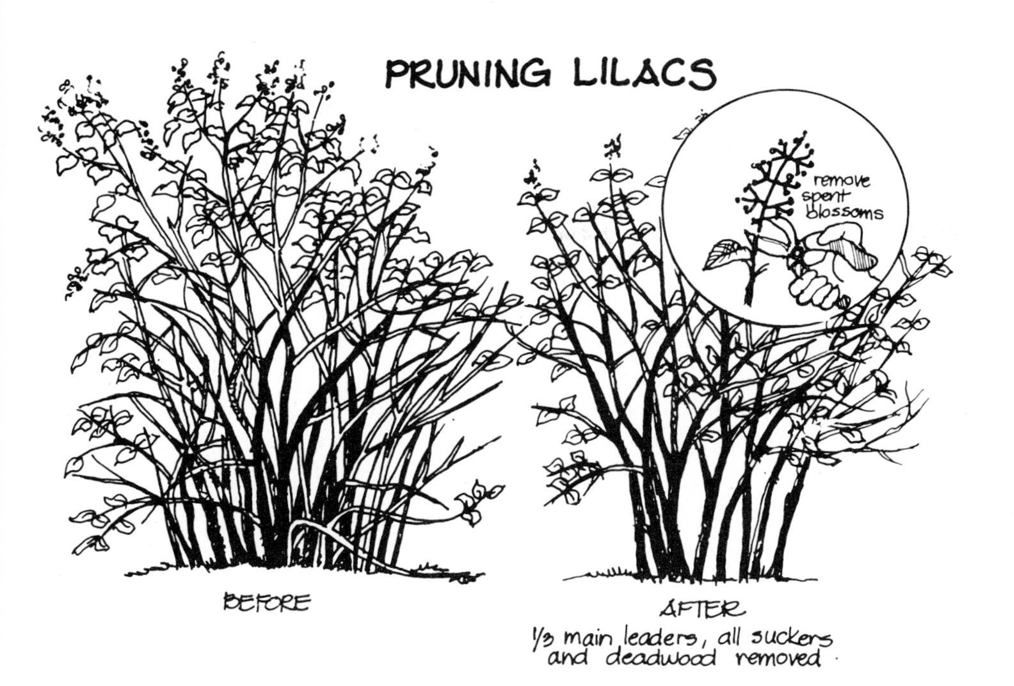

Lilacs respond wonderfully to this kind of attention.

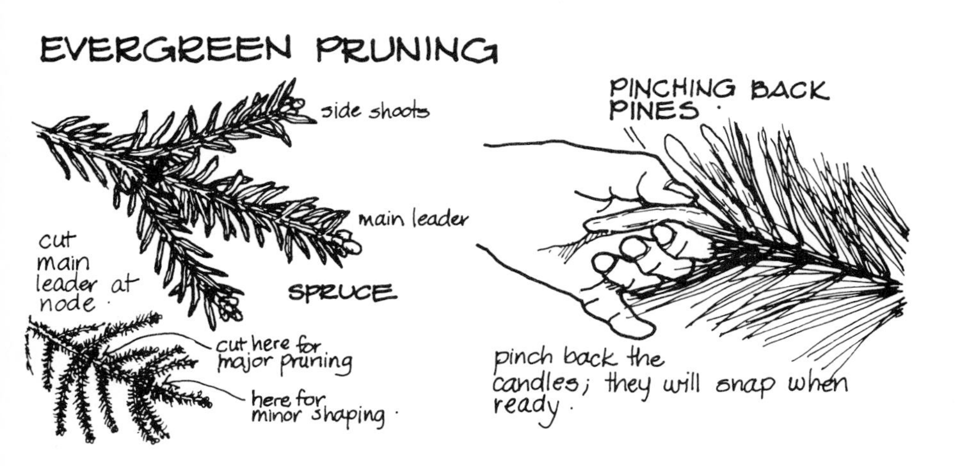

Pinching and pruning as appropriate keep evergreen trees' sizes within bounds.

new growth; this will promote compact, bushy growth without deforming the plant.

Propagation by Simple Layering Simple layering means reproducing plants by fastening a portion of a branch (or branches) to the earth and keeping it in position until it roots. This form of propagation — unlike propagation by cuttings (January and June Landscape Tasks) — often occurs spontaneously in nature and is therefore very easy to do successfully. Azaleas and rhododendrons are among the plant types easiest to reproduce this way; others (see the list on page 175) include many shrubs and even trees whose lower branches naturally bend close to, or touch, the soil.

For simple layering, all you need is patience. It can take as long as 18 or 24 months for a layered stem to acquire a root system ample enough to withstand transplanting. And successful transplanting and es-

Judicious removal of branches helps enhance the shape of weeping white pine.

tablishment of the new plant is (as with softwood cuttings) often the trickiest phase of the whole project.

Ahead of time With simple layering as with hardwood and softwood cuttings, you'll have the best results if you prepare the plant ahead. In this case, prune the desired branch or branches severely the preceding spring to encourage fast-growing new shoots. These artificially promoted shoots will root far more readily than shoots of the same age produced by the plant in its normal course of growth.

When to layer Rooting capacity is at its peak during the peak growth period: that is, early spring. It's worth trying from spring into midsummer, however.

Preparing the soil Choose a location with a good amount of sun, since warmth hastens rooting. Cultivate the soil well; it should be friable, with good moisture-retaining capability, but never soggy. If necessary, lighten it with sand, peat moss, or compost. Then firm it gently.

Preparing the stem Choose a flexible shoot of the previous year's growth. Remove leaves and side shoots from 4 to 24 inches back from the tip. Layers usually root best if the stem is wounded or girdled at a spot about 9 inches behind the tip. To girdle it, wrap a piece of copper wire around it and twist it snug; or peel off a 1-inch ring of bark. To wound it, you can make a diagonal cut about ½ inch long, reaching halfway through the stem, and prop the cut open with a pebble or piece of wood. Or some gardeners prefer to take the shoot in both hands and give it a sharp twist; or simply to shave a ¼-inch slice off the underside of the stem.

Pegging down the layer Make a 6-inch-deep trench in the earth. Secure the wounded or girdled portion of the stem in it with a stake, forked stick, wire hoop, rock, or anything that will hold the stem firmly in place. For more vertical growth, you can also prop the end of the layer upright by driving a dowel into the soil and tying the tip to it with soft garden twine. Finally, fill in the trench with soil, firm the soil gently, and water well.

Layer care For the rest of the season and possibly the next season too, keep an eye on the layer. You are waiting for the layer's tip to put up vigorous new growth, showing that it has rooted. See that the soil is kept moist, since drying out sets back or even kills the new roots. Weed the area. If the layer looks as if it will be ready to transplant in the fall, you can cut it back in late summer to encourage still more root production.

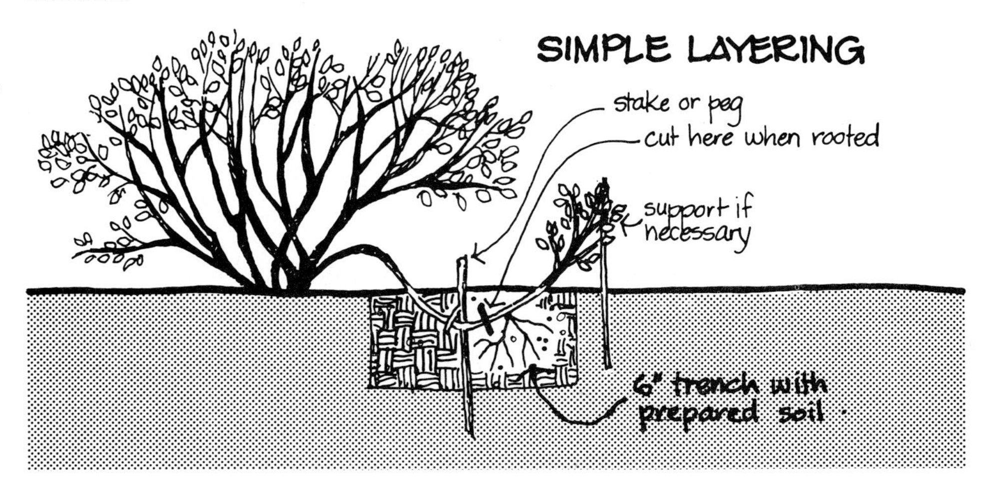

Layering: many plants can be reproduced by this simple method of vegetative propagation.

Transplanting The best time to lift and transplant a layer is in fall (if the roots are well established by then) or in the following early spring. Failing that, wait until the next fall. Begin by severing the stem that connects the layer to the parent plant. Then lift the new plant, using a spading fork and disturbing the roots as little as possible. Set it immediately in its new location; if for some reason it must wait, it should be heeled in. After transplanting, tend the layered shoot as you would any new plant. Cut back its top growth, give it light shade, and watch its water supply.

Other layering techniques Variations on the simple-layering theme are many, and you may enjoy exploring the literature and trying some of them. They include compound or serpentine layering (pegging down several sections of a long shoot or vine); tip layering; dropping; mound or stool layering; French layering; and air layering.

What to layer Very many vines naturally reproduce themselves by layering, so if you want to increase anything from akebia to wisteria I'd suggest trying simple layering first. Also, low-growing ground covers with creeping stems are excellent layering candidates by nature. As for trees and shrubs, I've listed here some popular types that lend themselves beautifully to layering.

Trees and Shrubs to Propagate by Layering

Shadblow, juneberry, or serviceberry (*Amelanchier* spp.)
Katsura tree (*Cercidiphyllum japonicum*)
Quince (*Chaenomeles speciosa*)
White fringe tree (*Chionanthus virginicus*)
Dogwood (shrub types) (*Cornus* spp.)
Smoke tree (*Cotinus coggygria*)
Cotoneaster (*Cotoneaster* spp.)
Hawthorn (*Crataegus* spp.)
Redvein enkianthus (*Enkianthus campanulatus*)
Euonymus (*Euonymus* spp.)
Beech (*Fagus* spp.)
Forsythia (*Forsythia* spp.)
Fothergilla or witch alder (*Fothergilla* spp.)
Witch hazel (*Hamamelis* spp.)
Rose-of-Sharon or shrub althea (*Hibiscus syriacus*)
Holly (shrub types) (*Ilex* spp.)
Juniper (*Juniperus* spp.)
Kerria (*Kerria japonica*)
Leucothoe (*Leucothoe* spp.)
Privet (*Ligustrum* spp.)
Honeysuckle (*Lonicera* spp.)
Andromeda or pieris (*Pieris* spp.)
Azalea and rhododendron (*Rhododendron* spp.)
Lilac (*Syringa* spp.)
Viburnum (*Viburnum* spp.)

Detailed information and recommended varieties can be found in Part III.

Watering and Mulching The month of May is sometimes quite dry, so keep an eye on any newly planted shrubs or trees, and water them if there's an extended drought. By way of prevention, mulches around the bases of plants help conserve moisture in the soil. You can use shredded pine bark, bark nuggets, wood chips, pine straw, stones, or gravel. As a fringe benefit, a good thick mulch will stop many weeds from growing. The weeds that do make it through to daylight will be leggy and easy to pull out by the roots.

JUN

Landscaping Opportunities
Planting in Woodland Shade

Plants for a Purpose
Ground Covers and Vines

Materials and Construction
Decks and Trellises

Plants by Design
June Bloomers

Landscape Tasks for June

Layers of white, pink, and red azalea bloom carpet this woodland floor.

June is the month when the hours of daylight are longest and the sun rides highest in the sky. Sunny gardens are a mass of brilliant color now. Yet as the days grow hotter, it's also a pleasure to turn to the cooler, shadier areas of the landscape. Gardening in full shade is my first topic this month, followed by ground covers and vines — often among the top choices for shady locations. For outdoor leisure on long June days I'll consider decks and trellises in the Materials and Construction section; and I'll recommend June-blooming trees and shrubs to keep your yard in flower throughout the month.

Landscaping Opportunities

PLANTING IN WOODLAND SHADE

Even with homesites on generally open land, there are areas of shade: day-long "open shade" along the north side of a house, a wall, or a stand of evergreens; the filtered "light shade" under fine-foliaged trees or under trellises or other open canopies; or the "half shade" or "partial shade" of an area that's in sun half the day, shadow the other half, like a yard at the east side of a house.

The plant lists throughout this book contain many good candidates for open shade, light shade, and partial shade situations. But what about the day-long unbroken shade under a canopy of mature woodland trees? That is what's known as "full shade under trees," and it is a special case.

Every plant needs some light. The question is how little you can get away with. Let me start with one warning: if the woods in question are low-branched, closely planted evergreens (like hemlocks, firs, or immature pine forest) you can probably forget about growing anything under them. You should also keep your ambitions firmly in check if you're working under large deciduous trees with wide-sprawling, shallow root systems: maples and beeches are the worst.

But if the woodland consists of tall, open deciduous trees or conifers that have lost a lot of their lower branches and are beginning to permit the growth of an understory of vines, shrubs, and ground covers, there's a lot you can do.

A clump of fern and a large group of laurels thrive in this shady woodland setting.

Planning a Woodland Garden One of my favorite places to visit is the Garden in the Woods in Framingham, Massachusetts, which was started many years ago by a landscape architect and gardener and is now headquarters for the New England Wildflower Society. The feeling of the place is that of a natural woodland; yet the understory trees, shrubs, and ground covers have been planned and shaped to blend into the most marvelous composition of colors, textures, and forms. It is breathtaking. And if you have some time to dedicate to the project, you can achieve the same kind of rich yet natural effect (on a more modest scale) in your own woodland setting.

Before you begin, take a look at what you have. If nothing at all is growing under the trees, you may be faced with one of those worst-case scenarios I mentioned above. More typically, however, you'll find an interesting tangle of low-growing ground plants, high-growing briers, shrubs, small trees, and vines. Even with a good handbook, some of these may be tough to identify. But don't just rip everything out wholesale.

Take photos and cut leaf samples of a good number of varieties, and send these materials to your state university extension specialist for identification.

Believe it or not, you'll find this exercise enormously helpful. Knowing the likes and dislikes of the plants already thriving in your potential woodland garden, you'll have a huge head start on finding plants that are equally well adapted to the site but more to your personal taste.

Also, you could well discover that one or two of the components of your existing jungle are plants recommended in the woodland plant list that follows. If so, you may want to build them into your design — which gives you a head start of another kind.

A second thing not to do at the outset is to clean up all the mess of leaves, rotted branches, and nameless organic matter that carpets the woodland floor. That litter, as it decays, is an important moisture-retaining, weed-suppressing mulch and a source of nutrients for the trees and shrubs growing in it. Since competition for nutrients is right up there with absence of light as a liability of woodland life, you want to do all you can to sustain and even augment the bacterial and chemical processes that are already in action. Depending on what plants you will be installing, you may need to add extra mulch, peat moss, compost, or fertilizer to the soil under the trees.

Approach the woods with respect; the indigenous communities of plants and wildlife have formed a network of interdependencies, and you want to beware of disrupting things. Be conservative.

You should also approach a woodland setting with patience — and with a certain philosophical attitude. Plants adapted to woodlands are usually (by nature) very slow-growing: expect to wait several years for the effects of your design to be apparent. And all that shade and competi-

Play of contrasting textures in a Washington, D.C., woodland garden: large shiny leaves of hosta (above) and fine-foliaged ground covers (below) capture light in distinctive ways.

tion with large trees for light, water, and nutrients is a strain on even the best adapted plant, so prepare yourself for a few failures along the way.

Selecting, Planting, and Maintaining Woodland Plants

Beyond conservatism, patience, and resignation to the inevitability of occasional setbacks, I can offer a few concrete guidelines.

Emphasize native plants The majority of plants I'll suggest for shaded woodland locations are natives. Many of these can survive with as little as one-tenth the light demanded by sun-loving species. In addition, they are equipped to hold their own in their ongoing competition with the larger plants whose roots, trunks, and foliage will be above, below, and all around them. Many natives among the plants listed here can be collected from fields and woods near you; or buy them at a good nursery. (For more discussion on choosing and using native plants, see March.)

Establish colonies Most native plants tend to grow in colonies anyway, and you want to capitalize on their self-propagating tendency, not fight it. And if some members of a colony fail to thrive, their neighbors can fill in for them. Also, in terms of scale and balance, the sheer size and strong forms of the trees in a wooded environment really call for underplantings with a good deal of substance — and colonies of growth can provide that where single specimens might not. Finally, as a bonus, the bird and wildlife population will flock to enjoy the cover, nesting areas, and food supplied by densely clustered growth.

Mix generations If a garden is flourishing in full shade, the corollary is that it will fail in full sun (or, often enough, even in half shade/half sun). I've seen beautiful woodland plantings suffer terribly from

The bright yellow-green color and dainty texture of sweet woodruff make it a perfect choice for heavily shaded spots.

shade deprivation when a great old tree died and had to be removed. So endeavor to keep a cross-section of young, old, and middle-aged trees growing together. That way, when old cover is damaged or destroyed, new cover can fill the gap.

Irrigate and mulch Particularly for the first two years, and particularly with nonnatives or with the less determined natives, a boost from you in the form of mulch and water can make or break a woodland planting. Plants respond heartwarmingly to this kind of attention while they're getting established.

A shaded landscape is always a challenge, but it's a cornucopia of possibilities as well. At every season, and especially at midsummer, it can be a place of pure delight.

Plants for Shady Woods

Trees and Shrubs

Shadblow, juneberry, or serviceberry (*Amelanchier* spp.)
Red chokeberry (*Aronia arbutifolia*)
Black chokeberry (*Aronia melanocarpa*)
Barberry (*Berberis* spp.)
Redbud (*Cercis canadensis*)
Summer-sweet clethra (*Clethra alnifolia*)
Flowering dogwood (*Cornus florida*)
Redvein enkianthus (*Enkianthus campanulatus*)
Fothergilla or witch alder (*Fothergilla* spp.)
Witch hazel (*Hamamelis virginiana*)
Inkberry (*Ilex glabra*)
Winterberry (*Ilex verticillata*)
Mountain laurel (*Kalmia latifolia*)
Drooping leucothoe (*Leucothoe fontanesiana*)
Regel privet (*Ligustrum obtusifolium regelianum*)
Spicebush (*Lindera benzoin*)
Native azaleas (*Rhododendron calendulaceum, R. nudiflorum, R. visocosum*)
Native rhododendrons (*Rhododendron carolinianum, R. maximum*)
Chenault coralberry (*Symphoricarpos chenaultii*)
Coralberry or Indian currant (*Symphoricarpos orbiculatus*)
Canadian yew (*Taxus canadensis*)
American arborvitae (*Thuja occidentalis*)
Canadian hemlock (*Tsuga canadensis*)

Ground Covers

Bugleweed (*Ajuga* spp.)
Bearberry (*Arctostaphylos uva-ursi*)
Sweet woodruff (*Asperula odorata*)
Lily-of-the-valley (*Convallaria majalis*)
Bunchberry (*Cornus canadensis*)
Ferns (many genera and species)
Daylilies (*Hemerocallis* spp.)
Plantain lilies (*Hosta* spp.)
Evergreen candytuft (*Iberis sempervirens*)
Partridgeberry (*Mitchella repens*)
Japanese spurge or pachysandra (*Pachysandra terminalis*)
Canby paxistima (*Paxistima canbyi*)
Bloodroot (*Sanguinaria canadensis*)
Stonecrop (*Sedum* spp.)
Blueberry (*Vaccinium* spp.)
Vinca, periwinkle, or myrtle (*Vinca minor*)
Violets (*Viola* spp.)
Yellowroot (*Xanthorhiza simplicissima*)

Vines

Wintercreeper (*Euonymus fortunei* vars.)
English ivy (*Hedera helix*)
Climbing hydrangea (*Hydrangea anomala petiolaris*)
Virginia creeper (*Parthenocissus quinquefolia*)

Detailed information and recommended varieties can be found in Part III.

Vinca, a wonderful standby ground cover for shady places, will also flourish in sun.

Plants for a Purpose

GROUND COVERS AND VINES

Not only in shady spots (although they are wonderful there) but throughout the landscape, ground covers and vines have important parts to play. In fact I often allocate 10 to 15 percent (or more) of a total planting budget to these hardworking plants. Some ground covers and vines are unobtrusive mats of green; others have gorgeous flowers or dramatically textured or variegated foliage. Whatever their texture or color, they give definition, character, and life to large forms and spaces. They contribute the final brushstrokes to the landscape picture.

Vines and ground covers also have very practical uses. They are frequently the only way to cover an arid bank or shady woodland floor. They're wonderful for shading out weeds at ground level among larger plantings of shrubs or trees. Growing over trellises or arbors, vines provide welcome summer shade to houses and grounds. Growing over fences, they curtain out unwanted views.

Almost every plant listed here is very easy to propagate and, given soil and conditions that are to its liking, virtually maintenance-free. The one exception I would make to that statement is that many of this group are by definition vigorous spreaders — or, in the case of vines, rampant climbers and twiners. Containment of spreading rhizomes, or annual or biennial prunings, may be called for. If you want to avoid that kind of chore, just stay away from the most eager growers among the lists that follow.

Ground covers and vines are a hugely wide-ranging assortment of plants, spanning succulents, grasses, perennial flowers, herbs, low-growing shrubby plants, and large climbing vines; and including both woody plants (evergreen and deciduous) and herbaceous perennials. That's why there are five lists here: evergreen and deciduous nonherbaceous (woody) ground covers, herbaceous perennials, and evergreen and deciduous vines. The woody ground covers are basically low-growing, spreading shrubs. The herbaceous ground covers and the vines, however, call for a little explanation here.

Herbaceous Perennials Unlike every other kind of plant listed in this book, most of these ground covers are not visible in winter, dying back completely and then reemerging with new growth in spring. (There are some evergreens among them, however, as noted in their descriptions.) Many of these plants are covered with flowers for short periods; in fact that is sometimes a problem, if their vivid yellows or pinks or reds compete with flowering shrubs just when you want to give the shrubs priority. My solution to this (although many fine gardeners do not share my view) is to use the bright-flowering herbaceous ground covers as color features in nonflowering settings, such as gardens consisting mainly of grass and conifers. Where there are flowering trees and shrubs, I tend to choose ground covers more for foliage than for flowers.

Vines Many vines make excellent ground covers — but they also tend to scramble up any and all upright objects they encounter. This makes them great for shading, draping, curtaining, and screening purposes. It also means that they can kill trees and shrubs by slow strangulation; so if you're using vines in the same area with other plantings, you have to give them their own supports and keep an eye on them.

Dwarf eared coreopsis is one of many herbaceous perennials that make fine ground covers when planted in large drifts.

Some vines, such as wisteria, twine themselves bodily up and around in a spiraling pattern. Others, like grapes, send out little tendrils to hold onto whatever they're climbing. Still others have tiny rootlets at intervals along the stems (like English ivy) or put out little adhesive holdfasts (like Boston ivy).

These varying means of support determine where and how you can use different vines. Ivies, for instance, should never be grown against a wooden structure because the rootlets or holdfasts damage the wood. A big vine like grape or wisteria needs a wire, pipe, or wood support of its own. If you're growing a twining or tendril-twisting vine — like five-leaf akebia or pink anemone clematis — against your house, you should provide support other than the house itself. And if the outside of your house is painted, it would be smart to make the vine's support system removable so that you can hinge it away from the house at painting time.

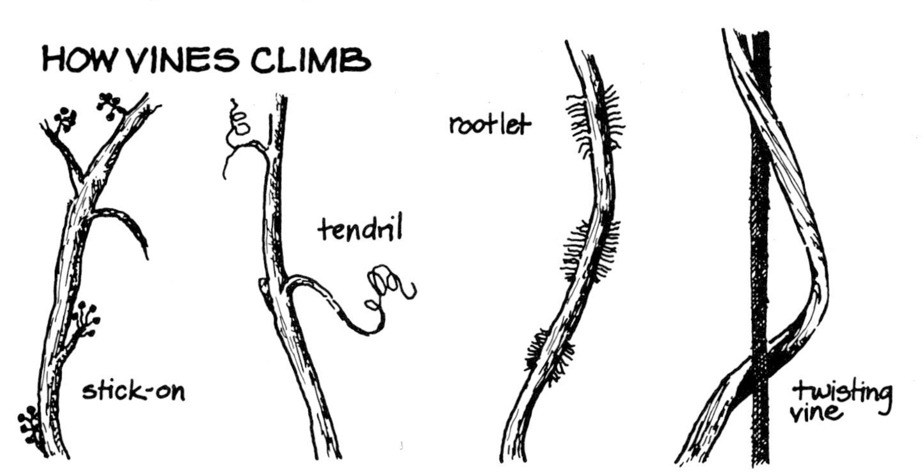

A vine's individual personality results partly from the way it attaches itself to its substrate as it climbs.

Above left, common Boston ivy and a small-leaved variety grow together on a wall for a pleasant interplanted effect. Above right: delicate-leaved ferns are perfect for a moist niche, and this variety has lively fall color too.

The sampling of vines listed here is drawn from among innumerable possibilities.

Ground Covers and Vines

Nonherbaceous Deciduous Ground Covers

Black chokeberry (*Aronia melanocarpa*)
Sweet fern (*Comptonia peregrina*)
Bunchberry (*Cornus canadensis*)
Crown vetch (*Coronilla varia*)
Bronx forsythia (*Forsythia viridissima* 'Bronxensis')
Virginia rose (*Rosa virginiana*)
Memorial rose (*Rosa wichuraiana*)
Daphne spirea (*Spiraea japonica* 'Alpina')
Lowbush blueberry (*Vaccinium angustifolium*)
Yellowroot (*Xanthorhiza simplicissima*)

Evergreen Ground Covers

Bearberry (*Arctostaphylos uva-ursi*)
Skogsholmen bearberry cotoneaster (*Cotoneaster dammeri* 'Skogsholmen')
Purple wintercreeper (*Euonymus fortunei* 'Colorata')
Wintergreen (*Gaultheria procumbens*)
Candytuft (*Iberis sempervirens*)
Japanese garden juniper (*Juniperus chinensis procumbens*)
Sargent juniper (*Juniperus chinensis sargentii*)
Creeping juniper (*Juniperus horizontalis*)
Drooping leucothoe (*Leucothoe fontanesiana*)
Partridgeberry (*Mitchella repens*)
Japanese spurge or pachysandra (*Pachysandra terminalis*)
Canby paxistima (*Paxistima canbyi*)
Goldmoss stonecrop (*Sedum spurium*)
Houseleeks or hens-and-chickens (*Sempervivum tectorum*)
Canadian yew (*Taxus canadensis*)
Vinca, periwinkle, or myrtle (*Vinca minor*)

Herbaceous Perennial Ground Covers

Pink yarrow (*Achillea millefolium* 'Rosea')
Goutweed or bishop's weed (*Aegopodium podagraria*)
Bugleweed or carpet bugle (*Ajuga reptans*)
Rockcress (*Arabis procurrens*)
Moss sandwort (*Arenaria verna*)
European ginger (*Asarum europaeum*)
Lily-of-the-valley (*Convallaria majalis*)
Dwarf eared coreopsis (*Coreopsis auriculata* 'Nana')
Pinks (*Dianthus* spp.)
Siberian draba (*Draba sibirica* 'Repens')
Mock strawberry (*Duchesnea indica*)
Epimediums (*Epimedium* spp.)

Ground Covers and Vines (*continued*)

Ferns (many genera)
Sweet woodruff (*Galium odoratum*)
Prostrate baby's breath (*Gypsophila repens* 'Rosea')
Daylilies (*Hemerocallis* spp.)
Plaintain lilies (*Hosta* spp.)
Creeping jenny or moneywort (*Lysimachia nummularia*)
Creeping mint (*Mentha requienii*)
Persian ground-ivy (*Nepeta faassenii*)
Ribbongrass (*Phalaris arundinacea picta*)
Moss pinks or ground pinks (*Phlox subulata*)
Solomon's-seal (*Polygonatum biflorum*)
Pearlwort (*Sagina subulata*)
Bloodroot (*Sanguinaria canadensis*)
Ground bamboo (*Sasa pumila*)
Thymes (*Thymus* spp.)
Allegheny foam-flower (*Tiarella cordifolia*)
Violets (*Viola* spp.)
Barren strawberry (*Waldsteinia fragarioides*)

Deciduous Vines

Five-leaf akebia (*Akebia quinata*)
Porcelainberry or porcelain ampelopsis (*Ampelopsis brevipedunculata*)
Trumpet vine or common trumpet creeper (*Campsis radicans*)
Bittersweet (*Celastrus scandens*)
Sweet autumn clematis (*Clematis dioscoreifolia robusta*)
Pink anemone clematis (*Clematis montana rubens*)
Climbing hydrangea (*Hydrangea anomala petiolaris*)
Henry honeysuckle (*Lonicera henryi*)
Hall's honeysuckle (*Lonicera japonica* 'Halliana')
Virginia creeper or woodbine (*Parthenocissus quinquefolia*)
Boston ivy (*Parthenocissus tricuspidata*)
Chinese or silver fleece vine (*Polygonum aubertii*)
Grapes (*Vitis* spp.)
Japanese wisteria (*Wisteria floribunda*)

Evergreen Vines

Wintercreeper (*Euonymus fortunei* vars.)
English ivy (*Hedera helix*)

Detailed information and recommended varieties can be found in Part III.

Climbing hydrangea is splendid topping a fence or a masonry wall.

Materials and Construction

DECKS AND TRELLISES

Enjoying the outdoors is high on June's agenda. A natural setting such as a woodland garden is one fine place to do that; another is an outdoor deck.

Wood (see May Materials and Construction) is the primary material for both decks and trellises, and primarily the softwoods that do such a good job in outdoor use: redwood, cedar, cypress, spruce, or white pine.

If you want a high and dry raised terrace or patio, but can't or don't want to build on grade because of a problem like sloping topography, you're talking about a deck: an elevated wooden platform.

And if you wish to provide some sun screening, an arbor for vines, or just an ornamental overhead structure, whether related to a deck or elsewhere, you're talking about a trellis: an open-air overhead structure.

The Architecture of Decks and Trellises Decks and trellises are often thought of and referred to as part of the landscape — yet I feel they're more aptly considered architecture. They are usually closely related to the house in location, style, materials, or all three. Also, they definitely function as outdoor rooms. A deck is a floor, a trellis a ceiling. Add a few vertical elements such as hanging or potted plants, a railing, some trees, or the side of the house — and presto, a well-defined space, or "room."

Uses and locations First, consider how you are going to use the spaces you create. Will you be relaxing, dining, sunning, swimming, partying, viewing, or all of the above? Plan for comfortable circulation between and within these outdoor spaces. Let the purposes you have in mind determine their location and orientation, just as the purposes of an indoor room would determine its position in the house.

Modular deck sections — versatile, easy to install, and practical — require good drainage and good wood. Here, redwood decking atop a gravel bed makes a handsome parquet.

Above left: a "floating" deck allows an unobstructed view from within the house and draws people out for a new perspective. Above right: an attached deck makes a graceful transition from the first floor of the house to the lawn two feet lower down.

Most people put decks immediately outside the house, an inch below floor level, and with sliding doors connecting to the interior of the house — usually to the living room, dining room, or family room. Such a deck directly extends and opens up the living area. It's easily accessible and welcoming to visitors.

But sometimes a "floating" deck is the answer, away from the house, perhaps with a bridge or path connecting it to one or more convenient entrances. With a floating deck, you can often design in some grade variations or even different levels for the deck itself. This treatment can open up new and more enticing views and better separate the various landscape spaces. Also, when the deck in question is to be on a level with an upper floor of the house, the space beneath it is apt to be dark and uninviting; but a separated deck allows light to penetrate both beneath it and through to the windows of the house. A freestanding deck will, however, require more elaborate bracing than one connected to the house.

Materials As always, try to integrate and coordinate as best you can with the architecture of the house. Too many decks convey a tacked-on feeling. Even if your deck is a late addition, it does not have to look that way. Many neutral styles and finishes will blend with almost any architecture. Just stay away from violent contrasts like a heavy, timbered rustic deck up against a white clapboard Colonial.

Before you get into detailed design or construction, stand back one last time and make sure that a deck is really the best answer. Sometimes a hasty decision results in a deck being built where a stone or brick terrace on grade would have been a more natural choice, and a forced look is the outcome.

Decks You build a deck or a trellis from the bottom up (footings, post anchors, posts, beams, joists, finally decking) — but you design a deck from the top down. First you determine the size and shape of deck surface that will meet your needs and fit your location. Then you select the decking material and decide which direction you want the decking boards to run. All other structural specifications follow from these initial decisions. (Shown on page 188 is a schematic representation of decks' and trellises' structural parts.)

Angled decking boards lend extra structural strength and can be exciting to look at, but they do entail waste and thus extra expense. In general, for a deck adjoining a house, I prefer decking boards parallel to

Nomenclature and basic components of deck and trellis structures.

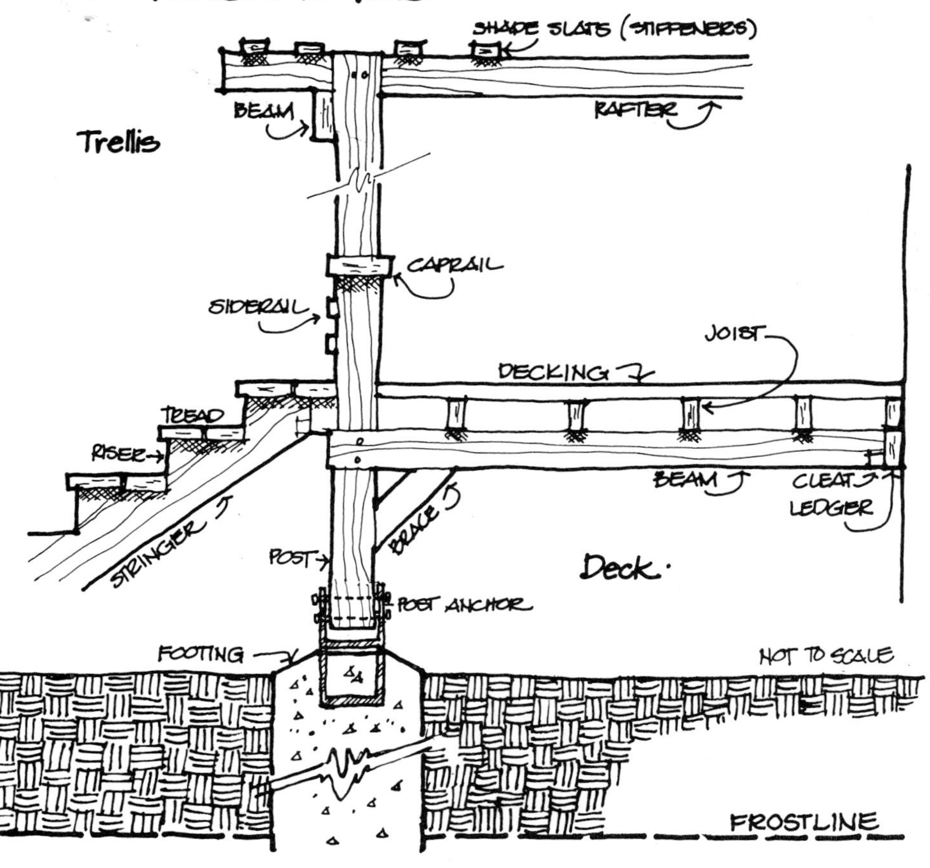

This low railing is simply an extension of the deck's main support posts: an easy and sturdy approach to railing construction. (Use higher railing in dangerous conditions.)

the house wall, since a more restful or harmonious feeling results. The exceptions are cases where you want to direct the view outwards by using deck flooring perpendicular or at an angle to the house.

My first and last word of advice on designing these structures is to keep them extremely simple — or consult a professional. A good carpenter may be your best bet for advice (and help, if needed) on the job, if you can find one who's willing. Or talk over your plans with a landscape architect, an architect, or a structural engineer. If your design is really complex, the structural engineer may be brought into the picture anyway. The point is that if it's not designed and built for decades of use and weather resistance, a deck can turn into a serious safety hazard. It must be not only attractive and useful, but strong and durable.

Railings Railings may be built on extensions of the deck's support posts or attached separately to joists, beams, or fascia boards. Benches or wide rails are often attractive, provided a fall over the edge would not be hazardous: the deck should not be at too great a height, and there should be grass or shrubbery underneath, not sharp rocks. The railing requirements in local building codes vary greatly, so before you plan your deck's railing, check the codes for your area. That goes for both basic railing structures and benches or low, wide rails suitable for sitting.

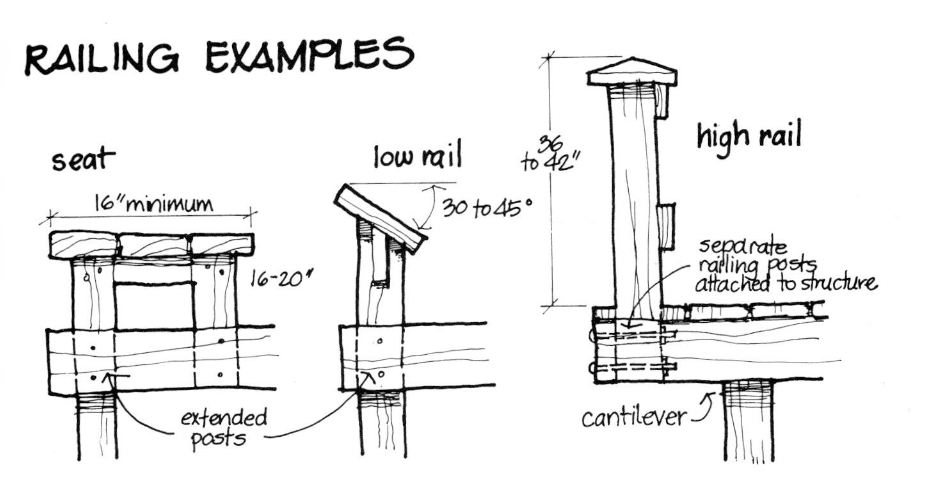

Railings: always check local building codes. If the view through is important, use a transparent type; and if young children may climb, use vertical balusters.

Vertical balusters work well with post-and-beam construction. And since railings are a key safety factor, vertical balusters — which are tough to climb — are my choice if young children will be using the deck. I use balusters no more than 6 inches apart (between edges) and no less than 40 inches high: an unclimbable height for small children.

Stairs With all wood stairs, follow the formula 2R + T = 27 for proper riser and tread proportions, where R = riser height in inches and T = tread depth in inches. Using this formula and the standard lumber sizes available, you can determine the most comfortable and economical dimensions for your deck's stairs.

For treads, use lumber to match the decking; for risers (if any) lumber should match joists or fascia boards; and stair railings should match deck rails.

This simple arbor, in Ann Hathaway's cottage garden in England, is made from peeled branches.

Trellises With a trellis, you may want to design as much from the bottom up as from the top down. The size and spacing of the posts supporting the overhead structure may be as important to you as the size and spacing of the horizontal members above.

The enormous latitude of possible dimensions, densities, and designs for trellises makes it hard for me to give you firm guidelines — beyond strongly encouraging you to give any trellis a clear 8- to 8½-foot height to its underside. A lower ceiling feels cramped and tight outdoors, unless it is very small.

Trellises are perfect for hanging things: furniture, lights, plants, hammocks. Take advantage of the opportunities a trellis offers — but as always, don't let the hanging motif become too much of a good thing.

One good choice for a trellis structure is an egg-crate system with square or rectangular openings. This kind of arrangement gives you great flexibility: you can insert mats or louvers in openings as you wish, moving them around seasonally for varying areas of shade. You can obtain still further shading with roll-down screening between the posts, either along the outside edge or inside the line of the "roof" of the trellis.

Before you translate your ideas into wood, make a reasonably accurate mockup of the trellis you plan to build and test it out at different times of day to see the approximate quality of the shade it will cast.

Plants by Design

JUNE BLOOMERS

Early June

White fringe tree (*Chionanthus virginicus*)
Yellowwood (*Cladrastis lutea*)
Siberian dogwood (*Cornus alba* 'Sibirica')
Kousa or Japanese dogwood (*Cornus kousa*)
Drooping leucothoe (*Leucothoe fontanesiana*)
Flame azalea (*Rhododendron calendulaceum*)
Catawba rhododendrons (*Rhododendron catawbiense* vars.)
Rugosa rose (*Rosa rugosa*)
Late lilac (*Syringa villosa*)
Arrowwood (*Viburnum dentatum*)
Linden viburnum (*Viburnum dilatatum*)
Black haw (*Viburnum prunifolium*)

Mid-June

Washington hawthorn (*Crataegus phaenopyrum*)
Mountain laurel (*Kalmia latifolia*)
Privet (*Ligustrum* spp.)
Tulip tree (*Liriodendron tulipifera*)
Hall's honeysuckle (*Lonicera japonica* 'Halliana')
Roses (*Rosa* — many spp.)
Tree lilac (*Syringa amurensis*)

Late June

Virginal mock-orange (*Philadelphus virginalis*)
Rosebay rhododendron or great laurel (*Rhododendron maximum*)
Anthony Waterer spirea (*Spiraea bumalda* 'Anthony Waterer')

Detailed information and recommended varieties can be found in Part III.

Rhododendrons in every size, shape, and color are in all their glory this month.

LANDSCAPE TASKS FOR JUNE

Lawn Maintenance For weed control and a healthy lawn, it's best to mow your lawn no shorter than 2 or 2½ inches. The shade cast by the blades of grass serves to prevent broad-leaved weeds' seeds from sprouting: it's too dark down there. It also keeps moisture in the earth, thereby cutting down on your watering time and expense.

Crabgrass Control If you have problems with crabgrass, postemergent weed controls will kill the seedlings as they appear. The packages of the various weed-killing chemicals provide instructions for their use. Be sure to follow the instructions carefully if you go this route. I'd recommend using these herbicides only as a last resort, however. By far the best way to suppress weeds is to promote a sturdy, dense growth of grass (see the April and September sections on lawns and their installation and maintenance) and cut it at the appropriate length.

June Pruning

Spireas, forsythia, lilac, and quince that finish blooming in June should be pruned as soon as their flowering season ends. Pruning procedures for lilacs and spireas are detailed in the May chapter; forsythia and quince can be rejuvenated either by removing their oldest stems or by cutting the whole shrubs back to 6 inches from the ground. A more moderate trimming is also acceptable if you want to avoid the crew-cut look.

Low-growing perennials like rock cress, evergreen candytuft, or moss pink should be cut back severely once they finish flowering, to encourage compact, sturdy growth for next year.

Shade trees are often best pruned in full foliage — that is, now. You may be thinning them in order to open up a summer view or increase light filtration to the ground level; if so, doing the job now enables you to tell exactly what results you are getting. Or you may want to remove lower branches to accentuate the lines of a tree's trunk, or to clear space for people and air circulation beneath. Or you may simply be keeping the tree healthy, by lopping crossing branches or dead or diseased limbs (which can harbor rot and insects), or by preventing it from shading its own foliage too densely.

For any of these purposes, there's a right way to prune a shade tree. Use clean, sharp equipment; a pole pruner with a saw on the end is

A professional tree man works at pruning a big shade tree.

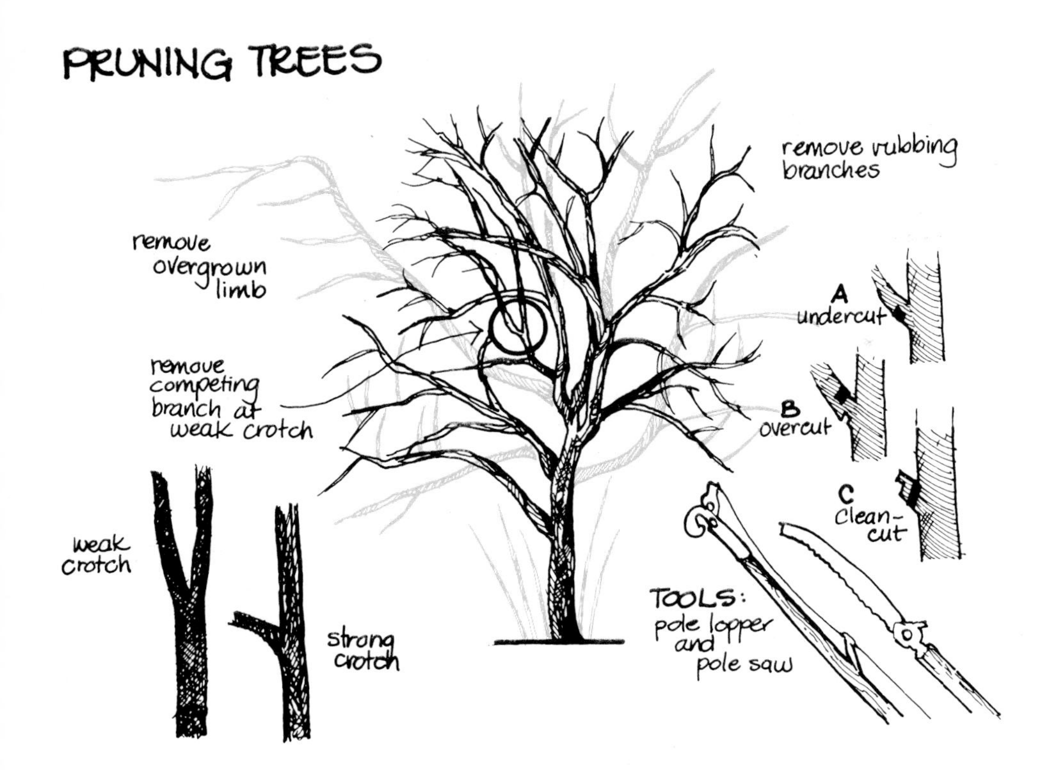

When pruning a tree of any size, consider the overall form and balance of branches in the crown as well as the tree's health and well-being.

a good multipurpose tool, but for more maneuverability I prefer two poles, one with a saw and another with a pruner. Start from the top, thinning judiciously and checking often to make sure you're not distorting the shape of the tree or creating unsightly gaps. With each branch, first make a cut into the underside of the branch several inches from the crotch (see figure A, above), to forestall the bark's tearing all the way to the trunk. Cut off the limb several inches farther out (figure B), then cut off the remaining stump as close as possible to the trunk (figure C). Leave no crotch to trap moisture (which causes rot) and slope the cut surface down, away from the trunk, so as to shed rain.

For large trees beyond the reach of the pole pruner, it may be best to hire a professional tree man — both to ensure the job's done right and to avoid the dangers involved in climbing and felling big limbs.

At this season the wounds heal rapidly, which is good for the tree. Even so, it's a good idea to paint or spray all cuts 2 inches or more in diameter with antiseptic tree paint, to prevent excessive loss of sap and to deter insects and fungus. Smaller cuts, less than 2 inches across, don't need to be painted.

Broad-leaved Evergreens If you haven't done it already (see May), give your rhododendrons, azaleas, andromedas, or laurels a thick acid mulch now (like pine needles, oak-leaf compost, or wood chips) to help keep their roots cool and their soil moist in the hot weather to come.

Continue breaking or cutting off the spent flower heads on late-blooming azaleas, andromedas, and mountain laurel. Be sure not to harm the new buds for next year, which will be coming along just below the remains of the old flowers.

Irrigation Deep watering of lawns and gardens is critical in June. Surface sprinkling, on the other hand, is worse than useless. Water early in the morning, before the heat of the day, and give each area of your grounds the equivalent of 1 inch of water per week, unless rainfall provides it. (Leave an empty straight-sided container outdoors to check.)

Propagation Project: Rooting Softwood Cuttings This method of propagation is a good deal trickier than rooting hardwood cuttings (see January), since every phase of the procedure is fraught with hazards to tender young shoots; but success is definitely feasible with several popular landscape plants, so you may enjoy giving it a try.

This method of propagation, like others involving rooting sections of stems, works much better if you prepare a young plant with a rigorous pruning ahead of time. For softwood cuttings, cut back during the dormant season — any time from late fall through winter — to promote a surge of new growth in spring.

Some trees, shrubs, ground covers, and vines that often root successfully from softwood cuttings taken at this season are listed here. The starred plants can often be propagated from cuttings — which become known as "semiripe," then "hardwood," as the season advances — throughout the summer, fall, and early winter.

English ivy, shown growing companionably with sweet woodruff, can be propagated practically any time.

Plants for Propagating from Softwood Cuttings

Barberry (*Berberis*)
Butterfly bush (*Buddleia*)
*Boxwood (*Buxus*)
Cotoneaster (*Cotoneaster*)
Dogwood, shrub types (*Cornus*)
*Euonymus (*Euonymus*)
Forsythia (*Forsythia*)
Ginkgo (*Ginkgo*)
*English ivy (*Hedera*)
Hydrangea (*Hydrangea*)
*Holly (*Ilex*)
*Juniper, creeping (*Juniperus*)
Kerria (*Kerria*)
Privet (*Ligustrum*)
Honeysuckle (*Lonicera*)
Magnolia (*Magnolia*)
Dawn redwood (*Metasequoia*)
*Japanese spurge (*Pachysandra*)
Boston ivy (*Parthenocissus*)
Mock-orange (*Philadelphus*)
Andromeda (*Pieris*)
*Firethorn (*Pyracantha*)
Azalea and rhododendron (*Rhododendron*)
Rose (*Rosa*)
Willow (*Salix*)
Spirea (*Spiraea*)
Stewartia (*Stewartia*)
Lilac (*Syringa*)
*Yew (*Taxus*)
Viburnum (*Viburnum*)
Wisteria (*Wisteria*)

*Can often be propagated from cuttings throughout summer and fall and into early winter. Detailed information and recommended varieties can be found in Part III.

When to cut Softwood is the plant's new spring growth, and it is ready for cutting when its leaves are fully out and fully colored. If it bends but won't break, or if new leaves are still emerging at the tip, it's too young. If it is too stiff to snap readily, it's too old. If it snaps crisply, it should be about right. Choose healthy-looking normal growth from the outside of the plant, not outsized shoots or spindly growth.

Advance preparation Before you cut, have a container of powdered rooting hormone on hand and prepare the sterile rooting medium.

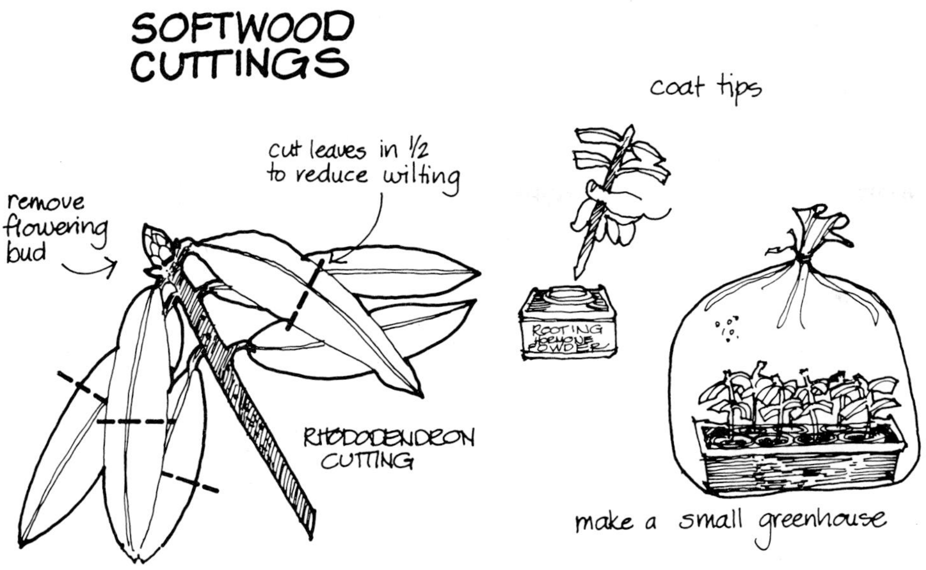

SOFTWOOD CUTTINGS

remove flowering bud
cut leaves in 1/2 to reduce wilting
RHODODENDRON CUTTING
coat tips
ROOTING HORMONE POWDER
make a small greenhouse

Try your luck with softwood cuttings. Many desirable landscape plants can be reproduced this way throughout spring, summer, and even fall.

You can use sterile sand, vermiculite, perlite, or a mixture of sand and peat moss. Whichever medium you use should be kept moist but not soggy. Flower pots, flats, or boxes make fine containers.

Making cuttings Choose a cool early morning to start. Using a very sharp, thin-bladed knife, take cuttings of terminal growth about 2 to 6 inches long. Make the cuts at about a 45-degree angle. Large-leaved plants like rhododendrons require longer cuttings; small-leaved ones like privet, shorter cuttings. Remove the leaves from the bottom third of each stem. If the cutting has large leaves, cutting off the outer half of each leaf will diminish transpiration and make the cutting less apt to wilt. As you make each cutting, immediately put it between damp sheets of paper or cloth. Drying out at this stage is fatal.

Cuttings into medium Once your collection is complete, use a pencil to make a hole in the rooting medium where each cutting is to go. Dip the tip of each cutting in the rooting hormone powder (see instructions on the hormone container) and insert the bottom third of the cutting in the medium. Gently firm the medium around it. Keep the cuttings in a warm place — ideally 70° to 80°F — and protected from direct sunlight. To keep both the medium and the atmosphere around the cuttings humid, cover them with a plastic cover, put them in a plastic bag, or place a glass jar over them.

Rooting and hardening off Some cuttings will send out roots in a couple of weeks; others may take as long as 3 months. Keep the medium moist, watch, and be patient. Once they have roots about 1 inch long (pull them out to check) you can start hardening them off by removing their coverings for longer and longer periods each day. After a week or so you can carefully transfer them to potting soil in pots in a bright window or greenhouse.

Once new top growth has started, the cuttings can be treated like any young plants: they can move outdoors if the weather is still mild, or wait in the greenhouse or cold frame to be planted outdoors next spring.

JUL

Landscaping Opportunities
Planting in and around Water

Plants for a Purpose
Shade Trees

Materials and Construction
Water in the Landscape

Plants by Design
July Bloomers

Landscape Tasks for July

Flowering perennials and annuals come into their own in my herb garden in midsummer, stealing the scene from the trees and shrubs.

The longest day of the year was the June 21 summer solstice, so midsummer has officially passed by the time July begins. July *feels* like midsummer, though, and keeping cool is a high priority. This month I'll consider some cooling topics: plants to grow in and around water; pools and other water displays to delight the eye and ear and freshen the air around you; and big shade trees to relax beneath.

Water-loving plants such as willows, cattails, and red maples have a natural rightness around a pond, as in this autumn landscape.

Landscaping Opportunities

PLANTING IN AND AROUND WATER

There is no limit to the kinds of plants you can use around water. While potted flowers are pretty beside a pool, this section will focus on water plants as such, from plants that actually live in water to plants for edges and backgrounds of still or moving water.

Examples of the affinity between water and vegetation abound in nature. Think of a stream in the woods: hemlock and beech tower overhead and the rocks along the water's edge are covered with mosses, while ferns and bunchberry grow in the crevices. In the shallows of every pond or lake are rushes, sedges, and grasses; trees and shrubs like willow, birch, swamp oak, alder, and viburnum — to mention just a few — thrive on sloping banks nearby.

And the relationship is not just biological but visual. Reeds and water lilies need water, of course — yet in a sense the water needs the reeds and lilies too. They complement and enhance each other.

In the Water Water lilies are the plant of choice for midpond or midpool growing. There are two categories: tropical and hardy. *Hardy water lilies* are day bloomers and carry their flowers just above the surface of the water. *Tropical water lilies* have larger leaves and flowers; they hold their blossoms on tall stalks, well above the water (good for cutting); and some of them bloom at night. Many of them are fragrant. Both tropical and hardy types have been extensively hybridized and are available in a wide range of sizes and colors from suppliers who specialize in water plants. Be sure to select lilies in scale with your setting — some of the larger-leafed tropical varieties are really huge and demand large ponds to hold them.

Growing water lilies Among the hardy lilies, some are sufficiently tough to survive year-round in ponds and streams in the north, provided their roots are below the frost line. They die back to their roots under the ice, then reemerge in all their glory in June. If you have a natural pond that you can allow to freeze and thaw all winter, you're all set.

Artificial pools, however, present a different challenge. Usually they're drained for winter; if not, they often freeze solid. To avoid winterkill, take up hardy water lilies in fall after the first frost. Store them in a box of damp sand in a cool place (about 50°F) until early May, then replant them.

Tropical lilies really have to be considered annuals unless you have a greenhouse where you can overwinter and propagate them. Lacking a greenhouse, you should resign yourself to buying a fresh supply of tubers each spring. Set them out when your pond water is well warmed up, in June.

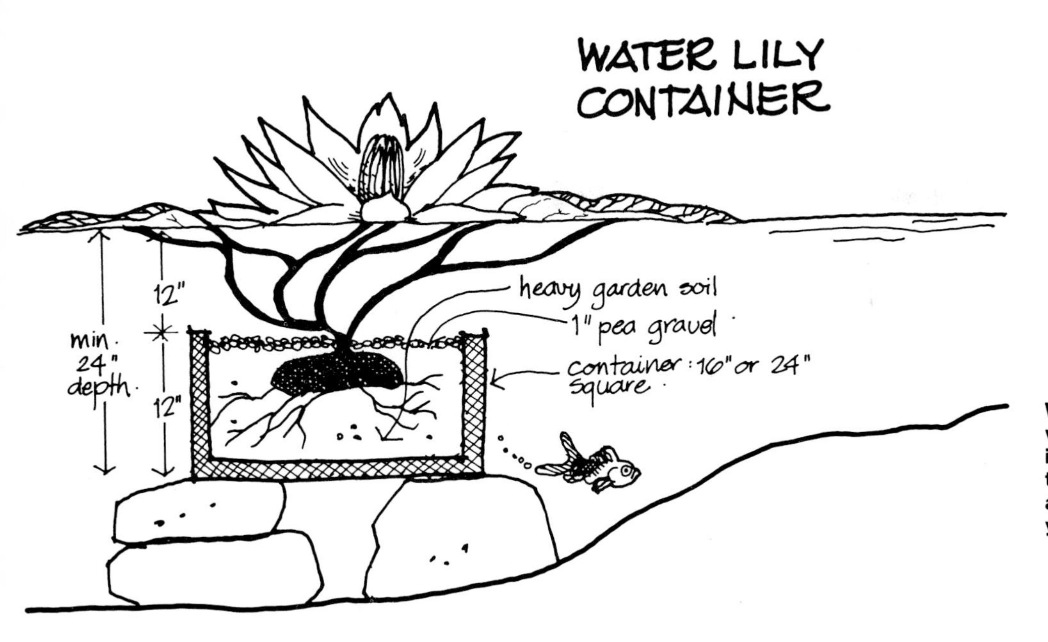

Water lilies need water at least 24 inches deep. Containers are readily available, or build your own.

Both types (except hardy lilies living in a natural pond) require a separate underwater container for each plant. This diagram shows the minimum dimensions. Fill the container with heavy garden soil mixed with well-rotted manure — no peat or compost, which would be too light. Top the soil with 1 inch of pea gravel to keep the water clean. The best material for the container (though the most expensive) would be redwood or cedar; pine or fir, while acceptable, will rot eventually. Steer clear of wood that has been treated with preservatives, which can be toxic to plants and/or fish.

Water-lily environments Water lilies need three things for their well-being: four to six hours of direct sunlight each day, ample space, and adequate oxygen.

Both for good design and for good plant culture, it's important not to have more than *half* your total water surface covered with plants. In addition, each individual water lily has its own territorial requirements. A large one needs 12 square feet of water surface; a medium one 10 square feet; small ones 4 square feet each. As you can see, one large lily or three small ones will demand a pool surface area of at least 24 square feet — that is, double the area required by the lilies themselves. Three large lilies will need a pool with not less than 72 square feet of surface area. Do your computations before you order your lilies.

There are two ways to ensure that your pool water contains ample oxygen for the support of water lilies. First, control algae, which tend to proliferate in still water and consume more than their share of the water's oxygen. A small recirculating pump will both aerate and move the water, which will discourage algae. You can also install floating plants to shade out sunlight and thereby prevent the growth of algae (they need light too). Choose floating sunshades (such as water chestnuts, water hyacinths, water lettuce, or water fern) whose size, character, and growing habits are in keeping with the overall effect you're after — be it bold and vivid or small-scale and restrained. If the floating plants become too nu-

Strong horizontal lines of water-lily pads and stiffly upright stalks of irises are in counterpoint, heightening each other's effects.

merous and start to take over the pond or pool, they're easy to control: just scoop them out.

The second approach to oxygen maintenance is to add oxygenating plants to your pool colony. Available from those same water-lily suppliers, they include eel grass, arrowheads, elodea (sometimes called anacharis), and water milfoil.

Plants for boggy edges There are many lovely plants that won't live in deep water but flourish at the shallow edges where only their roots are submerged. If yours is a natural or naturalistic pond or pool, and if you can arrange a trickle of water to prevent stagnation, you can cultivate varied and fascinating bog plants like baby's-tears, papyrus, arrowhead, horsetail, umbrella plant, water canna, water iris or flag, or water poppy.

Around the Edge Many kinds of herbaceous foliage and flowering plants lend themselves to planting around the edges of water displays. You can set these plants in pockets of soil between paving stones or rocks; use them as ground covers; or plant them in larger free-standing groups. For plantings near still water, I particularly like upright-growing plants like loosestrifes or ferns, which contrast with the horizontal surface of the water and make great reflections. Around falling water or fountains, cascading and spreading plant forms are appealing to echo the water's effect.

Among my favorite water's-edge plants are primroses; irises; orchids; buttercups; daisies; lilies, including garden lilies (*Lilium*), daylilies (*Hemerocallis*), and plantain lilies (*Hosta*); loosestrifes, ferns, grasses, rushes, sedges, and reeds. In addition, many ground cover plants grow beautifully in rock crevices and on banks. (For a selection of these plants, see June Plants for a Purpose.)

In the Background If you have the space to create a complete water garden setting, a progression from smaller herbaceous plants to shrubs and then trees will round out the picture. A word of warning, however: don't plant trees close to the water on any side, and don't plant them anywhere except to the north. Otherwise they will cast shade and inhibit the growth of all your other lovely water plantings. If they are too near the water (the distance depends on size and type of tree and force of prevailing wind), they will drop leaves and debris into the pool. Besides, their roots will be apt to invade piping and rock masonry or even crack the pool itself.

The plants listed below are all adapted to watery surroundings, and therefore have an air of rightness as background plantings for a pool or pond. Incidentally, many of these trees and shrubs are also fine candidates for any spot where wet soil is a problem, even without a pool, pond, or waterfall.

Plants with soft weeping and cascading forms make lovely reflections.

Background Plants for Pools and Ponds

Medium and Large Trees

Red maple (*Acer rubrum*)
River birch (*Betula nigra*)
Weeping European birch (*Betula pendula*)
Gray birch (*Betula populifolia*)
Sweet gum (*Liquidambar styraciflua*)
Weeping willow (*Salix alba tristis* or *Salix elegantissima*)
American arborvitae (*Thuja occidentalis*)

Small Trees

Cutleaf Japanese maple (*Acer palmatum dissectum*)
Allegheny serviceberry (*Amelanchier laevis*)
Redbud (*Cercis canadensis*)
Thread cypress (*Chamaecyparis pisifera* 'Filifera')
Kousa or Japanese dogwood (*Cornus kousa*)
Cornelian cherry dogwood (*Cornus mas*)

Shrubs

Buttonbush (*Cephalanthus occidentalis*)
Siberian dogwood (*Cornus alba* 'Sibirica')
Red-osier dogwood (*Cornus sericea*)
Japanese garden juniper (*Juniperus chinensis procumbens*)
Spicebush (*Lindera benzoin*)
Japanese andromeda or pieris (*Pieris japonica*)
Flame azalea (*Rhododendron calendulaceum*)
Pinxterbloom or pinxter azalea (*Rhododendron nudiflorum*)
Swamp azalea (*Rhododendron viscosum*)
Carolina rhododendron (*Rhododendron carolinianum*)
Goat willow or French pussy willow (*Salix caprea*)
Blueberries (*Vaccinium* spp.)
Viburnums (*Viburnum* spp.)

Vine

Japanese wisteria (*Wisteria floribunda*)

Detailed information and recommended varieties can be found in Part III.

Plants for a Purpose

SHADE TREES

In the full heat of summer there's nothing more delicious than the green shade under a big tree. But like the decision to get married, the choice of a shade tree involves a major long-term commitment. So approach it thoughtfully. Look beyond quick inducements and superficial charm, and consider the needs the tree will have and the contributions it will make ten, twenty, or fifty years in the future.

Without a doubt there's a tree to meet every individual landscaping requirement. It would be great if there were some one tree that combined all the most sought-after characteristics. It would have lovely foliage, flowers, fruit, form, and bark; its flowers would be fragrant and its fruit tasty but not messy; the fall foliage would look sublime but never demand raking; and the tree would be long-lived, hardy under every duress, stately, yet small enough to have charm as well. . . .

But there's no such thing around — at least not yet. Since the late 1960s the federal government has run an "urban forestry" program aimed at discovering and propagating the plant strains most perfectly suited to the city or suburban landscape; and several state universities are also working in this area. By the early years of the next century you may well be able to find trees that will meet a broad range of criteria without any of the drawbacks or weaknesses their species now possess.

Meanwhile, the first guideline for the selection of large trees is: restrain yourself. It's natural to yearn for the flowers of one tree, the fall color of another, the fast growth of a third. It's also natural to yield to the siren song of nurseries with bargain rates and bonus collections — "five trees for the price of two" and so on. But that way clutter lies. Before you know it you'll have a mini-arboretum in your front yard, like one family I know whose yard started as a naked expanse of earth when they first moved in: now, ten years later, it's a jungle of wildly various vegetation.

Another guideline: be brave enough to let a tree go if it's not right for your place. Very often, good landscape gardening consists of elimination as much as any other single activity. A frequent trap for the unwary is the tree that's already growing on your property, whether it's a volunteer seedling struggling up through the forsythia, or a sickly middle-sized shade tree, or a huge monster. For many people it's all but impossible to say good-bye to the seedling, the sickly, or the monstrous. But sometimes it has to be done. A weed is a plant out of place, and that applies equally to the grass in the flower bed, the lilies-of-the-valley sprouting between the bricks of the front walk, and the ancient Norway maple that's shading out or starving out every other plant you possess. Get rid of trees that are unhealthy, crowded, past their prime, out of keeping, or out of proportion, and you can often do more for your landscape than you could accomplish by installing a dozen new specimens.

That said, you may still be in the market for a new tree. Here are some general considerations and a few recommended candidates.

Choosing a Shade Tree The smaller your grounds and the fewer trees you need, the more of a challenge the decision-making process. The range of possibilities is vast. Your first job is to isolate the qualities most important to you: color of foliage, density of shade, fragrance of flower, appeal to birds, etc. The list on page 204 includes some exceptionally fine all-around trees; but if you're looking for some specific attribute such as fall foliage, form, texture, or bark color, you will find other ideas in the Plants by Design sections of October through February.

Remember the rule of proper scale. Be alert to the ultimate size of the tree you select and how it will relate to the scale of its surroundings. All the trees listed on page 204 are over 30 feet tall in maturity (trees for smaller spaces are listed in May). But there's wide variation even among these larger trees: a 40-foot yellowwood plays a very different part from an 80-foot beech.

Trees' fall foliage color often varies depending on location, climate, etc. Sassafras leaves can be yellow or red.

The old rule of simplicity also applies. Hard though it may be to restrict yourself to one or two types of trees, it's usually better to do so unless you have a very expansive territory to cover. If you plan to install three trees in one spot, it's better to plant three of one variety than one each of three types.

Keep in mind the branching habits of trees when they are mature. Do you want upswept branches, horizontal, or drooping; dense and twiggy or open and graceful? Sometimes this is hard to discern in a nursery sapling, so check Part III (or a nursery catalogue) when in doubt. Most trees do not assume a real individual character until they reach a trunk diameter of 4 to 6 inches.

Where fall foliage color is a factor in your choice, here are a few hints. It's the combination of cool nights and warm sun that brings out the most vivid oranges, reds, and red-purples; so trees in that color range will do best in a location with ample sun. Yet there is considerable variation in color from one plant to another within the same species, from one spot to another in the same neighborhood, and even from one year to another in the same plant. Some of these variations depend on the genetic makeup of the individual plant, others on annual vagaries of weather, others on topography and microclimates. For all these reasons, I always pick out red maples, sugar maples, and oaks in nurseries in fall so that I can be confident of at least their potential for color. Another trick is to take into account the angles of sun and sources of shade on your property. Often only the sides of plants exposed to southern and western sun will color up fully. (Similarly, shrubs or small trees in open or partial shade will not color like those in full sunlight.) So choose and position all your plants with this in mind.

Finally, some trees lend themselves especially well to grouping, and actually take on a stronger, richer appearance than if they were planted alone. Often these are trees that grow in clusters or colonies in natural situations, such as oak, American beech, ash, maple, hickory, or birch. Other trees, because of strong individuality or massive size, tend to be most effective as single, isolated specimens — like sugar maple, linden, or honey locust. But no tree can or should be pigeonholed strictly as a "grouping" rather than a "specimen" tree. Any big tree, growing by itself with no competition for sun, water, or soil nutrients, will mature into a specimen with character and stature it wouldn't ever have attained as part of a cluster or grove. The choice of handling depends on the effect you want.

Above, honey locust (left) and Amur cork tree (right) are shade trees with fine-textured summer foliage. The photo of the honey locust shows the delicacy of its branches and twigs in winter silhouette.

A Selection of Shade Trees

*Norway maple (*Acer platanoides*)
Red maple (*Acer rubrum*)
Sugar maple (*Acer saccharum*)
*Red horse chestnut (*Aesculus carnea*)
Horse chestnut (*Aesculus hippocastanum*)
Paper birch or canoe birch (*Betula papyrifera*)
*Cutleaf weeping birch (*Betula pendula* 'Gracilis')
*Katsura tree (*Cercidiphyllum japonicum*)
*Yellowwood (*Cladrastis lutea*)
American beech (*Fagus grandifolia*)
European beech (*Fagus sylvatica*)
White ash (*Fraxinus americana*)
Ginkgo or maidenhair tree (*Ginkgo biloba*)
Thornless honey locust (*Gleditsia triacanthos inermis*)
Tulip tree (*Liriodendron tulipifera*)
Black gum or black tupelo (*Nyssa sylvatica*)
*Amur cork tree (*Phellodendron amurense*)
Scarlet oak (*Quercus coccinea*)
Red oak (*Quercus rubra*)
Golden weeping willow (*Salix alba tristis*)
*Thurlow weeping willow (*Salix elegantissima*)
*Sassafras (*Sassafras albidum*)
Japanese pagoda tree (*Sophora japonica*)
Littleleaf linden (*Tilia cordata*)
*Crimean linden (*Tilia euchlora*)
Silver linden (*Tilia tomentosa*)
Zelkova (*Zelkova serrata*)

*Indicates trees that are medium-sized, with mature heights of approximately 30 to 50 feet. Other trees listed will reach 50 to 100 feet or more.

Detailed information and recommended varieties can be found in Part III.

Materials and Construction
WATER IN THE LANDSCAPE

Water is cooling to look at, to wade or swim in, and to listen to. It can also actually cool the air around you — both because of the refrigerating effect of evaporation, and because water retains coolness longer than air.

In the natural landscape there is no element more captivating, more irresistibly attractive than water. It speaks to every physical sense — and to our inner beings as well. Water is, after all, the primary component of every living thing on this planet.

From the simplest reflection mirrored in a quiet pool to the thunderous resonance of a mountain cataract, the spectrum of effects water creates in nature is nearly infinite. Man-made gardens have always celebrated water. Pools and fountains were the focal points of Roman atria, Moorish courtyards in Spain, Moghul palace grounds in India, palace gardens in China and Japan. All of these — and the extravagant water vistas of Italian villas, the artificial lakes of French châteaux, the ponds and lakes of the English country tradition — have their descendants in public and private gardens in this country. Still or flowing, falling or leaping, bubbling or misting, water in the landscape is a source of charm, mystery, an almost hypnotic fascination.

If you're lucky enough to have a wet lowland or a spring or stream on your property, use this section primarily as a source of design ideas. The construction end of things will really consist of adapting the natural topography and vegetation to suit your utilitarian and/or decorative ends. Consult your state university extension service or soil conservation service for guidelines on handling ponds or streambeds in your specific area. If necessary, you may want to introduce or recirculate water to supplement the natural supply during the dryest season.

Few homesites are blessed with existing water supplies, however. Nor do most people even have the kind of topography that will

Natural effects of water, from falls (below, left) to smooth sheets (below, right), suggest varieties of water display that can be adapted for the home landscape.

Water, not a cataract but a gentle trickle recirculated by a small pump, adds life and beauty to this rock ledge.

make falls or basins for water once it is brought in. So this section focuses on uses of water that include both importing water and constructing environments for it.

Water as Ornament As with so many facets of landscape design and construction, the first step in working with water is to look and think. Look at the forms and manifestations of water in nature, and think about how they work. How does water move along a steep or irregular bank, against a shallow beach, around rocks in a stream? What shapes does it take in open ponds or narrow channels? What land forms cause it to lie glassy smooth, to trickle quietly, or to splash energetically? With an awareness of natural forms of water activity (or inactivity), you can channel, direct, or contain water in effective and pleasing ways.

Forms of water display Ornamental water effects can be grouped into three categories, to be used singly or in combination:

- Piped water is pumped and propelled through nozzles or jets to form sprays, squirts, gurgles, splashes, or drips, as in all kinds of fountains.
- Falling water is pulled by gravity over drops in elevation, resulting in falls, spills, rapids, or eddies.
- Still water lies at rest, as in a lily pond, fishpond, reflecting pool, or birdbath.

You must decide what effect or combination of effects is appropriate for the scale and character of your setting. A quiet trickle into a sunken birdbath? A decorative spray that can be illuminated at night? A simulated streambed ending in a reflecting pool next to a terrace? You can let the water display blend with its environment, or design it to enhance the theme or overall motif you have chosen for the space.

Mechanisms for water display Both the location and the purpose of the water display will affect the details of its construction. A lily pond for a large sunny lawn will be designed differently, and have different mechanical requirements, from a naturalized pond in a shady low spot.

But a few basic items are common to all water displays from birdbaths to swimming pools. At the very least, you'll require a basin to contain water and a source of water to fill it. And, of course, if there is to be moving water, then a pump is needed to recirculate it. There should also be a bottom drain to permit cleaning the basin from time to time, and an overflow drain in case heavy rains or snow melt fill it beyond its capacity. If there's a pump, you'll need electricity to power it. And while you're installing electricity, you may want to consider installing lighting as well: the combination of water and illumination can produce wonderful effects at night.

One measure of good design and construction of any landscape fixture is that it should look as attractive in winter (five to six months of the year) as in summer. Therefore, no pipes, pumps, electrical cords, or lamps should be visible. They spoil the effect at any time, and they look particularly sad and out of place in winter when the pool or other display is drained.

Swimming Pools By far the most widespread use of water in the American landscape is the swimming pool. If you ever fly into or out of a metropolitan airport, look at the suburbs spread out beneath you: the turquoise rectangles, ovals, and circles dot the landscape with incredible density and regularity.

Swimming pools, dedicated to pleasing the sense of touch, can and should (though they seldom do) appeal to the eye and the ear as well. Unlike a lily pond, a reflecting pool, or a miniature waterfall, however, a swimming pool in a residential landscape is something of a bull in a china shop. It can't help but make a major impact on everything within range. Because a swimming pool is so cumbersome, so big, so visually potent, there is often a tendency for homeowners and contractors alike to put aside their good taste and training and just build the thing willy-nilly.

The rectilinear design of the swimming pool is integrated with that of the house close by, and the bottom of the pool is painted gray for an elegant subdued color of water.

But you can have the sensual delight of a cool dip on a sultry day and still create a pool habitat that is harmoniously integrated with its surroundings and a thing of beauty in itself. This doesn't necessarily involve great added cost. It's more a matter of thoughtfully taking stock of where and how you will build the pool, and of coordinating line, form, and materials with the existing setting. As with ornamental pools, an attentive eye is your most valuable tool.

I'll give you here what I consider the most important rules of thumb for designing swimming pools, based on my own experience with a large number of them.

Location If your pool is near your house (either because that's all the space you have or because you want the pool to be part of the view from your windows), I suggest that you put it very close to the house and key its size, shape, construction materials, furnishings, and plantings to those of and around the house. If you live in the North, however, and if you have enough space to let the pool occupy a separate self-contained area, I'd encourage you to go this route — primarily because in this climate, swimming pools are not very agreeable to look at for most of the year. And whether near or far from the house, a pool should not be under trees or downwind of them. Trees' falling leaves and detritus make a terrible mess of a pool.

Type I do not recommend an aboveground pool under any normal circumstances. It may be cheaper than an inground one, but it is bound to be an eyesore from at least one vantage point.

Shape Take your cues from the house, the space available, and the setting. Free-form pools are tricky to work with if they're right up against the straight lines of house, patio, and so on; they're easier if somewhat removed from the house in a natural area. Rectangular pools can work well anywhere. And keep practical considerations in mind when you choose the pool's shape: try to balance cut and fill, making use somehow of the material excavated from the pool.

Deck My own preference is for an exposed-aggregate concrete with round pebbles in a good range of colors — provided the job is expertly done. You can also build pool decks of wood; or of modular paving tiles, blocks, or bricks. Or stone: bluestone, granite, slate, limestone. Of all materials the least expensive is concrete, the most expensive stone.

A coping (a rounded, slightly protruding edge) offers an element of comfort and practicality. I do feel, however, that the standard foot-wide precast coping makes an extremely strong linear statement. Particularly near the house, it's sometimes preferable to let the edge of the deck be the edge of the pool.

Drainage is a major issue with decks. Slope all deck surfaces away from the pool, and arrange carefully for drainage of any planting areas around the deck. If water seeps below a concrete deck it will freeze and cause heaving and cracking.

Equipment As with ornamental pools, concealment of plumbing is mandatory. It sometimes comes as a shock to discover the amount of plumbing, power machinery, and other apparatus and chemical input a simple swimming pool involves. The minimum will be pump, filter, supply of chlorine, and algae control. If you're going to heat the pool you'll need heating units, fuel storage capacity, and so on. Plan for an enclosure for all this gear before the pool is built, not as an afterthought.

Fencing Fortunately (since town ordinances require it anyway), fencing affords great scope for ingenuity and creativity. How to make the pool secure, yet allow for air circulation and nice views while at the same time avoiding a fenced-in feeling — this challenge can be fun to meet. Wrought iron is costly but elegant for formal garden settings. The least expensive and most transparent fencing (in fact it's almost invisible) is a black-vinyl-coated wire mesh with rectangular openings, stretched between posts of wood or black-painted steel. I am not partial to chain-link fence, but if for some reason you are stuck with it you can soften the effect with shrubbery or vines. Other than metal, the best choice will be one of the almost unlimited forms of wood fencing. Depending on style and finish, wood fits into any design and blends with any surroundings.

Plants by Design

JULY BLOOMERS

Flowering trees and shrubs for summer color

Early July

Swamp azalea (*Rhododendron viscosum*)
Korean stewartia (*Stewartia koreana*)
Japanese stewartia (*Stewartia pseudocamelliia*)
Littleleaf linden (*Tilia cordata*)
Crimean linden (*Tilia euchlora*)
Silver linden (*Tilia tomentosa*)

Mid-July

Common trumpet creeper (*Campsis radicans*)
Golden-rain tree (*Koelreuteria paniculata*)
Sorrel tree or sourwood (*Oxydendrum arboreum*)
Memorial rose (*Rosa wichuraiana*)

Late July

Buttonbush (*Cephalanthus occidentalis*)
Summer-sweet clethra (*Clethra alnifolia*)
Rose-of-Sharon or shrub althea (*Hibiscus syriacus*)

Detailed information and recommended varieties can be found in Part III.

LANDSCAPE TASKS FOR JULY

Irrigation Keeping up the water supply of lawns, flowers, and shrubs — particularly evergreens — is a major July responsibility. Give each garden area an occasional deep watering, not frequent sprinklings (which really do more harm than good).

Newly transplanted trees and shrubs are particularly vulnerable to drought, and need watching. If you have a great many plants to attend to, a moisture-meter probe can be a help. This instrument consists of a thin probe with a meter on the end: you plunge the probe a foot deep in the soil, and the meter tells you the status of the soil moisture.

Wisteria Pruning After wisteria blooms it should be radically pruned. This promotes flower production and prevents the vines from getting too heavy and unruly — which can be a major threat when a vine is on a wooden porch, trellis, or arbor. I let each vine develop just a few main trunks, and cut back all lateral branches to 10 to 12 inches from the main stem.

Left to itself, wisteria will tear apart almost any trellis. Prune hard after bloom; the more you prune, the better for the vine (and the trellis).

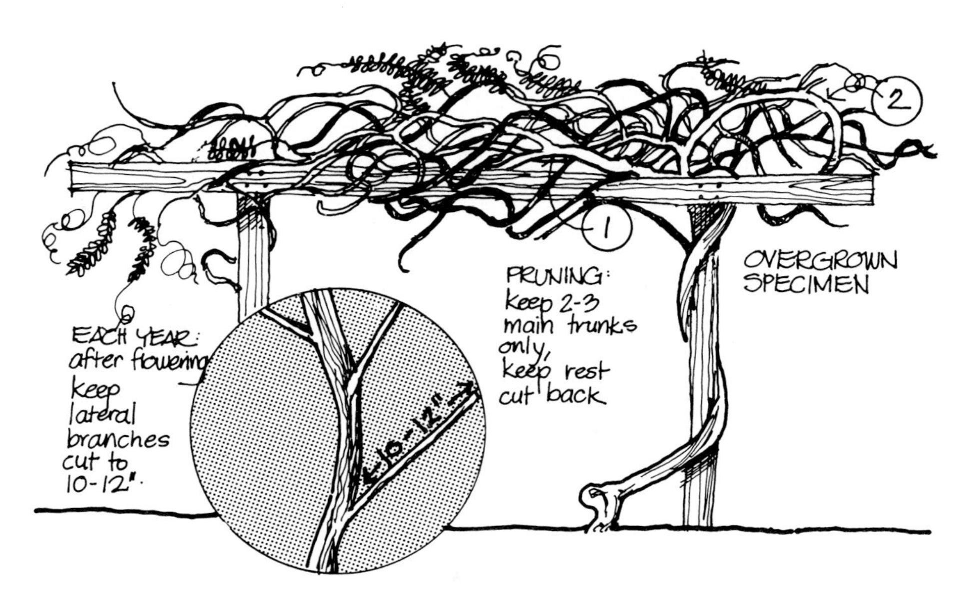

Hedge Pruning Keep up the trimming of deciduous hedges as needed (see November Plants for a Purpose for some guidelines). Many deciduous hedge plants call for several shapings a year.

Be sure to prune evergreen hedges by the end of the first week of July. Their annual growth period is ending then anyway, so a good shaping will last until the following spring. More important, you want to give any tender new growth that does come after pruning a chance to harden off before cold weather.

Pest Control

Red spider mites Watch for red spider mite damage to evergreens, particularly the close-needled dwarf varieties. These mites are most apt to invade in dry weather. If necessary, spray with a miticide such as malathion; two applications are usually needed. As always with poisons, follow the label directions to the letter.

Poison ivy This noxious and invasive plant definitely qualifies as a pest. If any poison ivy grows on your property you should stop it before it multiplies. If you catch it early, you can pull it out by the roots. Or there are a number of liquid and granular compounds on the market you can mix with water to spray on the plants. Pick a dry spell: if you spray just before a rain, the herbicide will wash off and leave the poison ivy as happy as before. Wear heavy clothing and gloves, and as always, be scrupulous about reading and following the directions for proper use of the spray.

Nursery Sales This is often a month for great markdowns at nurseries. If you're in the market for balled and burlapped or container-grown trees or shrubs, you may be able to get them now at a reduced rate and plant them successfully. Do, however, stick to a supplier you know and have confidence in; a tired or sickly plant is never a bargain.

AUG

Landscaping Opportunities
City Gardens

Plants for a Purpose
Plants for Small Spaces

Materials and Construction
Outdoor Furniture

Plants by Design
August Bloomers

Landscape Tasks for August

In sultry August weather, the pool imparts a sense of refreshment and repose to this Japanese garden.

"The old of the moon in August is the time to cut your brush," goes a true old saying. Brush cut now stays cut — because trees and shrubs have pretty much stopped growing for the year. Everything is slowing down. Nights are longer, lawns are dormant. In suburbs and cities, the cool evenings and gentler sun make outdoor greenery especially welcoming now. I'll look at some special aspects of gardening in the city this month — and at plants for small spaces (city or country); garden furnishings; and the select group of landscape plants that come into bloom in August.

Landscaping Opportunities

CITY GARDENS

Designing and building a city garden is worth all the ingenuity (and effort) you can put into it. Particularly in the heat of summer, nothing gives such wonderful respite from the clamor and bustle of city life as a garden.

Yet the fact remains that creating a city garden almost seems to define itself as a series of problems. The best way I know of to surmount these obstacles is to recognize and address them at the start. They will probably consist of some or all of the following:

Soil Most urban soils are better described as dirt, and consist of construction debris, gravel, and sand. If you're lucky enough to possess something resembling proper loam, it has probably been beaten down to the consistency of concrete. Porosity, fertility, and drainage capacity are probably going to be up to you.

Shade A city means density of both buildings and people. Even if your garden plot is not deeply shaded by abutting structures, you're likely to want to provide yourself with privacy by means of a wall or fence — and that means shade. Plants that require a lot of sun will stretch toward the light, growing leggy and frail. So you're probably going to have to stick to shade-tolerant plants.

Air City air is actually a mixture of air with dust, soot, carbon monoxide, sulfur dioxide, and other particles and gases, none of which are beneficial to plants (or people, for that matter). But for the foreseeable future, air pollution has to be considered a fact of urban life. Some plants and construction materials will suffer badly from the dust, soot, etc., and these you must avoid. Other plants are quite adaptable and, in their quiet way, improve air quality.

Accessibility Most city gardens seem to be relegated to leftover space. You may find that your only access to your city plot is through the laundry-room door, down a narrow alley, or even over a roof and down a fire escape. This will have a lot to do with how ambitious your plans for planting and construction can be.

Cost The cost of improving your soil, providing for drainage, installing some greenery, and possibly doing a little paving or construction may be somewhat daunting. But at least, since a city garden is almost always very small, its cost is finite. To do an equally good job on a suburban site would probably cost quite a lot more — without yielding such positively dramatic results.

Designing a City Garden The great opportunity and first priority in a city garden is to bring a bit of nature into an unnatural

The skillful use of shade-tolerant vines and broad-leaved evergreens creates a haven of beauty in a tiny walled city garden.

setting. Japanese bonsai, the art of cultivating individual specimens or groves of dwarfed trees in containers, can put a miniature living forest on a windowsill. You can think of a city garden as a larger kind of bonsai — a microcosm you can shape to evoke all the wonder of the natural world. The smallest, simplest things will do the trick: a tree with berries to attract birds, a source of running water, or a little patch of green where the sunlight falls.

The basic design guidelines I follow for a city garden are the same as those for any landscape (see Part I). But a few watchwords are in order here.

First, let simplicity be your guiding principle. It is often hard for the zealous gardener to resist cramming too lavish a variety of forms, colors, or textures into too small a space. But the effect can't help but be distracting and cluttered. In a city garden restfulness is the goal.

Second, think small, particularly when you select plants. Most plants that are well adapted to the shady, constricted, and polluted environs of a city garden are in fact modest in size. Don't be tempted by big forest trees or by the kinds of shrubs that send up hundreds of shoots every year so that they sprawl over the countryside. You won't be happy with the burgeoning habits of these plants for long, and they won't be happy with you.

Third, put practicality foremost, both in the construction stage and as you plan for future maintenance. For instance, if you're going to be hand-carrying paving material from the street, through the kitchen, and out into the garden, your paved area had better be small; and big stone slabs are not recommended. Or if you have no outdoor water source, keep your planting ambitions modest. In other words, think through not only what you're going to do but how you're going to do it. You may well find that the means dictate the ends, rather than the other way around.

Building a City Garden It should be all too clear by now that in a city situation, both the designing phase and the building phase will be as much a matter of coping with difficulties as anything else. I'll take the building process in the same order as the difficulties I listed at the beginning of this section.

I am assuming here that your garden is at ground level. (For a balcony, window-box, or rooftop garden, you'll be working primarily with containers — see the October Landscaping Opportunities section.) At ground level, your biggest chore and most important contribution will be to improve the soil. First, get a soil test (see March Landscape Tasks). "Proceeding without a soil test," an old-time gardener said to me, "is like building a house without a blueprint." A good way to tackle soil and drainage problems is to construct raised beds. If you can till the soil mechanically or by hand and bring in additional topsoil and organic matter (compost, manure, and/or peat moss), great. If you can't do that, you can still avail yourself of the benefits of raised beds by digging soil out of one place and piling it in another. Add peat moss and perlite, which both come cleanly bagged and are light to carry, to improve tilth (texture and porosity) and fertility. Install curbs of wood, stone, or brick; if you have raised your bed(s) only 6 inches, you'll have gained deeper and more friable soil. And if it's deep and friable, that is half the battle. Limestone, fertilizers, whatever you add now will have a proper matrix to be added to.

What to do about the place where you removed soil? Perhaps pave it, cobble it, or put a sandbox or a small pool in it; or install footings and a small deck over it. This is the sort of issue that makes practicality such a vital consideration at the design stage.

A narrow raised planting bed is easy to maintain and holds precious soil for ground covers and vines. (The newly repointed wall will look better when the mortar darkens.)

One way to deal with poor drainage is to build a drainage gutter or conduit that connects to a downspout from the roof. The downspout presumably leads to a drain, which leads to a storm sewer somewhere. If this is not feasible, you should consider a drywell or "French drain": a hole or trench filled with gravel, where water can collect and leach off slowly into the subsoil. (A drywell might be one good use for that spot where you excavated soil for your raised bed.) There's one possible hitch, however. Your subsoil may be so densely compacted, rocky, or clayey that it won't permit leaching. Check by digging a hole a foot across and several feet deep and filling it with water. If the water disappears overnight, your subsoil is probably in good shape for leaching. But if after 24 hours some of the water is still there, you are going to have to find another way to collect and dispose of excess rainwater.

You can't do much about the problem of shade from neighboring buildings, except to make allowance for it in your choice of plants and construction materials. But if part of your shade is going to result from your own construction of, say, a screening fence, you can have some impact. Try to pick a design that is at least partly open to sunlight (the November Materials and Construction section has some good suggestions).

The air-polluting particles and gases that will be the daily diet of your city garden also fall into the category of things you cannot change and will have to live with. The plants listed at the end of this section are all resilient and well adapted to survival in city air. If you decide to go beyond this list for some favorite of your own, do talk over your selection with a knowledgeable nurseryman to be sure your choices will be successful. Similarly, some garden construction materials will work better in polluted circumstances than others. Obviously, you should steer clear of white paint, pale masonry, and pale stones like limestone or marble. Choose wall and seating materials that show dirt as little as possible. For paving materials think in terms of surfaces that can be swept or hosed down with ease. And keep the questions of accessibility and cost always in mind.

Choosing Plants for the City Garden The plants listed here are chosen mainly for their ability to put up with city conditions, from shade to poor soil to dirty air; so this is a very strictly limited group. There are countless other good possibilities in this month's Plants for a Purpose section and in the lists of ground covers and vines in June. Just be sure not to pick anything that's specifically described as intolerant of urban life, and you may have good luck. A little adventurous experimentation is not out of line, when a green oasis is the goal.

Plants for the City Garden

Shade Trees

European hornbeam (*Carpinus betulus*)
Katsura tree (*Cercidiphyllum japonicum*)
Ginkgo or maidenhair tree (*Ginkgo biloba*)
Thornless honey locust (*Gleditsia triacanthos inermis*)
Japanese pagoda tree (*Sophora japonica*)
Littleleaf linden (*Tilia cordata*)

Smaller Deciduous Trees

Japanese maple (*Acer palmatum*)
Weeping European birch (*Betula pendula*)
White fringe tree (*Chionanthus virginicus*)
Flowering dogwood (*Cornus florida*)
Washington hawthorn (*Crataegus phaenopyrum*)
Star magnolia (*Magnolia stellata*)
Sorrel tree or sourwood (*Oxydendrum arboreum*)
Amur cork tree (*Phellodendron amurense*)
Bradford callery pear (*Pyrus calleryana* 'Bradford')

Evergreen Trees and Shrubs

White fir (*Abies concolor*)
Douglas fir (*Pseudotsuga menziesii*)
Umbrella pine (*Sciadopitys verticillata*)
Yews (*Taxus* spp.)
Canadian hemlock (*Tsuga canadensis* — dwarf vars.)

Deciduous Shrubs

Japanese barberry (*Berberis thunbergii*)
Flowering quince (*Chaenomeles speciosa*)
Summer-sweet clethra (*Clethra alnifolia*)
Cotoneasters (*Cotoneaster* spp.)
Redvein enkianthus (*Enkianthus campanulatus*)
Winged euonymus (*Euonymus alata*)
Showy border forsythia (*Forsythia intermedia* 'Spectabilis')
Rose-of-Sharon or shrub althea (*Hibiscus syriacus*)
Peegee hydrangea (*Hydrangea paniculata* 'Grandiflora')
Regel privet (*Ligustrum obtusifolium regelianum*)
Winter honeysuckle (*Lonicera fragrantissima*)
Vanhoutte spirea (*Spiraea vanhouttei*)
Black haw (*Viburnum prunifolium*)

Broad-leaved Evergreens

Boxwoods (*Buxus* spp.)
Boxleaf holly (*Ilex crenata* 'Convexa')
Inkberry (*Ilex glabra*)
American holly (*Ilex opaca*)
Mountain laurel (*Kalmia latifolia*)
Drooping leucothoe ((*Leucothoe fontanesiana*)
Japanese andromeda or pieris (*Pieris japonica*)
Laland firethorn (*Pyracantha coccinea* 'Lalandei')
Rhododendrons and azaleas (*Rhododendron* spp.)

Vines

Boston ivy (*Parthenocissus tricuspidata*)
Virginia creeper (*Parthenocissus quinquefolia*)
Japanese wisteria (*Wisteria floribunda*)

Ground Covers

Wintercreeper (*Euonymus fortunei* vars.)
English ivy (*Hedera helix* vars.)
Japanese spurge or pachysandra (*Pachysandra terminalis*)

Detailed information and recommended varieties can be found in Part III.

Plants for a Purpose
PLANTS FOR SMALL SPACES

How small is small? City gardens are small, of course, but in this section I am also considering everything from balcony or rooftop gardens to side yards in the suburbs and enclosed nooks next to houses or along walls in larger properties.

Not all small-scale situations require small plants, to be sure. If you have an old shade tree or a tall pine growing happily up and out of a narrow passageway or in the corner of a small yard, and if its location, condition, and appearance please you and create a pleasant canopy, by all means keep it.

But for the most part, gardens in circumscribed settings work best with modest-sized plantings. A big tree or large mass of shrubbery is apt to dominate everything else visually and give you a cramped, hemmed-in feeling. Big trees cast a lot of shade, making it hard for you to grow anything else under them, even grass. The roots of larger trees and shrubs take so much of the soil's moisture and nutrients that it is a constant battle for any other plant to survive near by. Besides, in their efforts to work their way out of confinement these hungry root systems will also tend to heave pavements or clog drains.

The plants listed on page 220, by contrast, make docile and cheerful citizens in close quarters. They're well suited to raised beds or containers, as well as to planting in the earth. They'll provide you with beauty of flower, texture, or form, as you choose, but without growing you out of house and home.

Japanese maple varieties offer many textures, from this fine cutleaf type to coarser lobed-leaved selections.

A scaled-down enclave of nature in a small entry yard: gray birches, dwarf shrubs, ground covers, and vines are selected for modest size and compatibility.

Designing a Small Garden The basic precepts of small-garden design are identical to those for the design of more roomy landscapes. First, it's important to plan. Sketch your design on paper; then measure it out and test it with mockups to see how it will work. Pay extra attention to proper scale, because it's extra important here.

Perhaps most important of all is simplicity. If ever there's a risk of developing a claustrophobic clutter, it is when space is limited. So restrain yourself. Tempting though it may be to try one of everything, you'll achieve a far happier effect if you stick to a few varieties. If necessary, group them for more mass or coverage.

Choosing Trees and Shrubs There are two large groups of plants not listed here that are in fact ideal for small spaces: ground covers and vines. (See the June Plants for a Purpose section.) Any number of ground covers can also be grown as container plants or in a rock-garden arrangement or as miniature shrubbery. And very often a vine can give you all the benefits of a tree or flowering shrub — but take up no more horizontal space then it needs for a foothold at the base of a wall or trellis.

Also, consider using shrubs as trees. Quite a few varieties in the June list of deciduous ornamental shrubs can be pruned to one to three stems and treated like small trees in a small garden, and they are lovely this way. Some that you might consider using are autumn olive, redvein enkianthus, shining sumac, or Siebold viburnum.

Finally, bear in mind that many deciduous and evergreen shrubs, broad-leaved evergreens, and small trees are now available in dwarf forms. Small cultivars of rhododendrons, azaleas, andromeda (pieris), lilacs, even hemlocks can be found. If your heart is set on a tree or shrub you've discovered elsewhere in this book, do ask your nursery if they have a reliable dwarf variety to fit your small plot.

That said, here is a selection of my own favorites for planting where space is at a premium.

Trees and Shrubs for Small Spaces

Deciduous Trees

Japanese maple (*Acer palmatum*)
Shadblow, juneberry, or serviceberry (*Amelanchier canadensis*)
Weeping European birch (*Betula pendula*)
Gray birch (*Betula populifolia*)
Redbud (*Cercis canadensis*)
White fringe tree (*Chionanthus virginicus*)
Flowering dogwood (*Cornus florida*)
Kousa or Japanese dogwood (*Cornus kousa*)
Cornelian cherry dogwood (*Cornus mas*)
Washington hawthorn (*Crataegus phaenopyrum*)
Star magnolia (*Magnolia stellata*)
Crabapples (*Malus* spp.)
Sargent crabapple (*Malus sargentii*)
Sorrel tree or sourwood (*Oxydendrum arboreum*)
Weeping cherry (*Prunus subhirtella* 'Pendula')
Bradford callery pear (*Pyrus calleryana* 'Bradford')
Korean stewartia (*Stewartia koreana*)

Deciduous Shrubs

Crimson pygmy Japanese barberry (*Berberis thunbergii* 'Crimson Pygmy')
Cranberry cotoneaster (*Cotoneaster apiculatus*)
Skogsholm bearberry cotoneaster (*Cotoneaster dammeri* 'Skogsholmen')
Compact winged euonymus (*Euonymus alata* 'Compacta')
Bronx forsythia (*Forsythia viridissima* 'Bronxensis')
Dwarf fothergilla or witch alder (*Fothergilla gardenii*)
Bush or shrubby cinquefoil, or potentilla (*Potentilla fruticosa*)
Korean azalea (*Rhododendron mucronulatum*)
Daphne spirea (*Spiraea japonica* 'Alpina')
Compact Korean spice viburnum (*Viburnum carlesii* 'Compactum')
Compact or dwarf cranberrybush viburnum (*Viburnum opulus* 'Compactum' or 'Nanum')

Evergreen Trees and Shrubs

Dwarf or pyramidal hinoki false cypress (*Chamaecyparis obtusa* 'Nana' or 'Nana Gracilis')
Dwarf golden thread false cypress (*Chamaecyparis pisifera* 'Filifera Golden Mop')
Dwarf Chinese garden juniper (*Juniperus chinensis procumbens* 'Nana')
Nest spruce (*Picea abies* 'Nidiformis')
Dwarf white pine (*Pinus strobus* 'Nana')
Dwarf Japanese yew (*Taxus cuspidata* 'Nana')
Hetz Midget arborvitae (*Thuja occidentalis* 'Hetz Midget')
Dwarf or weeping hemlock (*Tsuga canadensis* 'Bennett' or 'Coles Prostrate')

Broad-Leaved Evergreens

Littleleaf box (*Buxus microphylla* vars.)
Boxwood (*Buxus sempervirens* 'Vardar Valley' or 'Green Gem')
Hellers Japanese holly (*Ilex crenata* 'Helleri')
Dwarf inkberry (*Ilex glabra* 'Compacta')
Dwarf drooping leucothoe (*Leucothoe fontanesiana* 'Nana')
Canby paxistima (*Paxistima canbyi*)
Compact Japanese andromeda or pieris (*Pieris japonica* 'Compacta')
Carolina rhododendron (*Rhododendron carolinianum*)
Evergreen azaleas (*Rhododendron* 'Delaware Valley White,' *kaempferi*, 'Herbert,' 'Hinocrimson,' 'Hinodegiri')
Wilson rhododendron (*Rhododendron laetivirens*)
Purple gem rhododendron (*Rhododendron* 'Purple Gem')

Detailed information and recommended varieties can be found in Part III.

Materials and Construction
OUTDOOR FURNITURE

A beautiful landscape can be both enjoyed from a distance and cherished from within. Outdoor furniture lets you observe, participate, recreate, and relax in your landscape. This is just as true of furnishings in a spacious place as of seating and eating places in a tiny city patio. And a few hints may be helpful for both situations.

First, although you want to assemble furnishings that will comfortably meet your family's needs, you do not want to crowd your place with a hodgepodge of furniture and equipment — or break the bank, for that matter. Where should you start? What should you select? How much should you spend?

Begin by making list of all the areas you have available and of the activities requiring furniture that go on in each. It might look something like this:

Furniture Needs by Area and Activity

Place	*Activities*	*Furniture*
Under shade trees	Family and party dining, cocktails, conversation, resting	Picnic table, chairs, small tables, hammock?
Terrace next to a window	Breakfast, lunch, supper, sitting	Table and chairs; trellis for shade?
Barbecue	Cooking	Grille, utility table, bench for cook or guests
Flower garden	Sitting, viewing	Ornamental bench
Children's play area	Climbing, swinging, jumping, sliding, building, digging, acting, etc.	Play equipment

As you consider what to buy to fulfill the requirements of your own list, bear in mind the following ground rules.

- Don't try to stuff furniture for every conceivable purpose onto a small terrace or patio. If you have a little additional space, you can find separate homes for some activities and liberate the patio from clutter; if not, you'll need to make compromises, or perhaps include a small storage shed in your plans.
- Select good-quality furniture that combines sturdy construction and durable materials with restraint of design. In general, furniture should not dominate the landscape but blend into it. The possible exception might be a special piece or group of pieces that are intentionally chosen as an ornamental feature — such as a custom-made wooden settee, painted white, in an herb or flower garden.
- Try to avoid putting outdoor furniture directly in the line of a prime view.
- If you're working on furniture at the base plan stage of a landscape design, you can experiment with paper templates cut to scale. You'll probably discover that you want to make your ter-

Urban and suburban settings with similar background colors show the range of choices in outdoor furnishings. Formal wrought iron suits the city garden, above left. Above right, aluminum-framed furniture with white cushions contrasts starkly with the house.

race larger, or to put some of the furniture away from the house, or even to buy less furniture. That can be all to the good if it lets you invest in better quality in the items you do buy.

- If you aren't able to use a plan and templates (or indeed, even if you are), make a deal with the supplier to allow you to return your garden furniture if you are not happy with it once you see it in place. This is one component of the landscape that you can easily take back if it's not the way you pictured it, and you should.

Now for a few ideas on furniture to meet the needs suggested in the areas-and-activities list above.

Under shade trees (away from house) Here's the perfect place for a good big redwood or cedar table, benches, chairs, and maybe a small table or two. I prefer movable benches, since the fixed ones are hard for older people to get in and out of, and uncomfortable for small children. If you want to get fancy, you can add cushions; but they cannot stay out in the weather, so you need a place to store them and the patience to haul them out and back every time you use them.

A shady spot — ideally, under evergreens — is also lovely for a hammock. Children can't resist hammocks, though, so be sure to have a soft surface underneath, such as grass, shredded bark, or any soft mulch.

Terrace next to a window Since an area like this constitutes a view from inside the house as well as a comfortable, enticing outdoor living space, I'd choose chairs and tables that are modest-scaled, unobtrusive, more delicate than the rustic cedar type. There's furniture of thin steel with wire mesh fabric, all painted black, that practically disappears, so that it doesn't impinge on your view of your plantings. Or you can get furniture with aluminum or vinyl-coated parts and open fabric webbing; again, for easy maintenance and an inconspicuous quality, I recommend dark colors or neutrals if possible. Save lightweight aluminum furniture with multicolored webbing for the beach.

Barbecue There are many eminently satisfactory kinds of grilles, from the smallest hibachi to the most imposing masonry edifice. Whatever kind you prefer, I like to have a small table (about 2 by 3 feet) near by, where you can organize food supplies. Another amenity is a place where you can sit while the food sizzles, or where friends or family members can perch and keep the cook company.

Flower garden By "flower garden" here I'm suggesting any place designed primarily for viewing but where you'd like to set aside a spot to relax. Some unusual and beautiful form of seating, such as an English teak bench or a cast-iron Victorian grapevine settee, would be appropriate in such a place; and there are many less costly but well-designed and comfortable alternatives.

Children's play area Children do grow up. Play yards are temporary and should be designed accordingly; have in mind a second or ultimate role for the space once it's no longer used for children's play.

Furnishings for play areas should be sturdy and minimal. They can range from the standard sandbox, jungle gym, and swing set (wooden ones preferred: they're softer and warmer to the touch) to complex and expensive play systems. In my experience, however, children rapidly tire of most of this equipment and have far more fun inventing their own games wherever you least anticipated it. Besides, you get a much better ride on a long rope hung from a tree limb than on a swing set. There's no substitute, however, for the sandbox. All the kids love it. So do all the neighborhood cats. Put it in a place where you can grow flowers, herbs, or vegetables afterwards; my sandbox herbs are flourishing.

A decorative stone bench at Dumbarton Oaks in Washington, D.C.: more pleasant to look at than to sit on.

Plants by Design

AUGUST BLOOMERS

A few standouts in the later-summer landscape

Trees and Shrubs

Orange-eye butterfly bush (*Buddleia davidii*)

Summer-sweet clethra (*Clethra alnifolia*)

Rose-of-Sharon or shrub althea (*Hibiscus syriacus*)

Peegee hydrangea (*Hydrangea paniculata* 'Grandiflora')

Sorrel tree or sourwood (*Oxydendrum arboreum*)

Japanese pagoda tree (*Sophora japonica*)

Vines

Clematis (*Clematis* spp.)

Chinese fleece vine (*Polygonum aubertii*)

Ground Cover

Plantain lilies (*Hosta* spp.)

Detailed information and recommended varieties can be found in Part III.

Rose-of-Sharon or shrub althea (below left) and fragrant summer-sweet clethra (below right) are two of the relatively small group of trees and shrubs blooming in August.

LANDSCAPE TASKS FOR AUGUST

Lawn Upkeep You can, if you wish, allow your lawn grass to go dormant now. Growth will tend to slow down naturally, toward the end of July; and if you stop watering, it will come to a halt almost completely. It doesn't hurt lawn grasses to rest awhile before reviving with cooler weather and autumn rainfall. Besides, dormant grass doesn't take much mowing, so you get a rest too.

You may decide to keep up the watering, however, if you dislike the dull, dry appearance of a dormant lawn, or if your lawn gets the kind of strenuous wear (such as badminton or softball games) that would damage brittle grass.

Evergreen Pruning Firs and spruces have to be treated a little differently from pines and hemlocks and other needled evergreens, because they form new buds along the sides (not at the outer ends) of their twigs. Now through late fall, you can see where the new growth will come; so this is the time to cut back selectively and judiciously, saving some buds for next spring. (For pruning of other needled evergreens, see May Landscape Tasks.)

Trimming Deciduous Hedges In late August, you can give a final trimming to most deciduous hedge plants and they'll be all set until next spring. The prunings of this past spring and summer will have promoted dense growth of new shoots from the sides of cut twigs, but at this season the plants have pretty much finished growing for the year.

Euonymus Scale It's at this time of year that scale insects really do a job on evergreen euonymus (wintercreeper and similar types). The leaves and stems of the plant will be covered with white insects. Scale can do real damage to euonymus if you let it go unchecked. Spray with oil emulsion, summer strength.

Tools and Equipment As gardening chores slow down, go over all your gardening tools and get them into good condition. Clean, sharpen, and oil as appropriate, both for winter rustproofing and for the sake of a good start next spring.

SEP

Landscaping Opportunities
The Fruiting Garden

Plants for a Purpose
Small Trees for Flowers, Foliage, and Fruit

Materials and Construction
Brick and Pavers

Plants by Design
Notable Fruit Display

Landscape Tasks for September

A sweep of meadow grass just beginning to turn golden speaks of the end of summer.

The golden days of September are a time of ripening and harvest — and of new beginnings. This month I'll touch upon some of the glories and the liabilities of fruits and berries grown in the home landscape. I'll discuss small trees that are superb for foliage and fruit at this time of year, and plants noted for ornamental (as opposed to edible) fruit display. I'll introduce brick as a paving and building material, since this is a great month for building. And since September begins the fall planting season, when you can put new trees into the ground while you enjoy the fruits of the old ones, I'll delve into the procedure for planting trees and shrubs.

Landscaping Opportunities
THE FRUITING GARDEN

Not only do fruit-bearing plants produce delectable yields, many of them also hold their own as decorative members of the landscape plant community. As a group, fruiting trees, shrubs, and vines are probably the most maintenance-intensive plants you'll ever have to deal with. They seem to keep you busy with spraying, pruning, fertilizing, weeding, cleanup at every month of the year. In this necessarily brief section, I won't try to give you all the cultural specifications (the Further Reference offers some good sources) but will outline a general philosophy and some design tips for using fruit-bearing plants in your landscape.

Fruits for the Eating I have suffered some resounding defeats in my ventures with tree fruits, particularly with plums and cherries — and a few gratifying triumphs with peaches and apples. I've also met varying results with bush and vine fruits: fantastic raspberries and good grapes year after year, but only moderate success with blueberries. Despite all my tribulations, however, I firmly believe that fruiting plants are worth the struggle; because the kinds of fruits and berries you grow in your own yard are so good. They are completely unlike supermarket fruit. Commercial growers are forced to concentrate on specially bred types that can be picked unripe and that will keep their color and soundness throughout shipping and storage and on market shelves. They can't afford to grow the same mouth-watering varieties the home gardener can indulge in.

Since I grow fruits for the joy of eating them — often right off the bush, tree, or vine — I try to avoid pesticides. Of course, it's certainly true that many of the fruits and berries grown this way are far from unblemished. If perfection is important to you, or if you're considering marketing some of your crop, your garden center, university extension service, or county agricultural agent will be happy to give you bounteous information on fungicides and insecticides.

My own approach is to keep the plants I grow as healthy as possible. The most pest-resistant crop is one that grows vigorously and ripens fast. This means full sun, ample moisture, proper soil, and plenty of mulch where required. It also means clean growing practices, including regular removal of dead fruit and damaged branches in and around productive trees and shrubs. I do use a dormant oil spray as a preventive measure on peach, apple, and pear trees (see February and March Landscape Tasks). And finally, I try to temper with realism my expectations of the more difficult crops. Good years and bad years come and go, but there are some crops that seem to have nothing but bad years; and those I do without.

Landscaping with Productive Plants Many fruit-bearing plants, especially the trees, are beautiful in bloom and attractive throughout much of the rest of the year. They can play as big a part in your landscape as you want; they don't have to be relegated to far corners or tucked behind the garage. Apples, cherries, or pears can stand on their own as specimen trees or can be part of shrub borders. Highbush blueberries are handsome shrubs by any standard, fine for borders or grouped plantings. Lowbush blueberries are second to none as a ground cover for thin, acid soil, perhaps among oak trees or pines. A little ingenuity will suggest uses even for the more challenging plants. Grapevines are lovely growing across a trellis for shade, or along an open fence for added summer screening. A mass of raspberries or blackberries can be worked into a shrub border or used as an informal barrier or hedgerow.

What plants to grow and how to fit them in? A lot depends on the amount of space and sun you can provide. Soil type, exposure, drainage, and other growing conditions are important too. As a quick guide, this table indicates the basic space, soil, and time requirements of the various fruiting plant groups. When you've arrived at a preliminary list of the plants you'd like to try, talk to a dependable nursery or garden center in your area to determine what specific varieties will be best adapted to the conditions you have to offer and the time you'd like to put in.

Fruit-Bearing Plants

Fruit	*Spacing**	*Soil preference*	*Years until bears*	*Years bearing*
Raspberry	3–4 feet, with 6 feet between rows	Deep loam	2	8–10
Blackberry	3–4 feet, in a block or in rows 8 feet apart	Any fertile soil	2	Indefinite
Blueberry (highbush)	4 feet, with 6–8 feet between rows	Well-drained acid soil, not too fertile	3–4	Indefinite
Peach	16–20 feet	Sandy or stony loam	2–3	10–15
Plum	20 feet	Heavy silt or clay loam	3–4	20–30
Cherry:				
Sweet	25–30 feet	Sandy loam	3–5	40
Sour	20 feet	Clay loam	3–5	25
Apple	30–40 feet	Loam	6–8	40–50
Pear	30 feet	Clay loam	3–6	30–40
Grape	8–10 feet	Any fertile soil	2	50

*Spacing for dwarf and semidwarf trees (see discussion on page 230) can vary from 12 to 18 feet; consult nursery for instructions.

Above left: an apple tree provides both bounteous fruit at arm's reach and a foliar archway over the house entrance. Above right: a pear espaliered against a wall takes an enormous amount of care to grow and maintain.

Space Savers: Dwarf and Semidwarf Fruit Trees If your space is limited or if you crave fruit trees that are docile and easy to maintain, dwarf or semidwarf apples, pears, plums, or cherries may be for you. Dwarf fruit trees reach a top size of about 10 to 12 feet, semidwarfs 12 to 18 feet, with cherries slightly larger than other types in both categories.

Essentially these are trees of different desirable varieties that have been grafted onto slow-growing rootstocks. (There are also some genetic dwarfs, a new development.) The grafted rootstocks hold back the trees' annual growth rate, but otherwise the dwarfed trees are identical to their full-size counterparts. All you sacrifice is quantity of fruit, not quality or size of individual fruits.

You'll find that these trees not only save space but tend to begin fruiting at a younger age. Being modest in size they also ease the tasks of pruning, thinning, picking, and upkeep in general. Because the grafting of these plants requires experts — and because they take a longer time to train and grow to the size at which you buy them — you should be prepared to pay more for these trees.

Special training methods There are some specialized pruning and training systems to which dwarf and semidwarf trees are ideally

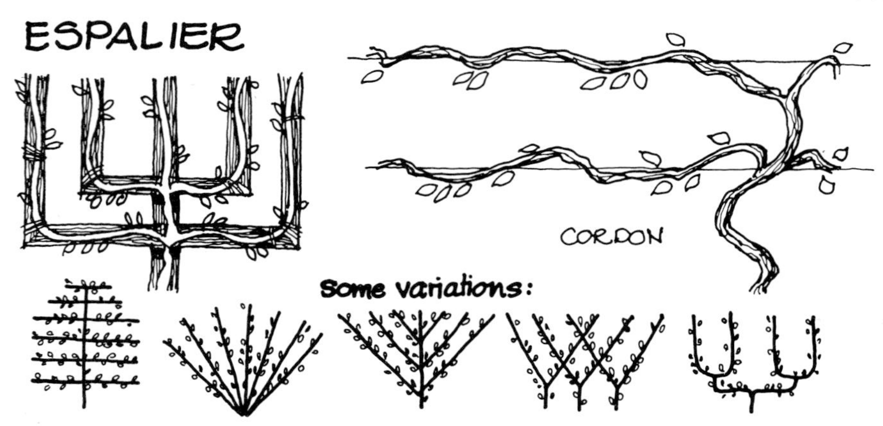

Save space, create decorative patterns, and (against a wall) have earlier fruit with plants trained in espalier forms. Here are some sample designs.

suited. These methods go back many centuries in European gardening, and the terms we use for them come from the French: *espalier* and *cordon*. Both systems involve training plants to grow against south-facing walls, trellises, or fences. They're a wonderful way to have the beauty and productivity of fruit trees in an absolute minimum of space, which was one of the reasons for their original development. In addition, you can often grow as espaliers varieties that would not necessarily be hardy as freestanding specimens, because of the shelter and extra warmth provided by the supporting wall. For the same reason, an espaliered plant usually bears fruit earlier than it would elsewhere.

Beyond all these practical arguments, espaliers make fascinating decorative plantings to soften or screen a bare wall. They're often the perfect answer in a city garden or small patio.

Creating and maintaining espalier fruit trees is a project, however. The steps involved include training from purchase to maturity, then annual maintenance for optimum bearing. Of all the fruits I've mentioned, dwarf apples and pears take best to this treatment. Peaches come next, then plums. For all of them, be prepared to spend plenty of time clipping, tying, coaxing, and cajoling to achieve the final artistic — and productive — result.

Plants for a Purpose

SMALL TREES FOR FLOWERS, FOLIAGE, AND FRUIT

There's no one month that I can single out as tailored to a discussion of small trees — because they do so much all year round. But the fruits of many of these plants definitely add to their appeal, so I have picked September.

Large trees offer big masses of shade or color, big architectural effects. For smaller-scale but no less important effects, small trees play a vital part in the landscape. What a small tree may lack in size it very often makes up many times over in a profusion of beauty.

Yet the appeal of small trees also stems partly from the very fact of their size. They're on a human scale. In a garden of limited size, such as a city or suburban plot, the large tree is a monster, the small tree a model resident. Small trees add more delicate textures, more encompassable forms to the landscape. They're ideal for locations close to houses and outdoor living areas, where the many charms of their flowers, foliage, fruits, bark, and branches are most visible and immediate.

What constitutes "small"? There's no clear demarcation line. Some "small" trees are also perfectly fine shade trees despite a mere 20 feet of overall height. Some "small" trees, supposed to top out at 30 feet, can fool you if conditions are perfect by growing on to 50 or 60 feet. For purposes of this section of this book, I'll arbitrarily put the bottom size limit of a mature small tree, as opposed to a shrub, at around 12 feet; the top at around 30 feet. (For deciduous shrubs see May, and for taller deciduous shade trees see July.)

You can use small trees in an almost infinite number of ways. They make fine isolated specimen plants for display on their own; they're good fillers in shrub borders; they provide summer shade near windows,

Weeping flowering cherry and magnolia, enchanting in spring bloom (as here), are small trees with much to offer in the landscape throughout the year.

Golden-rain tree really catches the eye when it's in flower. Bursts of yellow bloom cover the tree in late summer.

on lawns, or in patios. Whatever their functional role, their changing colors, forms, and lines are lovely throughout the year.

Flowers Perhaps the moment of greatest glory for many of the small trees listed in this section is the season of bloom: spring. The blossoms — often fragrant — are mostly in shades of white, pink, or yellow. Some of my favorite moments have been spent wandering through groves of blooming magnolias, crabapples, and cherries. It is a sensation you simply never forget.

There are also several small trees that bloom in mid- to late summer, so that you can spread your trees' blooming season throughout much of the year (as shown in the Plants by Design lists of March through August) — provided you have enough room. Room is a criterion because in a small property, as I've said elsewhere, too many different varieties can make for confusion. If you are working with limited space, try to limit yourself to just a few kinds of flowering trees.

Summer Foliage Spectacular though the blooming season is, the season of foliage is equally important and lasts a great deal longer. Some small trees' leaves are compound (sets of small leaves arranged on a stem); some are heart-shaped, star-shaped, or oval; most are somewhat smaller and finer in overall texture than those of bigger trees, so that they contribute variety to a landscape's patchwork of colors and textures. And in autumn, small-sized leaves tend to blow around and vanish into crevices and corners, not blanket the countryside with heavy accumulations demanding raking. For many people that's a very good thing.

Fruit and Fall Foliage Many ornamental trees produce fruit — in a spectrum of colors from yellow to red to blue-black. Some fruits, like red maple's, appear in spring and keep the tree's glow of color alight for weeks. Most, however, ripen in September and October (and this month's Plants by Design list includes many of the best). At this time of

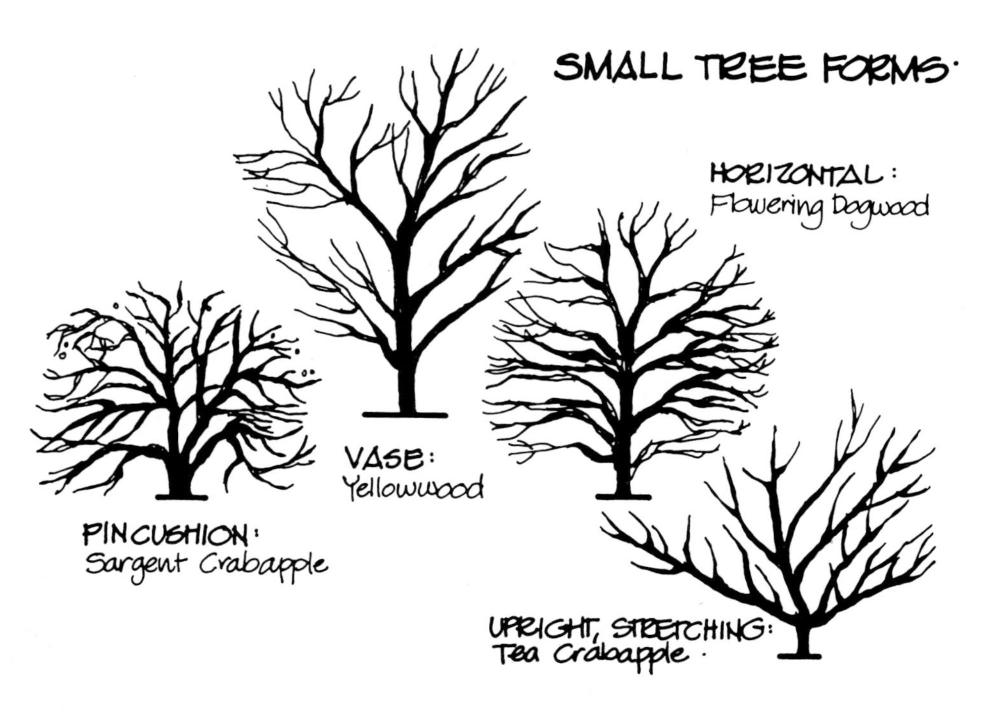

Even without leaves, many small trees have distinctive forms. This group includes representative favorites chosen for form.

year, the dried fruits, seeds, and pods of many small trees make wonderful accents for dried flower arrangements.

Some of the most cherished fruiting trees are those — like hawthorn and many viburnums — whose fruits hang on long into the cold season. The trees and the flocks of birds that visit them provide winterlong live entertainment.

(Be aware, though, that some fruiting trees can make quite a mess. Some drop their fruits en masse after the first few frosts; with others it is the feasting of birds and wildlife that generates the litter. In either case, if the plant in question is next to a paved area or refined lawn, cleanup can be a tiresome chore. Place your fruiting trees accordingly.)

The autumn leaf color of small trees can be every bit as vivid as that of large ones. You can choose colors ranging from the sunny yellows of birches to the deep scarlet of Japanese maple, with every hue in between.

Color, Form, and Line in Winter For locations around your house, where you'll be viewing them at close range throughout the long leafless season, consider the color and texture of bark and twigs as well as the overall branching habit, density, and form of the plant. There's a multitude of possibilities. The smallest Sargent crabapple has a low pincushion shape, much wider than it is tall. A yellowwood grows into a vase shape, up to 30 feet tall and equally broad at its top. The fine branches of flowering dogwoods or black haw take on striking horizontal lines. Kousa dogwood and tea crabapple seem to surge upward.

The trees listed here will afford beauty at every season of the year. If you have a specialized interest — such as in native plants, shade-loving plants, or fruit, fragrance, or bark color — you can find specialized lists in other sections of this book.

A Selection of Small Trees

Paperbark maple (*Acer griseum*)
Japanese maple (*Acer palmatum*)
Bloodleaf Japanese maple (*Acer palmatum* 'Atropurpureum')
Red cutleaf Japanese maple (*Acer palmatum* 'Atropurpureum Dissectum')
Green cutleaf or threadleaf Japanese maple (*Acer palmatum* 'Dissectum')
Shadblow, juneberry, or serviceberry (*Amelanchier canadensis*)
Allegheny shadblow or serviceberry (*Amelanchier laevis*)
Gray birch (*Betula populifolia*)
Redbud (*Cercis canadensis*)
White fringe tree (*Chionanthus virginicus*)
Yellowwood (*Cladrastis lutea*)
White flowering dogwood (*Cornus florida*)
Pink flowering dogwood (*Cornus florida rubra*)
Kousa or Japanese dogwood (*Cornus kousa*)
Cornelian cherry dogwood (*Cornus mas*)
Smoke tree (*Cotinus coggygria*)
Washington hawthorn (*Crataegus phaenopyrum*)
Chinese witch hazel (*Hamamelis mollis*)
Golden-rain tree (*Koelreuteria paniculata*)
Merrill magnolia (*Magnolia loebneri* 'Merrill')
Saucer magnolia (*Magnolia soulangiana*)
Star magnolia (*Magnolia stellata*)
Adams crabapple (*Malus* 'Adams')

Dogwoods head the list of small trees, and juxtaposing pink and white varieties brings out the best of each in the blooming season.

A Selection of Small Trees *(continued)*

Donald Wyman crabapple (*Malus* 'Donald Wyman')
Japanese flowering crabapple (*Malus floribunda*)
Tea crabapple (*Malus hupehensis*)
Mary Potter crabapple (*Malus* 'Mary Potter')
Red jade crabapple (*Malus* 'Red Jade')
Sargent crabapple (*Malus sargentii*)
Winter gold crabapple (*Malus* 'Winter Gold')
Zumi crabapple (*Malus zumi calocarpa*)
Sorrel tree or sourwood (*Oxydendrum arboreum*)
Sargent cherry (*Prunus sargentii*)
Paperbark cherry (*Prunus serrula*)
Oriental cherry (*Prunus serrulata*)
Autumn-flowering cherry (*Prunus subhirtella* 'Autumnalis')
Hally Jolivette cherry (*Prunus subhirtella* 'Hally Jolivette')
Weeping Higan cherry (*Prunus subhirtella* 'Pendula')
Yoshino cherry (*Prunus yedoensis*)
Bradford callery pear (*Pyrus calleryana* 'Bradford')
Korean mountain ash (*Sorbus alnifolia*)
Korean stewartia (*Stewartia koreana*)
Japanese stewartia (*Stewartia pseudocamellia*)
Japanese tree lilac (*Syringa reticulata*)
Black haw (*Viburnum prunifolium*)

Detailed information and recommended varieties can be found in Part III.

Materials and Construction

BRICK AND PAVERS

September and October are the last two months when the weather allows much outdoor construction work, if you live in a northern climate. So this month I'll look at one of my favorite construction materials, brick; and next month at terraces and patios, for which brick is one ideal choice.

Bricks are made of baked clay, one of the three time-honored building materials provided by nature and used by human beings since prehistoric times. (The other two, of course, are stone and wood.) To this day, brick finds almost limitless uses. In the landscape, it's perfect for walks, boundary walls, screening walls, posts, planters, steps, and pavements.

The color and texture of brick have a lot to do with its popularity. The natural earth tones of baked clay, in shades of red, brown, and yellow, fit perfectly into any outdoor setting and add warmth to the most bleak urban surroundings. The regular patterns in which bricks are laid, and the small sizes and matte surfaces of the individual bricks themselves, are easy on the eye.

Besides, in the United States, so much historic construction of the Colonial and Revolutionary periods was of brick that there's a faint nostalgic air about it. Brick evokes the heritage of the past.

Brick also possesses plenty of practical virtues as a material, particularly for the novice or do-it-yourself builder. For one thing, bricks are widely available in a good selection of types, sizes, and colors. For another, brick is relatively easy to work with and far more forgiving of trial and error than many materials. This is especially true of dry-laid brick used as a paving material. As for expense, even though the cost of anything whose manufacture uses fuel (as brick kilns do) continues to spiral, brick is still less expensive than most forms of stone.

Buying Brick As a general rule, the harder the brick, the better it will serve you in outdoor use. Hardness is arrived at by longer firing at higher temperatures. This causes the grains of the clay to fuse and the pores to close, making the brick impenetrable by water; and as with so many things in outdoor construction, water and ice are the big enemies of brick. If a brick is capable of absorbing more than 8 percent of its weight in water, it will crack or spall (chip) or flake apart when the absorbed water freezes. So impermeability by water is critical.

A visit to a brickyard may dazzle you (or daunt you) at first with the huge assortment of types, sizes, colors, and costs. But when you zero in on the kinds that are actually suited to landscape construction, your range of choices becomes more manageable. They include two basic types:

Building bricks come in many grades, depending on whether they are intended for indoor or outdoor use. For outdoor walls, the best bricks are the ones sold as "building brick type SW" — that is, building brick that will stand up to severe weathering.

Bricks, old and new. Below left: moss softens the running-bond pattern of old red bricks. Below right: brick soldiers are set flush with grade as edging for newly laid pavement.

Pavers are manufactured expressly for use in paving, and if paving is your goal you should stick to them. Very dense and hard, pavers are designed for extra-low water absorption and extra-high compressive strength: i.e., resistance to crushing.

Whether you are working with building bricks or pavers, you'll probably find a rich selection of colors and textures available. Your choice will be dictated partly by your own likes and dislikes; partly by the materials and colors with which you want to harmonize, such as those of your house or drive or other existing landscape structures; and partly by the functions the bricks are to fulfill. You'll see colors varying from pale cream, through golden yellows, to oranges, reds, and browns that range from russet to deep purplish hues. I prefer the middle to darker range in the red to brown hues. The many textures of brick include smooth, scored, combed or roughened, sandy or slick. All these textures result from the machinery used in the manufacturing process, where mold surfaces, extruding machines, or cutting devices leave their imprints on the wet clay before the bricks are fired. For outdoor use, I tend to favor a sand mold finish. This is produced when sand is sprinkled in the mold as butter is spread in a baking pan, to make the mold release the brick easily when it's overturned after baking. The grains of sand give the brick a slightly softened, worn appearance, unlike the more crisp surfaces obtained by other cutting or molding methods.

Although colors and finishes are a matter of your own taste and judgment, I will give you one firm word of advice about brick: don't buy salvaged brick for outdoor use. Old bricks may look charming, with their subtly toned colors and battered shapes. They may even be cheap, although that is by no means the rule. But they come from unpredictable or unknown sources and may be of many different degrees of hardness. If they're really old, they are almost certain not to be as hard-fired as bricks must be to endure the weather.

I learned this lesson the hard way. Every spring my patio is a shambles of cracked and flaking bricks — because I paved it with lovely old bricks that were never intended to stand up to rain, snow, ice, and the deep freezes of winter. That was before I knew better.

Designing with Brick As I've already said, there is an almost limitless variety of types of brick — and that goes for dimensions as well as colors and textures. The most common, however, are two standardized sets of measurements.

Brick sizes Bricks sized 4 by 8 by 1⅝ to 2¼ inches are often dry-laid and tightly fitted. Their 4 by 8–inch dimensions are the basis for the sizing of the other standard type, "modular" bricks.

Modular bricks measure 3⅝ by 7⅝ by 2¼ inches. With a little arithmetic you can see that a modular brick laid with ⅜-inch mortar joints or grouts will fit the 4 by 8–inch module.

The reason that standard sizes come under the heading of designing is that whatever you build, you'll have to compute quite carefully the dimensions and construction method before you can decide on what kind of bricks to get and how many of them. The numbers of bricks *without* mortar joints to make up one square foot of paved surface are:

Brick size	*Bricks per sq. ft.*
4 × 8 inches (flat)	4.5
3⅝ × 7⅝ inches (flat)	5.2
2¼ × 7⅝ inches (on edge)	8.4

Trimming the rough edge of a brick to fit a space in the pattern — a job to avoid as much as possible.

Bricklaying patterns There are many, many patterns you can follow when you lay out brick. Sometimes the most delightful effects are created by a combination of patterns; sometimes a single traditional pattern is the best. It depends on the context. The most familiar and widely used patterns are the classic running bond, stacked (or jack-on-jack), herringbone, and basketweave. These and some less traditional patterns and combinations are shown in the illustrations on page 238.

All these patterns can be accomplished with either standard 4 by 8–inch pavers dry-laid with butted joints, or modular bricks using ⅜-inch mortar joints. But if you use the smaller modular bricks dry-laid, only the running, stacked, and herringbone patterns are feasible, since the other patterns require that the width of each brick be exactly half its length. To make matters a little more complicated, if you use mortar joints with the full-size 4 by 8–inch pavers, forget the basketweave patterns: the width of the joints will throw off the overall fit.

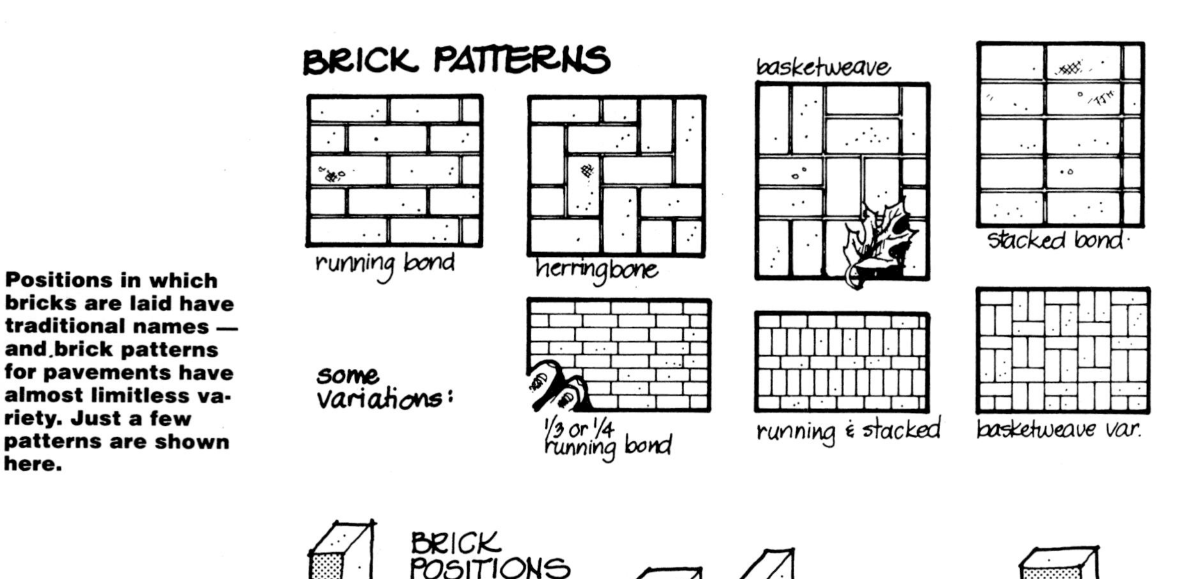

Positions in which bricks are laid have traditional names — and brick patterns for pavements have almost limitless variety. Just a few patterns are shown here.

Bricks can be laid up in walls, edgings, or pavements in different positions, called soldier, stretcher, header, and rowlock. Each has its uses and advantages depending on the situation, and playing around with alternatives is another pleasant facet of working with brick.

Brick Substitutes Your researches in your local brickyard will also introduce you to at least some of the many bricklike modular materials that are on the market. Asphalt and concrete "bricks" and blocks come in a wide variety of shapes and sizes. I have seldom found these very satisfactory for residential landscape use, however. Their prevalent colors are somewhat synthetic-looking grays, greens, and reds that (for me) do not coexist happily with natural landscape surroundings. And their textures are apt to be equally unappealing. But as you shop around you may just discover some locally available concrete or asphalt block that will suit your taste and pocketbook. So don't write these products off entirely until you have spent some time looking.

Plants by Design

NOTABLE FRUIT DISPLAY

Fruit with Unusual Form or Size

Honey locust (*Gleditsia triacanthos*)
Sweet gum (*Liquidambar styraciflua*)
Tulip tree (*Liriodendron tulipifera*)

Fruit with Notable Color

Red maple (*Acer rubrum*)
Barberries (*Berberis* spp.)
Bittersweet (*Celastrus scandens*)
White fringe tree (*Chionanthus virginicus*)
Dogwoods (*Cornus* spp.)
Cotoneasters (*Cotoneaster* spp.)
Hawthorns (*Crataegus* spp.)
Winged euonymus (*Euonymus alata*)
Winterberry (*Ilex verticillata*)
Hollies (*Ilex* spp.)
Privet (*Ligustrum* spp.)

The color of viburnums' fall fruit often makes as great a contribution as that of their spring bloom.

Notable Fruit Display *(continued)*

Honeysuckle (*Lonicera* spp.)
Crabapples (*Malus* spp.)
Bayberry (*Myrica pensylvanica*)
Firethorns (*Pyracantha* spp.)
Sumac (*Rhus* spp.)
Roses (*Rosa* spp.)
Elderberry (*Sambucus canadensis*)
Korean mountain ash (*Sorbus alnifolia*)
Blueberry (*Vaccinium* spp.)
Viburnum (*Viburnum* spp.)

Fruit Remaining into Winter

Red chokeberry (*Aronia arbutifolia*)
Barberries (*Berberis* spp.)
Bittersweet (*Celastrus scandens*)
Hawthorns (*Crataegus* spp.)
Winterberry (*Ilex verticillata*)
Bayberry (*Myrica pensylvanica*)
Scarlet firethorn (*Pyracantha coccinea*)
Meadow rose (*Rosa blanda*)
Rugosa rose (*Rosa rugosa*)
Coralberry (*Symphoricarpos orbiculatus*)
European cranberrybush viburnum (*Viburnum opulus*)
American cranberrybush viburnum (*Viburnum trilobum*)

Detailed information and recommended varieties can be found in Part III.

LANDSCAPE TASKS FOR SEPTEMBER

Starting New Lawns What with cool weather, plenty of rain, and the fact that grasses are entering a natural growth surge now, this is the best time of the year to get new grass started. (Another good time is the April growth period.) Whether a whole new lawn or a patch here and there, the basic procedures are the same. Cultivate the top 6 or 8 inches of soil. Work in lime and peat moss if needed (see Soil Testing in March). Add a high-nitrogen complete fertilizer like 10-6-4 or 20-15-10, or an organic fertilizer such as manure or cottonseed meal. Rake the soil smooth, roll it, then sow a good mixture of bluegrass and fescues that are adapted to your climate. A grass-seed spreader does the most even job of distribution. Rake lightly to cover the seeds with a little soil, then roll the area again.

For a week or so, sprinkle the newly seeded grass as often as necessary to keep it evenly moist until it sprouts. If traffic is a problem, protect the new lawn from dogs and passersby by spreading light brush, bramble cuttings, netting, or other barriers over it.

September Lawn Feeding If your lawn is already in place, this fall growing season is the proper time to feed and lime it. The April Plants for a Purpose section mentioned the fertilizing requirements of lawn grasses, but here's a reminder to keep you on schedule.

In the Northeast, where soil pH tends to drift lower (more acid) year by year, it's a good idea to apply 50 pounds of ground limestone per 1000 square feet of lawn in early spring every three or four years. (For your lawn's measurements, the base plan made in Part I is a helpful reference.) Lawn grasses like a minimum pH of 6.0, preferably 6.5.

As for feeding, there are many commercial forms of slow-release, high-nitrogen synthetic fertilizer available, and they carry their own instructions as to quantities per square footage of lawn. I tend to prefer cottonseed meal (although it's more expensive than the man-made products), which is very slow releasing and contains goodly amounts of phosphorus and potash as well as nitrogen. Fifteen pounds per 1000 square feet is ample. For an extra boost, you can also spread 5 pounds of bonemeal per 1000 square feet, to add extra phosphorus for strong stiff growth. Or alternatively, you can forget all the above and use dried or well-rotted cow manure at the rate of 100 pounds per 1000 square feet. My wife's grandmother always relied on manure from the local dairy farm, and she had the best lawn in her neighborhood.

Lawn Mowing Keep mowing, but now you can lower the height of the blade to 1½ inches if you want. Annual weed seeds are no longer sprouting; burning sun is no longer such a threat; and it will be easier to rake leaves off short grass as the fall wears on.

Lily-of-the-Valley Division Lily-of-the-valley will grow more thickly and bloom more lavishly if you divide the pips every three or four years — and now is the moment to do it. Dig everything up; choose the huskiest-looking pips; and replant them 6 inches apart from each other, just below the soil's surface. Enrich the soil with bonemeal and some well-rotted manure.

Wisteria If your wisteria failed to bloom, root-prune it (see March Landscape Tasks) this month. Then give it a high-phosphate feeding such as bonemeal, rock phosphate, superphosphate, or a commercial mix like 6-18-6. Leave it alone over the winter, then prune it drastically in February or March. The results will amaze you.

Ripening Harvests Each September-ripening garden fruit has its own set of needs.

Grapes ripen well in the heavy shade of their foliage, but do not ripen further after picking — so leave them on the vine until they're practically bursting.

Apples need bright sun to ripen. You may actually want to thin the foliage of the trees to let the sunlight get at the fruit. Apples should not be picked until they're ripe: that moment comes when there's no green color left (except with green apples, of course) and when a quick turn of the wrist pulls the apple loose.

Pears, by contrast, want to be picked while they are still firm, a week or so before they would have softened. Ripen them indoors in a cool, dark place.

Planting Trees and Shrubs

Deciduous ornamental trees and shrubs Most kinds can be planted in the fall. (For a list of exceptions, see the April Landscape Tasks.)

Evergreens Early this month is the optimum time to plant narrow-leaved evergreen trees or shrubs, or to move them from one place to another.

Broad-leaved evergreens Although early spring is by far the season of choice, broad-leaved evergreens such as mountain laurel, boxwood, rhododendrons, some evergreen azaleas, hollies, and so on can be planted in early fall if you are careful. Once in place they should be given a deep watering and a thick acid mulch such as pine needles, oak leaves,

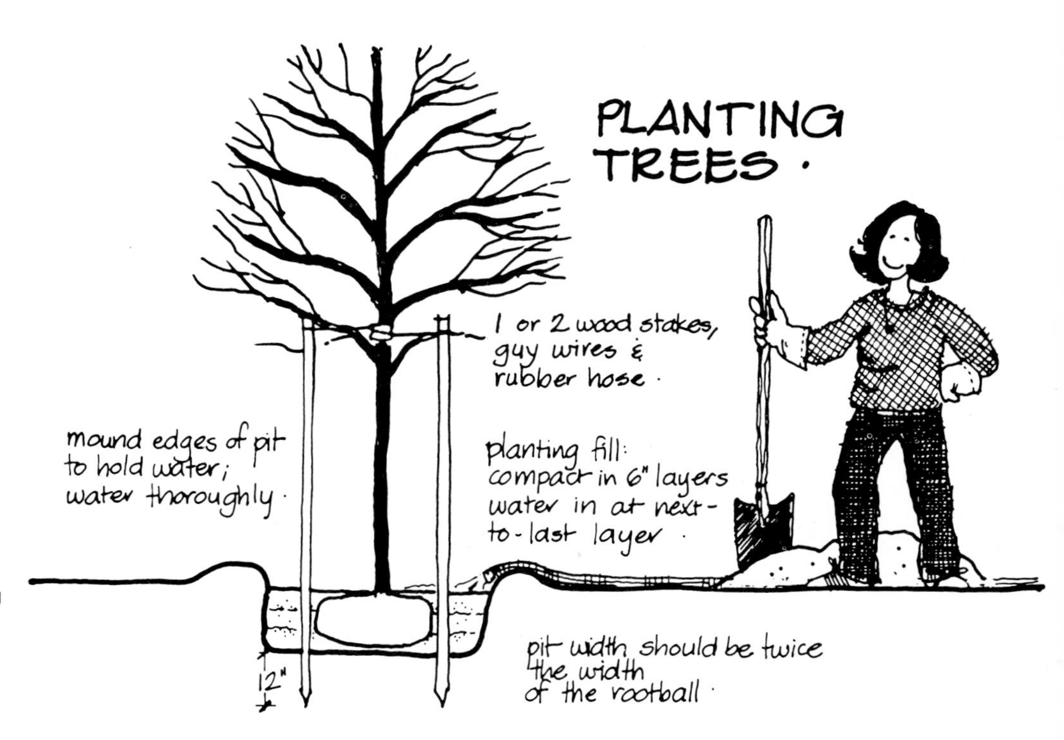

Planting a tree: be certain the pit is big enough and the soil is good enough.

or wood chips; and in a windy or sunny location they will benefit from an antidesiccant spray.

For all of the above, prepare in advance the place where the plant is to go. You want to be able to install it promptly after you bring it home or remove it from its present location. Make a planting hole twice the diameter of the root ball or container and about the same depth. For a bareroot plant, the hole should be about a foot wider than the spread of the roots, and just a bit deeper than they reach.

Enrich the soil you've excavated from the hole with manure and compost or peat moss, about one-fifth to one-quarter the volume of the soil, to have it ready for backfilling. Roughen and loosen up the soil around the sides and especially at the bottom of the hole: you want a gradual transition between existing topsoil (and/or subsoil) and the enriched mixture you'll be putting back in.

If you are putting in a tree bareroot, take care not to let its roots dry out while it awaits planting (see April for some suggestions on keeping roots moist).

If the plant is balled-and-burlapped, you can leave the burlap on (provided it's not plastic; in that event remove it). Real burlap will rot away in the ground and the roots will grow right through. If the plant is in a container, you may possibly be able to tap it out; more probably, you'll have to cut the container off with heavy shears or metal cutters.

Set the root ball or roots into the hole so that the plant's stem emerges from the ground at the same level as it did in the nursery. Work earth gently but thoroughly in among the roots of a bareroot plant. Fill in the earth in 6-inch layers, firming down each layer. Once the plant is settled, remove the cords that bound the burlap, if it was wrapped, and loosen the burlap around the top. With some extra soil, build a saucer around the plant to act as a reservoir for water. Then water thoroughly.

With a balled-and-burlapped deciduous tree, I usually cut out about a third of the branches after planting, so as not to overburden the already stressed root system. The tree recovers rapidly.

In fall planting, you should usually stake young trees with trunks 1 inch or more in diameter. A sturdy stake driven into the soil, plus a rope or guy wire run through a section of rubber hose (so as not to scrape the bark off), will keep the tree from swaying in autumn and winter gales and exposing its roots to the air. A single stake should be placed at the side from which the prevailing winter wind blows; or double stakes, for a tree with a trunk over 2 inches thick, on both sides. Stakes should stay in place for the first two years.

Another winter precaution: mulch or mound soil around the bases of plants newly installed at this season.

During the first few months especially, and throughout its first two years, make sure the newly installed tree or shrub is regularly watered, either by rainfall or by you. Getting it well established now will make all the difference to its long-term health and beauty.

Review and Planning While the successes and failures of the past growing season are fresh in your mind, make a map, list, or chart to remind yourself what to change and what new things to try next year.

OCT

Landscaping Opportunities
Container Landscaping

Plants for a Purpose
Broad-leaved Evergreens

Materials and Construction
Terraces and Patios

Plants by Design
Colorful Fall Foliage

Landscape Tasks for October

Foliage begins to turn color sooner in low-lying places.

This month I'm looking in two directions: outdoors, and ahead into winter. This is the season for really splendid fall color. The autumn foliage in the northeastern United States is about as spectacular as any in the world (only parts of our West Coast, northern Japan, and southwestern Europe have anything to rival it); and the trees and shrubs that produce this brilliant show should be a part of every planned landscape in this area.

October is the last dependable month for major outdoor construction, and the terrace and patio section here will give you ideas for an enjoyable outdoor living space for next spring, summer, and fall. Container plants, ideal for patios, are portable and versatile enough to contribute to every part of the landscape in every season, and that's the subject I'll talk about first.

Also, casting an eye ahead to the coming months, I'll introduce some of the handsomest plants of the winter landscape (and all year round): broad-leaved evergreens.

Landscaping Opportunities

CONTAINER LANDSCAPING

This rooftop garden shows the amazingly lush effects possible with containers. Baskets and pots of all sizes work together wonderfully here.

Containers add another dimension to a landscape even if you have plenty of ground space for planting — and in some places where the ground just won't do, they alone can make planting possible. They are the only answer to gardening on rooftops, stoops, or balconies. They are a wonderful solution to the problem of putting greenery or flowers in paved areas. They're just the thing if you want to break up an expanse of terrace and lawn but don't want to dig a bed. And they are mobile, so you can shift them to different locations as the spirit moves, or take them indoors for special occasions. Besides, many plants really show themselves off best of all in a pot or box or urn that brings them closer to eye level and gives them something from which their lower fronds or branches can gracefully hang down.

There's just one drawback to container gardening in any northern climate — winter. The cold does a job on many container plantings, for two reasons. First, few normal landscape plants can tolerate root temperatures below 20°F; but in a container outdoors, a plant will be exposed to cold far greater than that — usually with fatal results. Second, when soil freezes it expands, and a rigid container (earthenware, metal, plastic, even concrete) will crack.

So if you want to use containers for permanent plantings like shrubbery or perennials, you must have a winter plan. Here are a few ideas:

- Hardy yews and junipers in good big wooden planters will usually survive.
- Hollies, hardy azaleas, and broad-leaved evergreens will need shelter and a site chosen for minimal temperature extremes.
- For smaller shrubs, a greenhouse or coldframe is great for overwintering. Or you can remove hardy shrubs from their containers and bury them in the ground in an out-of-the-way spot for the winter.
- Nonhardy shrubs and some flowers can even be brought indoors to a cool, bright window.

- If the plants are neither hardy nor transportable, you'll have to discard them, store the containers in a dry place, and start again next year.

Designing with Containers Here you are bounded only by the limits of your imagination (and possibly your budget). There are scads of options both in plant materials and in container materials, designs, and arrangements. I won't attempt to cover them all, but again, here are the general guidelines I follow:

- I like to use groups of containers of different sizes, with the largest to the rear so I can build an ascending foliage mass. It often makes sense to use larger plants in the larger containers, as background for the whole arrangement.
- For a look of restraint combined with fullness, stick to one or perhaps two kinds of plants in the same grouping or large container.
- For a more lively or splashy effect, you can combine several varieties of plants in a grouping or a large container. If they're together in one container just make sure that it is big enough to house everything comfortably; see container dimensions below.
- Not all your pots need be ornamental in themselves. It's nice to have handsome wooden tubs, Italian ceramics, or elaborately molded concrete planters; but camouflage can give you flexibility, save weight, and save lots of money. For instance, a really big tub or sawed-off barrel can be given a homemade facelift. Or a cheap metal or plastic container looks fine inside an attractive woven basket.

Container Specifications Whether you build your own (see below) or choose from the enormous range of ready-made containers on the market — glazed or plain terra cotta, concrete, Plexiglas, plastic, cast iron, metal, wood, or stone — the basic criteria for their design are the same. Size, weight, and (as usual) drainage are the major issues.

Size Allow the right cubic footage of soil for the plant(s) you plan to grow. Too large a container will look ungainly in relation to the plant, will be unnecessarily heavy, and may present drainage problems. But too small a container is a more common and more serious problem. A container too small for its plant will cause the plant to become root-bound. This will make the plant look sickly, stunt its growth, and possibly kill it. Ascertain first what kind of plant you're going to put in a container; find out from the plant's supplier what its required volume of soil will be; then choose a generous-sized container to house it.

Shallow soil dries out quickly, so as a general rule I never use a soil depth of less than 10 inches; I prefer 12 inches as a minimum. A window-box-type planter should be at least 10 by 10 by 36 or 42 inches. Beware of bowl- or dish-shaped containers where the top flares outwards. The thin soil around the circumference will dry out much faster than the rest and will be useless for growing anything except perhaps succulents that tolerate near-arid conditions.

Weight If portability is a goal, consider both the weight of the container itself and the weight of the volume of soil it is designed to hold. Soil (including its moisture) weighs about 100 pounds per cubic foot. Lightweight planting mixes containing perlite as well as lots of peat moss weigh much less: 50 to 80 pounds per cubic foot when wet. All the same, you can see that a container a foot and a half square, with a plant growing in it, will be no picnic to move. Large planters, if they have to be moved, can be transferred on dollies. You can improvise with rollers and boards, or drag the container on a burlap bag or toboggan.

Drainage Water must not be allowed to accumulate in the bottom of a container, where it will cut off the oxygen supply to the roots and discourage or even kill the plant. Every planter should have plentiful drainage holes in its base. I don't recommend putting shards or pebbles in the bottom of containers for outdoor plants, however. This can cause too-swift drainage and drying out of the lower roots, particularly in hot weather. Instead, I put small pieces of screening over the drain holes.

In addition, a well-drained soil mix is a must for healthy plants. My favorite mix consists of one-third good garden loam, one-third sharp builder's sand, and one-third sphagnum peat moss. To lighten this soil, I'll often make up the basic mix, then add another one-third perlite (by volume). For acid-loving plants I reduce the loam and increase the peat moss by 10 percent each.

Often an old artifact makes a good container, as with this copper receptacle from England.

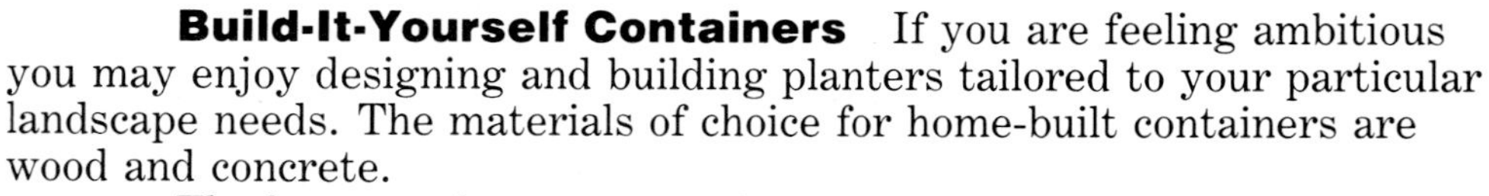

Build-It-Yourself Containers If you are feeling ambitious you may enjoy designing and building planters tailored to your particular landscape needs. The materials of choice for home-built containers are wood and concrete.

The best woods to use are the naturally rot-resistant cedar, redwood, or cypress. Or you can use wood that has been pressure-treated with preservative. Marine or exterior-grade plywood will also perform fairly well, although you have to cover up the raw edges to prevent water from seeping in. Alternatively you can have a galvanized metal liner made to fit your wooden container, which will make any kind of wood last much longer. Be sure that all metal hardware (nails, bolts, etc.) is galvanized; plain steel will rust out, and cause unsightly stains in the process.

Large molded concrete containers are generally beyond the scope of a home construction project. Small concrete troughs are certainly feasible, however. They can serve as beautiful settings for miniature plantings; or hold low-growing perennials or dwarf conifers or herbs; or even make excellent birdbaths.

Plants for Containers For many gardeners, the ultimate in container gardening is bonsai: the Japanese art of dwarfing large trees by pruning their roots and foliage and training them into carefully predetermined shapes. These miniature plantings make a fascinating and very time-consuming horticultural hobby; but they are not especially useful for the average patio or front stoop, since bonsai trees have to be studied up close in a properly scaled setting. They also need winter protection and careful monitoring of light and water. If bonsai is your interest, some good sources of further information are listed in the Further Reference.

Apart from bonsai, however, it's the smaller and slower-growing trees and shrubs that are best suited to growing in planters. When they become root-bound you can root-prune them (shave off the outermost 2 inches of roots all around), then replant in the same pot with new soil. Or repot them in a bigger container if you want them to continue growing.

The best adapted of all are dwarf and very slow-growing varieties — evergreen or deciduous, flowering or not — and small plants like ground covers. (The August Plants for a Purpose list focuses on trees and shrubs for small spaces, many well suited to containers; and the June list includes ground-cover plants.) With these you won't face frequent repottings, and the plants themselves will be contented rather than permanently thwarted in their natural growth patterns. A contented container plant is easy to maintain, so that with a minimum of annual upkeep you will have a charming decorative element for your landscape.

Plants for a Purpose

BROAD-LEAVED EVERGREENS

With winter around the corner, this is an appropriate time to start thinking about winter greenery — and broad-leaved evergreens' unique contribution.

When I think of broad-leaved evergreens in their full glory, I must admit it is the southern landscape that comes to mind. Southern hollies and magnolias, among others, are magnificent full-sized trees that stay green all year. The magnolia is surely the queen of broad-leaved evergreens.

Yet in the Northeast, those broad-leaved evergreens that will stand up to the climate are especially precious. They afford color and a sense of life even in the bleakest winter weather. Their textures and forms are utterly different from those of other northern winter greenery — the conifers, or "narrow-leaved" evergreens. Used as hedge plants, broad-leaved evergreens like boxwood or boxleaf holly do just as great a job in the winter as in the summer. And when spring comes, the flowering broad-leaved shrubs — azaleas, laurels, andromedas, rhododendrons — burst forth with blossoms in the most luscious array of colors. They are breathtaking. With all the varieties and cultivars that are available, you can plan for a sequence of bloom that will last from April into July, in as wide a spectrum of colors as you like, from white to blue-violet to pink to yellow.

Rich varieties of forms and foliar textures are available in rhododendrons.

In the North, however, there are no broad-leaved trees, as such, that will survive the winter except one or two species of hollies. So for Zones 4, 5, and 6, we're really talking about shrubs. For the most part they belong to a small group of genera: *Rhododendron* (which includes what we call azaleas as well as rhododendrons), *Ilex* (hollies), *Buxus* (boxwoods), and *Pieris* (andromedas or pieris).

Designing with Broad-leaved Evergreens There are some people who dislike rhododendrons and some of the other broad-leaved evergreens because they look so wizened in winter. A friend once said, "Rhododendrons make me feel cold just looking at them." I see what she meant — rhododendron leaves do curl up in self-defense against midwinter's dry cold. It is also true that in severe winters some boxleaf hollies and boxwoods have a tendency to turn a sickly yellow-brown, making you wonder if they will ever return to green again. American holly and the various types of mahonia are susceptible to a depressing brownish-gray tipburn. As for some of the evergreen azaleas, they simply drop their leaves altogether if things get too cold for them, and grow a new crop the following spring.

Yet these drawbacks have never bothered me particularly. It seems to me that the many assets of broad-leaved evergreens more than compensate for their one flaw of looking pinched in cold weather. Often, too, I believe that people's aversion to broad-leaved evergreens stems from unfortunate choices of location, which are by no means the plants' fault. It used to be very common for rhododendrons, laurels, and others of the larger broad-leaved shrubs to be promoted as "foundation plantings." So when people looked out their windows in winter the first thing they saw was a dismal mass of curled, leathery-looking, dark-green leaves. In fact it might be the only thing they saw, in older houses where the shrubbery had been allowed to get somewhat overgrown. No wonder that rhododendron phobia became a common malady.

There's a simple solution to this complaint Don't use rhododendrons or other large broad-leaved evergreens right around the house. (They don't do their best in hot south- or west-facing locations anyway. If you want them around the house, stick to the north or east sides for the best results.) Instead, think of broad-leaved evergreens as wonderful plants for the long view. They're great at the edge of a lawn under tall trees, for instance, where they'll get slightly filtered sun in summer and a modicum of shelter in winter. Not to mention the possibility of a nice acid mulch in the form of falling leaves or needles every autumn. Even if you don't have many tall trees, any reasonably distant location will do fine. Just so that you don't have to stare at forlorn curled-up or tipburned leaves right outside your window all winter long.

I have to confess to a partiality to broad-leaved evergreens in the wild. If you've ever been lucky enough to come upon a mass of native rosebay rhododendrons or mountain laurel flourishing by a streambed in the woods, you may agree. There is nothing quite so majestic, so completely and prosperously at home as these plants. They grow to a size and stature that make them more like trees than shrubs.

Even if you can't provide a wilderness, keep in mind how happy these plants are in a roomy setting, and avoid placing them in very tight arrangements or in very rigidly structured surroundings. Try to plan for a variety of textures. Combine smaller-leaved plants with the larger-leaved ones, and work into your design some deciduous shrubs — which could be deciduous azaleas — to add lighter summer color and provide airy breathing spaces in the winter composition. Provide for well-spaced blooming times and a variety of colors, too. See if you can combine some very early plants like andromeda and the earliest rhododendrons, some middle-blooming azaleas, and some late-blooming laurel, azaleas, and rhododendrons. Think about a palette of colors, perhaps from white to rose to red, or from lavender to deep blue-violet.

Buying Broad-leaved Evergreens The first thing you will learn when you start shopping for broad-leaved evergreens is that the range of choices is vast. There are always new cultivars being introduced and newly fashionable varieties being promoted. My best advice: seek out tried and true varieties whose virtues are well proven and whose needs you can easily determine. There's generally nothing like a plant that has stood the test of generations of gardeners and thousands of geographical locations.

Inkberry is good for informal hedges, and its black fruits are true to its name.

Different hollies have different fruit habits and leaf forms, as in longstalk holly (above left) and American holly variety (above right).

The broad-leaved evergreens listed here are all good and hardy in the north. They all will do their best, however, if you can give them at least some degree of protection from the bitterest winter wind. Some like full sun; others will prosper in filtered shade. The rhododendrons, azaleas, laurel, and andromeda will bloom approximately in the time periods indicated in their descriptions in Part III, so that you can decide on a rough calendar of bloom for your garden. But don't try to calculate this too precisely. Every plant has its vagaries, and all plants' blooming schedules are contingent on the weather of seasons past as well as present.

Broad-leaved Evergreens for Year-round Appeal

AZALEAS (EVERGREEN)
- Herbert azalea (*Rhododendron kaempferi* 'Herbert')
- Hinocrimson azalea (*Rhododendron obtusum* 'Hinocrimson')
- Hinodegiri azalea (*Rhododendron obtusum* 'Hinodegiri')
- Delaware Valley White azalea (*Rhododendron* 'Delaware Valley White')

Littleleaf boxwood (*Buxus microphylla* vars.)
Common boxwood (*Buxus sempervirens* vars.)
Boxleaf holly (*Ilex crenata convexa* vars.)
Inkberry (*Ilex glabra* vars.)
Blue holly (*Ilex meserveae* vars.)
American holly (*Ilex opaca*)
Longstalk holly (*Ilex pedunculosa*)
Mountain laurel (*Kalmia latifolia* vars.)
Coast leucothoe (*Leucothoe axillaris*)
Drooping leucothoe (*Leucothoe fontanesiana*)
Oregon holly-grape (*Mahonia aquifolium*)
Canby paxistima (*Paxistima canbyi*)
Mountain andromeda or pieris (*Pieris floribunda*)
Japanese andromeda or pieris (*Pieris japonica* vars.)
Laland firethorn (*Pyracantha coccinea* 'Lalandei')

RHODODENDRONS
- Boule de Neige rhododendron (*Rhododendron* 'Boule de Neige')
- Carolina rhododendron (*Rhododendron carolinianum*)
- Catawba rhododendron (*Rhododendron catawbiense* vars.)
- Chionoides rhododendron (*Rhododendron* 'Chionoides')
- Scintillation rhododendron (*Rhododendron fortunei* 'Scintillation')
- Wilson rhododendron (*Rhododendron laetivirens*)

Broad-leaved Evergreens for Year-round Appeal *(continued)*

Rosebay rhododendron or great laurel (*Rhododendron maximum*)
Nova Zembla rhododendron (*Rhododendron* 'Nova Zembla')
P.J.M. hybrid rhododendrons (*Rhododendron* 'P.J.M. Hybrids')
Purple gem rhododendron (*Rhododendron* 'Purple Gem')

Detailed information and recommended varieties can be found in Part III.

Materials and Construction
TERRACES AND PATIOS

October may have its frosty nights, but much of this month is truly delightful outdoors, just right for sunning on the patio. The joy of a terrace or patio is that it extends your daily living space. It's a cleaner, cozier, usually more private place than the rest of your landscape. A terrace or patio makes an enticing adjunct to the house for many months of the year, and I highly recommend that you have at least one — or more than one, if possible.

Planning and Design The best place for a terrace or patio is on the south side of the house. There you'll get the most use out of it spring, summer, and fall. The west side is a good second choice, although it misses the morning sun. Both south- and west-facing terraces need at least partial summer shading. Terraces facing east or north will be cool in summer, but less welcoming in spring and fall.

As with any outdoor construction, allow plenty of room. One of the most common failings of terraces and patios is being built too small. Start by thinking about an area double the size of your living room. You may find, when you stake it out on the ground, that that's really too big or impractical in your setting; if so, at least try to provide access to an adjoining lawn area that will take care of overflowing people and furniture when needed.

Overflow areas don't have to be on the same level as the basic

For entertaining on a small raised terrace or patio, it's important to plan an adjacent area where people can overflow.

terrace or patio. In fact there's no law that says the terrace or patio itself has to be on a single, continuous, level plane. That approach often works fine; but in many cases it works equally well to break spaces up with changes in elevation — with a broad flight of steps, for instance, or a planting bed or a pocket of trees.

The essential difference between a terrace and a patio is the amount of enclosure. A terrace is a generally level space abutting or nearby the house, but open to views both to and from the surrounding landscape. In addition to being an outdoor living room, a terrace often serves as the visual transition between the house and its larger environment. Therefore it is important that the terrace's location, size, proportions, materials, edge treatments, and so forth be in keeping with the landscape as a whole — as well as with the house to which it is linked.

A patio is also a level outdoor space, but by definition it is enclosed on at least three sides, either by the house or partly by house, partly by walls or other structures. Patios trace their ancestry to European courtyards and cloisters; they migrated to this country with the Spanish settlers of the Southwest. They carry on a tradition where a central garden was embraced and sheltered by living quarters. A patio is thus more closely related to the interior functions of the house and somewhat less involved with the surrounding landscape than a terrace. Often a patio can be relatively small in scale. The intimacy of its connection with the house means that details of its design and construction should be thought out with great care. Should there be a fence enclosing it, or a solid or perforated wall? How about a vine-grown trellis for shade over part of the area? How much privacy, how much shelter from wind? How much square footage for children's play or for plantings or for entertaining? The responses to these kinds of questions depend on the character of your house and its surroundings, the needs of the people who'll use the patio, the available space, and of course the available budget.

Paving Materials If walls — or absence of them — define the difference between a patio and a terrace, floors define the similarity. Both patios and terraces are floored, or paved, usually with something other than grass. That's what gives them their delightfully livable quality. The focus of this section is on the floors themselves.

Should your patio or terrace pavement be warm-colored or cool, fine-textured or coarse? The first thing to consider is the relationship between the color and texture of the paving material and those of the house: the two should make sense together. Also think about practical effects. A dark color in a sunny exposure will absorb heat and be scorching on a hot summer day. A very pale color in a south-facing spot will reflect a lot of light, sometimes blindingly so.

Then there's the question of formality or informality. For a tidy, formal appearance, the components of a pavement should be regular and repetitive, like brick, modular stone, or tiles. The joints between paving modules should be tight and evenly spaced. If a casual or countrified air is your goal, use irregularly shaped and sized paving materials like slate or bluestone slabs and lay them in random patterns.

After you've dealt with these preliminary issues, consider availability and cost — both the cost of the materials and the cost (in dollars or in time) of installing them. Your choices of design and materials will have a lot to do with the degree to which you're going to do the work yourself.

Time and money sometimes become tradeoffs, particularly where skills like stonecutting or bricklaying are concerned.

For instance, giant granite slabs are murder to handle. Modular brick is comparatively easy. Or you can order concrete delivered and lay it yourself without too much difficulty. If price is no object, or if do-it-yourself time is nonexistent, then you'll be thinking in terms of hiring the whole project out to a contractor. That opens up a great latitude of possible materials, approaches, and costs.

Again, beware of fantastic bargains on used materials. What looks like a bargain now may be a big liability in the long run. A friend of mine built his front walk out of irregularly shaped salvaged cobblestones; they didn't cost anything at the outset, but the cracks between them never fail to throw visitors off balance, particularly those wearing high-heeled shoes or no shoes at all. And he wrecks at least one snow shovel every year.

Modular paving materials include brick, cement blocks, bluestone, slate, and granite (among others). Each comes in the form of regularly sized and shaped blocks, usually rectangular or square, and well adapted to an infinite variety of patterns and designs. Irregularly sized and shaped stone pieces are also widely used to create informal or artistic effects.

Modular pavings can be wet-laid (cemented together with mortar) or dry-laid. Always use an edging with dry-laid modular paving, to prevent creep. For brick pavements, an attractive and easy edging is a row of brick "soldiers" set on end in the earth. Or use rot-resistant wood like cypress, heart redwood, or heart cedar; or pressure-treated fir or pine. Granite cobblestones or modular masonry blocks also serve well.

Stone I recommend that you have all stone cut for you by your supplier, particularly if you're planning on an irregular or random pattern. The supplier should also provide you with a joint pattern for a random design, because these are very hard to work out until you've had a good deal of training or experience. A rule of thumb for a good random pattern is that the same joint line should run along no more than 3 stones' sides before changing direction.

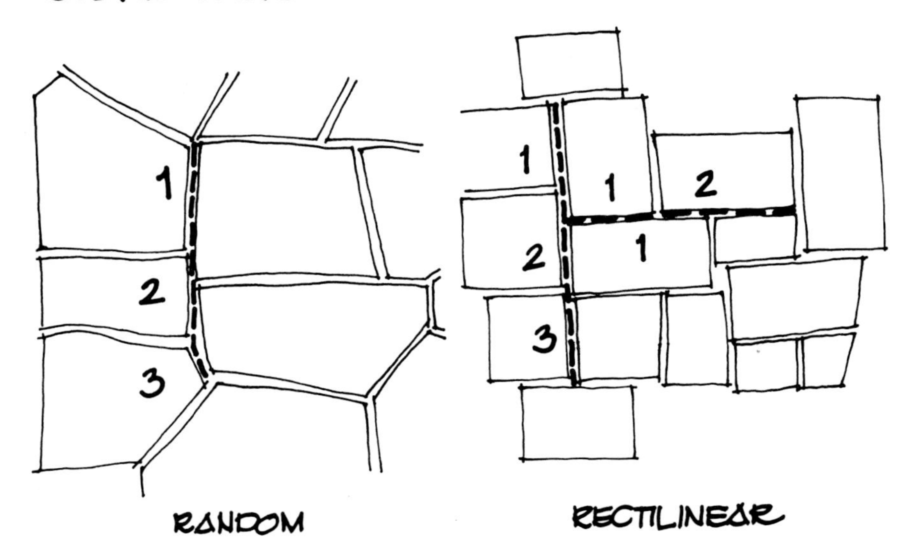

Never let a joint run along the sides of more than three paving stones in a row.

Bluestone set with butt joints on a gravel bed makes a refined surface for outdoor living.

Take with you to the supplier a cardboard cutout representing any curved or unusually shaped objects around which the stone pavement will have to fit. The supplier can use your cutout as a template.

There are some bluestones and slates you can cut yourself, and you may enjoy trying it, particularly if just a few cuts are called for. I always make sure to buy at least 10 percent more stone than the job calls for if I'm going to be cutting it, to make up for disasters and ordinary waste. Use a masonry blade in a skill saw to score the stone; then break it off the rest of the way with a rubber or wooden mallet. Or for really professional cuts, you can rent a water-cooled, table-mounted masonry saw.

Brick Unfortunately, the hard-baked pavers that are best suited to outdoor use are also very hard to cut. The best approach to cutting brick is to work out a pattern that cleverly incorporates all whole bricks with no ragged edges or gaps, so that you don't have to do any cutting at all. If you do have to cut a few, you can mark them with pencil and take them to your supplier to be trimmed down to size. To cut your own bricks, first practice on some waste samples until you feel competent. Use a mallet and "brick set," or brick chisel. Score the brick all the way around, then break it off with a sharp blow; or lay the brick on hard-packed wet sand and slice it in two with the chisel.

Granular paving Gravel, crushed stone or stone dust, crushed brick, ornamental stones such as river or beach pebbles, bark nuggets, or bark shreds: all these are what I call granular paving. They all make attractive surfaces, and they are all easy to install dry-laid. They do have certain liabilities, however. They're not suitable for use on sloped areas, where storms will wash them away, but only on level surfaces with good drainage. They're less easy to keep clean than harder surfaces, and weeds and grass invade them more swiftly. And they will "creep" unless you give them an edging to hold them in place. For edgings you can get specially made metal strips (Ryerson Steel) in 3⁄16 by 4–inch or 1⁄4 by 5–inch sizes. There are also several plastic edgings available, but in my opinion these are often too conspicuous. Most of them have a tube along the top edge that makes them feel and look bulky. They also tend to be so flexible that it's difficult to achieve a clean, unwavering line. But often the best solution to edging granular pavements is the same as for brick or stone: wood, cobblestones or masonry blocks, or bricks. These materials do the job they're intended for and enhance the overall appearance of the patio or terrace as well. With all materials, that final overall effect is something always to keep in mind.

Drainage As with every other phase of landscape construction, good surface and subsurface drainage is imperative for paved patios and terraces. Slope everything away from the house. Smooth-textured pavements — like concrete, or smooth stones or bricks laid in mortar over concrete — should be sloped at least 1 percent, or 1⁄8 inch per foot. More irregular surfaces, such as granular pavings, dry-laid brick or stone, or rough stone set in mortar, should be sloped at least 2 percent, i.e., 1⁄4 inch per foot.

If the surrounding soil offers plenty of absorption for runoff, simply sloping the pavement will be adequate. But if you have poorly drained soil, a high water table, or shallow soil over ledge, you should also provide drainage in the form of a drywell or a pipe to a storm drain.

Base Preparation You can't just slap paving down on unprepared earth. Thorough preparation of the underlying grade, as well as of the pavement's supporting and/or setting materials, is crucial to the finished appearance and durability of the pavement. The key word here is consistency. Beneath any kind of paving material there must be consistency of grades, of drainage, of compaction of soil. Otherwise you are bound to end up with uneven settling and cracking in due course.

A very common hazard is a site that is wholly or partly filled. Usually, the soil in the area of deepest fill is the most disturbed and the least compacted, and will therefore settle noticeably in the seasons after it's paved over. Make sure that fill goes in in 6-inch layers, with each layer watered and compacted evenly.

All pavements require some substrata under the surface material — usually well-tamped crusher-run (crushed stone and stone dust) or bank-run gravel. This table gives the requirements in a nutshell. There are, however, occasional situations where much of this preparation can be omitted, particularly for dry-laid pavements (brick, stone, or granular materials laid without cement). If you are lucky enough to have a porous sandy or gravelly soil and to live in an area where frost does not penetrate more than about a foot down, you can skip the base course of gravel or stone. Just prepare and compact the underlying surface evenly.

Base Preparations for Landscape Pavements

Paving Material	*Base*
Concrete	6 inches well-compacted gravel or crushed stone; base should extend 1 foot in all directions beyond edge of area to be paved.
Modular materials (stone, brick, concrete blocks, etc.)	*Wet-laid:* 6 inches well-compacted bank-run gravel or crushed stone, topped by 3- to 4-inch concrete base slab (reinforced with wire fabric mesh if necessary) and ¾-inch mortar setting bed. *Dry-laid:* 6 inches well-compacted gravel or crushed stone plus 1½-inch bed of sand or stone dust; edging to prevent creep.
Granular materials (gravel, crushed stone, ornamental stones, bark nuggets, etc.)	*Dry-laid:* 6 inches well-compacted crusher-run or bank-run gravel; edging to prevent creep.

Plants by Design

COLORFUL FALL FOLIAGE

Plants appearing in both yellow and red categories can have predominantly yellow, red, or purple coloration according to soil, sunlight, temperature, or a combination of variables.

YELLOW FOLIAGE

Small Trees

Shadblow, juneberry, or serviceberry (*Amelanchier* spp.)
Redbud (*Cercis canadensis*)
White fringe tree (*Chionanthus virginicus*)
Golden-rain tree (*Koelreuteria paniculata*)
Star magnolia (*Magnolia stellata*)

Medium to Large Trees

Norway maple (*Acer platanoides*)
River birch (*Betula nigra*)
Paper birch or canoe birch (*Betula papyrifera*)
European white birch (*Betula pendula*)
Cutleaf European birch (*Betula pendula* 'Gracilis')
Gray birch (*Betula populifolia*)
European hornbeam (*Carpinus betulus*)
Shagbark hickory (*Carya ovata*)
Katsura tree (*Cercidiphyllum japonicum*)
American yellowwood (*Cladrastis lutea*)
American beech (*Fagus grandifolia*)
European beech (*Fagus sylvatica*)
White ash (*Fraxinus americana*)
Ginkgo or maidenhair tree (*Ginkgo biloba*)
Honey locust (*Gleditsia triacanthos*)
Sweet gum tree (*Liquidambar styraciflua*)
Tulip tree (*Liriodendron tulipifera*)

Colorful Fall Foliage *(continued)*

Amur cork tree (*Phellodendron amurense*)
Black or rum cherry (*Prunus serotina*)
Littleleaf linden (*Tilia cordata*)

Shrubs

Summer-sweet clethra (*Clethra alnifolia*)
Witch hazel (*Hamamelis* spp.)
Spicebush (*Lindera benzoin*)

Vine

Bittersweet (*Celastrus scandens*)

RED, PINK, AND ORANGE-RED FOLIAGE

Small Trees

Japanese maple (*Acer palmatum*)
Shadblow, serviceberry, or juneberry (*Amelanchier canadensis*)
Allegheny serviceberry (*Amelanchier laevis*)
Flowering dogwood (*Cornus florida*)
Kousa or Japanese dogwood (*Cornus kousa*)
Cornelian cherry dogwood (*Cornus mas*)
Smoke tree (*Cotinus coggygria*)
Washington hawthorn (*Crataegus phaenopyrum*)
Sorrel tree or sourwood (*Oxydendrum arboreum*)
Callery pear (*Pyrus calleryana*)
Shining sumac (*Rhus copallina*)
Korean stewartia (*Stewartia koreana*)

Medium to Large Trees

Red maple (*Acer rubrum*)
Sugar maple (*Acer saccharum*)
Katsura tree (*Cercidiphyllum japonicum*)
American beech (*Fagus grandifolia*)
Sweet gum tree (*Liquidambar styraciflua*)
Black gum or black tupelo (*Nyssa sylvatica*)
Sargent cherry (*Prunus sargentii*)
Scarlet oak (*Quercus coccinea*)
Red oak (*Quercus rubra*)
Sassafras (*Sassafras albidum*)

Shrubs

AZALEAS
Flame azalea (*Rhododendron calendulaceum*)
Royal azalea (*Rhododendron schlippenbachii*)
Pink-shell azalea (*Rhododendron vaseyi*)
Japanese barberry (*Berberis thunbergii*)
Siberian dogwood (*Cornus alba* 'Sibirica')
Red-osier dogwood (*Cornus sericea*)
Redvein enkianthus (*Enkianthus campanulatus*)
Winged euonymus or burning bush (*Euonymus alata*)
Dwarf winged euonymus (*Euonymus alata* 'Compacta')
Fothergilla or witch alder (*Fothergilla* spp.)
Fragrant sumac (*Rhus aromatica*)
Rugosa rose (*Rosa rugosa*)
Virginia rose (*Rosa virginiana*)
Bridal-wreath spirea (*Spiraea prunifolia*)
Blueberry (*Vaccinium* spp.)
Arrowwood (*Viburnum dentatum*)
European cranberrybush (*Viburnum opulus*)
Black haw (*Viburnum prunifolium*)

Vines

Virginia creeper or woodbine (*Parthenocissus quinquefolia*)
Boston ivy (*Parthenocissus tricuspidata*)

PURPLE TO PURPLISH-RED FOLIAGE

Small Tree

Japanese stewartia (*Stewartia pseudocamellia*)

Medium to Large Trees

White ash (*Fraxinus americana*)
Red cedar (*Juniperus virginiana*)

Shrubs

Gray dogwood (*Cornus racemosa*)

Katsura tree foliage is yellow or multi-colored in fall, but the tree is valuable in the landscape all year round.

Colorful Fall Foliage *(continued)*

Cranberry cotoneaster (*Cotoneaster apiculatus*)
Drooping leucothoe (*Leucothoe fontanesiana*)
Regel privet (*Ligustrum obtusifolium regelianum*)
Bayberry (*Myrica pensylvanica*)
Canby paxistima (*Paxistima canbyi*)
Beach plum (*Prunus maritima*)
Chenault coralberry (*Symphoricarpos chenaultii*)
Korean spice viburnum (*Viburnum carlesii*)
Linden viburnum (*Viburnum dilatatum*)
Doublefile viburnum (*Viburnum plicatum tomentosum*)

Ground Covers

Purple wintercreeper (*Euonymus fortunei colorata*)
Andorra juniper (*Juniperus horizontalis plumosa*)

Detailed information and recommended varieties can be found in Part III.

Opposite: The red-orange foliage of red maple glows in the autumn sunlight and the satiny blackness of pond water makes a dramatic contrast.

LANDSCAPE TASKS FOR OCTOBER

Fall Planting Continued You can still plant many trees and shrubs this month. In fact, the preferred planting season for deciduous trees and shrubs (as opposed to lawns, broad-leaved evergreens, and needled evergreens) extends from now through the end of November. (See September Landscape Tasks for planting instructions for all trees and shrubs.)

Lawns and Leaves Keep the lawn mowed (see September) and rake leaves reasonably often to prevent them from matting and smothering the grass.

Your leaves are valuable. Don't bag them up and throw them away: pile them in the compost heap along with all the rest of your clean, disease-free garden refuse. Add limestone to speed the composting process come spring. Oak-leaf compost is particularly precious, being acid and therefore a great soil additive or mulch for azaleas, rhododendrons, and other broad-leaved evergreens.

Watering Azaleas and rhododendrons, evergreen trees and shrubs, newly planted trees, and newly installed perennials should all be kept watered. (Lawns, however, don't need it.) Monitor rainfall and irrigate accordingly.

Cleanup Hard though it is to get around to it, this is the time to clean, repair, and store garden furniture and equipment. Also clean up and compost all dead leaves and other garden debris, except material that harbors insects, weed seeds, or fungi. Get rid of this material; burn it if your local statutes permit, or send it to the dump if not.

NOV

Landscaping Opportunities
Energy-Efficient Landscaping

Plants for a Purpose
Hedges

Materials and Construction
Fences and Gates

Plants by Design
Foliage Texture

Landscape Tasks for November

Sugar maples cast dense shade for summer comfort and have unforgettable autumn color — but in November they are notable for vast leaf piles.

With shortening days, cold nights, early frosts, perhaps even a snow flurry, November is a chilly month. And for people in cold climates, the November fuel bill is almost as chilling as the weather. The hottest days of summer may have been uncomfortable, but they were nowhere near as expensive as winter promises to be.

This month, energy-efficient landscaping becomes a concern: planning your structures and plantings to maximize shelter from wind and retention of the sun's warmth in winter — and the opposite in summer. (It wouldn't make sense to try to plan for either season in isolation, since the structures and plantings stay in place all year.) Hedges and fences are important for both winter wind protection and summer shade, so they're included here too. And I'll provide some ideas on plantings for textural highlights — a year-round subject, but well suited to this month, whether you are actually installing trees now or just contemplating plans for next spring.

Landscaping Opportunities

ENERGY-EFFICIENT LANDSCAPING

Human beings have always tried to keep warm in winter, and in climates like that of the Northeast it has always been a dirty, time-consuming, and/or expensive job to do that — with the exception of the brief but luxurious period between 1900 and 1973.

Similarly, people have always tried to keep cool in summer, but with far less success, until air conditioning really took hold around 1960. Up until then it was a matter of staying in the shade and moving slowly.

For many people it was a rude shock to learn in 1973 that energy for heating and cooling would never again be both cheap and effortless to come by. Conservation of heat — and natural cooling techniques — were rediscovered as a top priority of architecture and landscape design. Energy-saving tactics that had been forgotten came to light once more.

Most of these tactics have a lot to do with simple common sense. But what's exciting about them is the very considerable difference they can actually make. A landscape designed to block summer sun and winter wind — and to capture winter sun and summer breezes — can reduce energy costs for a centrally heated, air-conditioned house by 30 percent or more per year. Consider the following facts and figures.

Warmth in Winter In winter sun is a friend, wind an enemy.

- Increase in heat loss from building surfaces is directly proportional to the square of increase in wind speed. That is, if wind speed increases from 10 to 20 mph (doubles), the heat loss will be 4 times as great.
- Wind velocity can be reduced by as much as 80 percent by a properly designed windbreak. I'm told that that amount of reduction in wind will cut heating bills by about 30 percent.
- If window overhangs and plantings let sun flow unobstructed into the windows of a house, the shortwave radiation of the sun's rays will warm up objects within the house; the objects will store the heat and help keep the house warm. The darker the color of the floors, furnishings, or walls where sunlight falls, the more heat will be retained. This is what's known as "passive solar" design and it involves no esoteric gear, just a little forethought.

Not England but Cambridge, Mass.: an outstanding example of an energy-efficient hedge. Above left, leafless European beeches let the winter sun filter through to the house. Above right, a dense screen for summer shade.

Summer Cooling Shading trellises or shade trees, vegetative ground covers, and wind tunnels in the form of hedges or structures can actually cool your house as well as its surrounding land.

- An unshaded asphalt pavement in summer can be 25°F hotter than the air above it.
- A structure such as a garage will be as much as 20° cooler in summer if shaded on the south and west by deciduous trees. (Deciduous because you don't want the shade in winter, of course.)
- Air temperature above a lawn is 15° cooler than above exposed earth. In the woods, it's 25° cooler than above exposed earth. And air temperature above a lawn mowed at a 3-inch height is 10° cooler than above one closely cropped to ½ inch. (As for astroturf, it heats the air up 50° hotter than above the close-cropped lawn.)
- The wind-chill created by air drawing through an evergreen tunnel on an 80° summer day makes the air feel as though it were 70°.

Designing for Comfort Your first move in planning an energy-saving landscape is to determine where the sun and the wind are coming from, winter and summer. Sun angles and directions vary continually and from place to place. Some seasonal observation and recordkeeping (perhaps in the form of notes on your base plan) will give you the data you need. Prevailing wind directions are also various, and for total accuracy they should ideally be measured by you (since local topography has a lot to do with wind flow). To determine prevailing winter and summer winds in your area, put up 6-foot posts or stakes here and there on your property; attach to the tops pieces of ribbon about 1 inch wide and 1 foot long; and record the wind directions daily for a couple of weeks in each season.

Sun In much of the United States we have sun for about half of all daylight hours, year round; in summer more, in winter less.

For winter, the diagrams on page 266 should suggest how to trap sun in and around your house. Eighty-five percent of the total energy from the sun flows our way between 9 A.M. and 3 P.M., and in winter the angle of the sun's rays between those hours varies from 10 to 30 degrees in this area. So try to orient living areas with lots of windows to the southeast. And avoid putting evergreens or other plantings where they'll shade windows, walls, or roofs in that southerly facing crescent during the peak sunlight hours.

On the south and west sides of the house, where you want the sun's warmth but where blinding reflected light from the snow may be a problem, you can plant a visual buffer of low evergreens. Or short deciduous trees will filter the light effectively, and give you a bonus of some shade in summer.

For summer, deciduous vines on upright screens or trellises do a great job of absorbing the sunlight, preventing it from turning a south-facing wall into a giant radiator.

On the east or southeast side of the house, small deciduous trees to screen windows from the potent late-morning sun are helpful. And on the south and west, overhangs and trellises to keep the sun out of the windows in summer can let it shine right in in winter, thanks to the different angles of the rays at different seasons.

Deciduous shade trees can cool your entire property as well as your house itself. Some cast deep, opaque shade; others a broken or filtered shade. The table here compares the percentages of visible sunlight blocked by various popular shade-tree species. I like different kinds of shade for different effects and purposes: heavy shade for a more intimate grotto or dense forestlike feeling; open, airy shade for simply breaking the direct sunlight with patterns of branching and foliage on the ground. Select your trees carefully for the quality of shade you have in mind.

Percentages of Sun Blocked by Various Shade Trees

85 to 90% blocked
Norway maple (*Acer platanoides*)
European beech (*Fagus sylvatica*)
Silver linden (*Tilia petiolaris*)

80 to 85% blocked
Red maple (*Acer rubrum*)
Sugar maple (*Acer saccharum*)
Red oak (*Quercus rubra*)
Weeping willow (*Salix* spp.)
Littleleaf linden (*Tilia cordata*)

75 to 80% blocked
Shadblow or serviceberry (*Amelanchier* spp.)
Shagbark hickory (*Carya ovata*)
Katsura tree (*Cercidiphyllum japonicum*)
Japanese pagoda tree (*Sophoria japonica*)

60 to 70% blocked
Honey locust (*Gleditsia triacanthos*)
White pine (*Pinus strobus*)

Shade out summer sun and introduce warming rays in the winter by adjusting the height and dimensions of a trellis or overhang. (Don't let evergreens block winter sun.)

Wind For winter, windbreaks are the name of the game. They are most effective if they're solid masses of evergreens positioned perpendicular to the flow of the prevailing wind — because evergreen trees will grow taller than any wall. A good solid windbreak should be planted as broad as it is tall. It will reduce wind velocity up to 80 percent for a distance of 3 to 5 times its height. This should help you figure out how tall a windbreak you want and how close to the house (or other area to be sheltered) it will need to be.

Another way to insulate the house in winter is to plant low evergreen or deciduous shrubs against the foundation or walls of the house on the sides facing the winter wind. These plants will trap snow and create pockets of dead air: both effective forms of insulation.

For summer, trapping and funneling the wind to ventilate both outdoor and indoor living spaces is your goal. The increased wind velocity caused when a broad flow of air is channeled through a narrow opening, called the Venturi effect, is shown here. The wind-trapping barriers can be hedges, walls, shrub masses, even other buildings. A breezeway does a terrific job if you orient it right.

All in all, the arrangement of your landscape can make a tremendous difference to your comfort, not to mention your expenditures on heating fuel or air-conditioning electricity. It's fun to see it happen.

An evergreen arborvitae hedge forms a year-round visual screen and muffles sound from the adjacent roadway.

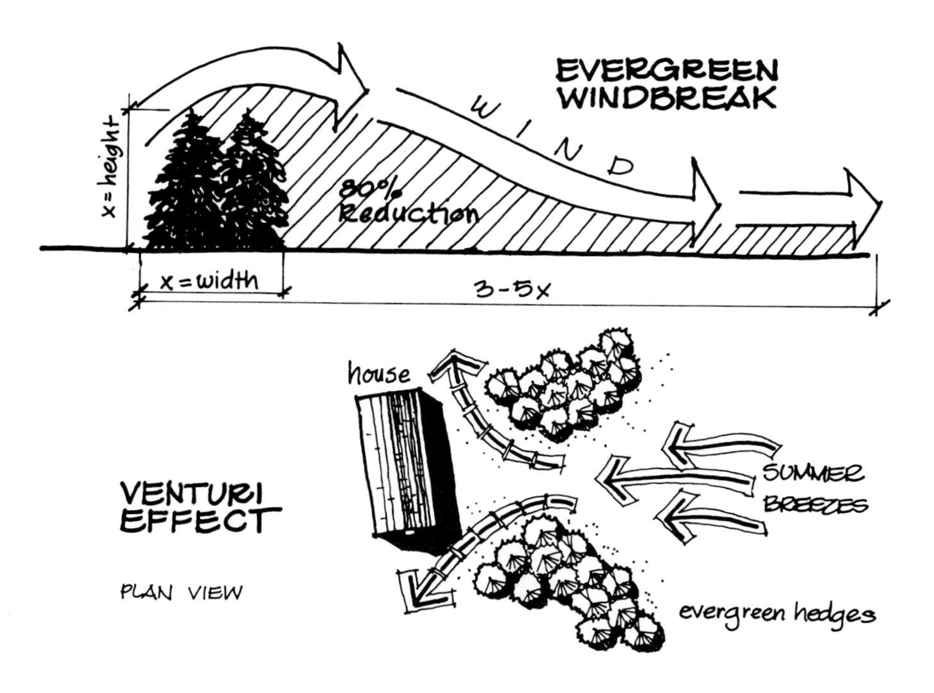

Reduce or increase velocity of seasonal winds by manipulating the air flow as suggested here.

Plants for a Purpose
HEDGES

Arranging plants together to form rows or walls of green is a practice as old as landscape gardening itself. For thousands of years, people have used hedges as barriers, privacy screens, backgrounds for other types of planting, or ornamental borders or edgings. They've also used them to block cold winter winds or to funnel breezes for summer cooling or provide summer shade, as detailed in the preceding section.

In this section I'll look at some uses of hedges and some essentials of hedge care and maintenance. And I'll list some of the plants best suited for use in hedges, either because of their own natural sizes and shapes or because of their tendency to respond to pruning with vigorous bushy growth.

Hedges for Screening Hedges can be massive or diminutive, evergreen or deciduous, transparent or opaque. Let me say right here that if complete privacy is the goal in your situation, you should probably invest in a fence or wall instead of a hedge. There are environmental hazards that can and do open gaps in even the sturdiest of hedges — ice storm damage, falling branches, or excessive zeal on the part of the end on the local touch football team.

Next to a wall or fence, the most effective year-round screen is an evergreen hedge, with the individual plants set in at least two staggered rows, so that if one is lost the others will fill in and the green wall will remain opaque. Many narrow-leaved evergreens like yews, juniper, or arborvitae do well. So do broad-leaved evergreens like inkberry, boxwood, or boxleaf holly — but be cautious with these last plants if the hedge's functions include winter wind protection, because many of them are subject to winterburn.

Even for purposes of privacy or visual screening, you may find that a deciduous hedge will serve your needs perfectly. If the hedge is used for summer shade but the shade is no longer wanted in winter — and/or if the hedge screens an area where you don't spend much time in cold weather — perhaps you can let the leaves go for the sake of the added light and sense of space. Again, the plants in a deciduous hedge

Colors and textures of evergreens used along a bank and as barriers accentuate the intriguing quality of the entry at the top of the flight of garden steps.

should be staggered, for summer privacy and for an air of fullness in winter. The range of deciduous hedge plants is vast — from shrubs like lilacs, honeysuckle, and privet, to trees like hawthorn and even lindens and beeches.

The height of a screening hedge depends on its location and function. Usually, hedges for privacy are taller than eye level; but if all you want to do is screen a view seen from a sitting position, you may not need such a tall hedge.

Hedges for Borders Low hedges make elegant edging or borders, and very effective physical barriers as well. They can be evergreen or deciduous, formal or informal. As backgrounds, they set off other plants through contrasting color and texture. As boundaries, they contain and define spaces. They can also be transitional elements, where they ease the eye from the softness of the natural landscape to the hard-edged forms of buildings or other structures.

In these more decorative roles, the best hedge plants are usually smaller or dwarf plants with finer textures, to fit their uses in smaller-scale or more structured surroundings. If you want an ornamental hedge to keep out unwanted visitors as well, choose a particularly dense or even a prickly plant, like a hedge yew, barberry, or rugosa rose.

Some Hedge How-Tos Think carefully at the outset about what you want from the plants you choose. The maintenance of a hedge doesn't have to be a major project, if you choose dwarf plants or plants with naturally compact forms. But if — for whatever reasons — you want to use bigger, more aggressive plants, then plan realistically on spending some time keeping them under control, one to three times a year.

Be conscious of the growing conditions of the area where you contemplate installing your hedge. Imagine what will happen if the hedge is in full sun for half its length, in dense shade for the other half; or if part of the hedge has its roots in well-drained soil, part in a soggy low spot. If you want a consistent hedge, you'll have to find or develop consistent conditions.

When you prune and shape your hedge, there's a right way and a wrong way to do it. Whether squared-off or rounded in form, all hedges should be allowed to grow wider at the base than at the top. Wider top growth — or even equal widths at top and bottom — will shade the bases of the hedge plants, often causing loss of lower foliage and an open, scrawny look along the bottom of the hedge.

What if your hedge is scrawny all over? It is sometimes best to start anew: dig the whole thing up and replant, perhaps with a different kind of shrub. With a deciduous hedge, however, you may be able to stop short of total demolition. Many an old and sad deciduous hedge can be restored to youthful exuberance by being cut right back to 6-inch stumps in early spring. If they're sufficiently vigorous, the plants will send out

HEDGE PRUNING

Basic rule of hedge pruning: shape the hedge to allow as much light as possible to reach all foliage, top and bottom.

multiple shoots of new growth to compensate for their loss. To test whether the plants do possess the needed degree of vigor, experiment on an inconspicuous part before attacking the whole hedge.

Evergreen hedges, however, don't respond to this kind of treatment. In fact they may die if you try it. But regular annual trimmings will keep them thick and bushy without any trouble. Prune evergreens just after their spring growing season, but no later than the Fourth of July. If you wait longer, the new growth that comes after pruning may not have time to harden off before cold weather, and the plants may suffer needless winter damage.

A hedge that is to serve purposes other than hedging has some special care requirements. Many people like to make hedges of plants that will bloom in spring, and perhaps also produce edible seeds or fruits. But productive plants usually can't undergo the kind of regular trimming that hedges receive and still produce. The trimming removes flower buds and throws off the plants' blooming and fruiting schedule. So if you do want to establish a multipurpose hedge, allow it plenty of room. You won't be able to repress it with any severity. Prune discreetly right after flowering, and leave much of the current year's flowering growth intact if you want to have seeds or fruits later on.

Plants for Hedges You can make a hedge out of virtually any tree or shrub that will grow in your climate (although some will work a lot better than others). In some gardening traditions, the creation of hedges out of unlikely material represents the ultimate in hedge culture. European hedges sometimes consist of old beech trees, dwarfed to 6-foot size by pruning since they were saplings — while their unpruned brothers stand 100 feet tall near by. Wandering across the English rural landscape there are 3-foot hedges of hawthorn trees, which if left to themselves would grow 30 feet tall. At Dumbarton Oaks in Washington, D.C., you can see an enclosure of hornbeams that are kept in shape by dint of week-long clipping sessions several times a year. These, however, are heroic measures, and not really pertinent to the common or garden residential hedge.

Whether hedges are made of artificially dwarfed forest trees or of naturally compact shrubs, we usually think of them as consisting of a single variety of plant. But even that isn't necessarily the rule. In Japan it's typical to have several different kinds of plant in the same clipped hedge, making a tapestry of foliage and branch textures. It can be a fascinating effect. My only word of warning, if you are considering trying the Japanese approach, is that such a hedge should stand pretty much alone. With other plants around it, a multiplant hedge can give a somewhat busy feeling, particularly in surroundings where space is limited.

The raison d'être of all hedge plants is dense growth and finite size. If you choose trees or shrubs that are innately large, you'll have to keep them in fairly strict bondage by cutting and shaping; and your efforts will inevitably prevent the plants from fulfilling their natural cycles of blooming and fruiting. Some people feel uncomfortable with plants forced into artificial shapes and sizes. If you are of that school of thought, or if you simply haven't a great amount of time, interest, or equipment to dedicate to hedge care, your best choices will be self-limiting smaller shrubs of naturally bushy character. There are plenty of those in the list that follows, small plants that can go a year or three without any pruning at all.

If you are considering a more ambitious hedge, look to the larger evergreen and deciduous shrubs and trees listed here. It will take more work on your part to keep them within bounds, but they'll lend themselves to effects of great substance and even grandeur.

Plants for Hedges

Large Evergreen Tree Forms (look for compact or dwarf varieties in your nursery)

Norway spruce (*Picea abies*)
Austrian pine (*Pinus nigra*)
Douglas fir (*Pseudotsuga menziesii*)
Douglas arborvitae (*Thuja occidentalis* 'Douglas Pyramidal')
Canadian hemlock (*Tsuga canadensis*)

Large Evergreen Shrubs

Common box (*Buxus sempervirens*)
Intermediate yew (*Taxus media* 'Densiformis')
Hatfield yew (*Taxus media* 'Hatfieldii')
Hicks yew (*Taxus media* 'Hicksii')
Hetz Wintergreen arborvitae (*Thuja occidentalis* 'Hetz Wintergreen')

Medium Evergreen Shrubs

Japanese box (*Buxus microphylla japonica*)
Dwarf Japanese yew (*Taxus cuspidata* 'Nana')

Small Evergreen Shrubs

Hellers Japanese holly (*Ilex crenata* 'Helleri')
Nest spruce (*Picea abies* 'Nidiformis')
Dwarf Canadian hedge yew (*Taxus canadensis* 'Stricta')
Hetz Midget arborvitae (*Thuja occidentalis* 'Hetz Midget')

Large Deciduous Trees

European hornbeam (*Carpinus betulus*)
American beech (*Fagus grandifolia*)
European beech (*Fagus sylvatica*)
Littleleaf linden (*Tilia cordata*)

Small Deciduous Trees/Large Deciduous Shrubs

Cornelian cherry dogwood (*Cornus mas*)
Washington hawthorn (*Crataegus phaenopyrum*)
Winged euonymus (*Euonymus alata*)
Rose-of-Sharon or shrub althea (*Hibiscus syriacus*)
Amur honeysuckle (*Lonicera maackii*)
Sargent crabapple (*Malus sargentii*)
Chinese lilac (*Syringa chinensis*)
Arrowwood (*Viburnum dentatum*)
European cranberrybush (*Viburnum opulus*)
Black haw (*Viburnum prunifolium*)

Medium Deciduous Shrubs

Japanese barberry (*Berberis thunbergii*)
Dwarf winged euonymus (*Euonymus alata* 'Compacta')
Showy border forsythia (*Forsythia intermedia* 'Spectabilis')
Tatarian honeysuckle (*Lonicera tatarica*)
Vanhoutte spirea (*Spiraea vanhouttei*)
Dwarf Korean lilac (*Syringa palibiniana*)
Persian lilac (*Syringa persica*)
Doublefile viburnum (*Viburnum plicatum tomentosum*)

Small Deciduous Shrubs

Red-leaved Japanese barberry (*Berberis thunbergii* 'Atropurpurea')
Regel privet (*Ligustrum obtusifolium regelianum*)
Rugosa rose (*Rosa rugosa*)
Anthony Waterer spirea (*Spiraea bumalda* 'Anthony Waterer')
Dwarf European cranberrybush (*Viburnum opulus* 'Nanum')

Detailed information and recommended varieties can be found in Part III.

Inkberry is used effectively as a screening hedge; vinca planted along the base is very similar in texture.

Materials and Construction
FENCES AND GATES

When you're looking for an energy-efficient landscape, security, or privacy immediately — and you want it to last a good long time — a fence is often the way to go. And this month you can still build fences, even the concrete footings, if you pick your time astutely. Well-built fencing may represent a substantial investment compared to a planted border or hedge, but over the long haul it also represents a quick, enduring, and maintenance-free answer to your needs.

With maximum longevity the goal, it is important that fences and gates be not only well built but thoughtfully selected. A stopgap solution generally turns out to be unsatisfactory in one way or another. But (possibly for the very reason that fences can be put up relatively swiftly) mistakes are often made with fences, to their owners' lasting chagrin. To help you make a choice you'll live with happily, I'll start by outlining a few of the most common errors made in fence design and construction.

Fencing Pitfalls Other than exercising excessive haste, people usually go astray in deciding on the size and type of the fence, its fit and relationship to its environment, or the amount of fencing used for the job at hand.

Wrong size or type You've probably seen plenty of ill-considered fences. A chain-link security fence usually imparts a feeling of being imprisoned rather than protected. A one-sided fence may look great in one family's yard but be a horrendous eyesore from the neighbors' vantage. An opaque fence designed for privacy can cut off light and ventilation as well as views in and out. Too tall a fence can make you feel more isolated than separated; this is particularly likely to happen in a small-scale place with a fence 6 feet or more high.

All fences fall into three groups: transparent, semitransparent, and opaque. On a slope, architectural fences should be stepped; informal ones can follow the topography.

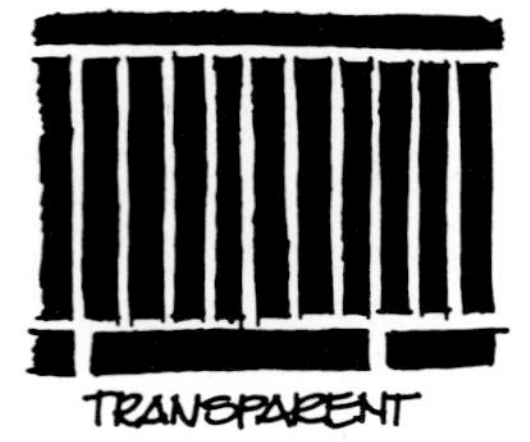

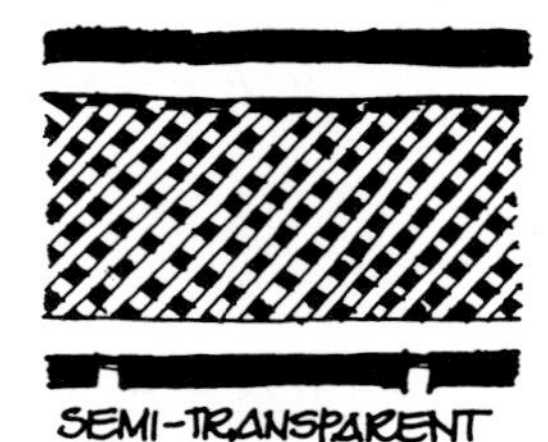

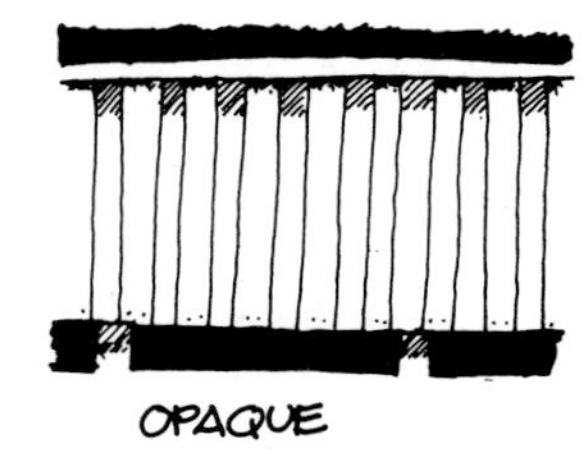

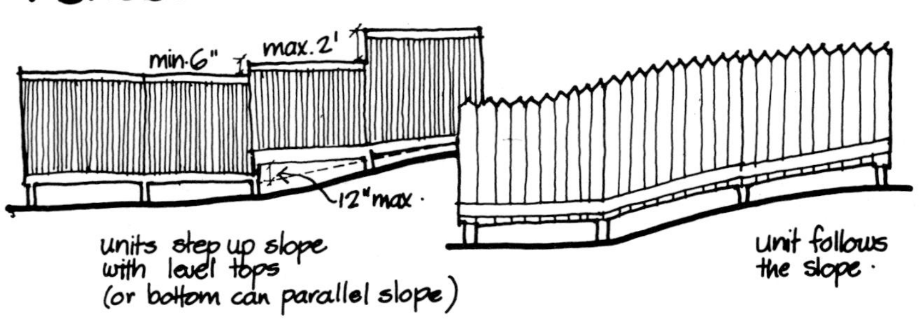

Faulty relationship to surroundings The materials, style, and finish of fencing should be in harmony with those of the house and other structures near it. Solid or semitransparent fences that are attached to the house or very close to it should be treated architecturally. That means that if the land slopes up or down, the fence should be stepped and the top of each segment kept level.

Transparent fences, on the other hand, can be allowed to follow the lines of the topography. So can fences (even solid ones) that are at a distance from the house. Let them be related primarily to the landscape rather than the house itself.

Too much fencing The most common mistake of all may be to use too much fencing, or at least too much of one type. It's rare indeed that fencing is needed around an entire property. But in cases where a complete surrounding fence is called for, it usually works best to use one major type with perhaps a compatible variation to meet the needs of some specific area (privacy, screening, security, traffic control, or whatever) or to afford visual relief, rather than one homogeneous type all the way around.

Planning Fences and Gates Let's look at the main considerations that enter into a wise choice of fencing for your property. Before you begin, check into your town's published zoning regulations to see if there are limitations on fence height, setback from property lines, direction of best face, etc. You want to do fencing only once and do it right.

Location This is the most important issue to resolve. Think about fences as walls or dividers that separate and define outdoor spaces or landscape "rooms," and you're 90 percent of the way towards a satisfying and functional fencing plan. Before you start building you need to be able to visualize very concretely what the finished effect will be. Test out the proposed placement of your fence by stringing clothesline where the fence is to run; drape sheets or blankets over it if necessary for an even greater sense of the visual effect. This will also help you decide two other important questions: what type of fence to build and how high it should be.

Type of fence The location and purpose will determine the overall type of the fence: opaque, semitransparent, or transparent.

Opaque fencing offers complete privacy but will cut off light, air

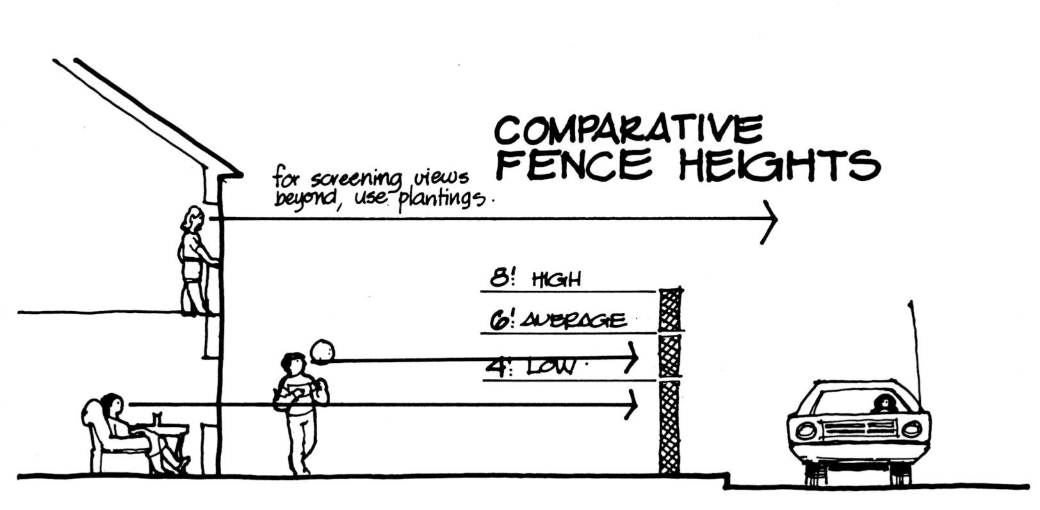

Fences are effective screens at lower levels, but they have their limitations. For screening second-story views, use plantings.

Fence types: a custom-made redwood fence (above left) is close to the house and architectural in feeling, while this stockade-type border fence at the property line (above right) has plantings at its foot and overflowing its top that integrate it with the natural surroundings.

circulation, and views to the outside. You have to weigh your need for privacy against your desire for summer breezes or a feeling of openness.

Semitransparent fencing permits a good deal of air and light to pass through; it allows you glimpses or an impressionistic sense of views beyond; and it affords considerable privacy from passing cars, although not from the view of people on foot outside. This is the kind of fence I use most often. Very often, too, I combine opaque and semitransparent types in one fence. Semitransparent and opaque sections one above the other, for instance, can give complete privacy to a sitting area while allowing views and air circulation through the upper part of the fence. Vertical louvers can be angled to permit views in one direction only and yet let air circulate. I think that the ideal semitransparent fence would be one with movable vertical louvers that you could adjust to changing wind and sun directions and differing needs for privacy, like a vertical venetian blind. It would be expensive to build, although you could probably do it with simple hardware like that used in the old wooden shutters. I've never yet had a chance to try one.

Below, a decorative lattice, scalloped gate, and scrolled steel arch welcome visitors.

Transparent fences often perform utilitarian roles, such as restricting children or animals, or surrounding swimming pools. A secure fence that allows unobstructed views is the wrought-iron type. (For complete transparency it should be painted a dark color.) Or transparent fences can be used as purely visual or decorative borders, like rail fences or traditional picket fences.

Size of fence Keep fencing as low as possible for the effect or purpose intended — provided that you also keep it in scale with surrounding structures and plantings. Here again, your clothesline-and-blanket rig is an invaluable aid to planning. You can determine whether the height you have in mind will just screen the view you want to screen or whether you're in danger of overfencing. The diagram on page 273 gives you the accepted maximum and minimum heights for various purposes.

Style of gate Where a space is enclosed with fencing, a gate is sometimes also needed. A gate can be a functional and pleasant part of the entry experience — or it can be merely exasperating.

Make sure your gate is big enough for the traffic it will have to bear, including lawn mowers, leaf carts, or other vehicles. And above all, a gate should work. Gates are as fussy to hang as doors, and there's the added dimension of the weather to contend with: wetting and drying and freezing and thawing play havoc with moving parts. Be sure your gate is built with appropriate hardware and sturdily braced against sagging.

Fencing affords scope for whimsy (left) — but be careful. At right, the sturdy service gate is well braced, not designed as an invitation for use by visitors.

Like other parts of a fence, a gate should be stylistically in keeping with the rest of the landscape. Usually this means using the same materials as the fence proper. But I don't recommend making a gate identical (except for its hinges) to the fence. A gate should convey a greeting and a sense of welcome. Try to give it some special quality: change the spacing or size of its members, or express its supporting structure, or give it a different height or outline.

Finishes for Fences and Gates You may choose to let wooden fences weather naturally. But if a fence abuts or runs very close to your house, particularly if you have wood trim or siding, it should be the same or a complementary color; and this may mean paint or stain. For long life and ease of maintenance I'd usually recommend wood-preservative stain rather than paint on wooden fences and gates. Paint tends to capture moisture in joints so that the wood rots underneath — but the object of finishing the wood in the first place is to keep moisture away from end grains and joints.

Foliage textures are used for landscape effect. Highlighting this textural tapestry are white birchbark and variegated hosta.

For this same reason, and whether you paint or stain, it's best to treat all members before you assemble them and touch them up afterwards. It is very difficult to get into all the nooks and crannies, and impossible to get into the joints, once the fence is built.

After the finish Very often the real finishing touch for a fence consists of the plantings along it. A fence can be an ideal backdrop for flowers, shrubs, or trees. Or you can design it specifically to serve as a framework for vines or espaliers. Foliage and flowers are the perfect camouflage for any little flaws or awkward corners in a fence; they soften stark lines and rough edges; and they complement the colors and textures of fencing materials.

Plants by Design

FOLIAGE TEXTURE

Textural high spots for the landscape: plants with very coarse and very fine foliage textures

The softness of white pine foliage texture is especially appreciated against a contrasting wall.

COARSE-TEXTURED PLANTS

Deciduous Trees

Horse chestnut (*Aesculus hippocastanum*)
Sweet gum tree (*Liquidambar styraciflua*)
Tulip tree (*Liriodendron tulipifera*)
Saucer magnolia (*Magnolia soulangiana*)
Red oak (*Quercus rubra*)

Deciduous Shrubs

Fothergilla or witch alders (*Fothergilla* spp.)
Witch hazels (*Hamamelis* spp.)
Hydrangeas (*Hydrangea* spp.)

Needled Evergreens

White fir (*Abies concolor*)
Hinoki false cypress (*Chamaecyparis obtusa*)
Norway spruce (*Picea abies*)
Japanese black pine (*Pinus thunbergiana*)

Broad-leaved Evergreens

Rhododendrons, large-leaved (*Rhododendron* spp.)

Vines

Bittersweet (*Celastrus scandens*)
English ivy (*Hedera helix*)
Boston ivy (*Parthenocissus tricuspidata*)
Grapes (*Vitis* spp.)

Ground Covers

European ginger (*Asarum europaeum*)
Drooping leucothoe (*Leucothoe fontanesiana*)

FINE-TEXTURED PLANTS

Deciduous Trees

Japanese maple (*Acer palmatum*)
Birches (*Betula* spp.)
Hornbeams (*Carpinus* spp.)
Beeches (*Fagus* spp.)
Honey locust (*Gleditsia triacanthos*)
Golden larch (*Pseudolarix amabilis*)
Weeping willow (*Salix* spp.)

Deciduous Shrubs

Barberries (*Berberis* spp.)
Cotoneasters (*Cotoneaster* spp.)
Privet (*Ligustrum* spp.)
Azaleas, small-leaved (*Rhododendron* spp.)
Spireas (*Spiraea* spp.)
Blueberries (*Vaccinium* spp.)

Needled Evergreens

Junipers (*Juniperus* spp.)

Foliage Texture *(continued)*

White pine (*Pinus strobus*)
Hemlock (*Tsuga canadensis* vars.)

Broad-leaved Evergreens

Boxwood (*Buxus* spp.)
Japanese holly (*Ilex crenata*)

Vine

Common trumpet creeper (*Campsis radicans*)

Evergreen Ground Covers

Bearberry (*Arctostaphylos uva-ursi*)
Japanese garden juniper (*Juniperus chinensis procumbens*)
Canby paxistima (*Paxistima canbyi*)
Vinca, periwinkle, or myrtle (*Vinca minor*)

Detailed information and recommended varieties can be found in Part III.

LANDSCAPE TASKS FOR NOVEMBER

Last Call Many trees and shrubs can still go into the ground now — but this is it. You can also dig, divide, and replant lily-of-the-valley if you haven't gotten around to it before. (See September for both procedures.)

Pools and Ponds Drain and clean artificial pools; remove and store hardy water lilies, or discard tropical ones. You can cover your pool with boards or a tarpaulin or other covering, or fill it with leaves and lay branches over the top. The protection will reduce the stress of winter's repeated wettings, freezings, and thawings.

Lawn Mower Send the lawn into winter at a height of no more than 2 inches. Then clean the lawn-mower blades, and have them sharpened and adjusted if necessary. Don't procrastinate; in spring every lawn-mower shop will be inundated with urgent business.

Leaves and More Leaves When the last of the leaves have fallen, give a final raking and mulching all around. You can let leaves remain around the edges of shrubbery, perennial beds, and so forth as an informal mulch; or if that looks too untidy to you, put all leaves on the compost heap and mulch your plants and beds with straw, bark chips, salt-marsh hay, pine straw, or any mulch of your choosing.

Tree Guards It's wise to protect young fruit trees, ornamental cherries, or crabapples with wire netting, wood, plastic coil wraps, or heavy paper if there are any rabbits, mice, or deer in your neighborhood. These animals like to chew on tender bark in the lean winter months, and their "girdling" can kill a young tree.

Lilacs Cut away all the suckers at the bases of lilacs. Spread manure around them, leave it over the winter, and work it in in spring, to nourish new growth and promote bloom.

Hardwood Cuttings Take hardwood cuttings now from forsythia, privet, or mock-orange. Bundle them up and store them buried in damp sand in a cold place (a cellar or cold frame is good) during the winter. They'll root swiftly if you plant them in the earth in spring.

DEC

Landscaping Opportunities
Night Lighting Outdoors

Plants for a Purpose
Needled Evergreens

Materials and Construction
Metal

Plants by Design
Form

Landscape Tasks for December

This lake in Callaway Gardens, Georgia, mirrors the splendor of a December sunset.

This wintry month it's natural to think about light. The winter solstice and the holidays arrive simultaneously — the former bringing the longest night of the year, the latter all kinds of festivities and the man-made illuminations to go with them. Evergreens are a natural topic here too, December being practically synonymous with the rich greens and woodsy scents of pine, spruce, and fir. Along with evergreens let's look at the forms of trees that make distinctive statements in a landscape composition — since one of the great contributions of evergreens is that their forms stay the same through every season. And for the concluding Materials and Construction section, metal seems a resoundingly good choice: a material as cold and crisp as this season, and more important in the landscape than you might suppose.

Landscaping Opportunities
NIGHT LIGHTING OUTDOORS

Most houses are built with a bare minimum of outdoor lighting: a floodlight or two, perhaps, and a lamp beside the front door. But floodlights are essentially security lighting. Designed to repel burglars or illuminate the area in emergencies, they glare or even blind you. They're far from welcoming. The same wattage can be put to work in other, far more attractive ways. Consider reserving your floodlight for real emergencies and installing other forms of outdoor lighting for beauty and safety combined.

Some of the most stunning effects of outdoor lighting occur when there's snow on the ground and on the branches of trees, and December often obliges with a light fall of snow. Yet at every season, well-designed lighting can create beauty or excitement around your house at night.

Outdoor lighting takes many forms. A simple homemade fixture (left) is a safety factor on a sloping walk with steps. A sophisticated arrangement (right) is built into a trellis.

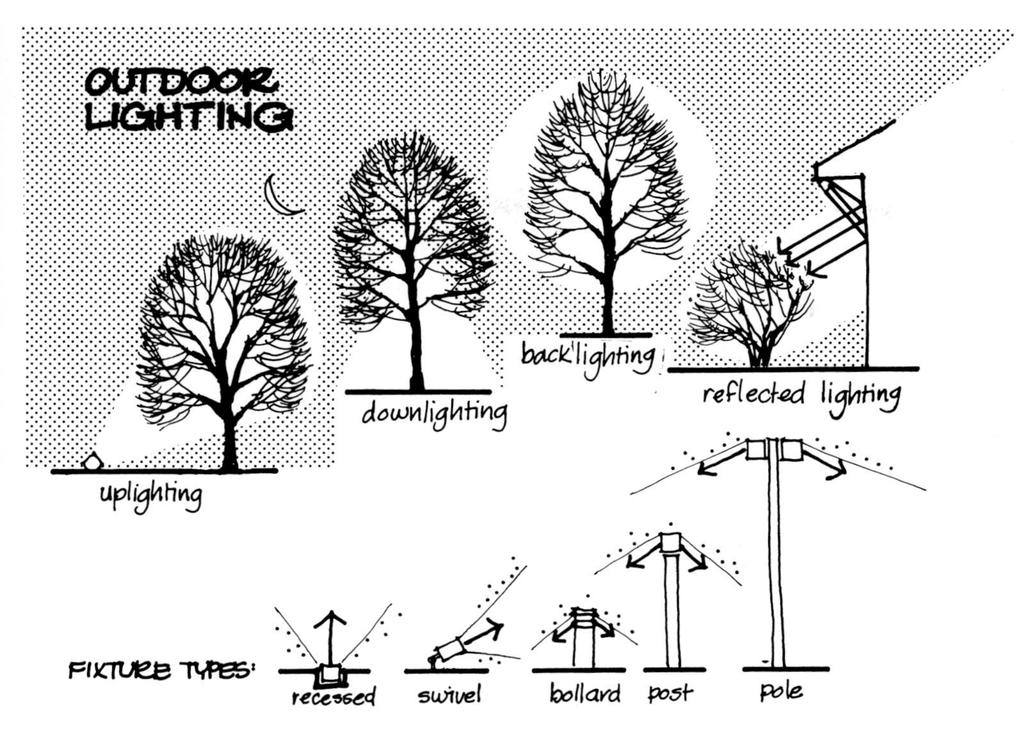

Sketched here are some often-used ways to create appealing effects with outdoor lighting, and some typical outdoor fixtures.

Lighting for Safety Lighting belongs first and foremost where hazards exist. A hazard is anything that might cause you or your guests to slip, stumble, or fall in the dark: steps, abrupt changes in grade, or changes in the material you walk on (pavement to grass, for instance).

The figures here show some of the types of fixture that you can use to make your property a safe and hospitable place after dark. There are posts with lamps mounted at or above eye level, to give off a gentle area light. Or there are lamps on shorter posts, which direct illumination onto the ground in a clear-cut pattern. Some short, fat "bollard" fixtures — 2 to 3 feet tall and 6 or 8 inches in diameter — contain lamps within the post itself. Other fixtures are boxes with lamps recessed to cast a soft glow, like the lights in movie-theater aisles.

As you look at these fixtures in a store or catalogue, you'll see that some cast light from a concealed or cutoff source while others are designed so that the bulb itself, as well as the light it casts, can be seen. If you don't want any visible bright spots of light, but you like a feeling of restrained elegance or a mysterious quality, concealed-source lighting may be the best approach for you. I must admit that in some instances I like to see lamps sparkling along a long path or driveway, or a handsome fixture atop a post at the beginning of a front walk. This approach is more animated and exciting. The lights seem like a greeting from the house and the people within. But it is important to make sure that the fixtures and their bulbs don't generate annoying glare.

Lighting for Effect Outdoor lighting can also be used chiefly for effect. In many cases lighting for visual interest can satisfy utilitarian purposes too, and that is always my goal.

A couple of examples: a spotlight in a cylindrical fixture high in a tree can cast wonderful shadows on the ground and still illuminate the path to the front door. Or a lamp attached to a roof soffit to create a wash of light down a textured stone wall can also make the adjacent steps negotiable. In the first example the light is direct; in the second the light is reflected, or indirect. Both forms of lighting are designed for appearance, but they also enable people to move safely around the landscape at night.

Lighting to enhance the beauty of the night landscape usually takes one or more of the forms shown on page 281: uplighting, downlighting, backlighting for silhouettes, reflected lighting, lighting for shadows or textures, and moonlighting (using lamps positioned to simulate moonlight). Some of these give a simple, straightforward look; others create an air of mystery or a theatrical mood.

Installing Outdoor Lighting It's not hard to install a low-voltage system yourself, if your house boasts a waterproof outdoor electrical outlet. You just purchase a 12-volt transformer, some wire (up to about 100 feet), and the fixtures you need; plug the transformer into the outlet; and arrange the lights where you want them. You can bury the wire in the ground or conceal it under mulch or thick shrubbery. You can even build fixtures to your own design, using materials suited to the setting.

There are some major drawbacks to a low-voltage system like this, however. You are limited to 5 or 6 fixtures on the circuit, and the bulbs can be no brighter than 75 watts. The longer the run of the wire, the dimmer the lights will be. And the standard plastic fixtures available are seldom attractive in themselves.

But if you can get around these disadvantages, there are two main arguments for using this kind of system. It is absolutely harmless because of its low voltage; and it is comparatively very economical to install and operate.

If the minuses of the 12-volt system outweigh its pluses for you, then a standard 120-volt system will be the solution. This will cost more to install and run, and its high voltage makes it more dangerous; but it will give you far more flexibility — and more light.

I would recommend that you have an electrician do all the wiring from the service panel to the switches to an outdoor junction box or panel. Then you can put in as many cables and fixtures as you like, provided you do not exceed the amperage limit for each circuit.

Be sure to use 3-wire direct burial cable and bury it far enough below ground so that a sharp shovel will not cut it. Be cautious about the locations of all buried fixtures: most "waterproof" fixtures leak, and a leaking fixture is dangerous.

I can't really recommend any standard line of outdoor lighting fixtures on the market. For some reason, good design and good materials are very hard to find; perhaps because the demand for outdoor fixtures is not great. The best insurance is to arrange ahead of time with your supplier to allow you to return any fixture that doesn't look right when you see it in place.

Plants for a Purpose
NEEDLED EVERGREENS

I usually think of needled evergreen trees and shrubs as background and frame for a landscape. Very often, though, they serve as important foreground plants. And sometimes they steal the entire scene.

They are necessary in every landscape — and so versatile that you can use them for any purpose at all.

Evergreens are such a mainstay because practically all of them retain their foliage, and therefore their mass, form, color, and texture, all year long. (The exceptions are interesting for reasons of their own.) Their forms run the gamut from prostrate creepers that carpet the ground to towering specimens with their heads in the clouds. As for their colors, the palette encompasses steely blues, bright to blackish greens, and greens variegated with white or yellow. Their textures are equally varied: some evergreens have flat frondlike scales, some short bristles, some long stiff needles, some short silky ones.

Umbrella pine holds its needles in a unique whorled pattern.

The big four among needled evergreens are pine, spruce, fir, and hemlock. These trees forest vast areas of the United States and yield much of the lumber used in building construction. Both the native species and the hundreds of introduced and cultivated varieties of these trees can make wonderful landscape plants — but most of the native species are basically large forest trees, and will grow into huge, overpowering specimens. Use these giants only on very large properties. For other settings, choose varieties bred for small size and/or slow growth. They'll give you equal drama without that looming effect.

More modest-sized evergreens are the junipers, yews, and arborvitae. Many of these plants will grow into small trees if you let them, but they're easy to restrain to shrub size and that is how they are most often used. Nestling near the house or at the edge of the lawn, they are companionable human-scaled plants.

Among the evergreens listed on page 284 are plants to serve all kinds of landscape functions. Some provide food and habitats for wildlife; some are natives, suitable for wild or naturalistic landscapes; some make great hedges; and there are ground covers, shade trees, specimens, and trees and shrubs for borders and screens.

Gold-tipped variegated false cypress catches the sun and helps warm the winter landscape.

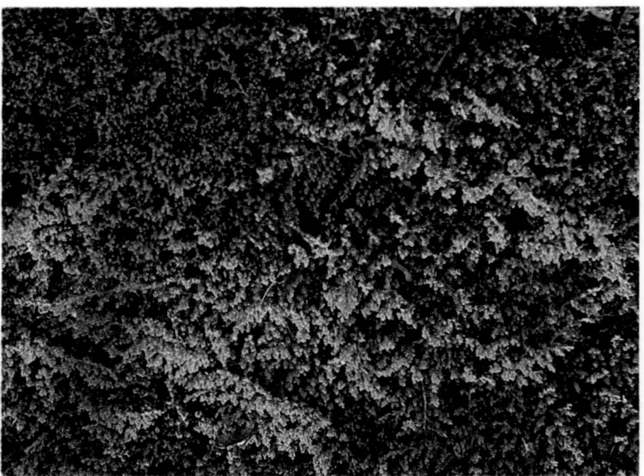

Above left: dark, shadowy pockets make the foliage of Hinoki false cypress seem to float in front of the plant. Above right: a very different effect is created by fine-textured dwarf prostrate juniper.

Needled Evergreen Trees and Shrubs

White fir (*Abies concolor*)
Hinoki false cypress (*Chamaecyparis obtusa* vars.)
Thread false cypress (*Chamaecyparis pisifera* 'Filifera' and vars.)
Chinese juniper (*Juniperus chinensis* vars.)
Creeping juniper (*Juniperus horizontalis* vars.)
Red cedar (*Juniperus virginiana* vars.)
Dawn redwood (*Metasequoia glyptostroboides*)
Norway spruce (*Picea abies* vars.)
Jack pine (*Pinus banksiana*)
Lacebark pine (*Pinus bungeana*)
Swiss stone pine (*Pinus cembra*)
Tanyosho pine (*Pinus densiflora* 'Umbraculifera')
Dwarf mugho pine (*Pinus mugo pumilio*)
Austrian pine (*Pinus nigra*)
White pine (*Pinus strobus* vars.)
Japanese black pine (*Pinus thunbergiana*)
Golden larch (*Pseudolarix kaempferi*)
Douglas fir (*Pseudotsuga menziesii*)
Umbrella pine (*Sciadopitys verticillata*)
Canada yew (*Taxus canadensis* vars.)
Dwarf Japanese yew (*Taxus cuspidata* 'Nana')
Intermediate yew (*Taxus media* vars.)
American arborvitae (*Thuja occidentalis* vars.)
Canadian hemlock (*Tsuga canadensis* vars.)

Detailed information and recommended varieties can be found in Part III.

Materials and Construction
METAL

Metals are not exactly the materials most prevalent in the landscape. Even so, they have quite a few uses: you'll find metals in fencing and railings, lighting fixtures and posts, drain frames and grates, bed edgings, and furniture — and in myriad forms of hardware and fastenings.

Most often you will be buying metal items ready-made. And for the most part you'll be dealing with ferrous (iron-containing) products, although you will probably also encounter nonferrous metals such as copper and aluminum and alloys such as brass and bronze.

Metal is capable of being bent, and as such is used to full advantage in this curved railing.

This section is by way of an introduction to the metals around you: their makeup, their properties, and some roles they play in the landscape.

Iron and Steel Steel as we know it has been around only since the 1850s. Before then, cast iron and wrought iron were manufactured by processes unchanged for 500 years.

Carbon content defines the differences between various types of iron and steel. Wrought iron is almost pure iron, containing less than 1/10 of 1 percent carbon. It is soft and malleable; when forged (heated to workable softness) it can be hammered into any shape required. Craftsmen in Colonial America and up to the early 1900s made wrought-iron tools, utensils, and furnishings a true art form.

Cast iron has a very high carbon content, 2 to 6 percent, almost the same as pig iron (unrefined iron smelted from crude ore). Iron of this type is brittle and nonmalleable. Melted and poured into forms or molds, it is the material of ornamental ironwork, rigid heavy objects like manhole covers, furniture, and hardware.

Steel comes in many categories for many purposes, and the carbon content of the different types varies from a mere trace (.05 percent) to a relatively high 1.5 percent. "Soft steel" is reserved for uses where strength and stiffness are unimportant, such as wire or pipe. "Mild steel" offers both strength and machinability and is used in everything from bolts to bridges to building construction. "Spring steel" is resilient enough for use in springs; "tool steel" is tough and high in carbon and is used for making precision instruments with close tolerances.

Stainless steel is an alloy that incorporates any of a number of other metals to provide rust-resistance and sheen. Added to stainless steel may be chromium, magnesium, or nickel in various proportions.

"Bright steel" means chrome-plated steel (commonly found in the form of nuts and bolts) and should never be used outdoors, as it will rust.

Weathering steel A special steel with a high phosphorus content, weathering steel rusts rapidly to a rich chocolate brown. It reaches its full color in about three years, then stops, having given itself a permanent finish that will never need attention. This material can be extremely handsome in the landscape, provided it's used in the right place. During the weathering process, large amounts of rust accumulate, wash off, and stain all surrounding surfaces; so you should never use this steel against any wall or on any pavement that will show the stains. Stone pebbles are an ideal edging or ground cover beneath a fence, gate, arbor, or lamppost made of weathering steel, because you can stir them around and somewhat conceal the staining.

Galvanized steel All steels except stainless steel need some form of protective finish or coating to prevent corrosion. Exposed nongalvanized steel of any kind should always be painted with a primer and rust-inhibiting paint. For longevity in outdoor use, the best treatment for plain steel is galvanizing, or coating with zinc. Most galvanized products you buy should be hot-dip galvanized. Electroplating results in a more uniform but thinner and less durable zinc coating; so ask for hot-dipped stock.

(Beware, however, of using galvanized nails or bolts or other connectors in visible spots on redwood or red cedar construction. Both these woods contain an acid that makes the zinc corrode and stain. Use aluminum or aluminum-coated steel nails and fasteners instead.)

In order to paint galvanized steel, you have to roughen its surface. You can do this by letting it weather a year until it "pickles" (turns a chalky gray). Or you can etch it with a 5 percent solution of hydrochloric, phosphoric, or acetic acid in water. After weathering or etching, use a zinc chromate primer before applying finish coats of paint. A far easier approach, and my own preference in most situations, is to leave galvanized steel alone. The color of the weathered zinc coating blends pleasantly with woods that have also been left to weather to a silvery gray.

A few words of warning about corrosion of unlike metals are in order here. When different metals are in contact in a moist environment, one will corrode the other. This phenomenon is called galvanic action; it results from warring between the metals' electrons, and will wreak havoc where it occurs. (It is a problem well known to anyone familiar with boats.) The solution is never to mix metals. Don't use brass, bright steel, or plain steel bolts or screws with zinc-coated hinges, for example. Never combine bright steel nuts with galvanized bolts.

Old iron Antique (or used) artifacts of wrought or cast iron make wonderful garden features. I am always searching for old ornamental grilles, gates, posts, and newels, as well as old garden furniture. Often I'll design an entire outdoor setting around one or two of these pieces. If you are lucky enough to have access to old ironwork, just be sure to use it with restraint and incorporate it carefully into surroundings of fitting character.

Aluminum Steels are capable of being cast, forged, wrought, rolled, and welded; but they cannot be extruded (forced under pressure through a die), and that is where aluminum comes in. Aluminum is easily extruded into complicated fluted, grooved, or ridged shapes, so that it is the material of choice for many a handrail, screen, and window or door frame. Once exposed to the weather it forms its own protective coating, aluminum oxide, an inert grayish film. It needs no other other protection — although you can buy it painted, vinyl-coated, or "anodized" in various colors. Anodizing is a form of electroplating. I find that under heavy traffic it tends to scratch and wear off, so I don't advise it for uses such as doorsills or handrails where deteriorating appearance will be a problem.

Antique cast-iron fence sections can often be incorporated in designs for small gardens.

You can use aluminum as a structural material in applications where light weight is a key criterion, such as large gates or movable planters. It's made in many of the same forms and dimensions as steel. Aluminum chairs and tables are often marketed as patio furniture: they are reasonable and portable, but not very stable, permanent, or (in my opinion) attractive.

If you are putting in or replacing screening in windows, doors, or porches, I strongly recommend black aluminum mesh, which is darkened by a process called "alodizing." It does not reflect indoor light as does shiny aluminum, and therefore it yields a wonderfully clear view. (Old-fashioned copper screening, now too expensive to use, darkened naturally over time with the same satisfactory result.) I stumbled upon this fact by accident when replacing one of two screens in a door. Oblivious to what the hardware store was cutting for me, I took the screen home to find that the old mesh was shiny, the new one black. The contrast was remarkable.

Copper Copper makes a wonderful roofing material for a small garden structure. Its velvety jade-green patina "sets" in eight to ten years and forms a permanent, insoluble protective coating. Or if you prefer to keep the original warm reddish color alive, you can do so with a yearly application of linseed oil.

Copper also, needless to say, finds uses in flashing, drain pipes, and fountains and their plumbing.

This decorative copper water fountain accents a city garden. Copper and water have visual (and practical) affinity.

Brass and Bronze These two alloys of copper are probably the most esoteric and expensive of landscape metals, but I mention them because they definitely have their places as architectural highlights. A shiny brass name or number plate adds an accent of charm and dignity to a front door. A rich golden-brown bronze railing or banister is elegant in its own right.

Brass is a blend of copper and zinc in variable proportions; the more zinc, the more silvery and bright the brass. Bronze combines copper and about 10 percent tin. Tin is much in demand for other commercial uses, and as it becomes more rare and costly, so does bronze.

From fencing to plumbing to railings to statuary, metal plays many parts as no other material possibly could. If you have a place for metal in your landscape you'll find there is excitement in shopping for it, designing with it, and enjoying it over the years.

Plants by Design

FORM

Large and small trees for character and emphasis

Above, the dogwood's rounded shape breaks the line of a fence. Opposite, the lofty pyramidal form of a dawn redwood is echoed where the trunk widens at its base.

Vase/Fan-Shaped Forms

Yellowwood (*Cladrastis lutea*)
Kousa or Japanese dogwood (*Cornus kousa*)
Tea crabapple (*Malus hupehensis*)
Japanese pagoda tree (*Sophora japonica*)
Zelkova (*Zelkova serrata*)

Pyramidal Forms

White fir (*Abies concolor*)
Sweet gum (*Liquidambar styraciflua*)
Dawn redwood (*Metasequoia glyptostrobides*)
Spruce (*Picea* spp.)
Korean mountain ash (*Sorbus alnifolia*)
Korean stewartia (*Stewartia koreana*)
Japanese stewartia (*Stewartia pseudocamellia*)
Littleleaf linden (*Tilia cordata*)
Hemlock (*Tsuga canadensis*)

Oval to Round Forms

Japanese maple (*Acer palmatum*)
Norway maple (*Acer platanoides*)
Sugar maple (*Acer saccharum*)
Horse chestnut (*Aesculus hippocastanum*)
Redbud (*Cercis canadensis*)
White fringe tree (*Chionanthus virginicus*)
Flowering dogwood (*Cornus florida*)
Cornelian cherry dogwood (*Cornus mas*)
Washington hawthorn (*Crataegus phaenopyrum*)
Beeches (*Fagus* spp.)
White ash (*Fraxinus americana*)
Saucer magnolia (*Magnolia soulangiana*)
Crabapples (*Malus* spp.)
Red oaks (*Quercus rubra*)
Willows (*Salix* spp.)
Lindens (*Tilia* spp.)

Weeping Forms

Weeping European beech (*Fagus sylvatica* 'Pendula')
Weeping cherry (*Prunus subhirtella* 'Pendula')
Weeping willows (*Salix* spp.)
Sargent weeping hemlock (*Tsuga canadensis* 'Pendula')

Columnar or Fastigiate Forms

Paper birch (*Betula papyrifera*)
Gray birch (*Betula populifolia*)
Pyramidal hornbeam (*Carpinus betulus* 'Columnaris')
Red cedar (*Juniperus virginiana*)
Hicks yew (*Taxus media* 'Hicksii')
American arborvitae (*Thuja occidentalis*)

Detailed information and recommended varieties can be found in Part III.

LANDSCAPE TASKS FOR DECEMBER

Bird Feeding If your yard is abundant in plants with seeds and fruits for birds, you may not need to supplement their diet with store-bought seeds. If not, now is the time to set up a feeding station or three. Warning: this is a winter-long commitment. It is not fair to accustom wildlife to feeding, then withdraw the supply. If you start now, plan to continue putting out provender until April.

Snow Stamping After a heavy snowfall, trample down circles around young fruit trees. This will protect them from tunneling rodents; the packed snow is hard to dig.

Protect tender plants from the full brunt of winter wind. This is one method; battens nailed outside burlap will keep the fabric from tearing loose from the stakes.

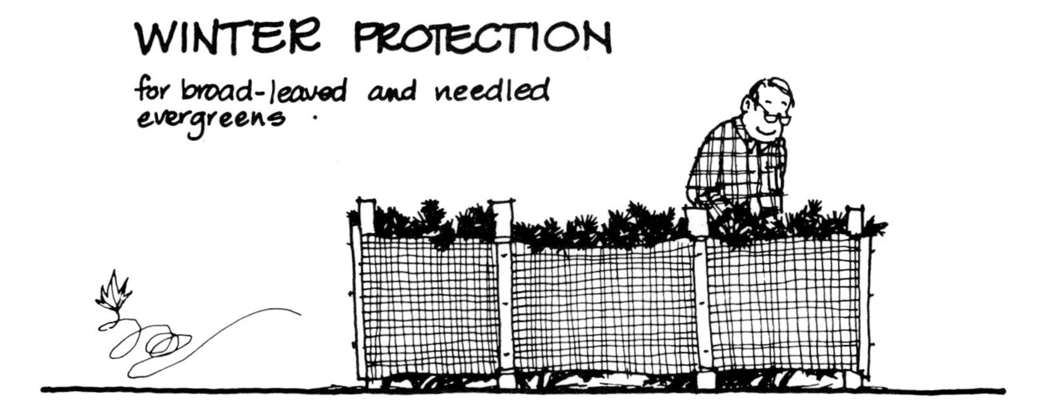

Needled and Broad-leaved Evergreens Until the ground freezes, water newly planted needled evergreen trees and shrubs. Once the ground is frozen, give them a thick mulch of straw or matted leaves to reduce damage from freeze-thaw cycles. Burlap windscreens to shelter evergreen shrubs from the prevailing winter wind are a good idea, too. Don't wrap the plants tightly, just create a barricade by driving stakes around them, then stretching the fabric around the stakes. Or build an informal A-frame of scrap lumber.

If you have boxwood or boxleaf holly plants in an exposed location, they too will benefit from burlap windbreaks.

Rhododendrons, azaleas, mountain laurel, and andromeda (pieris) will endure the coming months better if you can give them a few final waterings before the ground freezes solid. If they're not already well mulched, do it now. Antidesiccant spray can be applied to newly planted broad-leaves during a mild spell (40°F or up), to forestall damage from severe winter drying.

The flattened oval of a Japanese maple on an upper terrace stands out against an evergreen backdrop, especially in fall when the foliage turns scarlet.

Salt Advice Some gardeners find that a light application of commercial fertilizer melts ice from walks as effectively as salt — at least, as long as the cold is not too intense. If you must salt, keep the stuff away from lawns, shrubs, and all garden plantings. It is harmful to plants. It's also harmful to groundwater and aquifers, and should be used only when ice endangers life and limb.

One More Chance Here are a few samples of things you can still do if you've missed getting around to them before. It may be late, but it's still definitely beneficial to:

- Mulch perennials, shrubs, and all fruit-bearing garden plants with materials like oak leaves, pine straw, straw, bark chips, or evergreen boughs (except hemlocks, which rapidly lose their needles).
- Protect fruit trees, particularly young ones, with collars to fend off hungry animals.
- Clean up the dead remains of last summer's vegetation.
- Stake newly planted trees for support.
- Clean and oil those garden tools.
- Make lists of good ideas for next year.

Advance Notice At the other extreme, some tasks usually reserved for early in the new year can just as well be done now. For more details on all of these, see January:

- Send for seed catalogues and get your orders in early.
- Take hardwood cuttings of trees and shrubs.

December may seem a quiet month in the landscape. Summer's flowers and fruits have long since died or been harvested. Trees and shrubs and lawns are dormant. It's too cold to build anything. People are busy with other things; they haven't time even to page through the garden and nursery catalogues, much less make ambitious plans for redesigning the front entry area or planting dogwoods under the oaks. But don't let December fool you. This is really the upturn, the beginning of the great rebirth. The pace has been slowing; now it's about to speed up. As the days begin almost imperceptibly to lengthen at the end of this month, I like to look ahead to the new year, the coming spring, and everything starting anew once more.

PART III PLANT DESCRIPTIONS

Every plant recommended in this book is described here. This selection is by no means exhaustive; it represents many tough choices, for there are thousands of wonderful plants available. But at the least it should give you a good head start on deciding what plants will work for your landscape.

Opposite: forms, colors, and textures of conifers bring a winter landscape alive.

Type/Size Groupings For easy reference the descriptions are grouped according to type and approximate mature height of plant:

- Deciduous trees — small, medium, large
- Deciduous shrubs — small, medium, large
- Needled evergreen trees and shrubs
- Broad-leaved evergreens
- Deciduous ground covers
- Herbaceous perennial ground covers
- Evergreen ground covers
- Deciduous vines

These groupings are intended only as the most general guide. The maximum heights of trees and shrubs are very difficult to pinpoint; depending on genetic heritage and growing conditions, what looks like a big plant in the description may actually stay very modest in size, or vice versa. So don't let the size categories discourage you or tie you down.

Needled evergreen trees and shrubs are a somewhat special case. Many needled evergreen "shrubs" used in the landscape are actually dwarf or compact varieties of huge evergreen trees. But multiple descriptions would have required excessive repetition; so the small needled evergreens are included in descriptions with their large-sized ancestors. Be sure to glance through the descriptions to see what compact and dwarf plants are available.

Alphabetization Within each grouping, plants are almost always organized alphabetically according to botanical (Latin) name. Shadblow, for instance — whose other common names include Juneberry and serviceberry — appears under A for *Amelanchier*, its genus. The names of the two species I've described, *canadensis* and *laevis*, determine the order of appearance of the two plants within the *Amelanchier* genus.

There is an exception to this alphabetization system, however. Azaleas, which are of the *Rhododendron* genus, can be found under A for

Azalea in the Medium Deciduous Shrubs and Broad-leaved Evergreens sections.

Varieties and Cultivars A variety of a species is given as an extension of the italicized Latin name — such as *Salix alba tristis* for golden weeping willow. A cultivar — short for "cultivated variety" — is given as a capitalized name in single quotes, such as *Salix alba* 'Tristis', another frequently used form of the botanical name of golden weeping willow. In this instance I use the first form. But they're both the same plant, and you'll see both forms of the name in the literature and in your visits to nurseries. There are many discrepancies in writers' and nurserymen's handling of botanical names, so don't be alarmed if you encounter them with or without italic, quotes, capitals, or whatever.

The varieties and cultivars I offer here are by way of a guide to some of the most popular and time-tested plants, and/or to those that I have had happy experience with. Again, however, my suggestions should by no means dictate or limit your choice. Nurseries make new introductions all the time; besides, regional availability is widely diverse.

Cross-references You'll often find a plant named in one section with a cross-reference to a description appearing in another. This happens because a given vine (for instance) can also serve as a ground cover, or because a given small shrub is actually a cultivar of a large shrub or tree species. I've tried to be very thorough in cross-referencing; but if you're interested in a certain type of plant — say, maples or viburnums — please check in all the size groupings as well as the index so as not to overlook the very plant you want.

Cultural Specifications Where appropriate, I've spelled out plants' needs for sun, soil, shelter, etc. Where these are not mentioned, you can assume the plant is adaptable — but always consult your nurseryman about the particular variety you're considering.

Zone/Origin/Height Lines With each description (usually at the end) I've given the plant's northernmost hardiness zone, using the USDA zones shown on the map on pages 346–347. These zones reflect minimum winter temperatures, the lowest the plant will tolerate. The plant's origin, whether native to North America or imported from Europe or Asia, is shown next, followed by the *approximate* maximum mature size of the species named at the start of the description. Needless to say, many trees (particularly) take 20 or 50 or 100 years to reach the size indicated. And in many instances, compact or dwarf varieties suggested within the description are far smaller than the species height at maturity.

SMALL DECIDUOUS TREES

Approximately 12 to 30 feet mature height.

Acer griseum (paperbark maple) is named for its delicately peeling cinnamon-brown bark, and the bark is one of its great landscaping assets. Its other contributions are dainty three-part compound leaves, whose summer green changes to rich russet and red in fall; and a compact, upright, oval shape that makes this a good specimen plant for even a small garden. It tolerates soil of almost any type, including clay soils, although it prefers well-drained moist soil and a location in full sun.

Zone 6 / China / 20 to 30 feet

Acer palmatum (Japanese maple): The deeply lobed, star-shaped leaves of this small tree are a familiar sight in home landscapes — and no wonder. The Japanese maple is a picturesque plant, with pale gray branches that spread horizontally to create layers of light and color among the foliage and a low, rounded overall shape. You can grow it as an accent or specimen tree, or encourage multistemmed growth in a shrub border. Japanese maple prefers a moist, well-drained, slightly acid soil and a location where there is some protection from strong sun and drying winds. There are countless cultivars. Many have foliage in shades of red all season long, like bloodleaf Japanese maple (*Acer palmatum* 'Atropurpureum'), which like the species can grow into a sizable small tree up to 30 feet tall. Others have leaves that are cut between the lobes, like green cutleaf or threadleaf Japanese maple (*Acer palmatum* 'Dissectum') and red cutleaf Japanese maple (*Acer palmatum* 'Atropurpureum Dissectum'), which are smaller, more umbrella-shaped trees seen in Japanese gardens. Look for these and other time-tested cultivars at a reliable local nursery, since some of the newer or more esoteric cultivated varieties can be unpredictable.

Zone 6 / China, Korea, Japan / 30 feet

Amelanchier canadensis (shadblow) is so named because it blooms when the shad run upriver, in parts of the country where they have shad. It also goes by the names shadbush, downy serviceberry, juneberry, and service-tree — among others. This tall shrub or small tree is valuable for its white flowers in early spring, its streaky gray bark year-round, its brilliant yellow to red autumn color, and its berries, which are appetizing to birds. Its many stems and fine branches can form a rounded crown in an open sunny spot, although in the woods shadblow is more leggy. It thrives in moist or even wet acid soil and will tolerate full sun or partial shade. I like to use it in naturalistic plantings, woodland edges, or shrub borders.

Zone 5 / Native / 6 to 20 feet

Amelanchier laevis (Allegheny serviceberry) is very similar to its close relative, shadblow (*Amelanchier canadensis*). It's a lovely tree, with white flowers that bloom briefly in early spring, purplish young leaves that mature to green, then turn yellow or red in the fall; and sweet black berries that are great bait for birds and wildlife. It does well in acid soils and is ideal for naturalistic or woodland plantings. It is not temperamentally suited (or sufficiently pollution-tolerant) for urban settings. This is one *Amelanchier* that looks best as a single-stemmed tree, whereas the others lend themselves to growing with multiple stems or trunks.

Zone 5 / Native / 20 feet

Betula populifolia (gray birch) does have its liabilities — chiefly, a tendency to be fragile, with weak crotches, and to perish at the early age of fifteen or twenty years — but it is still a valuable plant for naturalistic landscapes where the more imposing native or European birches might be out of keeping, or (because of its size) for smaller properties. The gray birch has, despite its name, white bark. It usually grows multistemmed, and its delicate beauty derives both from that clustering effect and from the fine, dark green foliage that turns a glittering yellow in autumn. Given conditions to its liking, gray birch will colonize itself by seed or create thickets of suckers. It tolerates almost any soil: wet, dry, poor, rocky, even sterile burnt-over soil. (Maybe that's why it is sometimes called "poverty birch.") It will put up with full sun or partial shade, although it does not thrive if there's much competition from larger, hungrier plants.

Zone 4 / Native / 20 to 40 feet

Cercis canadensis (redbud): Also called eastern redbud or Judas tree, redbud has large, lustrous, heart-shaped leaves. Its trunk usually divides near the ground into several stems, and its ascending branches form a broad, spreading, flat-topped to rounded crown. Redbud is a member of the pea family; it bears pinkish-purple flowers in spring before its leaves emerge, making it a wonderful candidate for flower displays, and it produces pealike pods in fall. It does well in deep, well-drained, moist but not wet soils. Cuttings can be taken in midsummer if you want to propagate this tree. It's an all-purpose plant, attractive in woodland or wild landscapes, in group plantings, in shrub borders, or even as a specimen plant.

Zone 5 / Native / 20 to 30 feet

Chionanthus virginicus (white fringe tree): This small, spreading tree (or large shrub) blooms in June and looks like a snowstorm, covered with very pungently fragrant tassels of white. The male plants are more showy in flower than the females, but if you have a female fringe tree it will reward you in September with dark blue fruits that are a major attraction to birds. The leaves come out very late in the spring; they are lustrous and quite large, giving the fringe tree a relatively coarse foliage texture. In the right spot and with harmonious surrounding plantings, this is a wonderful specimen plant or candidate for grouped plantings or borders. It's especially valuable in city gardens or around large buildings, since it stands up to pollution and will tolerate a good deal of shade (although it will do best in full sun). Plant it in spring in moist, deep, somewhat acid soil. It almost never needs pruning.

Zone 5 / Native / 10 feet (30 in wild)

Cornus florida (flowering dogwood): This small tree is justly known as the best ornamental of all trees native to the northern United States. It holds its branches horizontally, and its spreading form is often wider than it is tall at maturity. Its beautiful white spring "flowers" are, like poinsettia "flowers," actually bracts, and they appear before the leaves. Flowering at the same time, pink flowering dogwood (*Cornus florida rubra*) makes a splash of clear, rosy coral. On both varieites, summer foliage is dark green and turns to purplish red in the autumn. The red berries of the flowering dogwood are loved by birds, and in winter its reddish young twigs add color to the landscape. Flowering dogwoods should be moved balled and burlapped, and need a well-drained, moist, acid soil. They thrive in partial shade although full sun will do. The only conditions they cannot survive are poorly drained soils or protracted drought. They will be beautiful wherever you put them, whether in groups or as specimen trees, near or at a distance from the house. A backdrop of dark color will show off the white-flowering ones especially well.

Zone 5 / Native / 20 to 40 feet

Cornus kousa (Kousa dogwood or Japanese dogwood) blooms about three weeks later than flowering dogwood (*Cornus florida*) and is a fuller, more densely branched tree. Its abundant white bracts — what we usually think of as its flowers — are pointed at the tip in contrast to the notched petals of the flowering dogwood. They are best viewed from above, since they are borne upward. Kousa dogwood not only blooms in spring, but it produces red fruits that look like raspberries in early fall, and scarlet to purple fall foliage; and its attractive exfoliating bark peels off to show cream and reddish patches that are a note of warmth in the winter landscape. This is a marvelous all-around tree for every kind of use — as a specimen, in grouped plantings, around buildings, in shrub borders. Its horizontally layered branches make a crisp counterpoint to the dominant vertical lines of buildings or other trees. It does demand a well-drained, moist, acid soil that is high in organic matter, and plenty of sun.

Zone 6 / Japan / 20 feet

Cornus mas (Cornelian cherry dogwood): See Large Deciduous Shrubs.

Cotinus coggygria (smoke tree): Among the virtues of this small tree (sometimes considered a large shrub) are its adaptability and ease of transplanting. You can move smoke tree bareroot or balled and burlapped, and it will survive in almost any well-drained soil. Once established, it demands almost no upkeep. It has a loose, open habit of growth — you might even say unkempt — so I plant several together for a better overall effect. Smoke tree has medium-textured blue-green foliage. It gets its name from the long, drooping, pinkish-grayish clusters of flowers it bears in midsummer, which do give the whole tree a smoky, cloudy appearance. A perfectly beautiful variety that is a favorite of mine is purple smoke tree, *Cotinus coggygria* 'Purpureus'.

Zone 6 / Southern Europe to China / 15 feet

Crataegus phaenopyrum (Washington hawthorn): This small tree, with its picturesque thorny branches and beautiful, jagged-edged leaves, has something to offer in every department. Its clusters of dainty white flowers come in June; its fall foliage is a handsome red-orange; its glossy red fruits ripen in autumn but remain on the tree all winter, which contributes color to the landscape and appeals to the bird population. Washington hawthorn is great for hedges and screens, since it does not mind being clipped or pruned, but it also makes an attractive accent plant. It does have a couple of liabilities, however. Its thorny twigs can be treacherous to the uninitiated; so put it in a place where traffic is infrequent. Also, some people dislike the smell of the flowers — another reason for putting the tree a distance from the house, preferably in a spot with full sun.

Zone 5 / Native / 25 to 30 feet

Enkianthus campanulatus (redvein enkianthus): See Large Deciduous Shrubs.

Hamamelis mollis (Chinese witch hazel): See Large Deciduous Shrubs.

Koelreuteria paniculata (goldenrain tree): In mid-July this small shade tree produces a glorious show of large, drooping clusters of yellow flowers — "very lovely to look upon and lie under," one writer says, and I agree. The many-lobed leaves are almost fernlike in complexity, and they make a dense, neatly rounded mass in summer; the slightly ascending branches are not dense, however, and in winter they are a delicate fan against the sky. Goldenrain tree will prosper in a sunny location with any kind of soil. Another big point in its favor is that it will survive drought, heat, wind, alkaline soils, and polluted air. Prune it for shape or size during winter; its flower buds will form on the spring's new growth.

Zone 6 / China, Korea, Japan / 30 feet (equally wide)

MAGNOLIA SPP.

Magnolias should be planted in early spring only. They need deep, moist, acid soil with ample organic matter. Give them full sun, or at most some light shade. Although these are small trees above ground, they need ample room for their roots to develop. Avoid putting magnolias against south-facing walls, where the sun's heat will bring their buds out early, only to be nipped by the year's last spring frosts.

***Magnolia loebneri* 'Merrill'** (Merrill magnolia): The notable attribute of this hybrid is that it grows much faster and flowers younger than most other magnolias — even younger than star magnolia. It is a vigorous, spreading, sturdy tree. If you have the patience, it can easily be propagated by softwood cuttings.

Magnolia soulangiana (saucer magnolia): If you appreciate the flowers of this tree you will forgive them their habit of dropping messy brown petals all over the lawn after they bloom. The blossoms are as much as 10 inches across and shaped more like cups or goblets than "saucers." They range in color from lavender to deep magenta-purple. Emerging in April before the leaves, they make a stunning display. This tree is slow-growing (although it blooms at a very young age) and as wide-spreading as it is high. It often produces multiple stems like a shrub.

Magnolia stellata (star magnolia) is one of the earliest magnolias to bloom; one of the hardiest of the Asiatic varieties; and a much-loved, much-used specimen flowering tree that never wears out its welcome. The fuzzy, silky buds and lavish white April flowers with their 12 to 15 floppy petals give this tree a special place in people's hearts. They make a stunning contrast to city walls — or to the browns of rural landscapes where few other trees or shrubs have come alive yet.

Zones 5 to 6 / Japan, China / 15 to 30 feet

Malus **(flowering crabapple) variety.**

MALUS SPP.

Flowering crabapple (or crab, for short) varieties, clones, and cultivars are so numerous that I can't even tell you how many there are. New ones are being discovered or developed as you read this, because crabapples hybridize themselves with reckless abandon. A good nursery, however, will offer a few fine proven varieties. You can choose the particular size of tree, overall branching form, shade of blossom, and color and size of fruit that appeal to you. Do be sure to pick varieties known to be resistant to fire blight and apple scab, two scourges of crabapples. All types mentioned below are resistant, with the possible exceptions of *Malus hupehensis* and *Malus* 'Red Jade' — but these two are great favorites with which I've always had good luck, so I include them for your consideration.

Give any flowering crabapple a moist, well-drained, acid loam and plenty of sun. If pruning is necessary, do it very discreetly right after flowering in early June. Most flowering crabs will be hardy in Zone 5. In height most of these trees range from 15 to perhaps 30 feet, but their different shapes and branching habits are as numerous as their varieties.

Malus floribunda (Japanese flowering crabapple) is one of the choicest of all. Clothed in fragrant white blossoms in early May, it is a miraculous sight. It's hard to overuse a tree like this. Plant it as a single specimen, in a cluster, at the edge of woodland, next to a house, in a patio, in a shrub border, or wherever. Japanese flowering crab offers a neat rounded form and fine foliage texture all summer — and its small red fruits give it particular appeal to birds in the autumn.

Malus hupehensis (tea crabapple) is one great favorite for its vase-shaped form. Its branches spread out and upward to give it a shape like a fan or inverted triangle. In spring, pink buds open to fragrant white flowers all along its branches and twigs; and in fall the fruits are greenish-yellow to red.

***Malus* 'Mary Potter'** (Mary Potter crab) is another type with pink buds and white blossoms, but with profuse red fruits, a wide, upright form, and picturesquely curved branches.

Malus sargentii (Sargent crabapple): See Large Deciduous Shrubs.

Other good varieties are 'Adams', for pink flowers and long-lasting, cherry-sized fruit; 'Donald Wyman', whose low, broad, mounded shape is a mass of white bloom in spring; 'Red Jade', which is named for its abundant and enduring bright-red fruit, and which boasts gracefully weeping branches and white flowers; 'Winter Gold', another white-flowered type with beautiful yellow fruits in the fall (but they darken after frost); and the hybrid *zumi calocarpa*, most noted for its glowing red fruits that hang on the tree — for color and for bird appeal — all the way into February.

Oxydendrum arboreum (sorrel tree or sourwood) is sometimes called lily-of-the-valley tree for the clusters of sweet-smelling flowers, similar to lilies-of-the-valley, that it bears in August to September. But its flowers are just one of its fine attributes. The leaves are a lustrous dark green and shaped like the leaves of laurel (to which sorrel tree is related); but in fall, unlike laurel leaves, they turn a gorgeous scarlet. The bark is gray, deeply furrowed, with scaly ridges. The overall shape is a tidy round-topped pyramid, with drooping branches. All in all, this is a born specimen tree: a star at every season, not a plant to be relegated to a background role. Move it balled and burlapped into a good location in full sun (where its flowering and fall color will be at their best) or in partial shade. Sorrel tree should have an acid, peaty, moist, well-drained soil.

Zone 5 / Native / 25 to 30 feet (75 in wild)

PRUNUS SPP.

Flowering cherry: Many of these beautiful ornamental trees come to this country from the Orient, bringing with them the elegant decorative quality that we associate with classical Chinese or Japanese design. The *Prunus* genus includes a vast and complex diversity of species, natural varieties, and cultivars and hybrids — among them all the cherries, native and imported, as well as all the apricot, plum, prune, peach, nectarine, and almond species. (Think of their stone pits and you'll see the family resemblance.) All I'll do here, however, is touch upon a selection of the most tried and true flowering cherries for spring display.

Cherries are very flexible as to soil, provided it is well drained. They need full sun for good flowering, which at best lasts no longer than 10 days. They do not do well in badly polluted circumstances. Cherries are relatively short-lived plants — many varieties live only about 20 years. But these few drawbacks should not deter anyone from enjoying their extraordinary loveliness while they last.

Prunus sargentii (Sargent cherry): See Medium Deciduous Trees.

Prunus serotina (black or rum cherry): See Large Deciduous Trees.

Prunus serrula (paperbark cherry) comes from China, and although it can be hard to find in nurseries it is worth the search. Its bark is a beautiful, lustrous, dark mahogany-red, a wonderful asset in winter. The May flowers are white and pleasant, although not as spectacular as the bark. This is a small, vigorous tree that reaches a top height of 30 feet and is hardy in Zone 6.

Prunus serrulata (Oriental cherry): Oriental cherries are mainly available in the form of cultivars — of which there are about 120 in existence, with at least 50 sold in the United States. Every good nursery will offer a few. Oriental cherries are usually upright or vase-shaped, with white, pale pink, or deep pink blooms, many double. The 'Kwanzan' cherry, one of this group, is a highly popular and hardy double-flowering type. It has deep-pink blossoms and heavy vase-shaped branching with glossy bark. Another popular form is 'Amanogawa', which grows narrow and tall and makes a good hedge or barrier. It has large double light pink flowers. Oriental cherries grow to 20 feet or so; they are indigenous to China, Korea, and Japan and are hardy in Zone 6 or Zone 7, depending on the variety.

Prunus subhirtella (Higan cherry) from Japan, is another plant seen mostly in the form of specific varieties and cultivars. And they are remarkable. In height they range from 15 to 30 feet. One is the weeping cherry (*Prunus subhirtella* 'Pendula'), with pink flowers that bloom in April on slender, gracefully weeping branches — the tree looks like a fountain of pale pink. Another cultivar, autumn-flowering cherry (*Prunus subhirtella* 'Autumnalis'), produces pink flower buds in summer that will open in a mild autumn, then bloom fully again the following spring. A popular cultivar is Hally Jolivette cherry (*Prunus subhirtella* 'Hally Jolivette'), a small plant with delicate pink blooms and multiple slender stems. As a group, Higan cherries are hardy in Zone 6.

Prunus yedoensis (Yoshino cherry) is also Japanese. It is one of the taller cherries, at 40 feet, and its spreading tiers of fragrant white to pale pink blossoms are a beautiful sight in May. This variety makes up the majority of the Washington, D.C., tidal basin cherry-blossom display. It is hardy in Zone 6.

Rhus copallina (shining sumac): See Large Deciduous Shrubs.

Syringa reticulata (Japanese tree lilac): Unlike the better-known shrubby forms of lilac, this is a true tree, with bark like a cherry's. Its stiff, spreading branches make a rounded umbrellalike crown. The large, pyramidal, creamy-white flower clusters bloom in mid-June. Their scent is heavy, almost annoying to some people. You can use Japanese tree lilac as a specimen tree, or in groups, or even as a street tree — it's very pest-free and easy to care for. Give it rich soil, an airy location, and full sun for best flowering.

Zone 5 / Japan / 20 to 30 feet

Viburnum prunifolium (black haw): Although it's a member of the viburnum group, black haw is often seen not as a shrub (like many viburnums) but as a small tree. It's very adaptable as to soil and sun. It resembles a hawthorn in habit: stiffly branched and twiggy, upright and round-headed overall. You can encourage multi-stemmed growth and use it as a hedge plant, or train a single stem and let it develop as a specimen or as a component in a shrub border or massed planting. Its dark green foliage turns red to bronze in the autumn. Its large, creamy-white flat-topped flower clusters appear in mid-May. The clustered fruits are interesting: as they ripen they pass from yellow to rose to blue-black, and often you'll find all hues represented in one cluster. Birds eat them up. People relish them too, and have used them for preserves since Colonial times.

Zone 4 / Native / 12 to 20 feet

Viburnum sieboldii (Siebold viburnum): See Large Deciduous Shrubs.

MEDIUM DECIDUOUS TREES

Approximately 30 to 50 feet mature height.

Acer platanoides (Norway maple): I recommend using one of the reliable cultivars (see below) of this tough and versatile shade tree. Unlike some other maples, Norway maple will tolerate street fumes and city pollution, and it will get along in hot, dry conditions and poor soils, even sand or clay. With all these sterling qualifications it's easy to see why Norway maple is sometimes considered overused. It casts a thick shade in summer. In fall its big star-shaped leaves are bright golden yellow; and there are tons of them, so be prepared to rake. Give this tree plenty of room, both for its rounded, densely branched crown and for its shallow but spreading root system (which makes growing anything under it, including grass, nearly impossible). Two excellent cultivars are 'Emerald Queen', a rapid grower with great resistance to pests and diseases and an upright oval form; and 'Summer Shade', a similar tree but with leathery dark green leaves.

Zone 4 / Europe / 40 to 50 feet (90 in wild)

Aesculus carnea (red horse chestnut) a hybrid with deep-pink flowers and far darker green leaves than the common horse chestnut, is valued both for its mid-May blooms and for its dense, rounded form. It shares many of the liabilities as well as the assets of other horse chestnuts (see horse chestnut, *Aesculus hippocastanum,* in Large Deciduous Trees, below) and should be used only if you have plenty of space so that its untidiness won't be a problem. It likes well-drained soil in light shade or full sun. A strikingly handsome variety in bloom is the ruby horse chestnut (*Aesculus carnea* 'Briotii'), with extra-large clusters of deep rose to red flowers.

Zone 4 / Hybrid (Europe) / 30 to 40 feet

Betula nigra (river birch, also called red birch) is one birch that thrives in wet acid soils. And in fact its fondness for wet feet is one of its main claims to fame. It also, however, has fine-textured foliage and russet-tinged exfoliating bark, so that it lends a lively accent of texture and color to the landscape. It is an excellent specimen tree for wild or wide-open landscapes. The trunk often divides near the ground, so that each tree looks like two or more trees growing together. The overall form of the tree is pyramidal to oval-headed, but growing more rounded in maturity.

Zone 5 / Native / 40 to 90 feet

Betula pendula (weeping birch or European white birch) has white bark at an earlier age than paper birch (see *Betula papyrifera* in Large Deciduous Trees), and is a very graceful, very popular tree for the residential landscape. Its fine, slightly drooping branches and delicate twigs form a symmetrical pyramid. Its leaves are glossy and even smaller and more triangular than those of the paper birch; they stay green relatively late in the fall, then turn yellow-green or yellow. Weeping birch is fast-growing and hardy, although like many birches it tends to die young. It's easy to transplant and tolerant of many soils. If it needs pruning, do it in summer or fall, since late-winter or early-spring pruning will cause copious "bleeding." Cutleaf weeping birch (*Betula pendula* 'Gracilis') is another vigorous, rapid grower, with an elegant upright form, pendulous branches, and deeply cut leaves that grow on clustered stems, giving the foliage a fine lacy texture.

Zone 3 / Europe / 40 to 50 feet

Cercidiphyllum japonicum (Katsura tree) has leaves much like those of redbud (*Cercis canadensis,* in Small Deciduous Trees) — shaped like plump, rounded hearts — but smaller, and slightly scalloped all around. In fall the foliage is yellow-orange to scarlet. The bark is brown and rather shaggy in maturity. This makes a lovely, fine-textured specimen tree for shade. It's untroubled by pests and diseases and very adaptable as to soil, provided it gets enough moisture. It prefers to be planted in early spring. You can let Katsura tree develop with multiple stems, or limit it to one. If kept to one central trunk, it will be a slim upright oval for its first 20 years or so, then grow more massive and spreading in old age.

Zone 5 / China, Japan / 40 to 60 feet

Cladrastis lutea (American yellowwood) is a small shade tree that grows as broad as it is tall, with a rounded crown of delicate branches. Its extremely smooth gray bark makes a handsome winter accent; its white early-June flowers are abundant and popular with bees; and its bright yellowish-green foliage is another asset. Yellowwood can be transplanted balled and burlapped into well-drained soil, and it is not particular as to alkalinity or acidity. Prune yellowwood only in summer — it will "bleed" profusely at other seasons. It is lovely as a specimen or in groupings.

Zone 4 / Native / 30 to 50 feet

Phellodendron amurense (Amur cork tree): The short, stout trunk of the cork tree separates just a few feet from the ground into several large, outspread branches that grow up and out to give the tree a low, spreading, open-topped shape. Its small, yellow-green compound leaflets cast a light, open shade. When amur cork tree is old (but not until then) the bark forms the beautiful corklike ridges for which the tree is named, and the overall form is extremely picturesque. This is an unusual and decorative plant for large properties, but both its branches and its shallow, fibrous roots are too wide reaching for any spot where space is at a premium. It will thrive in any soil and happily endures both drought and pollution. It does best in ample sun.

Zone 4 / China / 30 to 45 feet (equally wide)

***Prunus sargentii* (Sargent cherry).**

Prunus sargentii (Sargent cherry) is a big tree as cherries go, occasionally reaching a height of 50 feet or more, and spreading to be as broad as it is tall. Its pink flowers are the earliest to bloom of all cherries, coming in late April to early May; its leaves are a shiny dark green, changing to deep red-bronze in fall; and its berries, ripening in midsummer, are black and elongated.

Zone 5 / Japan / 50 feet

***Pyrus calleryana* 'Bradford'** (Bradford callery pear) is one of the very few pears sufficiently resistant to pear trees' many blights and pests to qualify as a top-notch ornamental tree. Its uplifted branches form a tidy pyramid, and in spring the tree is a cloud of purest white bloom. The leaves are a glossy, deep green and change to rich red or purple late in the autumn. Don't expect a harvest from this tree, however: there aren't any fruits. Bradford callery pear is wonderful for a suburban street or city tree, since it tolerates pollution, dryness, poor soils, and cramped quarters (although it is subject to damage from ice storms). Try to give it full sun for the best bloom and leaf color. Try not to prune it, since its tightly branched limbs help support each other.

Zone 5 / China (clone) / 30 to 50 feet

Salix elegantissima (Thurlow weeping willow): The leaves of this elegant tree are narrow slivers of dark green, hanging on long, graceful branches that sweep down all the way to the ground. The younger twigs are also green. As a whole the Thurlow willow is upright and moderate in size, not built on so grand a scale as the golden weeping willow (*Salix alba tristis*, in Large Deciduous Trees). It is perfectly hardy as far north as Zone 5. Beautiful near water, where reflections enhance the effect of weeping, this willow will grow in any damp or moist soil. Give it full sun, and prune in summer or fall if necessary.

Zone 5 / Hybrid (China) / 40 feet

Sassafras albidum (sassafras): Although this tree can be tricky to transplant (having a deep taproot), once established it thrives in poor, gravelly soil. It will generate multiple shoots around its base — gradually turning its trunk into a wonderful free-form sculpture. Its form is pyramidal at first, then irregularly flat-topped, with short, stout, contorted branches. Sassafras leaves come in all shapes, from elliptical to mitten-shaped or three-lobed; in autumn they change to yellow, orange, deep scarlet, or purple. The fall foliage alone makes this an outstanding ornamental tree. The roots and the corky, dark reddish-brown bark contain an aromatic oil and were used by early settlers to make sassafras tea. Sassafras is usually found as a container plant in the nursery. Give it a well-drained, loamy, acid soil with full sun or light shade. It's a good specimen tree, or attractive in small groups or naturalistic plantings.

Zone 5 / Native / 30 to 60 feet

Sophora japonica (Japanese pagoda tree): See Large Deciduous Trees.

Sorbus alnifolia (Korean mountain ash) is a modest-sized but upright tree, with smooth, dark gray bark and bright green leaves that bear a strong resemblance to beech leaves. Its white flowers form large, flat-topped clusters in May. The September fruits are handsome red-orange berries, also appearing in clusters, and the fall foliage turns orange and scarlet to match. This is a great all-around specimen tree for lawns in country or suburban areas, but it will not stand city pollution. Other than that it is most flexible and undemanding and will perform well in just about any well-drained soil. (I would not recommend other species of mountain ash, however. They are seriously disease-prone.)

Zone 6 / China, Korea, Japan / 40 to 50 feet

Stewartia koreana (Korean stewartia): Like all stewartias, this tree can be hard to find commercially and is relatively fussy to transplant (in spring only, please). Yet in every way and at every season, Korean stewartia is a real star in the landscape. Its form is a dense, upright pyramid. In July it bears large, cup-shaped, white flowers with prominent yellow stamens. The camellia-like leaves are a glossy deep green; in fall they turn brilliant orange or scarlet. The bark is a dark brown that flakes like a sycamore's to reveal patches of green beneath. Give this tree a moist, acid soil with plenty of peat moss or compost added, and try to provide a sheltered location with sun most of the day, but not during the hottest hours.

Zone 6 / Korea / 35 to 45 feet

Stewartia pseudocamellia (Japanese stewartia), another member of this elegant genus, can grow considerably taller than Korean stewartia. Its form is pyramidal; its bark is a strong red-brown, peeling in long plates; and its fall foliage is purplish-red. The white camellia-like flowers, somewhat smaller than those of Korean stewartia, are a lovely sight blooming in July against the dark green foliage. Move this tree with tender loving care (see Korean stewartia) and only in spring. Give it moist, acid, humusy soil and protection from burning sun.

Zone 6 / Japan / 60 feet

Tilia euchlora (Crimean linden): This lovely hybrid linden forms an upright, symmetrical pyramid, its branches extending outward or drooping slightly from its straight trunk. The glossy bright green leaves are heart-shaped, and the small yellow flowers contribute a delightful fragrance in late June or early July. A vigorous grower, Crimean linden does a great job as a shade tree and tolerates street and city circumstances well. It requires a good deal of sun and a good, moist soil. (For larger lindens, see Large Deciduous Trees.)

Zone 5 / Hybrid (Europe) / 40 to 60 feet

LARGE DECIDUOUS TREES

Approximately 50 to over 100 feet mature height.

Acer rubrum (red maple): The branches of this tall shade tree form a pyramidal or elliptical shape in maturity. The bark is a light gray that stands out in winter woodlands; the trunk grows more and more rough and scaly in old age, while the branches stay a smooth gray. The red maple is named not for its foliage (as is sometimes said) but for its small spring flowers. They are so profuse that they give the woods a red haze in early April, and they're followed by fruits that continue the color. The fall foliage ranges from yellow to crimson. Also called swamp maple, this tree is a fast grower, tolerates damp conditions, and prefers an acid soil. Red maple is beloved of birds for both food and cover. One cultivar that's particularly glorious in its fall foliage is the aptly named 'October Glory'.

Zone 4 / Native / 60 feet (120 in wild)

Acer saccharum (sugar maple), often called rock maple or hard maple, is another wonderful shade tree for large lawns or wild landscapes. It does poorly, however, in crowded circumstances, it can't handle pollution, and de-icing salts kill it; so it is not a city tree. Its fall foliage is chiefly brilliant yellow to burnt orange or reddish — the mainstay of New England's fall color extravaganza. Sugar maples tolerate some shade, and like a well-drained, fairly moist, fertile soil. 'Green Mountain' is a cultivar that withstands dry conditions well and has the added virtue of vibrant orange to scarlet fall foliage. Unless you have an awful lot of sugar maples, a lot of space, and a lot of time, I don't recommend that you try to make maple syrup. You have to boil down over 4 gallons of sap for every pint of syrup you get.

Zone 4 / Native / 60 feet (120 in wild)

Aesculus hippocastanum (horse chestnut): This is one of those trees that used to be fashionable and therefore widely planted, but now have fallen out of style. Yet there are those who love it, for three reasons. The first is its white mid-May flowers, which resemble little Christmas trees or candelabra all over the tree, each 10-inch cone of blossoms held upright atop a platter of outspread leaves. The second is its silken-skinned brown nuts, nested singly or in pairs inside their spiky hulls, which plop to the ground in September to delight the squirrels and schoolchildren. The third reason derives from its former popularity: the horse chestnut was part of many people's youth and evokes a nostalgic warmth in their hearts. If you want to have horse chestnuts, a roomy property is the best. They're too messy for use on small lawns or along streets, since they're always dropping leaves, twigs, or fruits. Plant horse chestnuts in well-drained soil in light shade or full sun. 'Baumannii' is a good choice; its flowers are long-lasting and it doesn't produce any of those prickly chestnuts. (For the smaller red horse chestnut, see Medium Deciduous Trees.)

Zone 4 / Southern Europe / 50 to 75 feet

Betula papyrifera (paper birch or canoe birch) starts out in life with brown bark, and its younger branches stay reddish-brown; but by the time the tree is about 15 feet tall the trunk turns a chalky white with faint horizontal black markings. The bark peels in thin layers: this is the stuff of birchbark scrolls and birchbark canoes. A much-loved tree and a native fixture of the American landscape, paper birch can have multiple stems or a single sturdy trunk, and either way it is a beautiful tree for larger lawns or large area plantings. Its youthful pyramidal form gives way to an irregular, more or less oval form in older age. The leaves are small and pointed, almost wedge-shaped. The foliage, when stippled with sunlight, makes glittering patterns in the wind — the more so when autumn turns it bright yellow. Give paper birch ample sun and a well-drained soil; it does best in an acid, moist, sandy or silty loam.

Zone 3 / Native / 50 to 70 feet (90 to 120 in wild)

Carpinus betulus (European hornbeam): This elegant tree has striated gray bark and graceful slender branches. Its dense foliage is dark green in summer, yellow or yellowish-green in fall, and virtually pest-free. The European hornbeam is also wonderfully adaptable: it will grow in almost any well-drained soil; it will tolerate light shade or prosper in full sun; it does fine around large buildings, along streets, in paved areas, and in landscape groupings; and it puts up with shearing to the extent that it can even be used as a hedge plant.

Zone 5 / Europe / 40 to 60 feet

Carya ovata (shagbark hickory): This large, beautiful tree is named for its dark gray, deeply fissured, shaggy bark. It usually develops a straight, cylindrical trunk and tall crown. The fragrance of hickory smoke is familiar to everyone, if only in the form of smoked ham — and all hickories have edible nuts, some more edible than others. A cousin of the shagbark hickory, for instance, is the pecan tree. There are just a few drawbacks to hickories as landscape plants. For one thing, they are almost impossible to transplant because of their very deep taproots. For another, they have a tendency to drop bits and pieces all year long: leaves, stems, fruit, or all three. They are also very tall when they reach their growth; they're not for the small yard. But if you have an open or wooded area with hickories in it, by all means keep them (or plant new ones). They are lovely to have.

Zone 5 / Native / 60 to 120 feet

Fagus grandifolia (American beech) is a magnificent forest or parkland tree, although not at all a tree for a small yard or urban setting. On top of that, it grows quite slowly (if you plant a young beech it will attain its mature glory in your great-grandchildren's time) — so I don't recommend that you go shopping for beeches unless you're adding native trees to your woodland setting. If you have an American beech on your property, you are lucky. The smooth, silvery bark is elegant all year round. The tall, straight trunk supports many horizontally spreading branches with delicate twigs, and the bright foliage captures sunlight all summer and turns a beautiful golden bronze in fall. Sometimes the dry leaves hang on through the winter. The shallow roots spread picturesquely around the base of the tree, stopping growth of anything else there except moss; and the prickly nuts attract many of the most appealing wild birds and small animals. Beeches prefer acid soil, full sun, and plenty of room.

Zone 4 / Native / 70 to 120 feet

Fagus sylvatica (European beech) has been loved and cultivated for centuries, here and in Europe. It is a gorgeous, symmetrical tree that grows almost as broad as it is tall, with light gray bark that takes on a sculptural quality. Its shimmering deep green foliage often sweeps the ground, and the branches spread out and upwards from a base low on the trunk. It is not for small properties. Left to grow unimpeded as a specimen tree, European beech will attain a huge height and girth (there's one in England with a trunk 21 feet around); but it also takes to pruning and shaping, to the degree that it can be used as a hedge plant. Like the American beech, it has bronze fall foliage and seeds that are much appreciated by wildlife. It is almost as hardy as American beech, and prefers moist, well-drained soil with plenty of sun. One of the most famous cultivars of European beech is the copper beech (*Fagus sylvatica* 'Atropunicea' or 'Cuprea'); another fine purple-leaved cultivar is the Rivers beech (*Fagus sylvatica* 'Riversii'). Weeping beech (*Fagus sylvatica* 'Pendula') has gracefully drooping branches that give it a special gravity and elegance in winter.

Zone 5 / Europe / 50 to 100 feet

Fraxinus americana (white ash) is a big, rangy, fast-growing tree. In the wild its seeds rapidly create thickets of young trees, and these can be a nuisance if they get out of control. If you can contain it, however, white ash makes a handsome shade tree, with dense summer foliage, good fall color (anything from yellow to red to purple), and impressive overall size. Besides, it is very flexible as to soil type and other growing conditions — although it prefers full sun. The best white ashes for residential landscapes are cultivars, which tend to be more modest in size and less vulnerable to blights and pests than the basic species. One excellent type is 'Rosehill', which has reddish-bronze fall foliage; tolerates poor, alkaline soils; and won't produce seeds, so that you won't be overrun by ash seedlings.

Zone 4 / Native / 50 to 80 feet (120 in wild)

Ginkgo biloba (ginkgo or maidenhair tree): This prehistoric plant has survived virtually unchanged for 150 million years. Its leaves are unique and unmistakable: small green fans that shed a dappled, open shade and turn a buttery yellow in fall. The dark, rigid branches with their many short twigs are as distinctive in winter as the whole tree is year round. Ginkgo is very adaptable and immune to insects and blights. It prefers a sandy, deep, moist soil but will grow almost anywhere and in soil of any acidity or alkalinity; it's a fine tree for difficult situations, including city conditions, as long as there's ample sun. Generally, male ginkgos are the only ones offered for sale, since the females' seeds create a messy maintenance job and have a foul smell too.

Zone 5 / China / 50 to 80 feet

Gleditsia triacanthos (honey locust) has wicked thorns all over its trunk and branches, so that it's not really a tree for the domestic landscape; but its thornless varieties (*Gleditsia triacanthos inermis*, available in many cultivars) are very popular for their delicate pealike foliage and outstanding adaptability. They are tolerant of salt, drought, alkaline soils, and pollution, so they're much loved by city dwellers and people with seaside gardens. Besides, their roots run deep and won't heave sidewalks, and their small leaves require no raking to speak of. As with a few other trees and shrubs I'll mention, the honey locust has suffered somewhat from overuse by urban landscape architects and highway planners — but it can still be a lovely solution for a difficult site where very light, dappled shade is the goal. Consider the cultivars 'Halka', 'Shademaster', and 'Skyline', which offer steeply uplifted branches and symmetrical forms.

Zone 5 / Native / 30 to 100 feet

Liquidambar styraciflua (sweet gum tree), named for its fragrant, sticky sap, needs plenty of space around it for its wide-reaching roots, so that it's not a tree for a city garden. But given room enough, this is a most elegant, symmetrical specimen tree. Its serrated star-shaped leaves are an exceptionally beautiful green in summer and turn anything from yellow to scarlet to purple in the fall. Its fall fruits are round, spiky brown clusters of seed capsules, popular for Christmas decorations although somewhat messy under foot. Plant sweet gum in the spring, in deep, moist, slightly acid soil. Give it full sun. It takes a while to settle down, but once established it is no trouble to maintain.

Zone 6 / Native / 60 to 75 feet (120 in wild)

Liriodendron tulipifera (tulip tree) is one of those plants that people persist in loving even despite a few rather serious liabilities. It is very large in maturity; it is somewhat weak-wooded; and it suffers dreadfully from scale and aphid infestations and related fungus diseases. Nevertheless, its large, cup-shaped greenish-yellow-orange June blossoms, bright yellow autumn color, and handsome pyramidal form have earned it a place in the landscape. It is definitely a specimen tree for roomy locations. Its large leaves cast a dense shade. There are some 100-foot-tall tulip trees on the lawn at Mount Vernon, with trunks 6 feet in diameter. As a child I dug a small tulip tree out of the woods and transplanted it; at first the leaves withered and dropped, but an old gardener friend cut it back and it survived. Now, thirty years later, it stands 70 feet tall and has a trunk 2 feet across. Plant tulip tree in early spring, and give it full sun and a deep, moist, well-drained loam.

Zone 5 / Native / 70 to 150 feet

Metasequoia glyptostroboides (dawn redwood): This tree is something of a curiosity in the average landscape, but a very handsome one that deserves your consideration. It needs a sunny, large-scale setting. It is a deciduous conifer of very ancient pedigree (50 million years old, a survivor from the earth's prehistoric forests and thought to be extinct until found in China in 1944). Both its overall form and its trunk are conical: the trunk is fluted or buttressed at the bottom and dwindles upwards to its straight, slender top, so that it has a unique appearance in winter. The bark is reddish and exfoliates in long strips. The branches are held outwards horizontally or droop slightly, and the twigs are very fine. The fronds of bright green hemlocklike needles give a soft texture to the tree in summer. Dawn redwood likes moist (or even damp), slightly acid soils. It is easy to establish and grows rapidly into a very large specimen.

Zone 6 / China / 100 feet

Nyssa sylvatica (black gum or black tupelo) grows wild on hillsides and in swampy places throughout the eastern United States. This can be a superb ornamental tree — the only difficulty being that it is somewhat tricky to transplant because of its deep taproot. But plant it with care into deep, moist, acid soil, and you will have a specimen plant of singular beauty. The form of black gum is pyramidal in youth but more round-topped in maturity, with close-set, horizontal or slightly pendulous branches. Its bark is almost black and eventually grows cracked and ridged into an alligator texture. The lustrous dark green leaves change to vibrant, glowing yellows, oranges, and scarlets in fall. Black gum prefers sun or semishade; it is not tolerant of air pollution, so it grows best in open areas or in naturalized or woodland plantings.

Zone 5 / Native / 90 feet

Prunus serotina (black cherry or rum cherry) can grow to be a very big tree with dark brown bark, drooping branches, and graceful, lustrous dark green leaves. Its branches are covered with pendulous clusters of white blossoms in May; the blossoms are succeeded by fruits that ripen from colorful red to black in August and September. This hardy native grows wild almost everywhere, from moist, fertile soils to gravelly uplands to dry, sandy locations. Too often passed up (both by nurserymen and by consumers) in favor of less sturdy imported plants, black cherry is a fine tree. It has been valued since earliest Colonial times for its lumber — and since long before that for its fruits, which make fine wine and jelly as well as fine provender for birds. (Also see Small Deciduous Trees for a group of lovely Oriental flowering cherries.)

Zone 4 / Native / 50 to 60 feet (100 in wild)

Pseudolarix kaempferi (golden larch), also called *Pseudolarix amabilis*, is a rare member of the select group of deciduous conifers. Its cones are striking (although borne high in the tree so that they can be hard to see): they are a handsome reddish-brown and shaped like roses in full bloom. In the fall the long, soft, light green needles of golden larch turn a bright yellow. Its winter skeleton is a broad pyramid of fine brown twigs. With its open texture and wide-spreading, horizontal branches, this tree has a lovely profile in the landscape year-round. It can eventually reach a great height, but it is so slow growing that it will fit comfortably in modest-scaled surroundings for many human generations. It needs a deep, moist, acid, well-drained soil, and it is happiest if afforded some shelter from wind.

Zone 6 / China / 50 to 120 feet

Quercus coccinea (scarlet oak) has glossy, deeply cut leaves that turn a striking deep scarlet in the fall, and the acorns and furrowed bark typical of oaks. This is not the most massive of the oaks; even so, it is a big, stately tree with a wide-open habit of growth and does best in large-scale naturalistic landscapes. It is often found growing wild in dry, sandy soils. Not always available through nurseries, scarlet oak is nevertheless a tree to cherish if you can find it or if you have it growing on your land. I prefer it to pin oak (*Quercus palustris*), which has much the same habit and leaf except that its lower branches tend always to bend toward the ground.

Zone 5 / Native / 75 feet (100 in wild)

Quercus rubra (red oak): The many fine qualities of this oak make it one of the best choices as a lawn tree, for large open areas, or for wild landscapes. Red oak grows quite fast; it has a handsome round-topped form; it's easy to transplant and widely available; it withstands city pollution; and, like all the native oaks, it is a great haven and source of food for birds, squirrels, and other small wildlife. The bark is rough, ridged, and gray-brown. The leaves, deeply cut although not as fine-textured as those of scarlet oak, turn russet-red in fall. Their one flaw is a tendency to hang onto the tree for a good part of the winter; this can be annoying to people who like their landscapes tidied up in due season. Give red oak a well-drained, acid, sandy loam, and full sun.

Zone 5 / Native / 60 to 75 feet (100 in wild)

Salix alba tristis (golden weeping willow) is a tree that needs no introduction. It's one of the hardiest and most beautiful of all willows, with golden-brown bark and golden twigs and narrow, silvery-green leaves. Wonderfully adapted to wet ground, it will grow rapidly in almost any adequately moist soil. It is fibrous-rooted and no problem to transplant. Willows as a group are quite subject to disease and insect damage, but this is one of the toughest available. Pruning it (in summer or fall) and fertilizing it will lengthen its lifespan. If you're shopping for golden weeping willow through commercial suppliers, you may find it listed as *Salix alba* 'Niobe' or *Salix vitellina* 'Pendula' or even just *Salix niobe*. They all mean golden weeping willow.

Zone 3 / Europe, Northern Africa, Western Asia / 75 to 100 feet

Stewartia spp. (stewartias): See Medium Deciduous Trees.

Sophora japonica (Japanese pagoda tree) does not bloom until late July or August; then it produces long clusters of creamy-white pealike blooms. This is a graceful, round-headed tree, extremely tough, and disease and pest resistant. It will survive in poor soils, shade, drought, heat, even city pollution. Its compound leaves cast a finely dappled shade. Its younger branches and twigs are green (a pleasant touch in winter in the city) and its bark is a pale grayish-brown, deeply ridged. A good cultivated variety is the regent scholar tree (*Sophora japonica* 'Regent'), which is faster- and straighter-growing and which flowers at only 6 or 8 years of age, as opposed to 10 or 15 for the basic species.

Zone 5 / China, Korea / 50 to 75 feet

Tilia cordata (littleleaf linden) is a wonderfully tidy, organized tree to look at. Its form is a tight, regular pyramid of small, leathery, heart-shaped leaves. The neat shape (and pollution tolerance) of littleleaf linden has given it great popularity as a street tree — but it's a lovely shade tree for a lawn or patio, too. Its flowers appear in late June or early July, small and inconspicuous but very sweetly scented and enticing to bees (linden-flower honey is delicious). Plant it into any moist, well-drained, fertile soil; it's not particular about pH. Give it full sun if possible. Often used in Europe as a hedge plant, this linden responds well to severe pruning or even shearing. The cultivar 'Greenspire' is relatively fast-growing; and its trunk does not divide but heads skyward in a perfectly straight line, proving the aptness of its name.

Zone 4 / Europe / 60 to 70 feet

Tilia tomentosa (silver linden) takes its name from the white undersides of its leaves; they create a soft shimmering effect when stirred by the wind. This is an exquisite tree for lawns and other residential areas. It has smooth, light gray bark when young (although the bark darkens and furrows somewhat in the older tree), and the bark color is particularly handsome if you grow it as a multistemmed specimen. Silver linden has a regular pyramidal to oval habit, and its late-blooming flowers are sweetly fragrant. It has the added virtue of tolerating heat and drought better than many other lindens. It likes a moist, fertile, well-drained soil and ample sun. In its native Europe it has been planted and admired as a shade tree for thousands of years. (For a somewhat smaller linden, see Crimean linden — *Tilia euchlora* — in Medium Deciduous Trees.)

Zone 5 / Europe / 50 to 70 feet

Zelkova serrata (zelkova, or Japanese zelkova) is a member of the elm family and shares some of the grace and grandeur of the American elm — but not, luckily, its susceptibility to Dutch elm disease. It is vase-shaped in youth and retains that form in old age. Its leaves are small, very similar to elm leaves. A handsome shade tree for lawns, streets, or any area with plenty of room, it prefers deep soil and tolerates drought well. An extra-hardy and rapid-growing zelkova cultivar is 'Village Green', whose foliage turns russet-red in fall and whose trunk is straight and smooth.

Zone 6 / Japan, Korea / 50 to 80 feet (equally wide)

SMALL DECIDUOUS SHRUBS

Approximately 5 feet and under mature height.

Abeliophyllum distichum (Korean white forsythia) is not really a forsythia, although it looks like one in some ways. This is an unassuming small shrub, multistemmed and rounded in habit, with medium-textured foliage. In early spring it comes into its own with pretty and extremely fragrant white flowers. The flowers are borne all along the leafless stems in April (or earlier, depending on the location) and look very handsome in company with the yellow true forsythias. Korean white forsythia is tough and adapted to many soils. It likes full sun or light shade. It can be renewed by being cut back severely after flowering. In severe winter climates, give it protection from wind and cold.

Zone 6 / Korea / 3 to 5 feet

Azaleas: See Medium Deciduous Shrubs.

Berberis thunbergii (Japanese barberry): Valuable for hedges and groupings and for its appeal to birds and wildlife, the Japanese barberry is a low-growing, dense, prickly shrub. Its small oval light green leaves turn orange to scarlet in the fall, and its bright red berries hang on most of the winter. Japanese barberry does best in full sun but will tolerate some shade; it is easily transplanted bareroot, and will survive in just about any kind of soil, even dry. It does have a couple of drawbacks, however. If you ever have occasion to prune it (for shape or size), you'll need thick gloves and a lot of fortitude: the thorns are terrible. Also, its fine tangled thorny stems have a habit of trapping dry leaves and other unsightly debris all winter. Still, Japanese barberry is a good old landscaping standby — and it makes a great hedge if you want to keep dogs or other visitors off your property. To add a dash of color to your landscape, try red-leaved Japanese barberry (*Berberis thunbergii* 'Atropurpurea'), which has reddish-purple leaves all summer and abundant red berries in fall and winter — or the red-leaved dwarf 'Crimson Pygmy', another good one. These varieties do require full sun for full color.

Zone 5 / Southern Europe to China / 3 to 6 feet

Cephalanthus occidentalis (buttonbush): See Medium Deciduous Shrubs.

Comptonia peregrina (sweet fern): See Deciduous Ground Covers.

Cornus sericea (red-osier dogwood): See Medium Deciduous Shrubs.

Cotoneaster apiculatus (cranberry cotoneaster) grows low and dense. It is popular as a ground cover, a facer plant for shrub borders, or even a bank cover plant. Its only liability is that its stiff, tangled stems clamber over each other to form an impenetrable mound that snags all manner of dead leaves and other debris, often creating an unsightly mess in winter. At other times of year this is a beautiful shrub. Its glossy little dark green leaves turn bronze-red or purplish in autumn and hold their color for a long time. Its crimson berries, ripening in August through September, are enormously decorative. You can grow cranberry cotoneaster in practically any fertile, friable, well-drained soil in full sun. It will tolerate dry soils and seaside locations. Prune it any time at all.

Zone 5 / China / 3 feet

***Cotoneaster dammeri* 'Skogsholmen'** (Skogsholmen bearberry cotoneaster): See Evergreen Ground Covers.

***Euonymus alata* 'Compacta'** (dwarf winged euonymus): See Large Deciduous Shrubs.

***Forsythia viridissima* 'Bronxensis'** (Bronx forsythia): See Deciduous Ground Covers.

Fothergilla gardenii (dwarf fothergilla): See Medium Deciduous Shrubs.

***Hydrangea arborescens* 'Annabelle'** (Annabelle hydrangea) is a cultivar of the native smooth hydrangea (*Hydrangea arborescens*), a round, mounded shrub with big leaves and many fast-growing stalks. It boasts huge, symmetrical spheres of white blossoms, and it holds its flowers nicely erect on their stems. Annabelle hydrangea starts flowering in July and goes on into late summer. To encourage sturdy growth and bounteous bloom, cut this hydrangea to the ground in late fall or early spring, and let it grow back like a peony or other herbaceous perennial. It flowers on the spring's new growth. It does best in rich, moist, well-drained soil in partial shade; in prolonged dry spells, water thoroughly.

Zone 5 / Native / 3 feet

***Kerria japonica* 'Pleniflora'** (kerria or globe flower): This shrub offers green twigs in winter plus pretty yellow flowers in May. The weight of the round, buttonlike flowers actually bends the slender branches down, giving them a graceful arching line. The overall form of the shrub is rounded and its foliage and twig textures are fine. Give kerria partial or full shade and a well-drained, only moderately fertile loam. It needs frequent removal of dead wood. This makes a good massed planting for a shady, sheltered spot; or use it as a facer plant in front of leggy taller specimens.

Zone 5 / China / 4 to 6 feet

Ligustrum obtusifolium regelianum (Regel privet): For deciduous hedges, you can't go wrong with privet. A mass of fine-textured green in summer, a privet hedge is a haze of slender grayish twigs in winter. In between, in September, the plants bear blue-black berries that persist into the winter and are well liked by birds. And the June flowers, although some don't like the smell, are rather pretty to look at: small and pure white against the dark green foliage. A variety of border privet, Regel privet is extremely hardy. It grows low and spreads its branches horizontally, making a strongly horizontal form. Plant privet bareroot — it can handle just about any soil except an extremely wet one, and will survive city soot and smoke, full sun, or half shade. After it has flowered it can be pruned as drastically as you like. To rejuvenate old plants, just cut them back to stumps.

Zone 4 / Japan / 4 to 5 feet, spreading

Potentilla fruticosa (bush cinquefoil): Also known as shrubby cinquefoil or potentilla, this plant has a dainty air at every season. Its unique claim to fame is the length of its blooming period: from late spring until the first fall frost it is dotted with neat yellow blossoms the color and size of buttercups. Setting off the flowers, its leaves are fine-textured, deep green, and pest-free. In winter the shrub is a rounded mass of wispy upright stems. Bush cinquefoil grows very slowly and never gets much more than 4 feet tall and wide; it's an ideal plant for small gardens or for borders or massed plantings. It transplants with the greatest of ease and will grow in poor, dry soils and extreme cold; the one thing it demands is plenty of sun. You can find several good varieties of bush cinquefoil, some larger in size or with larger leaves, some with white, creamy, or orange flowers.

Zone 3 / Native / 1 to 4 feet (equally wide)

Rhus aromatica (fragrant sumac), unlike the more leggy tree sumacs, is a low-growing shrubby plant with a definite tendency to march across the landscape. Its roots send up suckers, and its stems take root where they touch the ground. As a result, fragrant sumac can do a great job of covering sunny banks or other problem bare spots with dense growth. It has rather nice yellow flowers in March. Its aromatic leaves are jagged-edged and glossy; they grow in clusters of three; and they turn vivid orange, red, or purple in fall. The furry red fruits ripen in August and September. Fragrant sumac is easy to transplant and happy in most soils, although it prefers light well-drained ones.

Zone 4 / Native / 2 to 6 feet (6 to 10 wide)

***Rosa* spp.** (rose): See Medium Deciduous Shrubs.

***Spiraea* spp.** (spirea): See Medium Deciduous Shrubs.

***Stephanandra incisa* 'Crispa'** (Crispa cutleaf stephanandra) is a very small and dense cultivar of cutleaf stephanandra that's ideal for use as a ground cover, bank cover, facer plant, or low hedge or border. It has finely cut leaves that give it a lacy summer texture, and in fall its foliage turns deep red or purple. The slender stems spread gracefully outwards. This shrub grows happily in full sun or light shade, and although it prefers a moist, highly organic soil, it will tolerate almost any soil that is well drained. It's easy to propagate by cuttings or by lifting and dividing older clumps.

Zone 5 / Japan, Korea / 1½ to 3 feet (equally wide or wider)

Symphoricarpos chenaultii (Chenault coralberry) will grow in almost any soil, including clays and alkaline soils. It thrives in shade, so it's useful in woodland settings. Its abundant berries ripen in fall, sometimes in such numbers that they bend the slender branches to the ground under their weight. The berries are pink, or pink shading to white where they're out of the sun. The very low-growing, arching habit and densely massed fine twigs of Chenault coralberry make it a good woodland understory plant or even ground cover. It spreads vigorously by suckering around its base, and it demands little in the way of upkeep.

Zone 5 / Hybrid (native) / 3 feet

Symphoricarpos orbiculatus (coralberry or Indian currant) is a hardy native and thrives in just about any soil in sun or shade. It spreads like wildfire, so it works well as a holding plant for shaded banks, cuts, or fills. Low, arching, and fine-twigged, coralberry needs no upkeep and has no pests. Its chief ornamental asset is its fall crop of smooth, round, fleshy purplish-red berries. They are very striking and they persist long into the winter.

Zone 3 / Native / 2 to 5 feet

***Syringa* spp.** (lilac): See Medium Deciduous Shrubs.

***Viburnum* spp.** (viburnum): See Medium and Large Deciduous Shrubs.

Xanthorhiza simplicissima (yellowroot): See Deciduous Ground Covers.

MEDIUM DECIDUOUS SHRUBS

Approximately 5 to 10 feet mature height.

Aronia arbutifolia (red chokeberry) has berries so sour, as its name suggests, that even the birds won't eat them. The masses of glowing crimson berries stay right on the shrub all winter long, making a cloud of color. Red chokeberry is an upright, open, multistemmed plant. Its fall foliage is red to purplish. It tolerates almost any type or condition of soil, though it does its best in good soil with full sun. Unlike many native shrubs, it is not an overly aggressive spreader. Thanks to that fact and to its adaptable nature, you may like to use red chokeberry in borders, grouped plantings, or any spot where a dash of red is called for.

Zone 6 / Native / 6 to 10 feet

AZALEAS

Azaleas are so widely known and so much loved that there's little I can say to promote their fame any further. They are some of the most beautiful shrubs known to man, that's all. I will confine myself here to summarizing the basic facts of azalea culture and to listing and describing a few hardy deciduous azaleas, several of them natives, that are sure to be star performers — even in our northern climate. (There are also some evergreen varieties described under Broad-leaved Evergreens.)

All azaleas share with other members of the *Rhododendron* genus a need for acid soil. If you live in the Northeast, your soil is probably already somewhat acid. Amend it with acid organic matter such as peat moss or oak-leaf compost, and there you are. The plants will also benefit from fertilizer (manure or other balanced fertilizer) and from mulching year-round with leaves, bark chips, pine needles, or any good acid mulch. Thicken the mulch in winter, after the ground freezes solid.

Azaleas are happiest in a humid environment, and they require some degree of shelter from the hottest summer sun and the most biting winds of winter. Surrounding trees and shrubs can provide such shelter; or plant azaleas near a rise in ground level, or along a fence, building wall, or woodland edge.

Plant azaleas in the late fall or early spring. You may also enjoy propagating them by simple layering (see May) or by softwood or semiripe cuttings (see June).

Rhododendron calendulaceum (flame azalea) is the most vivid and showy of native American azaleas. It bears its yellow, orange, or scarlet blooms in loose clusters in early June. It is an open shrub, growing as broad as it is tall, anywhere from 4 to 10 feet. Flame azalea is perhaps most beautiful in naturalistic plantings where it can be massed for maximum impact. It is hardy in Zone 6.

***Rhododendron* 'Exbury Hybrids'** (Exbury hybrid azaleas) include a large group — also sometimes called Knap Hill or de Rothschild hybrids — with upright forms, bright green foliage, and large, luxuriant blossoms in many shades of white, yellow, orange, pink, and red. They bloom in mid- to late May, and they are hardy in Zone 6. For an orange azalea that's hard to beat, try the Exbury clone 'Gibraltar'.

Rhododendron gandavense (Ghent azaleas) are even hardier than the Exbury hybrids, surviving nicely as far north as Zone 5. They grow 6 to 10 feet tall, and their late May flowers come in pure white, pure yellow, and numerous shades and combinations of pink, orange, and scarlet. Some of the flowers are double, with ruffly overlapping petals. 'Narcissiflora' is one of these: a lovely, fragrant double-flowered yellow variety.

***Rhododendron* 'Jane Abbott Hybrids'** (Jane Abbott hybrid azaleas) are an introduction of Weston Nurseries in Massachusetts. They are outstanding for large, fragrant, true-pink flowers in late May. They are robust growers and hardy in Zone 5.

Rhododendron mucronulatum (Korean azalea): The specialty of this species is its very early bloom. It bears its rosy-lavender blossoms before its leaves appear, in March or early April. Because of this it requires protection from the southern or southwestern sun. Strong sun will open the flower buds prematurely and expose them to fatal frostbite. Korean azalea grows 4 to 8 feet high and equally wide. It's hardy in Zone 5. Its fall foliage is colorful, turning yellow or russet-red.

Rhododendron nudiflorum (pinxterbloom, pink pinxter azalea, or downy pinxterbloom) is the hardiest of all the native azaleas (Zone 4). In May, before its leaves come out, it bears fragrant blossoms that range (depending on variety) from almost white to pale pink to deep rose-violet. The summer foliage is a bright green. Pinxterbloom grows low, densely branched, and shrubby, reaching a top height of 4 to 6 feet. It has a tendency to spread by shoots, so it's a fine plant for naturalizing. It is well adapted to dry, rocky, sandy soil.

Rhododendron roseum (rose-shell azalea, or early or honeysuckle azalea) is another hardy (Zone 4) and beautiful native shrub. Its bright pink flowers have a sweet, clovelike scent and bloom in May, just as or before the leaves emerge. The dense, spreading branches of rose-shell azalea make it as wide as it is tall — and in the wild it can grow as tall as 15 feet, although it's usually found in more modest sizes ranging from 2 to 8 feet. It will tolerate neutral or even alkaline soils.

Rhododendron schlippenbachii (royal azalea): This import from the Orient is a true aristocrat in the garden. It has handsome foliage, dark green above and pale beneath, that turns yellow, orange, or crimson in the fall. But its flowers are its real claim to fame. Exquisite pale-pink to rose single blossoms grouped together in clusters of three to six, they bloom in May just as the leaves begin to emerge. Royal azalea grows 6 to 8 feet high and is upright and rounded. It is hardy in Zone 5.

Rhododendron vaseyi (pink-shell azalea), a native of North Carolina, does fine as far north as Zone 5. Its clear rose flowers bloom before the leaves appear, in mid-May; and its foliage puts on an autumn display of rosy red. It will reach a height of 5 to 10 feet, and has an irregular upright form. As a bonus attraction, pink-shell azalea tolerates moist soil conditions exceptionally well.

Rhododendron viscosum (swamp azalea) is the most fragrant of native azaleas, bearing its spicy-smelling snowy-white flowers in June or July after the leaves are fully out. It is open and spreading in habit, and can range from 2 to 9 feet in height (and breadth) — or even, rarely, to 15 feet. As its name suggests, swamp azalea will flourish in amply moist soils. There are some cultivars and naturally occurring varieties that have pink flowers, and these too are particularly lovely, hardy shrubs, fine in Zone 4.

Buddleia davidii (orange-eye butterfly bush) usually dies back to the ground over the winter and blooms the following August on the current year's growth; so treat it like a large herbaceous perennial. This vigorous multistemmed shrub is widely available in many varieties, boasting showy flower spikes in assorted shades of white, pink, red, purple, and blue. Many of the flowers have orange "eyes." All hues and varieties are immensely attractive to butterflies, which flock around the plant and add to its lively effect. Orange-eye butterfly bush has coarse-textured foliage. It will thrive in any soil, without any attention to speak of; and it's simple to propagate from softwood or hardwood cuttings.

Zone 6 / China / 8 feet

Cephalanthus occidentalis (buttonbush) loves wet soil and can often be seen growing wild by ponds and streams or in soggy ditches. Its chief attraction is its creamy-white rounded flower clusters (like buttons), which bloom in August at a time when little else is in flower. The sweet, privetlike fragrance of the flowers gives this shrub its other familiar name, "honeyballs." The foliage of buttonbush is rather glossy and appealing, although coarse; and the compound nutlets hang on all winter. This shrub has a loose, gangly form, and isn't really a distinguished landscape plant except for wet or waterside locations. It's easy to divide, transplant, or propagate from cuttings.

Zone 5 / Native / 3 to 15 feet

Chaenomeles speciosa (flowering quince): Considered by some to be an undistinguished shrub 50 weeks out of the year and a winter trash-trapper to boot, the common flowering quince is nevertheless an old favorite and truly lovely in its brief season of bloom. The orange-pink, rose, red, or white blossoms on their stiff, spiky twigs make lovely Oriental-style flower arrangements for the house, too. With bees in the neighborhood you may even have a few sour yellow fruits for quince jelly. You can use flowering quince for massed plantings, shrub borders, or barrier hedges. Give it full sun for best flowering; it will grow in almost any kind of soil. Keep it vigorous by pruning out older stems in late spring. You can also renew it by cutting it back to 6-inch stumps after it finishes flowering.

Zone 5 / China / 6 to 10 feet (equally wide)

Clethra alnifolia (summer-sweet clethra) is sometimes called summer-sweet, sometimes clethra, and sometimes both. It is a great shrub for massed plantings or borders, almost completely pest-free, and a perfect solution to the problem of what to put in wet ground, shady areas, places with particularly acid soil, or even salty seashore environments. Besides having dense, deep green summer foliage and attractive gray stems for winter color, summer-sweet clethra bears small, pretty, deliciously fragrant white flowers in midsummer (July to August). The bees love it. Plant summer-sweet clethra in moist soil with plenty of organic matter. Or it's quite easy to propagate from cuttings taken in summer. It should be pruned in spring.

Zone 4 / Native / 3 to 8 feet

Cornus alba 'Sibirica' (Siberian dogwood), one of the colored-stemmed shrub forms of dogwood, makes its main splash in winter with its loose, upright stems of vivid coral-red. In a roomy situation Siberian dogwood is wonderful for display in a large mass, especially beside water. Its fall foliage is a good reddish-purple. It is not such an enthusiastic colonizer as the native red-osier dogwood (*Cornus sericea*), which makes it a good alternative for locations where excessive spreading would be a problem. It's a hearty grower that will take hold in sun or partial shade in any well-drained soil. Remove its oldest stems regularly, since the younger growth has the color. Siberian dogwood cuttings taken at any time of year root with the greatest of ease.

Zone 3 / Siberia to Northern Korea / 8 to 10 feet

Cornus sericea (red-osier dogwood) is most dramatic in winter, when the glowing red color of its stems shines out against dull grasses or white snow. This is a many-stemmed, medium-sized shrub, rounded in overall shape; it spreads rapidly by means of shoots from the base of the plant. The leaves are dark green in summer, purplish-red in fall. Red-osier dogwood grows wild in open, swampy areas and is well suited to damp soils; it's adaptable and easy to transplant either bareroot or balled and burlapped. I like best to use it in massed plantings in spacious settings, where it can spread more or less to its heart's content; but it is also good for shrub borders. A compact dwarf variety is 'Kelseyi', which reaches only 2 feet or so in height. You can use it as a ground cover or as a facer plant for more leggy shrubs in borders. Another variety, yellow-twig red-osier dogwood (*Cornus sericea* 'Flaviramea'), has stems of a potent sulfurous yellow that makes a very strong statement. For the most intense color, cut it back heavily every other spring.

Zone 3 / Native / 7 to 9 feet

Corylopsis glabrescens (fragrant winter hazel): See Large Deciduous Shrubs.

Forsythia intermedia 'Spectabilis' (showy border forsythia) is an old favorite among the several varieties of border forsythia. This shrub can stand almost any growing conditions, so it's a good choice for city gardens or difficult soils. It puts up with rigorous pruning; and if it's pruned at the correct season (spring, right after blooming) it comes back the next year with an undaunted display of big, bright yellow flowers in earliest spring. It flowers most abundantly in full sun but will tolerate partial shade. Showy border forsythia is upright and bushy (not droopy, like some of its species) and fine for hedges, shrub borders, massed plantings, or planting on banks.

Zone 5 / Asia; European hybrid / 8 to 10 feet

Forsythia suspensa sieboldii (Siebold weeping forsythia) is a very slender-branched form of weeping forsythia, with arching, trailing branches that gracefully sweep the ground. Its small golden-yellow flowers appear all along the branches in April, before the leaves emerge. This shrub has long been popular for growing over rocky banks or walls or beside water. It will endure city conditions, although it should have full sun for the best flowering. Plant it in just about any loose, well-drained soil. Or propagate it by cuttings taken at any time of year; June and July softwood or semiripe cuttings root especially easily. Siebold weeping forsythia will also propagate itself if you allow it — the tips of its branches send out roots and start new plants wherever they are in contact with moist soil.

Zone 6 / China / 8 to 10 feet (10 to 15 wide)

Fothergilla spp. (fothergilla species or witch alders) really come into their own in autumn, when the glorious colors of their foliage range from bright yellow to vivid scarlet. But they're useful and attractive in shrub borders and other grouped plantings throughout the year, being compact shrubs with spiky white flowers in spring, dense dark green summer foliage, and a neat low form. Dwarf fothergilla (*Fothergilla gardenii*) is the smallest; large fothergilla (*Fothergilla major*) has a more pyramidal form and a top height of 9 or 10 feet. All fothergillas require acid, peaty loam with good drainage. Plant in sunny or partially shaded spots, although they'll have the best flowers and fall color in full sun. Or you can try propagating them from softwood cuttings taken in late spring.

Zone 6 / Native / 2 to 10 feet

Hamamelis vernalis (vernal witch hazel): This is the smallest of the witch-hazel group and has the smallest flowers, tiny yellow or reddish blooms with ribbonlike petals. The flowers are very fragrant. They bloom in February or March, and on very cold days the petals roll themselves up tightly to protect themselves from frost. Vernal witch hazel is a dense multistemmed shrub, not open and gangly like its larger relatives. Its stems are an appealing grayish-brown; its dark green summer foliage gives way to brilliant yellow fall color. This is a resilient and useful shrub for massed plantings, screens, or borders — or for any soil where wetness is a problem. It will grow on stream banks and in clay soils. It blooms well in either full sun or shade. For other witch hazels, see Large Deciduous Shrubs.

Zone 5 / Native / 10 feet

Hibiscus syriacus (rose-of-Sharon or shrub althea): See Large Deciduous Shrubs.

Ilex verticillata (winterberry) is an appealing shrub, a member of the holly family but not evergreen like many others of its species. Given a male winterberry somewhere in the neighborhood, a female winterberry will produce lovely red berries that stay on the plant into late December or even January, providing a feast for birds. Winterberry grows densely, with many fine twiggy branches, so it's good for massed effects or for single specimens in shrub borders. Its foliage, deep green in summer, turns black after frost, which is why one familiar name for the plant is black alder. Winterberry does best in an acid, moist soil; in the wild it colonizes swampy areas. It will prosper in full sun or partial shade.

Zone 4 / Native / 9 feet

Kerria japonica (kerria): See Small Deciduous Shrubs.

Lonicera fragrantissima (winter honeysuckle) produces its delightfully lemon-scented white flowers in early April, and follows up in May with translucent red fruits that the birds enthusiastically eat. This is a wide-spreading, irregularly shaped shrub whose branches form a tangled mass. The small blue-green leaves hang on well into late fall; in fact this honeysuckle is considered semievergreen in the South. It's a good component of a shrub border or hedge, or in any spot where you can enjoy the fragrance of the flowers. Plant winter honeysuckle in any well-drained loamy soil. It likes full sun and won't stand for wet feet. Prune it after it flowers; or to renew it completely, cut it to the ground and let it develop new shoots from scratch. (For other honeysuckles see Vines and Large Deciduous Shrubs, as well as tatarian honeysuckle, below.)

Zone 6 / China / 6 to 10 feet

Lonicera tatarica (tatarian honeysuckle) is often thought of as the best of the honeysuckles for all-around use, very hardy, vigorous, prolific of flower, dense of foliage, with attractive red berries in summer, and with tangled gray stems that make a nice contribution to the palette of winter color. This shrub has been much cultivated, and varieties are available with flowers that range from white to pink, rose, even rosy-red. All bloom in mid-May; and all the flowers are almost intoxicatingly fragrant. There's nothing like a honeysuckle growing in the warm sun near a western wall of a house, where the fair-weather breeze carries the scent through the windows and throughout the house. It will adapt to most soils except waterlogged ones and likes full sun. If you want to prune it, cut it back after it finishes blooming; if it grows tangled or overlarge, you can cut it all the way back to low stumps, and it will bounce back with aplomb.

Zone 4 / Central Asia to Southern Russia / 10 to 12 feet

Myrica pensylvanica (bayberry) is a shrub that's easily remembered if you have seen it — and smelled it — once. Low-growing and apt to spread by shoots into thickets of shiny green, bayberry has small, gray, waxy berries that are the basis for perfumed wax candles. You can enjoy the same spicy, aromatic scent by rubbing a leaf between your fingers, or just by standing in the middle of a clump of bayberry on a hot day and inhaling. This plant is a familiar occupant of sand dunes and sandy seashore locations, and it's excellent for massed plantings in any sunny spot where dry, sterile soil or salty surroundings present a challenge. If the winter is mild enough, bayberry will hold on to its leaves; if not, it is deciduous. In summer the branches make attractive greens for indoor arrangements.

Zone 3 / Native / 9 feet

Philadelphus virginalis (virginal mock-orange), a hybrid with many fine cultivars, is cherished for its sweet-smelling June flowers. Except when it is in bloom there's little remarkable about this shrub — but to many people the scent of the blossoms during their 2-week peak is enough. Multistemmed, rounded, with arching or upright branches, virginal mock-oranges have extra-large white flowers, often double (depending on variety). They are easy to establish and to maintain; impartial as to sun, shade, and soil type; and extremely tolerant of drought. They'll do their best, however, in good, highly organic soil. They are a breeze to propagate by cuttings taken almost anytime. I'm especially partial to the double-flowering cultivar 'Virginal'.

Zone 6 / Hybrid (Europe) / 4 to 9 feet

Prunus maritima (beach plum) is really a shrub for seashore gardens. It thrives in light, sandy soil and is undaunted by heavy doses of salt spray, although it cannot cope with pollution. Given conditions it likes, it grows dense, rounded, and compact. The white flowers bloom in May, followed by bluish or reddish fruits that ripen in late summer and make wonderful jams and jellies. Birds like them, too. Beach plum does best in full sun, and it needs well-drained soil.

Zone 4 / Native / 6 feet

ROSA SPP.

Rose: The subject of roses fills many a volume, and the cultivation of roses amounts to a consuming passion for many a gardener. Symbols of love, life, truth, and beauty, roses have held a special place in the heart of humankind since time immemorial. There just aren't words in the lexicon that can capture the qualities of this "best and sweetest flower that grows."

For purposes of this book, however, a rose is a rose is a deciduous shrub. I certainly encourage you to study, plant, and enjoy the glorious hybrid tea roses, grandifloras, floribundas, or climbing roses that are the pride of the flower garden; and some good reference works on roses are listed in Further Reference. But in this section I'll focus on just a few of the "species" roses that qualify as shrubs with year-round value in the landscape.

Rosa blanda (meadow rose) is a native rose that contributes red twigs to the winter landscape as well as lovely spring and summer bloom and dense masses of summer foliage. It's a broad and spreading shrub, reaching a height of about 6 feet, and hardy even in Zone 3's coldest winters. Its single pink flowers are up to 2½ inches across and very fragrant.

Rosa hugonis (Father Hugo rose) has arching canes and a broad, rounded overall habit; it will grow 6 to 8 feet tall and equally wide, or wider. A native of China, it is hardy in Zone 6. It has exquisite single canary-yellow flowers that bloom abundantly all over it in May and June. Its leaves are small. Its dark red to black fruits ripen in August. Like all roses it needs ample sun and well-drained soil; but unlike most roses it flourishes best without fertilization, even in poor soil.

Rosa rugosa (rugosa rose), sometimes called saltspray rose, is native to the Orient but grows up and down the Eastern Seaboard wild among dunes and along rocky shores. It perfumes the air with the sweetness of its purplish pink or white blossoms in late June, and provides a dazzling display of orange foliage and large red rose-hips in the late summer and fall. But you don't have to live by the ocean to make use of this sturdy, vigorous rose. It is fine for massed plantings, and being very prickly it makes an impenetrable hedge. It is spreading in habit and reaches a top height of 4 to 6 feet. Hardy in Zone 3, it's a good solution for problem areas like banks, cuts, sandy soils, or salty environments. Give rugosa rose a sunny, open location and well-drained soil with plenty of organic matter worked in.

Rosa virginiana (Virginia rose) bears its profuse single pink flowers in June, then yields shiny red fruits that persist on the plant into the winter. The foliage puts on a fiery display of autumn color, and the prickly canes are bright red. Virginia rose makes an impassable hedge or barrier; it grows well in sandy soils; and it's happy by the seashore as well as inland. This robust native is hardy in Zone 4. It's naturally low (with a maximum height of 6 feet) and is apt to form a dense mass of upright stems. Prune it as you wish, or cut it to the ground in early spring for overall renewal.

Sambucus canadensis (elderberry or American elder): The heavy clusters of blue-black fruit borne by this shrub are great bait for birds; they're definitely edible by human beings, too, in the forms of jellies, preserves, and even elderberry wine. Elderberry is a hard plant to fit comfortably into the average residential landscape, however. It is a multistemmed, round-topped, sprawling shrub, with medium-textured compound leaves and a very coarse texture of branches and twigs in winter. It produces large, saucer-shaped clusters of small white flowers in June. It is easily established and adaptable as to soils. The best uses for elderberry are in wild landscapes, near wet areas, for roadside plantings or other wide-open areas, or at the edges of woodlands. It also prospers next to a compost pile.

Zone 4 / Native / 5 to 12 feet

SPIRAEA SPP.

Spirea comes in many varieties and cultivars — a large and well-loved family of useful shrubs originating in the Orient. Most spireas grow dense, rounded, multistemmed, and reasonably low. They like full or partial sun and make great hedges, shrub masses, borders, or facer plants for groups of taller, leggy plants. Spireas' flowers range from white to red and bloom any time from April to August, depending on the variety. They are hardy in Zone 5. Most spireas flower on the current year's new growth, so that you can prune them in very early spring, before growth begins — or right after they finish blooming. They grow well in any well-drained soil. Softwood cuttings taken in June or July will readily take root.

***Spiraea bumalda* 'Anthony Waterer'** (Anthony Waterer spirea) is very low-growing (2 feet), bears deep pink flowers in late June, has dark bluish-green foliage, and will grow practically anywhere. It is an excellent spirea for hedges.

***Spiraea japonica* 'Alpina'** (daphne spirea), a variety of pink-flowering Japanese spirea, blooms in June and July. This is a very dainty little shrub, only about a foot high at maturity, with small flat-topped clusters of flowerets and fine-textured blue-green foliage. It's useful for low borders or edgings, or for grouping in small gardens or even rock gardens.

***Spiraea nipponica* 'Snowmound'** (Snowmound Nippon spirea): Growing rounded and dense, as broad as it is tall, this is a tidy and adaptable shrub with a top height of 3 to 5 feet. The snow-white flower clusters appear in late May or June. The small, oval leaves are a cool blue-green; their denseness and fine texture are reminiscent of boxwood, and in fact this is sometimes called boxwood spirea. Prune it before it blooms for larger and splashier flowers; or to renew it from the ground up, cut it back to short stumps in early spring.

Spiraea prunifolia (bridal-wreath spirea), an old-fashioned shrub that some plantsmen consider positively out of date, remains popular for its button-like double white flowers that bloom in May. It can grow to a height of 4 to 9 feet, with a loose and open habit. Its small leaves are a glossy dark green in summer, its fall foliage reddish to orange, in contrast to the total lack of fall color of most other spireas.

Spiraea vanhouttei (Vanhoutte spirea) is a fine hybrid, perhaps the toughest of all spireas. This shrub tolerates urban pollution as well as most other hardships. Vanhoutte is a relatively tall member of the spirea group (8 to 10 feet), with leaves of a soft blue-green and graceful, arching branches that form a broad mound. Its showy white flowers appear in late April to May.

SYRINGA SPP.

Lilacs first came to this country from Europe around 300 years ago, and they've become part and parcel of the American scene. Dozens of species and hundreds of varieties, all stemming from European and Asian ancestors, are now grown and widely sold. The enchanting fragrance of their blossoms — which come in shades of lavender, purple, white, or pink — draws crowds to parks and public gardens for "lilac days" in May and June; but lilacs are equally desirable in your yard or outside your window. Their lovely color and perfume will pervade your life for many weeks.

Like many flowering trees and shrubs, lilacs put on their most spectacular show every other year, with lean years in between. That's to be expected; but you can boost their performance in all years by keeping them properly pruned (see May Landscape Tasks) and properly fed. They appreciate a friable, well-drained soil that is only slightly acid (limestone may sometimes be called for), plus plenty of sun and an occasional fertilizing. Cut out most of the suckers that appear around the base, cut out dead wood promptly, and remove spent flower heads. If you're pruning for shape, do it right after lilacs finish flowering, since next year's flowers will come on this year's growth.

Many lilacs fall victim to powdery mildew in late summer. This gives the leaves a dirty, whitish, dusty look that is unappealing but not really threatening to the plant or to its blooming capacity for the following spring. If powdery mildew bothers you, there are fungicides that can help control it if you follow the instructions religiously.

Syringa chinensis (Chinese lilac), a hybrid, blooms in mid-May like its parent, common lilac (*Syringa vulgaris*). Its flowers are a rich lilac-purple, slightly more delicate than those of common lilac, and deliciously fragrant. The arching branches of this fine shrub give it a broad, round-topped form 8 to 15 feet high. This is an adaptable plant and not fussy. Do prune it regularly, removing old stems and thinning shoots, to keep it in good form. (This is sometimes found listed as *Syringa rothomagensis*: same thing.) Zone 6.

Syringa palibiniana (dwarf Korean lilac) is one of the smallest lilacs around, and a favorite of mine. With a top height of 6 feet, it is compact but broad, with small, dark green leaves that turn a coppery color in autumn. Its dainty flowers are pinkish lavender. Because of its dense foliage and restrained size, I often choose this lovely shrub for screens, hedges, and borders. Zone 6.

Syringa persica (Persian lilac) is small-leaved and modest-sized, with profuse, delicate, sweet-smelling lavender flowers that come in late May. Its foliage is a bluish green and very pretty. Persian lilac has upright, arching branches and grows dense and spreading; it can reach 4 to 8 feet in height, 5 to 10 in breadth, so that it makes a fine flowering hedge or shrub border. Zone 6.

Syringa potaninii (Potanin or daphne lilac): Blooming in mid-May along with the many varieties and cultivars of the common lilac, this is prized for the color of its flowers: a clear pink. In addition it is very fragrant. With ample sun it will continue to produce occasional blooms throughout the late spring and summer. It has a graceful upright form and can be as tall as 9 feet. Zone 6.

Syringa villosa (late lilac) blooms in June, after most of the other popular lilacs, and as such it plays a distinctive role in the landscape. It is compact and tidy (6 to 10 feet), with very prolific, lightly fragrant pinkish-lilac to white blooms. This makes a good plant for the shrub border; it's dense and bushy, with many stout stems and a moderate overall size. For best bloom, remove suckers and cut down old stems periodically; and pinch off spent flower clusters every year, as with other lilacs. Zone 3.

Syringa vulgaris (common lilac) is the oldest lilac to be grown in this country and the parent species of anywhere from 400 to 900 named varieties. It's the archetypal pale-lavender-flowering shrub, tall and leggy (up to 15 feet) in maturity, eventually forming a spreading rounded head, and found in thousands of overgrown hedges and borders or even growing wild across the landscape. Kept properly thinned and pruned, however, it makes a reliable hedge or border plant; and its flowers smell as sweet as any exotic variety. It is easy to plant balled and burlapped, or try propagating it by softwood or hardwood cuttings — or better yet, simply dig up and replant any of the abundant crop of suckers that appear annually around its base. Zone 4.

Vaccinium corymbosum (highbush blueberry): This open, small-leaved shrub has small white flowers, tasty berries, and dark blue-green foliage that turns crimson in the autumn. With its many spreading stems it's a little tall and loose for formal settings, but looks attractive in massed plantings or borders, in naturalistic landscapes, or as part of a productive garden planting. For the best berry yield, check with your local agricultural agent or extension service for the cultivar(s) best adapted to conditions in your area. Plant highbush blueberries in acid, highly organic, moist but well-drained soil in full sun or partial shade. Or propagate them by means of softwood cuttings taken in June; these will often root successfully. Highbush blueberries appreciate a good acid mulch. Prune them as soon as the fruiting season is over.

Zone 4 / Native / 6 to 12 feet (equally wide)

Viburnum burkwoodii (Burkwood viburnum) is a hybrid that offers sturdy growth and good blight resistance together with wonderful spring fragrance and handsome summer foliage. The pink flower buds open to rounded clusters of waxy white bloom in May, filling the air with spicy-sweet scent. The leaves are a dark, lustrous green above and lighter beneath; they hold their green color late into the fall. Use Burkwood viburnum in borders or massed plantings. It is attractive combined with broad-leaved evergreens. It will flourish in any well-drained soil, but prefers a slightly acid environment.

Zone 6 / Hybrid (Asian) / 6 to 10 feet

Viburnum carlesii (Korean spice viburnum): This is one of those beloved shrubs that many experts feel should be replaced by newer, superior strains — but that keeps its loyal following among the gardeners of the world. I think the reason is its fragrance. Nevertheless, I should point out that there are numerous good cultivars and related hybrids, many offering resistance to the troublesome blight that afflicts this plant in maturity. Find out what your nursery recommends. The basic species is a modest-sized shrub with dense upward-spreading branches and crisp, dark foliage that turns wine-red in autumn. The flowers open in April or May; although the buds are pink the blooms are pure white "semi-snowballs" of close-packed flowerets, each a perfect little four-pointed star. As with other viburnums, plant Korean spice viburnum in any moist, well-drained soil; it will bloom best with plenty of sun, but it tolerates some shade. Prune it for size or shape immediately after flowering. If you need a smaller, more dense plant, try the variety 'Compacta', which grows only two-thirds as tall. (For other viburnums see Large Deciduous Shrubs.)

Zone 5 / Korea / 4 to 8 feet (equally wide)

Viburnum dilatatum (linden viburnum): Wide, flat-topped clusters of white bloom practically blanket this shrub in May to June; but it's not so much the flowers as the fruits and fall foliage that set the linden viburnum apart. It is dense-growing, broad, and rounded in habit. The cherry-red fruits ripen in showy clusters in September and often persist on the plant into December. Meanwhile the foliage turns a lively russet-red, adding to the overall effect. Linden viburnum yields the best fruit in full sun, but it has no other special requirements.

Zone 6 / Asia / 8 to 10 feet

Viburnum opulus 'Roseum' (European snowball viburnum or guelder-rose): See Large Deciduous Shrubs.

Viburnum plicatum tomentosum (doublefile viburnum) has been described as "the most elegant of flowering shrubs," and this is indeed a dramatically lovely plant in bloom. The mid-May flowers are of the lace cap type, with tiny flowers at the center of a ring of larger, more showy ones, the whole cluster forming a flat saucer 3 to 4 inches across. In the case of doublefile viburnum these saucers are arrayed in two rows along the top of each branch — hence "doublefile." Since the branches are long and very horizontal, this creates broad, spreading layers of pure white among the green leaves. Come fall, the tiers of foliage turn reddish-purple, also very handsome. The cherry-red fruits borne in clusters along the branches are pretty, but quickly eaten by birds. Like other viburnums, the doublefile viburnum is adaptable and sturdy; it will bloom and thrive in sun or shade, and it's very easy to propagate from cuttings. It is wonderful for massing, screening, or border plantings, or for use near a house where its horizontal lines set off the verticals of the building. A larger-flowering cultivar, and probably the best one for fruiting, is 'Mariesii', which you'll find widely available.

Zone 5 / China, Japan / 8 to 10 feet (wider than tall)

LARGE DECIDUOUS SHRUBS

Approximately 10 feet and over mature height.

Amelanchier canadensis (shadblow): See Small Deciduous Trees.

Cephalanthus occidentalis (buttonbush): See Medium Deciduous Shrubs.

Chionanthus virginicus (white fringe tree): See Small Deciduous Trees.

Cornus mas (Cornelian cherry dogwood) could be treated as a large shrub or as a small tree; either way, it grows dense, multistemmed, and rounded. It is a fine plant for hedges, borders, all sorts of grouped plantings around buildings. Its yellow flowers (really bracts) bloom in very early spring; they are small but so profuse that they completely clothe the tree or shrub in a cloud of yellow. The foliage is a good dark green, reddish in the fall. The cherry-red fruits are good for syrups and preserves, as well as appealing to birds and wildlife. Cornelian cherry dogwood adapts to most soil and light conditions, short of dense shade, although it flourishes best in rich, well-drained soil.

Zone 5 / Europe, Western Asia / 25 feet

Cornus racemosa (gray dogwood) is a shrub with a slight tendency to walk across the landscape: it sends up fast-growing new shoots from its roots. These newer stems are reddish brown, while the older growth is silvery gray, so that the overall appearance in winter is particularly lively. Gray dogwood boasts white spring flowers, white berries in summer, and dense, purplish fall foliage. Because it grows so thick naturally it is well suited for use in borders, particularly at the edge of woodland, or in massed plantings or naturalistic plantings; and cutting it back in early spring will make it grow all the thicker. It sprawls a little too much, however, to be the ideal hedge plant. It seems to be able to stand poor soil conditions and all kinds of other hardships.

Zone 5 / Europe and Western Asia / 15 to 20 feet

Corylopsis glabrescens (fragrant winter hazel), given a dark backdrop of evergreens to show off its drooping sprays of dainty yellow blossoms, makes an enchanting harbinger of spring. The fragrant bell-shaped flowers appear before the leaves in early April, earlier than those of any other flowering shrubs except witch hazels — to which it is related. Fragrant winter hazel is a dense, multistemmed, spreading shrub with a flat-topped to rounded form. Its flowers are vulnerable to late frosts, so provide it with shelter from southern sun (which will hasten its bloom) as well as from cold winds. It prefers a moist, acid, peaty, well-drained soil.

Zone 6 / Japan / 8 to 15 feet (equally wide)

Elaeagnus umbellata (autumn olive) is best known as a plant for saltwater locations, where it does exceptionally well. This shrub (or small tree) has lovely gray-green foliage and rather leggy, twisted stems whose bark is silver-gray. The berries, silvery deepening to red in color, are most appetizing to birds. Autumn olive is hardy and adaptable. The cultivar 'Cardinal' is very fast growing and naturalizes easily; it makes a wonderful wildlife planting for larger properties.

Zone 4 / Southern Europe to Central Asia and Japan / 12 to 18 feet

Enkianthus campanulatus (redvein enkianthus) can take the form of a narrow, upright shrub or of a small tree. It holds its branches in stratified tiers and its bright green foliage in tufts. Its May flowers are small, pale yellow bells with delicate red veins. At first they hang downward in clusters, then (when spent) turn upward like little chandeliers. They're best appreciated at close range, which is one reason to use enkianthus as a patio or terrace plant. It also makes a sprightly companion to rhododendrons or other broad-leaved evergreens. Its autumn foliage is a brilliant orange to red. Like rhododendrons, it demands a cool, moist, acid soil with plenty of peat moss or compost worked in, and preferably some shelter from intense heat and cold.

Zone 5 / Japan / 6 to 30 feet

Euonymus alata (winged euonymus), sometimes called burning bush, is the shrub you notice along roadways and in suburban yards in October, covered with glorious, medium-fine-textured, rose-red foliage. It is a wonderful shrub, broadly vase-shaped in its natural form, but well adapted to heavy clipping and shaping for use in screens and hedges. It's also distinguished enough to serve as a specimen plant, as well as in all kinds of group plantings. In addition to its brilliant autumn color, its bristling, ridged (or "winged") branches and twigs are a spirited note in winter — and especially lovely when frosted with snow. Winged euonymus is very hardy and tough, and tolerates almost any soil and light conditions. If this plant has any flaw, it is that it has been overused in some areas; but that shouldn't deter you from choosing it for your landscape.

If you want a smaller version with many of the same splendid qualities, the dwarf cultivar *Euonymus alata* 'Compacta' is widely available. This is not a tiny plant, but smaller, denser, more rounded, and extremely well suited for use in hedges. It'll scarcely need any pruning at all.

Zone 4 / Northeastern Asia / 9 to 20 feet

Hamamelis mollis (Chinese witch hazel): Growing happily in full sun or shade, this tall, open shrub or small tree produces sweetly fragrant yellow blossoms in earliest spring, February through March. It does best in a sheltered location that will protect its flowers from freezing in bud or after they bloom. The foliage turns a clear yellow in fall. Plant Chinese witch hazel in any moist soil, even stream banks or wet gravelly soil. It's a good shrub for open landscapes, naturalistic settings, shrub borders, or plantings in open shade. One cultivar is 'Brevipetala', whose abundant butter-yellow blooms have petals like ribbons. They look like miniature cheerleaders' pompoms and they smell wonderful.

Zone 6 / China / 30 feet

Hamamelis virginiana (common witch hazel) is the only one of the *Hamamelis* species to bloom in the fall. Its small yellow flowers appear in October, November, or even December — while at the same time its foliage also turns bright yellow. This tall shrub is best for wild or naturalistic plantings. The large, crooked branches of common witch hazel form an irregular vase shape in maturity. It grows in most soils, but it does best with plenty of moisture. In full sun it attains its fullest, most shapely growth, but it will manage perfectly well in shady locations.

Zone 5 / Native / 15 to 20 feet

Hibiscus syriacus (rose-of-Sharon or shrub althea) is an old American favorite for its showy, roselike blossoms. This is definitely a shrub for borders or hedges, not for a specimen role. The three-lobed leaves emerge late in spring, and the branches are dense and upright. The blossoms form on the current year's growth: you prune rose-of-Sharon in early spring, and it blooms in late summer. Without pruning, the individual flowers will be plentiful but small. Depending on the variety (there are hundreds in cultivation) the flowers may be anything from white to pink to crimson, or from lavender to deep purple. Rose-of-Sharon tolerates any kind of soil, provided it's not too dry or too wet; it thrives in highly organic soil; and it will grow in full sun or partial shade.

Zone 6 / China and Northern India / 8 to 12 feet

Hydrangea paniculata 'Grandiflora' (Peegee hydrangea): Named for the "*paniculata* 'Grandiflora'" in its botanical name, this spectacular late-blooming shrub bears wonderful long-lasting flower clusters. Peegee hydrangea grows upright and round-topped, with arching branches and coarse foliage. It is best planted as a group of specimens in the lawn. Its great pyramidal flower clusters appear in July and stay in place long into the fall, changing from white to pinkish-purple, then brown, as the season advances. It will bloom in sun or partial shade, but it wants a rich, loamy, well-fertilized and mulched soil (it is a heavy feeder). Do not trim it but cut out its oldest stems completely in early March: this will help it renew itself.

Zone 5 / China, Japan / 20 to 30 feet

Lindera benzoin (spicebush): The small, fragrant yellow flowers of this shrub appear in April, before its leaves are out, making it very pretty in shrub borders or naturalized landscapes — particularly along stream beds. It does well in wet soil and in partial shade, since it's native to woodlands. Its foliage turns bright yellow in autumn. The other assets of spicebush include its very aromatic leaves, twigs, and stems; and (on fertile plants) its scarlet fruits. All of these can be used to make tea. For a fruiting spicebush, make sure you get a pistillate (fertile) specimen.

Zone 5 / Native / 15 feet

Lonicera maackii (Amur honeysuckle) can be something of a threat if it is not in a controlled landscape, because the birds enjoy its berries and scatter its seeds around the countryside — and rapid propagation is the result. But if you can restrict it to its proper home, this is a great shrub for hedges and screening plantings. Its white flowers bloom from May into June, deliciously sweet-smelling and ambrosial to bees. Amur honeysuckle grows quite tall and upright for one of its family, and its dense dark green foliage stays on the plant well into late autumn, making a handsome backdrop for the glassy red berries. It's very hardy, and adaptable to most soils and growing conditions (but not very wet situations). It prefers full sun. After it flowers, prune it as severely as you need; cutting it back to the ground will encourage it to grow more dense clumps of stems. Rem Red honeysuckle (*Lonicera maackii* 'Rem Red') is a USDA introduction that I particularly like. (For other honeysuckles, see Vines and Medium Deciduous Shrubs.)

Zone 3 / China / 12 to 15 feet

Malus sargentii (Sargent crabapple): There are literally countless exquisite varieties of crabapple tree (see Small Deciduous Trees) — but Sargent crab is the only one you can really think of as a plant or a flowering screen or hedge. It is shrublike in its low, spreading, multistemmed habit of growth. Apart from that special characteristic, it's a typical crabapple: that is, a wonderful plant that will add beauty and charm to any landscape at any time of year. Its masses of fragrant, pure white flowers appear in spring, followed by very dense apple-green foliage, then abundant dark red fruits that last long into the winter, to the pleasure of the birds. Give Sargent crab a well-drained, moist, acid loam and full sunlight if possible. It should be pruned by early June — immediately after flowering — although you can do some careful removal of suckers or thinning of old growth later in the season.

Zone 5 / Japan / 10 feet (spreading)

Rhus copallina (shining sumac): Of all the sumacs, this is the most desirable garden plant — but even this is best for banks, open spaces, naturalistic plantings, or wild landscapes rather than disciplined residential backyards. It can grow into a small tree, but it's usually used as a shrub. The pointed compound leaves are a glossy deep green. In autumn they turn fiery tones of red, so that both in shape and in color they resemble flames; and in fact this tree is sometimes called flameleaf sumac. It has fuzzy red fruits that also ripen in autumn. As a young plant shining sumac is compact and dense; as it ages its branches spread up and outward and it becomes more open and picturesque. The great asset of shining sumac is that it is easily transplanted and will thrive in poor, dry, rocky soil and full sun.

Zone 5 / Native / 20 to 30 feet

Salix caprea (goat willow, or French pussy willow): This large shrub or small tree is usually the source of the "pussy willows" sold in florists' shops in March and April, since its silken gray catkins are larger and more showy than those of the true pussy willow (*Salix discolor*). Apart from the catkins, goat willow has limited landscape use. It's susceptible to the splitting, breakage, blights, and pests that beset many willows. It will, however, live cheerfully in soggy conditions; it's easy to propagate and an irrepressible grower. Goat willow can be renewed by being cut back to a stump in early spring. It will send up a forest of long shoots the minute your back is turned.

Zone 5 / Europe to Northeastern Asia / 15 to 25 feet

Sambucus canadensis (elderberry): See Medium Deciduous Shrubs.

Spiraea spp. (spirea): See Medium Deciduous Shrubs.

Syringa spp. (lilac): See Medium Deciduous Shrubs.

Viburnum dentatum (arrowwood): This hardy native is named for the strong, straight shoots that grow from its base, which the Indians used to make arrows. It grows into a dense, multistemmed, delicately branched shrub. Its flowers are borne in creamy-white flat-topped clusters in late May to early June, and give way to blue-black October fruits that are much relished by birds. The jagged-edged leaves are lustrous in summer and turn yellow, orange, red, or purplish-red in autumn. Arrowwood makes a marvelous screen, hedge, or filler in a shrub border. It grows quickly in any kind of soil, even in wet locations; and it tolerates shade well. You can propagate it from softwood cuttings taken in June, but you may find that repressing its natural self-propagating tendencies is your primary chore.

Zone 3 / Native / 6 to 15 feet (equally wide)

Viburnum dilatatum (linden viburnum): See Medium Deciduous Shrubs.

Viburnum opulus (European cranberrybush): This viburnum has three-lobed leaves like maple leaves and contributes a dash of purplish-red color to the autumn landscape. Its chief assets, however, are its showy mid-May flowers and its long-lasting berries. The blossoms are flat-topped clusters of white flowerets, arranged in a pinwheel pattern with small flowers at the center, larger ones around them. The clustered berries are translucent and bright red, persisting well into late fall or winter. European cranberrybush is upright and multistemmed; its form grows more rounded with age as the branches lengthen and arch over toward the ground. It is happy in many different soils and conditions, and makes a distinctive component of shrub borders or massed plantings.

A beautiful cultivar of this shrub is the European snowball viburnum or guelder-rose (*Viburnum opulus* 'Roseum'). Its spheres of white flowerets — "snowballs" — bloom in May; but they are sterile, so there's no fruit to follow. Another nonfruiting variety is a dwarf that's excellent in hedges, the small-leaved, dense *Viburnum opulus* 'Nanum'. Compact European cranberrybush viburnum (*Viburnum opulus* 'Compactum') is a great choice for small gardens or massed plantings; its flowers are lovely and it puts on a glorious display of crimson fruit, but it's only half the size of the species.

Zone 4 / Europe / 8 to 12 feet (equally wide)

Viburnum plicatum tomentosum (doublefile viburnum): See Medium Deciduous Shrubs.

Viburnum prunifolium (black haw): See Small Deciduous Trees.

Viburnum sieboldii (Siebold viburnum) in maturity looks more like a small tree than a shrub: it is sturdy, open, and upright in habit. It can stand alone as a specimen plant or can be used in taller grouped plantings. Its flowers are abundant saucer-shaped clusters of creamy white, practically smothering the plant in late May. The leaves are a crisp deep green. The spectacular fruits ripen from rose-red to black in September to October. Birds devour the fruits themselves, leaving behind the red stems — which give the plant a glow of rosy color for another few weeks. Siebold viburnum is tough and trouble-free, but it does demand adequate moisture. It will tolerate light or partial shade. (For another tree-sized viburnum, see black haw in Small Deciduous Trees.)

Zone 5 / Japan / 15 to 30 feet

Viburnum trilobum (American cranberrybush or highbush cranberry) isn't a cranberry at all. But its fruits resemble cranberries — shining red berries growing in clusters, ripening as early as July and persisting on the shrub throughout the late summer, fall, and most of the winter. These fruits are edible both by wildlife and by people; they make excellent jam. American cranberrybush also has handsome foliage and flowers: the leaves are large and three-pointed, similar to maple or ivy leaves in shape; and the flat "lace cap" clusters of showy white flowers, appearing in mid-May, alone could justify this as a plant for anyone's garden. The dense, round-topped form of this shrub makes it well suited for borders or massed plantings. Like all viburnums it is simple to propagate from softwood cuttings. It will bloom in sun or partial shade, suffers few pests or diseases, and is generally unfusy and a pleasure to have around.

Zone 3 / Native / 8 to 12 feet (equally wide)

NEEDLED EVERGREEN TREES AND SHRUBS

Abies concolor (white fir, or Colorado fir) has stiff upright clusters of 2-inch gray-green and bluish-green needles and a bristly, almost furry overall texture. It makes a very dense, sturdy cone of green at every age — although when the species is old, it can be a very large cone indeed. While this fir does best in full sun and rich, well-drained soils, it will tolerate thin rocky soils as well. It will also endure heat, cold, strong winds, partial shade, and even city conditions. Transplant it balled and burlapped. It's normally free of pests and diseases. Unlike some other firs, especially in less than ideal circumstances, it holds its needles well. A reliable standby for any spot that calls for an opaque evergreen tree.

Zone 5 / Native / 50 to 120 feet

Chamaecyparis obtusa (Hinoki false cypress) is often called just Hinoki cypress. It is most often seen in the form of its small cultivars; but the basic species is a very tall, slender, round-topped pyramidal tree. With its reddish-brown shredding bark and its picturesquely fanned, waxy, scalelike foliage, this evergreen makes a beautiful specimen or accent plant. Some varieties have blue-green foliage, some dark green, a few yellow-green. Dwarf Hinoki false cypresses are fine in city gardens, containers, or rock gardens, where you can appreciate the beauty of the coral-formed foliage at close range. Hinoki false cypresses prefer well-drained moist soil, plenty of sun, and shelter from drying winds — a humid atmosphere is best of all. Soils should be neutral to acid. Among the many cultivars are 'Gracilis', a dark-foliaged, compact pyramidal form; 'Nana', a tiny and very slow-growing dwarf that may reach a height or 2 or 3 feet; and 'Nana Gracilis', topping out at 4 feet, with foliage of a lustrous deep green.

Zone 5 / Japan / 50 to 75 feet (species; vars. much smaller)

***Chamaecyparis pisifera* 'Filifera'** (thread false cypress): Beautiful for its lacy-textured, light green foliage and for the slender, open branches that form an upright pyramid, this variety of Sawara false cypress makes a dramatic specimen plant. Like other false cypresses it prefers a rich, moist, well-drained, neutral-to-acid soil, in full sun or partial shade. It does best in a damp climate. You can install it in fall or early spring; and you can prune it in spring, or remove branches at any season. Compact thread cypress (*Chamaecyparis pisifera* 'Filifera Nana') has drooping frondlike branches that create a dense mound 6 to 8 feet high. The yellow-foliaged dwarf cultivar 'Golden Mop' looks, oddly enough, just like a small golden mop, and is a pleasant accent in a coniferous evergreen grouping.

Zone 4 / Hybrid (Japan) / 50 to 75 feet (species; vars. much smaller)

Juniperus virginiana (red cedar): Eastern red cedar, as it's also known, may be known best for its beautifully streaked, spicy-smelling wood, which is much used in storage chests for clothes and blankets (since the aroma is as repellent to moths as it is attractive to humans). But this hardy tree has plenty of landscape value, too. The erect, pointed forms of cedars are a familiar and appealing sight in overgrown pastures in New England, particularly near the sea — proof of this tree's affinity for poor, rocky, and even alkaline soils. The reddish bark that peels in long papery shreds is another asset. Still another is the dense evergreen foliage, which makes for excellent windbreaks or sheltering hedges. Plant red cedar ideally in a sunny, airy location with good moist soil. The variety 'Canaertii', which has a compact form, dark green foliage, and abundant blue berries, is smaller overall than the species. (For other junipers, see Evergreen Ground Covers.)

Zone 3 / Native / 40 to 50 feet (species; vars. much smaller)

Metasequoia glyptostroboides (dawn redwood): See Large Deciduous Trees.

Picea abies (Norway spruce): Because it grows very fast when it is young, Norway spruce has long been popular for shelter or screening uses. As a specimen tree it reaches a great height, and I admire it in wide-open spaces or large suburban properties where the sweeping branches with their pendulous branchlets lend a graceful note to the landscape. I would not recommend it as a plant for a small yard, however. There are several smaller cultivars of Norway spruce, many of which demand almost no pruning to stay within bounds, so that they are suitable for an opaque hedge all year long. A particularly low-growing, flat-topped one is nest spruce (*Picea abies* 'Nidiformis') — but your nursery can show you a selection to choose from. Norway spruce is easy to move because of its shallow root system, and thrives in a sandy, moderately moist, well-drained soil. It does best in a cold climate.

Zone 3 / Northern and Central Europe / 60 to 100 feet (species; vars. much smaller)

PINUS SPP.

Pine: These beautiful trees, a mainstay of the modern lumber industry and the source of wood products from paper to turpentine, are also a mainstay of the American landscape. Of all the many sizes and shapes of pines, only a small selection are described here; but even among these few you'll find plants to meet a great range of requirements.

Pines are generally tougher and more adaptable than spruces or firs. Their one important demand is to be either moved very young or carefully root-pruned in the nursery. The reason is that pines often develop a taproot that makes transplanting more and more difficult as they mature. Pines can also be pruned for thick, compact growth in hedges or screens: if you remove one-half of each "candle" of new growth in late spring, multiple buds will form below the cut.

All pines fall into three categories according to the number of needles grouped in each sheath. The 5-needle pines, like white pine and Swiss stone pine, have the softest texture because of their soft, feathery, densely grouped needles. Next come the 3-needle types, such as lacebark pine. The 2-needle types include mugho pine, Austrian pine, Jack pine, and Japanese black pine, all of which have a coarser, more bristly texture because of their more widely spaced, relatively rigid, sharp-pointed needles.

Many of these are large trees, reaching a mature height of 35 to 75 feet or more. A few, as noted below, are small or even shrubby.

Pinus banksiana (jack pine) is a utility tree for difficult situations. It will cling stubbornly to life in wretched soil where better-quality pines or deciduous trees won't grow. In maturity it spreads into a shrubby, flat-topped shape, perhaps 35 to 50 feet tall. Its mature bark furrows into thick plates, and its shortish, stiff, paired needles are dark green. This hardy native flourishes on dry banks, in full sun, and in sandy, gravelly, and/or acid soil; and it can take intense cold. Zone 3.

Pinus bungeana (lacebark pine) has beautiful red-brown bark that exfoliates like that of a sycamore, showing creamy-white patches beneath. Of Chinese origin, this is a specimen tree for viewing at close range, near the house or terrace. It has stiff, dark green needles in sets of three. Pyramidal in youth, often multistemmed, it develops slowly into a 30- to 50-foot-tall and picturesquely spreading tree in old age. Lacebark pine prefers well-drained soil and full sun, and tolerates limestone soils. Zone 5.

Pinus cembra (Swiss stone pine) comes from Europe. It requires a loamy, well-drained, slightly acid soil with full sun and very good circulation of air. It transplants more easily than most pines. When young it is a very slender pyramid, almost columnar; it becomes more open and flat-topped in maturity. It is slow-growing and stays a modest size (about 25 feet) for many years. The needles of Swiss stone pine, growing in fives, are quite long and dense, giving it a soft foliage texture. This makes a lovely specimen tree or mass planting. Zone 3.

***Pinus densiflora* 'Umbraculifera'** (Tanyosho pine) is a variety of Japanese red pine. Its bark is a striking orange-red. Its long, soft, twisted bluish-green needles, growing in pairs, are uniquely decorative. So is the form of Tanyosho pine: it develops into a small (10 to 12 feet) umbrella-shaped tree, usually with picturesque multiple trunks and dense spreading branches, like a scaled-up bonsai tree. This is a dramatic accent plant. It needs sunny conditions and a well-drained, somewhat acid soil. Zone 5.

Pinus mugo pumilio (dwarf mugho pine): This sturdy plant is descended from trees native to Europe's mountain ranges. It is low-growing, spreading, or even prostrate, and can be used in groups or planted as an individual specimen. Very hardy and a slow grower, it can be pruned for thickness and small size. It does best in deep, moist loam; it tolerates partial shade. Its rigid paired needles are a medium green, and its stems are held upright, giving it a bristly, brushlike texture overall. Zone 3.

Pinus nigra (Austrian pine) is moderate-sized, with handsome, stiff, shining dark green needles and cinnamon-brown bark, both of which you can appreciate best at close range. It tolerates shade, dirt, and pollutants and is flexible as to soil type and condition, so that it's at home in or out of the city. It does not suffer from alkaline soils, wind, or exposure to salt spray. You can prune its young growth in spring, for screening or hedging purposes; or plant it in groups or as a specimen. Dense and pyramidal when young, a mature Austrian pine — which can reach 50 feet — becomes flat-topped, with a stout trunk and stout, spreading branches. Zone 5.

Pinus strobus (white pine) has a windswept look in old age: a tall charcoal-gray trunk and clouds of soft blue-green foliage like feathery plumes against the sky. For its first half-century, however, it has a plump, pyramidal shape most distinguished for the softness of its texture and color. This is a beautiful tree, a basic component of the North American landscape since time immemorial. If you use white pine in a wild landscape it will rapidly colonize from seed. Or if you have plenty of space you can grow it as a specimen or in groupings; or you can shear it into a hedge of whatever dimensions you desire. Left to itself it will grow to 50, 80, even 100 feet or more. White pine will grow in nearly any well-drained soil. It needs plenty of light but will tolerate some shade, although shade will make it grow somewhat spindly. It will not, however, put up with salty conditions or urban air pollution. Zone 4.

Pinus thunbergiana (Japanese black pine) can stand large amounts of salt water, even drenchings by winter storms and hurricanes, so it is invaluable as an accent plant for seaside locations. It's a beautiful, picturesque, spreading tree with dense foliage. The needles are twisted, dark green, lustrous, and quite long; they grow in pairs. The mature bark is a blackish gray, fissured into irregular plates. This tree prefers full sun; it makes its best growth in good, moist soil, but it also does well in sandy soils. Its mature height ranges (depending on the circumstances) from 20 to 80 feet. Zone 6.

Pseudolarix kaempferi (golden larch): See Large Deciduous Trees.

Pseudotsuga menziesii (Douglas fir) is a noble forest tree by nature, growing to a height of 200 feet or more in the wild. But in smaller-scaled residential landscapes it contributes a wonderfully dense, regular pyramidal shape. Its needles are short and soft (not stiff like those of spruces), and blue-green or gray-green to green. It will do best in a moist, well-drained, neutral to slightly acid soil. It flourishes in a sunny, open location and prefers a somewhat humid atmosphere. High winds can damage it, the more so the bigger it gets. You can find slow-growing, pendulous-branched, or dwarf varieties of Douglas fir; the dwarf types are naturally the best suited to use in hedges, but bigger varieties also make fine screens and windbreaks as well as specimen plants for large properties.

Zone 5 / Native / 80 to 250 feet (species; vars. much smaller)

Sciadopitys verticillata (umbrella pine) is so named because its glossy dark green needles are held in whorls that radiate from the stem like the ribs of an umbrella. The tree is roughly pyramidal, but the foliage is so distinctive that it's the detailed texture rather than the overall form that matters in the landscape. The grayish-brown bark exfoliates in long strips. This is a wonderful specimen plant for use near houses, around rocks, or in small gardens. An extremely slow grower, it does best if sheltered from hot sun and freezing winds. Transplant it balled and burlapped into rich, acid soil with plenty of moisture, plenty of sun, and good ventilation.

Zone 6 / Japan / 30 to 90 feet

Taxus canadensis (Canada yew), one of just two yew species native to this country, is primarily of use as a ground cover or understory planting in shady naturalized or woodland situations. The hardiest of all yews, Canada yew is a low, sprawling plant with leaders that often root where they encounter the ground. Like other yews it has flat, shiny, dark-green evergreen needles and pretty (but mildly poisonous) red fruits. It likes a fertile sandy loam with top-notch drainage: it won't survive heat, drought, or bad drainage. Dwarf Canadian hedge yew (*Taxus canadensis* 'Stricta') is less sprawling, with more upright branches and a tighter general habit — but it shares the shade tolerance and great hardiness of the basic species, for people with shady or very cold locations. As its name implies, it is tailor-made for evergreen hedges.

Zone 3 / Native / 3 to 6 feet (6 to 8 wide)

***Taxus cuspidata* 'Nana'** (dwarf Japanese yew): This yew will perform well in sun or in shade, in city or in country, heavily pruned or not at all. It is also adaptable as to soil, although (like all yews) it does demand excellent drainage. This is a tidy, compact, slow-growing variety of Japanese yew, with spreading branches that give it a broad, low form. Its foliage is a lustrous dark green and somewhat tufted, making attractive patterns of light and shadow. The new spring growth is a very pretty bright yellow-green. You can prune dwarf Japanese yew just about any time, but I recommend doing it early in the growing season if possible, so as to allow the new growth that follows pruning to harden off before winter.

Zone 5 / Manchuria, Korea, Japan / 10 feet (20 wide)

Taxus media (intermediate yew) is more a group than a single type of plant. You'll find it mainly in the form of its many cultivars, each with its characteristic size and growth habit; each with its special assets; and each deservedly popular as a maintenance-free, symmetrical, slow-growing evergreen shrub. The cultivar 'Densiformis' is particularly dense, ideally suited for use in hedges or borders, and twice as wide as it is high (it can grow to 10 feet or more in height). Hatfield yew (*Taxus media* 'Hatfieldii') has a broad, compact form but holds its branches and branchlets erect; its top height is around 12 feet. Hicks yew (*Taxus media* 'Hicksii') is an upright, columnar variety that can grow 20 feet or more tall, with several stems but not nearly as broad and bushy a habit as many yews. All these yews like moist, sandy loam and will thrive in sun or shade. The female plants bear fleshy, mildly toxic red fruits that can be quite decorative against the dark-green foliage. Intermediate yews are excellent for hedges (pruned, of course), groupings, and massed plantings; or use them as facer plants below taller trees.

Zone 5 / Hybrid (England and Japan) / Various sizes

Thuja occidentalis (American arborvitae) is another reliable evergreen tree that's generally available in the form of one or another of its many cultivated varieties. Its lacy, fine-textured foliage makes a pleasant contrast to the foliage of needled or broad-leaved evergreens in winter, and to the leaves of deciduous plants in summer. With the basic species, however, the foliage often suffers from winter browning that spoils its looks; and in severely icy or snowy winters there is a tendency for one of its paired or clustered stems to split and droop sideways, giving the tree a very disheveled appearance. That's why the cultivars are usually recommended. One tall and vigorous type for backgrounds or hedges is 'Douglas Pyramidal'. Its fernlike foliage can be trusted to stay a good dark green year round. So can the foliage of 'Hetz Midget' arborvitae, a very slow-growing, ball-shaped dwarf plant for borders or low hedges. 'Hetz Wintergreen' is a narrow, upright, fast-growing variety that is ideal for a tall hedge (it can reach 60 feet) and keeps its color beautifully. All American arborvitaes are easy to propagate from softwood cuttings taken in fall or winter. They like full sun and a humid atmosphere as well as abundant moisture in the soil, which should be a deep well-drained loam. They tolerate alkaline soils well.

Zone 3 / Native (hybrids) / Various heights

Tsuga canadensis (Canadian hemlock), left to itself, will grow into a towering pyramid whose bottom branches create a cave of darkness 20 or 30 feet across. So this is not a tree for a small property unless you keep it small by regular pruning (as in a border or hedge) or use one of its small cultivated varieties. For larger areas or woodlands, Canadian hemlock is magnificent: rapid-growing, densely branched, with small flat needles of a very deep dark green (but bright yellow-green new growth in May and June). Birds and wildlife cherish its fine twigs and close-set branches for shelter and nesting, and its tiny round cones for food. Canadian hemlock prefers a soil that is acid, with ample moisture and good drainage; but it will do fine in sandy soils or even on rocky ledge. It won't tolerate pollution, drought, or heavy winds, however. It responds nicely to pruning, and makes a graceful evergreen hedge or screen. Among dwarf varieties, *Tsuga canadensis* 'Bennett' is compact and spreading, growing broader than it is high. 'Coles Prostrate' literally crawls over the ground, but can also be trained on stakes in any form you wish until the trunks grow sturdy enough to be self-supporting. Sargent weeping hemlock (*Tsuga canadensis pendula* or *sargentii*), the most beautiful weeping conifer, forms a broad dense mound of fine-textured drooping foliage.

Zone 4 / Native / 40 to 100 feet (species; vars. much smaller)

BROAD-LEAVED EVERGREENS

AZALEAS

There are just a few azaleas hardy enough to be considered evergreen in Zone 6 or north; and in a severe winter, even these selections should be expected to lose a good many leaves. Deciduous azaleas, described under Medium Deciduous Shrubs, are a much larger group. Like all members of the *Rhododendron* genus, azaleas need humidity and acid soil. In the north, shelter from hot summer sun and drying winds is beneficial; and azaleas like a thick acid mulch to keep their roots moist and cool in summer. Given these conditions, they'll afford matchless spring beauty, fine-textured summer foliage, and color and mass for the winter landscape. The choices listed here are all low-growing, almost dwarf plants, which is characteristic of azaleas that are evergreen in the north. For more impressive dimensions combined with small leaf texture, some of the small-leaved rhododendrons may be good alternatives.

***Rhododendron* 'Delaware Valley White'** (Delaware Valley white azalea) offers bright-green foliage and clear white blossoms, and reaches a top height of 4 feet. Zone 6.

***Rhododendron kaempferi* 'Herbert'** (Herbert azalea) is a hybrid with Japanese ancestry, and produces dark reddish-purple flowers. Zone 6.

***Rhododendron obtusum* 'Hinocrimson'** (Hinocrimson azalea) is a spreading, dense shrub with small glossy leaves — a hybrid of a Japanese mountain plant. The flowers are an intense crimson. Zone 6.

***Rhododendron obtusum* 'Hinodegiri'** (Hinodegiri azalea) has flowers that are a vivid rose-red; in addition it's especially compact, and can be shaped for a clipped hedge or border. Zone 6.

Buxus microphylla (littleleaf box or boxwood) is a dense evergreen shrub with small, glossy leaves — a classic favorite for all sorts of low hedges and borders. You can buy it in containers or balled and burlapped, and it will do fine in most well-drained soils, although it prefers mulching to keep its roots cool. It's also best used in locations where it has some protection from the strongest sun, drying winds, and winter cold. The basic species is only barely hardy in Massachusetts (one plantsman describes littleleaf box as turning a "repulsive yellow-green-brown" in winter); but the variety *japonica* and newer cultivars like 'Green Beauty' and 'Wintergreen' (*Buxus microphylla koreana* 'Wintergreen') have been bred specifically for attractive winter color in this climate. Look for them.

Zones 5 to 7 (according to variety) / Japan / 3 to 4 feet

Buxus sempervirens (common box or boxwood): This is much larger than its cousin littleleaf box, so it can be used not only in hedges and borders but as a specimen or in massed plantings. It's another dense, multibranched evergreen shrub, with a medium-fine foliage texture. Like littleleaf box, the basic common box prefers a mild climate and can just barely survive extremes of heat and cold; but many sturdy smaller cultivars have been developed that are tailored to the needs of gardeners in the Northeast. Some that have stood the test of many difficult seasons are 'Vardar Valley', 'Green Gem', 'Green Velvet', and 'Green Mountain'. Many of these are hardy even well into Zone 5.

Zones 5 to 6 / Southern Europe, Northern Africa, Western Asia / 15 feet (species; vars. much smaller)

***Cotoneaster* spp.** (cotoneaster): See Small Deciduous Shrubs and Evergreen Ground Covers.

***Ilex crenata* 'Convexa'** (boxleaf holly) is also called convex-leaved Japanese holly; by either name, it is one of the most useful and hardy broad-leaved evergreen shrubs available to northern gardeners. It doesn't seem to suffer from crowded, dirty city conditions, and it will endure severe pruning, so it is ideal for hedges. Prune it after its current season's growth has hardened off. Boxleaf holly is dense and low-growing; its small, oval leaves are a glossy dark green like those of most hollies. Its flowers and small black berries are inconspicuous (and anyway it won't bear fruit unless it's a female with a male near by). It prefers a light, acid soil. There are many fine cultivars; a couple of reliable ones are the dwarf 'Compacta' and the even more compact dwarf 'Helleri'.

Zone 6 / Japan / 9 feet (24 wide)

Ilex glabra (inkberry) is a popular and adaptable native shrub, a member of the holly family. Its clusters of small, shiny, oval leaves add a sprightly touch to the winter scene. Inkberry (so called for its black berries) will grow happily in wet soil; it prefers acid soil, but also does well in salty (alkaline) surroundings. It is best used in massed plantings. You can prune it as heavily as necessary, or alternatively let it expand into a broad mass, which it does by sending up shoots or suckers from around its base. 'Compacta' is a good dwarf form of inkberry.

Zone 4 / Native / 6 to 8 feet (8 to 10 wide)

Ilex meserveae (blue hollies or Meserve hollies) are a fairly recent introduction — a cross between English holly (*Ilex aquifolium*) and prostrate holly (*Ilex rugosa*), with the virtues of both and the failings of neither. These hardy hybrids have a distinctive bluish tinge to their foliage and make striking accent plants. The typical spikiness of the leaves makes blue-holly hedges impervious to man or beast. If there is a male blue holly in the vicinity, the female blue hollies will bear lovely red berries. Blue holly cultivars named 'Blue Angel', 'Blue Princess', 'Blue Prince', and the like come in assorted sizes and growth habits. They are all adaptable as to soil and sun conditions, and maintain their notable color throughout the winter.

Zone 5 / Hybrids / 6 to 20 feet

Ilex opaca (American holly), growing in the wild, forms a large and beautifully symmetrical cone of lustrous green. Its brilliant red berries stay on the tree well into the winter, and are much sought after for decorations around Christmastime. As with all hollies, only the female tree bears fruit, and it requires a male nearby for pollination. Holly prefers loose, moist, acid soil; it won't survive in extremely dry locations or in poorly drained soil, and it requires shelter from strong winds. If you're in the market for a specimen holly or for hollies for grouping, shop around a little. There are about 300 cultivars of American holly available. Look for varieties of proven worth that are known to flourish in your particular set of climatic and soil conditions.

Zone 6 / Native / 40 to 70 feet

Ilex pedunculosa (longstalk holly): This is a hardy, upright shrub or small tree with handsome, laurellike leaves and bright red berries the size of peas, borne singly on long stalks, not in clusters like those of American holly. This exceptionally resilient member of the holly group will stand up to drying winds, summer heat, and poorly drained soils. Its foliage is very dense, and it makes a strong statement as a specimen plant or in massed plantings. It is a kind of a Cinderella among hollies — a plant that many experts consider too little appreciated and deserving of much wider popularity.

Zone 6 / Japan and China / 20 to 30 feet

Ilex verticillata (winterberry): See Medium Deciduous Shrubs.

Kalmia latifolia (mountain laurel): This broad-leaved evergreen shrub has been loved by generations of gardeners up and down the East Coast. I mention the east because mountain laurel requires soil acidity; given that and a cool, moist, well-drained loam, it will prosper in considerable shade as well as in full sun. It is marvelous for massed plantings, borders, or even naturalizing on larger properties. Its June flowers are extraordinary: clusters of small 10-sectioned cups that are rosy in bud, white in full bloom, and as crisply perfect as porcelain. The leaves, a deep glossy green, make fine winter arrangements inside the house as well as brightening the outdoor scene. There are several good cultivars and varieties, some more compact, some with red to pink flowers (such as the variety *Kalmia rubra* or the cultivar *Kalmia* 'Fuscata').

Zone 5 / Native / 30 feet

Leucothoe fontanesiana (drooping leucothoe) bears sprays of fragrant, white bell-shaped flowers in spring, and its lustrous leaves stay on the plant year round, deep green in summer and bronze-toned throughout the winter. The branches of this graceful shrub curve in fountainlike arches — hence the name. Use drooping leucothoe (pronounced lew-KO-tho-ee) in groupings; as a facer plant to hide bare stems of taller shrubs; as a cover for a shady bank; or as "understory" growth in naturalistic or woodland plantings. Like the better-known azaleas and rhododendrons, to which it is related, drooping leucothoe prefers an acid soil. It is best planted in spring; it needs a moist, well-drained soil high in organic matter, and will tolerate partial to full shade (although it can stand full sun if there's plenty of moisture). It will not tolerate drought or excessive drying. If drooping leucothoe becomes overgrown or leggy, restore bushy growth and vitality by cutting it back to the ground after it flowers. For a lower-growing, more spreading variety, look at coast leucothoe (*Leucothoe axillaris*); or at dwarf leucothoe (*Leucothoe fontanesiana* 'Nana'), which grows 2 feet high but 6 feet across.

Zone 5 / Native / 3 to 6 feet (equally wide)

Mahonia aquifolium (Oregon holly-grape or grape-holly) is classified as a broad-leaved "evergreen" shrub even though its leaves are actually a bronzed brown in winter. It is a good border plant for shady locations, with clusters of bright yellow flowers in spring, glossy leaves shaped like holly leaves, and blue-black late-summer fruits that closely resemble Concord grapes. Oregon holly-grape likes a moist, well-drained, acid soil, and at least partial shade. It requires protection from heat and drying.

Zone 6 / Native / 3 to 6 feet

Paxistima canbyi (Canby paxistima): Formerly called pachistima, this is a useful low-maintenance evergreen shrub, categorized as a "broad-leaved" evergreen although it's by far the narrowest-leaved plant to come under that heading. For that reason, and because it grows low to the ground and spreads horizontally, and because of its handsome bronze fall color, Canby paxistima is wonderful in combination with other broad-leaved or needled evergreens in grouped plantings or low borders. You can propagate it from cuttings taken in summer. In the wild it colonizes rocky soils, but it prefers a moist, well-drained soil with good organic content.

Zone 5 / Native / 1 to 2 feet (3 to 5 across)

Pieris floribunda (mountain andromeda or pieris) gives winter-long promise of spring, because its flower buds are formed in summer and are visible throughout the winter months, a pale greenish white against the plant's dense evergreen foliage. This is a lovely, low, rounded shrub — a perfect choice for grouped plantings of broad-leaved evergreens or for use in woodland borders or naturalistic plantings. In very early spring the fragrant white flowers bloom, held aloft in small spires. Mountain andromeda likes a light, peaty soil, although it's not as demanding of acidity as some other broad-leaved evergreens. Give it a location in partial shade if possible. Keep it away from windy places in full sun, where its leaves are apt to burn in late winter.

Zone 5 / Native / 2 to 6 feet (equally wide)

Pieris japonica (Japanese andromeda or pieris) is taller and more upright than the related mountain andromeda. Its flower buds are visible on the shrub all winter long and bloom in earliest spring; they are graceful cascading clusters of fragrant white bells, similar to lilies-of-the-valley. With its lustrous dark green foliage, Japanese andromeda makes a fine specimen plant or combines with other broad-leaved evergreens in massed plantings or shrub borders. Several cultivated varieties have been developed. A compact type (*Pieris japonica* 'Compacta') is smaller-growing and smaller-leaved, for smaller gardens; others offer pink flowers, variegated leaves, or leaves with decorative textures. Give Japanese andromeda a somewhat acid, well-drained, highly organic soil, and partial shade; it will do best if sheltered from strong winds. Prune it in spring, after its flowering.

Zone 6 / Japan / 9 to 12 feet (species; vars. much smaller)

***Pyracantha coccinea* 'Lalandei'** (Laland firethorn): One of the hardiest cultivars of scarlet firethorn, this is an outstanding broad-leaved evergreen for informal hedges or barriers or for training as an espalier plant against walls or fences. It's often just the thing for a walled city garden. Its small leaves are a glossy dark green and it bears white flowers in late spring. Its small but very abundant berries, ripening in September, are a brilliant orange-red; they persist on the plant well into the winter, giving it a festive look. The firethorn's thorns are long, straight, and sharp. It is flexible as to soil pH. It prefers a well-drained soil and will tolerate dry soil; and it will produce the best crop of berries if it gets a good amount of sun. Whether you are using firethorn as a free-standing plant or espaliered, you'll need to prune it often to keep it within bounds.

Zone 6 / Italy to Western Asia / 6 to 18 feet

RHODODENDRON SPP.

The genus *Rhododendron* incorporates all the plants commonly called azaleas as well as all the rhododendrons — but I've listed azaleas under "Azaleas" here and elsewhere in this book. The great majority of rhododendrons (unlike azaleas) really are evergreen in the north.

If you've investigated rhododendrons at all, you already know that this is a huge clan of shrubs. Indeed, a large body of literature and numerous horticultural organizations concern themselves solely with the subject of rhododendrons and their relatives. There are 900 identified *Rhododendron* species and uncountable varieties. What I'll offer here is a small sampling of reliable and widely obtainable varieties. Your nursery will be able to introduce you to other good ones.

All rhododendrons should be planted into acid, moist, highly organic soil. The top of the earth ball should be at the surface of the ground — don't plant them deep. They do best in a humid climate and will prosper in locations where there is shelter from extreme cold as well as from dry heat and drying winds. Prune rhododendrons early in spring, if necessary; and after they bloom, remove spent flower clusters to encourage the formation of abundant new buds for next year.

***Rhododendron* 'Boule de Neige'** (Boule de Neige rhododendron), a hybrid of Caucasian origin, is one of the finest white-flowering rhododendrons available, with clear, pure-white blossoms in late May. Zone 6.

Rhododendron carolinianum (Carolina rhododendron) is one of the best and most popular rhododendron species, with small dark-green leaves and pale rosy-purple flowers in mid-May. It's not a huge plant, but grows to a height of around 6 feet; it generally has a compact, rounded shape. Give Carolina rhododendron sun or partial shade and protection from strong wind and sun. It is a native, and fine for naturalizing. Zone 5.

Rhododendron catawbiense (Catawba rhododendron), another native species, can grow very large, and has medium-large leathery leaves. It's wonderful growing in large masses at the edge of woodland or in wild landscapes; and it is tough enough for cold or exposed locations. The species flowers around mid- to late May. The best flowering Catawba rhododendrons are its many cultivated varieties. 'Roseum Elegans' is a great standby, long loved and much used for its reliability in flowering and its ability to withstand extreme temperatures; its flowers are a clear lavender-pink. 'Compactum' also bears rosy-lavender blossoms, but is smaller and more dense and rounded. The variety *album* has large clusters of white bloom with yellow markings. 'Nova Zembla' bears gorgeous red flowers and is another type with exceptional resistance to heat and cold. Zone 5.

Rhododendron 'Chionoides' (Chionoides rhododendron) is a later-blooming cultivar with long, light green leaves and a compact, wide-growing form. The flowers are white with yellow "eyes," giving the shrub a very crisp, clean, springy look. Zone 6.

Rhododendron 'P.J.M. Hybrids'.

Rhododendron fortunei (Fortune rhododendrons) include many hybrid varieties, all with a common origin in eastern China. They can grow to 12 feet and have large, loosely clustered leaves. The late May blooms are fragrant and very large, and all in pink to red tones. One of my favorite *fortunei* cultivars is a Dexter hybrid called 'Scintillation', with pale pink blooms. Zone 6.

Rhododendron laetivirens (Wilson rhododendron) is a very hardy and charmingly compact and neat hybrid variety. Growing slowly to a top height of 4 feet or so, it is fine for small-scale gardens, even rock gardens, or for planting close to the house where larger types would be out of place. Its small, rose-colored to purplish flowers appear in early June, but they're almost incidental. The small leaves are glossy and similar in size and shape to those of mountain laurel: I use this shrub more for its great foliage than for its flowers. Zone 5.

Rhododendron maximum (rosebay rhododendron, or great laurel), may be the hardiest of all the larger rhododendrons — and it really is large. Under ideal conditions in the wild it can grow into a great spreading mound as much as 30 to 40 feet high at its highest point; but in cultivation it will stop at 10 to 12 feet. Rosebay rhododendron is valued primarily as a background planting, rather than for its flowers. It has large, leathery leaves and bears small, pinkish-purple blossoms in late June. It needs semishade, being a plant that thrives in open woodlands. Use it with caution on small properties. Zone 4.

Rhododendron 'P.J.M. Hybrids' (P.J.M. hybrid rhododendrons) bloom in late April, and so profusely that they are completely covered with brilliant lavender-pink, not a leaf showing. They make a stunning display, although I find the color somewhat overpowering; I'd recommend using P.J.M. hybrids in front of masses of other bright green foliage. These rhododendrons grow to be 3 to 6 feet tall. Their leaves are small, glossy, and dark green; they turn a rich purple-bronze or dark red in the fall. P.J.M.s are happy in sunny, exposed locations. Zone 4.

Rhododendron 'Purple Gem' (Purple Gem rhododendrons): These dwarf evergreen rhododendrons are tidy and rounded in form — ideal plants for the smaller garden. Their leaves are very small, and their profuse April flowers are a light bluish purple. They're hardy in Zone 5.

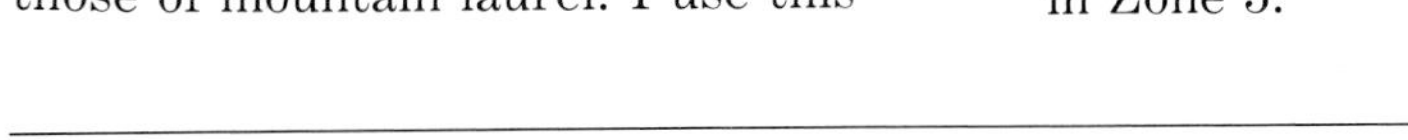

DECIDUOUS GROUND COVERS

Aronia melanocarpa (black chokeberry): This smaller relative of red chokeberry offers an interesting mixture of assets and liabilities. It's a wonderful shrubby ground cover for wet areas and for naturalistic landscapes. It is easy to propagate from cuttings; it tolerates shade; and it thrives in all kinds of soils, from boggy to sandy. Black chokeberry holds its abundant blackish-purple fruits most of the winter, so that a large mass makes quite an impact. On the other hand, it rapidly spreads across the countryside by sending up forests of suckers, so that you may find it hard to contain; it's not for use in disciplined landscapes.

Zone 6 / Native / 3 to 5 feet

Comptonia peregrina (sweet fern) is aptly named, for its aromatic dark green foliage is soft and feathery in appearance, like a bed of forest ferns. Its slender stalks create a broad flat-topped mound and it spreads and colonizes readily from suckers. Sweet fern is happiest in infertile, sandy, acid soils (give it lots of peat) and therefore makes a fine plant for banks and other poor-soil areas, provided they are adequately moist. I enjoy crushing several leaves and indulging in the redolent sweet yet spicy aroma.

Zone 3 / Native / 2 to 4 feet (4 to 8 wide)

Cornus canadensis (bunchberry) is one of the most beautiful of ground covers for naturalistic woodland settings. It is a member of the dogwood clan; its exquisite white flowers (actually bracts), blooming in May and June, are reminiscent of those of flowering dogwood. They're followed by clusters of bright red berries that are edible by human beings as well as wildlife. The leaves are carried in whorls like little pinwheels; they are a glossy dark green, changing to wine-red in fall. This plant needs cool, moist, acid soil, rich in humus and somewhat shaded. Probably the best way to get it started is to transfer sections of sod from established plantings. Given conditions it likes, bunchberry is wonderful under pines, broad-leaved evergreens, or other acid-loving plantings.

Zone 3 / Native / 3 to 9 inches

Coronilla varia (crown vetch) is chiefly useful for erosion control on steep, rocky banks. Its roots do a great job of holding soil in place, and its thick foliage shades out weeds. Don't try to grow it in a well-kept garden, though. It spreads like wildfire and will rapidly become a pest. Its compound leaves consist of many small oval leaflets, giving it a fine texture; and if you can mow it in spring it will make a dense, brilliant-green mat throughout the summer. It dies back to brown stems in winter.

Zone 4 / Europe / 2 feet

***Forsythia viridissima* 'Bronxensis'** (Bronx greenstem forsythia) flowers prolifically at a young age, but never grows more than a foot or so tall and twice as broad. It is very compact and bushy, with green stems and bright-yellow April blossoms. This little plant is at home in small gardens, rock gardens, patios, containers, or any sunny place where the cheerful air of forsythia is wanted but the site's dimensions require a dwarf. It also makes an excellent ground cover, turning a bank into a carpet of yellow. Like all forsythias it's very easy to propagate.

Zone 6 / China / 1 foot (2 wide)

Rosa wichuraiana (memorial rose): Easy to grow in poor soils, free from pests or diseases, and covered with fragrant snowy-white flowers in June and July, this rose is an appealing ground cover for banks and other informal open spaces. It has dark green, lustrous compound leaves. It is a fast spreader, growing as much as 10 feet in a season and multiplying itself rapidly. The canes trail along the ground, often rooting where they touch, and forming a tangled mat of foliage; or they will climb if you give them something to climb over.

Zone 6 / China, Korea, Japan / 1 foot

***Spiraea japonica* 'Alpina'** (daphne spirea): See Medium Deciduous Shrubs.

Vaccinium angustifolium (lowbush blueberry), a native inhabitant of the dry, acid, and infertile soils of former pastures in New England, makes a pretty and indestructible ground cover. The little bell-shaped pinkish-white flowers are followed in July by berries of an intense, dusty blue. These can be unpredictable in quantity, depending on the season; but abundant or not, their flavor is the very essence of summer. (The taste of wild or naturalized blueberries bears only a remote relationship to the blandness of the oversized cultivated berries you find in markets.) Blueberries grow on tiny bushes with woody stems; they're not a plant for walking on. The small leaves turn a rich scarlet in fall. You'll get the best berry crops if you have the plants in full sun, but they will also grow well in light shade or partial sun.

Zone 3 / Native / 2 to 8 inches

Xanthorhiza simplicissima (yellowroot) qualifies as a shrub, since it grows upward from the ground on woody stems to a height of 2 feet — but its great use is as a ground cover, particularly for banks or other challenging situations. It makes a dense mat of roots, stems, and foliage, and spreads rapidly across its allotted territory by means of underground stolons. It has cutleaf foliage like celery leaves. It will thrive in full sun or partial shade in almost any well-drained, adequately moist soil; it does especially well along stream banks or in other damp, lightly shaded areas. You can transplant it (take divisions of older plants) in spring or fall.

Zone 5 / Native / 2 feet

HERBACEOUS PERENNIAL GROUND COVERS

Achillea millefolium 'Rosea' (pink yarrow) will tolerate poor, dry soil and likes full sun. With feathery, finely cut leaves and small pink flowers all summer, it grows 6 inches to 2 feet tall. Zone 3.

Aegopodium podagraria (goutweed or bishop's weed): Low-growing (6 to 14 inches), sprawling, speedy to cover good or poor soil, this can be a pest if you don't contain it. It's happy in sun or shade. Especially handsome in shade is the variegated silveredge goutweed (*Aegopodium podagraria* 'Variegatum'). Zone 4.

Ajuga reptans (bugleweed or carpet bugle) makes a flat mass of interestingly creased and dimpled leaves 8 to 12 inches from the ground. It holds its clusters of small white bugle-shaped flowers above the leaves. Zones 3 to 4.

Arabis procurrens (rockcress) quickly creates a dense mat of shiny leaves in sun or light shade. Its white flowers bloom in April or May; it's pretty in rock gardens or as an edging plant. Zone 5.

Arenaria verna (moss sandwort) is great for planting among stepping stones or along pavement edges in sun or shade. It forms a 2-inch-high mat of fine, evergreen, mosslike foliage. It bears small white flowers in May. For contrast, a golden-leaved variety is *Arenaria verna* 'Aurea'. Zones 3 to 4.

Asarum europaeum (European ginger): Five inches tall, the glossy evergreen leaves of this wild ginger are 2 to 3 inches across and shaped somewhat like the foliage of violets. This is an elegant ground cover for shady or wooded situations. Zone 5.

Convallaria majalis (lily-of-the-valley): The sweet-scented bell-shaped white flowers of this plant need no introduction. This is a determined spreader, new plants popping up from rhizomes in the most unlikely places. Contain it with a physical barrier, or be prepared to weed it out of your lawn, walks, or patio. Lily-of-the-valley thrives in shade as well as sun. Zones 3 to 4.

Coreopsis auriculata 'Nana' (dwarf eared coreopsis) is an ideal rock garden plant in full sun. Its blossoms are orange-yellow, 2 inches across, and daisy-shaped; they bloom in June and July. Its overall height is 6 inches. Zone 5.

Dianthus spp. (pinks) have fine, soft, gray-green foliage; and their June flowers come in white, pink, scarlet, or purple tones. Sprawling and fuzzy-textured, they are lovely growing in low mounds over rocks in full sun. Zones 3 to 4.

Draba sibirica 'Repens' (Siberian draba) is a fast-growing, trailing plant, bearing large, open rosettes of leaves. Its dainty yellow flowers bloom in both spring and fall. It's attractive in rock gardens. Zone 4.

Duchesnea indica (mock strawberry) looks like a strawberry and spreads like a strawberry. Its runners create a thick mass of jagged-edged compound leaves about 2 inches off the ground, and it bears small yellow flowers. Zone 6.

Epimedium spp. (epimediums), otherwise known as barren-wort or bishop's hat, are excellent ground covers for full sun or for shade where the soil is good. Growing 6 to 12 inches high, their leaves are evergreen but turn reddish in winter. *Epimedium alpinum rubrum* has red and yellow flowers; *Epimedium pinnatum*, bright yellow; and *Epimedium youngianum*, white. Zones 4 to 6, depending on variety.

Ferns are not one genus but dozens, and I won't attempt to cover them all here. Their graceful, feathery forms and soft textures are familiar to nearly everyone. Suffice it to say that many ferns make fine ground covers for shady places, around water, or in large-scale open settings (depending on type of fern) — and that they are tough and easy to maintain once established in conditions appropriate to their needs. Some of my own favorite types are the following, all hardy in Zone 4. Hay-scented fern (*Dennstaedtia punctilobula*) is easy to grow and reaches a height of 2 to 3 feet, with fronds almost a foot across. It will thrive in most soils and it spreads by rhizomes, so it's great for shaded banks; in fact it can be somewhat invasive. Cinnamon fern (*Osmunda cinnamomea*) does well in moist soil and partial shade and grows up to 3 feet tall; in spring its curled fiddleheads are charmingly fuzzy. Royal fern (*Osmunda regalis*) is very tall — up to 6 feet — and needs an acid soil. I like to grow it beside water, where it makes sumptuous reflections. Lady fern (*Athyrium filix-femina*) is much smaller, reaching 2 feet or so, with wide, finely cut fronds. It is partial to limestone soils, well adapted to use around rocks, and no trouble to grow. Common polypody (*Polypodium vulgare*) is only about 10 inches tall, with fine-textured, evergreen fronds about 2 inches across; it's exquisite among rocky crevices and flourishes in shallow, rocky soils. Maidenhair fern (*Adiantum pedatum*) is dainty and delicate, with lacy bright green foliage on wiry stems. It grows up to 2 feet tall, and almost as wide; it likes cool, moist, shady spots, where it spreads slowly by rhizomes.

Galium odoratum (sweet woodruff), formerly known as *Asperula odorata*, bears clusters of exquisite, fragrant white flowers in May and June; its whorled leaves are sweet-scented too. Six inches tall, it is fine in texture. It flourishes in shade and does well among rhododendrons or in combination with English ivy. Zone 5.

Gypsophila repens 'Rosea' (prostrate baby's-breath) is a charming rock-garden plant with its fine, linear leaves and its low (6 inches) trailing habit. It likes full sun and a more alkaline soil if possible. Its tiny flowers are pale pink and bloom in clouds from June through July. Zone 4.

Hemerocallis spp. (daylilies): Most of these are ground covers of the tall persuasion, although there are some dwarf varieties. They grow with great vigor, sending their cheerful blooms to heights of 3 or 4 feet above their 1- or 2-foot foliage. Their flowers come in white, yellows, oranges, pinks, and reds. They don't need any care but they appreciate plenty of sun (although they tolerate partial shade). Zones 3 to 6, depending on variety.

Hosta spp. (plantain lilies): The large, glossy leaves of these durable plants come in many shades of green or variegated with white. Hostas are happy in partial shade, and produce spikes of white or purple flowers every summer no matter how resolutely you neglect them. Zone 4.

Lysimachia nummularia (creeping jenny or moneywort) is a creeping vine densely covered with small, round, flat leaves. Best suited to wet soils, it's perfect beside a pool or along a stream. It grows 2 inches high and bears abundant yellow flowers all summer. Zone 4.

Mentha requienii (creeping mint) has the smallest leaves of any mint (1/8 inch long), and it creeps along the ground, reaching a height of only 3 inches or so. It makes a delightfully scented, fine-textured ground cover for full sun and gives you a bonus of small pale-purple flowers in summer. Zone 6.

Nepeta faassenii (Persian ground-ivy): For full sun, this sprawling plant offers gray-green leaves with a wrinkly texture and bears clouds of lavender-blue bloom from May to July. It grows 8 to 12 inches high. (Sometimes offered in the trade under the name *Nepeta mussinii.*) Zone 4.

Phalaris arundinacea picta (ribbongrass) is a terrific ground cover for poor, dry soils or ornery banks in full sun. In such conditions it grows low and thick. Its leaves are attractively striped. It can be a pest if allowed to get out of control; keep it away from good moist soil and mow it down a few times a year. Zone 4.

Phlox subulata (moss pinks or ground pinks) form a 6-inch-deep mat of stiff, linear leaves. They are semi-evergreen and great for banks or rock gardens. In March they bloom profusely — white, pink, red, or blue according to variety. Zone 4.

Polygonatum biflorum (Solomon's-seal) is coarse-textured and too large for small gardens (its arching sprays are 2 to 3 feet tall); but it can be useful in full shade and moist soil. It bears pendant white bell-shaped flowers in May to June, and dark-blue fruits in fall. Zone 4.

Sagina subulata (pearlwort) is a mosslike, matted evergreen plant growing only 4 inches tall. It thrives in shade and is ideal for use among stepping stones. In July and August it produces profuse small white flowers. Zone 5.

Sanguinaria canadensis (bloodroot), a lovely ground cover for shady wooded settings, is notable not only for its red stems (and roots) but for its star-shaped white flowers, blooming in May, and its deeply cut, wavy-lobed foliage. Bloodroot grows 3 to 8 inches tall. It self-sows rapidly in the rich acid soil of its native woodlands; you can propagate it by division in spring or — preferably — fall. Zone 4.

Sasa pumila (ground bamboo) should be grown only in sun and restrained from sending out runners and taking over the landscape. Its attractive long narrow leaves reach a height of 12 inches. Zone 6.

Thymus spp. (thymes): With their fine-textured evergreen foliage and soft color, often grayish or gray-green, these aromatic plants are lovely along walks, among stepping stones, and in rock gardens in the sun. They grow very low to the ground. Many bear dainty flowers in various colors. Zones 4 to 6, depending on variety.

Tiarella cordifolia (Allegheny foam-flower) makes a wonderful ground cover for shady to partially shady places, particularly in wild or woodland gardens with rich, slightly acid soil. Its spires of white flowers bloom in April to July. Its deeply veined, jagged-edged leaves grow 6 to 12 inches from the ground. Zone 4.

Viola spp. (violets) grow 6 inches to a foot tall, with colors ranging from white to yellow to blue, violet, or rose. Their pretty heart-shaped leaves sprout in clusters, spreading joyfully in acid soil. Totally undemanding, violets flourish in partial shade. Small types are good in rock gardens; larger ones make attractive borders (if you can keep them from spreading) or woodland undergrowth. Zones 3 to 7, depending on variety.

Waldsteinia fragarioides (barren strawberry) is particularly well adapted to poor, dry soils in full sun, where it makes a flat evergreen bed of glossy strawberrylike leaves just 4 inches off the ground. Its enchanting yellow flowers bloom in May and June. Zone 5.

EVERGREEN GROUND COVERS

Arctostaphylos uva-ursi (bearberry) is a charming and sturdy fine-textured ground cover. Red berries appear in late summer and are much savored by wildlife. Happy in seaside locations and largely untroubled by pests or diseases, it thrives in poor sandy soils with very high acidity (pH 4.5 to 5.5). Its leaves are oval and a glossy dark green, turning bronze to reddish-purple. Growing under its preferred conditions, a single plant will form a dense mat up to 15 feet across. Plant bearberry on a slope or over a wall in any informal setting, in sun or partial shade.

Zone 3 / Native / 6 to 12 inches

***Cotoneaster dammeri* 'Skogsholmen'** (Skogsholmen bearberry cotoneaster) is an exceptionally vigorous variety of this sturdy semievergreen to evergreen ground cover. Creeping stems grow outward rapidly in all directions, taking root where they touch the soil and carpeting a large area in a short time. Or you can grow it espaliered against a wall, or treat it as a low shrub for banks or borders. The tiny oval leaves are a lustrous dark green, and in mild years stay on the plant (somewhat wizened) all winter. The berries are persistent and a perky bright red, but fairly sparse compared to the massed fruits of many other cotoneasters. Skogsholmen bearberry cotoneaster will put up with dry or rocky ground and even salt spray; but it will flourish and spread most briskly in fertile, peaty soil with adequate moisture.

Zone 6 / China / 1 to 1½ feet (6 or more wide)

Euonymus fortunei (wintercreeper) mutates readily and is available in countless forms. All are tolerant of sun and shade. All are evergreen, with more or less small, slightly serrated, oval or pointed-oval leaves. And all are capable of climbing or sprawling as needed, depending on variety. Wintercreeper is extremely easy to grow and to propagate from softwood cuttings; but you must watch out for and control euonymus scale, a pernicious insect that can really do a job on this plant. You can use wintercreeper as a ground cover, a vine, a low, spreading shrub, a border, or even a hedge plant. The variety *colorata* is a rambling ground cover type whose leaves turn purple in winter. Another variety, *radicans*, trails or climbs, and its glossy leaves have a wavy texture. 'Minima' is low-growing and fine-textured, with ½-inch leaves. 'Kewensis' is the smallest of all, a low-growing miniature with tiny leaves only about ¼ inch long.

Zone 5 / China / Ground cover or clinging vine

Gaultheria procumbens (wintergreen): Sometimes known as checkerberry, this is such an appealing ground cover for cool, moist situations with humusy acid soil that I include it here in case you can provide the conditions it requires. Tolerant of shade, it is lovely as a companion plant for broad-leaved evergreens or in wooded settings. It has glossy dark green leaves that turn reddish in winter, and red berries that ripen in midsummer and stay on the plant until the following spring. The leaves when crushed or chewed yield the delightful oil of wintergreen.

Zone 4 / Native / 6 inches

Hedera helix (English ivy), a familiar house plant, is also one of the most adaptable outdoor plants that exist. Like so many vines, its only failing is a slight tendency to travel where it is not wanted. It has glossy evergreen 3- to 5-lobed leaves (depending on variety), and it climbs by means of rootlets that adhere to rocks, masonry, tree trunks, or wooden structures. It will thrive in dense shade or full sun, and makes few demands except protection from the hottest sun and the coldest winds. You can use it as a vine to curtain any vertical surface, or as a spreading ground cover; or you can grow it in a container, train it as a

Hedera helix (English ivy).

shrub, or virtually anything else. A particularly hardy English ivy for northern gardens is the small-leaved variety known as *baltica*.

Zone 6 / Europe / Ground cover or clinging vine

Iberis sempervirens (evergreen candytuft) is charming in edgings, among rocks, or interplanted with flowering bulbs or among evergreen shrubs. Its lacy, fine-textured foliage is dark green, setting off the crisp white flower clusters that bloom in April and May. Candytuft is adaptable as to soil and sun, although it prefers good soil and ample sun. It's easy to propagate by softwood cuttings. It performs best if pruned heavily after flowering. Over time, it will sprawl and propagate itself (by layering) to form broad mats of foliage.

Zone 6 / Europe, Asia / 12 inches

Juniperus chinensis (Chinese juniper) in its native habitat is a slender, pyramidal tree that grows quite tall — but it is hardly ever seen in that form in the United States. Here it is the numerous cultivars that are widely known and very popular. Some are ground covers, some miniatures, some small evergreen shrubs; some make superb specimen plants, some are better suited to borders or massed plantings. The foliage is prickly and usually bluish or gray-green. Chinese junipers prefer well-drained, moist, alkaline soils and will do well in full sun or partial shade. Compact Pfitzer juniper (*Juniperus chinensis* 'Pfitzeriana Compacta') is a bushy, compact, gray-green variety. Chinese garden juniper (*Juniperus chinensis procumbens*) grows low — only up to 2 feet high — and is creeping or broadly mounding in habit. Its dense blue-green foliage makes a very handsome ground cover. A slow-growing dwarf cultivar of this same plant (*Juniperus chinensis procumbens* 'Nana') is rounded and spreading, holding its branches in flat layers; it never grows more than a foot high, and its foliage is blue-green and mosslike in texture. Another low ground cover or rock garden plant, Sargent juniper (*Juniperus chinensis sargentii*), has grass-green to blue-green foliage and is great for poor dry soils or seaside planting.

Zone 5 / China, Mongolia, Japan / All sizes

Juniperus horizontalis (creeping juniper), which comes in a vast assortment of cultivated varieties, is an enormously useful evergreen ground cover for difficult situations. It will happily take command almost anywhere, from an arid, rocky bank to an exposed, wind-chilled city corner lot. It derives its sturdy tenacity from its origins on and around North America's swamps, seaside cliffs, and gravelly slopes. Low-growing, fibrous-rooted, with a strong inclination to take over the landscape, creeping juniper flourishes in any soil. Its fine-textured and somewhat prickly foliage is a bluish gray-green, turning violet in the winter. The variety known as Andorra juniper (*Juniperus horizontalis* 'Plumosa') is a flat-topped and fast-spreading ground cover. 'Bar Harbor' is a ground-hugging creeper with a top height of 1 foot.

Zone 4 / Native / 1 to 2 feet (spreading)

Leucothoe fontanesiana (drooping leucothoe): See Broad-leaved Evergreens.

Mitchella repens (partridgeberry): This is a familiar Christmastime gift plant, sold in florists' shops in decorative glass bowls or rings; but paradoxically it is one of the most difficult ground covers to establish in the residential landscape. It is really at home only in wild woodlands. It needs moist, acid soil with some shade and plenty of humus. If you have the conditions it needs, partridgeberry makes a fine-textured low-growing ground cover. Its glossy white-veined leaves are dainty year round; it has tiny pinkish-white flowers in spring and summer; and in fall it bears sprightly scarlet berries that last into the winter.

Zone 4 / Native / 2 inches

Pachysandra terminalis (Japanese spurge or pachysandra:) Almost everyone is familiar with this indomitable, maintenance-free evergreen ground cover. It is happiest in light to deep shade, where it spreads rapidly by means of underground stolons and successfully crowds out all would-be weeds, forming a thick, dark green carpet of lustrous foliage. Japanese spurge tolerates many soils but ideally prefers well-drained acid soils with adequate moisture and lots of organic matter. With good soil, it has no objection to city surroundings.

Zone 5 / Japan / 6 to 12 inches

Paxistima canbyi (Canby paxistima): See Broad-leaved Evergreens.

Sedum acre (goldmoss stonecrop) is just one of over 300 species of *Sedum*. This is a hardy, tiny-leaved, mat-forming plant for use among rocks or around steps, or in any sunny spot where you want a sprightly ground cover with a soft, mossy texture. Its foliage is light green, and it bears small bright yellow flowers from late May through June. Goldmoss stonecrop is an eager spreader, even in poor soil, and very easy to propagate by division or cuttings.

Zone 4 / Europe, Asia / 2 inches

Sedum spurium (two-row stonecrop) creeps along the ground to create a dense mat of stems and foliage. It is one of the hardiest and best all-around ground covers for dry, sunny, exposed locations, being semievergreen and very pretty to look at in bloom. Its rounded leaves turn red in winter. Its 2-inch clusters of pink flowerets blossom in July to August. It spreads energetically, or you can easily multiply it by cuttings or division.

Zone 4 / Asia Minor / 3 to 6 inches

Sempervivum tectorum (houseleeks, or hens-and-chickens) look wonderful growing around steps, among rocks, or as a ground cover in any small-scale situation that lets you enjoy them close up. They are succulents shaped like rose blossoms. Each larger plant or "hen" (they grow up to 4 inches across) surrounds itself with various sizes of small plantlets or "chickens," and they make a tight ground-covering mass. The gray-green leaves are edged with reddish or purplish tones. The pink flowers bloom on tall fuzzy stalks. Given sun and good drainage, houseleeks will happily survive total neglect in the most exposed locations. You can also pot them up in fall to use as houseplants.

Zone 5 / Europe and Asia / 4 to 12 inches

Vinca minor (vinca, periwinkle, or myrtle) is another very well-known and long-loved evergreen ground cover. It can be slow to establish, but once settled in conditions to its liking it makes a beautiful carpet of fine-textured, lustrous, dark-green foliage. The dainty late-April flowers of the species are lilac-blue, and there are cultivars available in many shades of white, blue, and purple. Set vinca plants 1 foot apart in light or partial shade; and give them good, humusy, well-drained soil for best results.

Zone 5 / Europe and Western Asia / 3 to 6 inches

DECIDUOUS VINES

Akebia quinata (five-leaf akebia): Hardy, vigorous to the point of aggressiveness, and charming both in foliage and in flower, this twining vine will rapidly cover anything you allow it to: banks, walls, trellises, or even other shrubbery. Keep it within bounds. It has no insect or disease problems. The dainty 2- or 3-inch oval leaves are held in clusters of 5 and are a deep, rich green, keeping their color late into the fall. (In warm climates, in fact, they are evergreen.) Give five-leaf akebia deep, rich soil and room to grow in.

Zone 5 / China, Korea, Japan / Twining vine

Ampelopsis brevipedunculata (porcelainberry or porcelain ampelopsis): The great claim to fame of this vine is its fruit, which ripens in September and October. Each cluster may include berries of lavender, yellow, and the final vivid blue. The dark green leaves are 3-lobed like grape leaves. Porcelainberry grows well in any well-drained soil. It should be given something to climb over. It will fruit best in full sun and if the spread of its roots is restricted.

Zone 5 / China, Korea, Japan / Climbing vine

Campsis radicans (common trumpet creeper) produces clusters of gorgeous red-orange trumpet-shaped flowers in midsummer. The compound leaves are bright green and relatively fine-textured. If you have wet soil, dry soil, or any other problem conditions and need a durable climbing plant, this vine may be for you. It will grow practically anywhere and is definitely of the rampant persuasion. It grows into such a thick, heavy mass that it requires some support in addition to its own small rootlike holdfasts. It's easy to propagate.

Zone 5 / Native / Clinging vine

Celastrus scandens (bittersweet, or American bittersweet) is a fast-growing vine about which some people have mixed feelings. (Maybe that's why it is called bittersweet.) For all its virtues, it can be a menace to the landscape: it will swarm over every plant or structure in sight if it's not kept firmly under control. This means cutting it back at least once a year. I grow mine on a 7-foot post to keep it contained. Bittersweet is, however, adaptable to virtually any soil. And birds love it for its berries. The berries are bright yellow, and when fully ripe they split open to reveal a crimson seed inside; they make a popular addition to dried arrangements for the house. If you do decide to acquire some bittersweet, be sure the nursery labels the plants as to sex — because you won't get any berries at all unless you have both a female bittersweet and a male.

Zone 4 / Native / Twining vine

Clematis dioscoreifolia robusta (sweet autumn clematis): Formerly known as *Clematis paniculata*, this clematis bears fragrant white flowers in August and September. The cascades of feathery blossoms engulf the vine, and the vine has a habit of engulfing everything else. This is a vigorous grower that forms a lush mass of lustrous semievergreen foliage. If you can keep it from taking over the landscape, sweet autumn clematis is a very easy plant to grow; it positively thrives on neglect.

Zone 6 / Japan / Climbing vine

Clematis montana rubens (pink anemone clematis) bears its lavish rosy-red flowers in June, when it is a real showpiece in the landscape. It will grow into a bower of foliage over a trellis, fence, wall, or any structure that affords support for the twining tendrillike leaf stalks. Clematis flourishes best when it is given cool roots (a well-drained soil and ample mulch), and it needs at least some shade during the day. If you have to prune it, keep in mind that it blooms on the previous year's wood.

Zone 6 / Himalayas, China / Climbing vine

Euonymus fortunei (wintercreeper): See Evergreen Ground Covers.

Hedera helix (English ivy): See Evergreen Ground Covers.

Hydrangea anomala petiolaris (climbing hydrangea): This coarse-textured, vigorous climber is marvelous in large-scale settings where the masses and textures can support a hefty vine like this one. The resplendent white flower clusters appear in June. The leaves are an elegant, deep, glossy green. Leaves and flowers are borne on lateral branches that reach out 1 to 3 feet from the main stems. The whole plant can grow upwards as much as 60 or 80 feet; or it will clamber over a wall, trellis, or other free-standing structure. The weight of climbing hydrangea means that it must be given sturdy support if it's to go far. The vine is dramatic even in winter, when you can see its layered meshes of twigs all covered in shaggy exfoliating cinnamon-brown bark. Climbing hydrangea does best in deep, rich, moist, well-drained soil in eastern or northern exposures.

Zone 5 / China, Japan / 60 to 80 feet

Lonicera henryi (Henry honeysuckle) is a vine form of honeysuckle that makes an easy-care, sweetly scented ground cover without quite the rampant runaway qualities of some of its relatives. Nevertheless, it is vigorous enough so that you have to watch it and possibly cut it back from time to time. Its small oval leaves and thin, flexible stems develop into a dense tangle on the ground. The flowers are yellow to purplish red and bloom from June to August; the fruits that follow are black and well liked by wildlife. This honeysuckle tolerates some shade and many different soils; it cannot stand boggy situations, however. It is happiest with ample sun and well-drained, loamy soil.

Zone 5 / China / Twining vine

***Lonicera japonica* 'Halliana'** (Hall's honeysuckle) can be a menace if it gets out of control, rampaging over the landscape and smothering any tree or shrub it gets a purchase on. But there is just nothing like it for shrouding a fence, bank, or other barrier in dense dark-green foliage — with the added attraction of deliciously fragrant creamy-white flowers that perfume the air and delight the bees all summer long. This vigorous vine likes any loamy, well-drained soil but cannot tolerate wet situations. It is happiest in full sun. If it threatens to outgrow its intended site, cut it back ruthlessly: it can take it.

Zone 5 / Japan / Twining vine

Parthenocissus quinquefolia (Virginia creeper or woodbine) This vine is so tough and resilient that one friend of mine complains it's impossible to kill. If you use it appropriately, however, you shouldn't want to kill it. It holds on to any surface (it provides its own cement) so it makes a great "drapery" to add softness and color to walls. Its 5-part leaves are lustrous green in summer and change to rich purple-scarlet in early fall. Often, in fact, that first dab of red at the top of an old oak tree will be Virginia creeper, not oak. After the leaves fall — which they seem to do all at once, making a glowing carpet on the ground — you can see the small, blue-black berries that give the vine such a high rating with birds. The cultivar called Engelmann woodbine (*Parthenocissus quinquefolia* 'Engelmannii') is an attractive smaller-leaved version.

Zone 4 / Native / Climbing vine

Parthenocissus tricuspidata (Boston ivy): Neither an ivy nor native to Boston, this handsome clinging vine came to this country from the Orient. It achieved some slight publicity in 1982, when acres of it were stripped from the walls of the buildings of Harvard University so that old bricks could be repointed (the ivy's adhesive rootlets had not done the masonry any good), which deprived the campus of a hundred-year-old leafy look. The large, 3-lobed, glossy leaves of Boston ivy make a richly textured tapestry that undulates in the breeze. The blue fruits are greatly relished by birds. The leaves are most gorgeous in the fall, when they turn a deep ruby red. Then they drop, leaving a flat tracery of slender stems. This is a fine and indestructible plant for trellises where you want light to filter through in winter, as well as for walls or other stone surfaces. It will flourish in any soil and in any exposure at all. For smaller leaves and a finer texture, the cultivar 'Lowii' is a good choice.

Zone 5 / China, Japan / Climbing vine

Polygonum aubertii (Chinese fleece vine, or silver fleece vine) will completely blanket an unsightly fence with its bright green foliage in a matter of months. It is an irrepressibly energetic twining vine and can grow as much as 15 feet in one season. It offers the added feature of fragrant greenish-white flowers, borne in dense clusters in August. Chinese fleece vine will grow almost anywhere and in any amount of sun or shade. It spreads so rapidly (by rhizomes) that it can become a pest, but it's a useful workhorse where it can be contained.

Zone 5 / China / Twining vine

***Vitis* spp.** (grapes): For ornamental use, grape vines are a long shot in most settings. The hardy native fox grape (*Vitis labrusca*) is a ruthless smotherer that — much though the birds love it — I can't recommend for any landscape. Other species are somewhat more docile, and some gardeners like them for training over trellises, along fences, or over steep banks. Grapes are fast-growing and tough, with dense, coarse-textured foliage, picturesquely twisting stems, and papery reddish-brown bark. They are happy in well-drained or even dry soils and in partial shade to full sun (although for fruit they demand ample sun). The real joy of grapes, to me, is to have a trellis where you can shape and prune a fruiting vine. (See instructions in the January Landscape Tasks.) There are many marvelous strains adapted to Zones 5 and 6, often hybridized with *Vitis labrusca* for hardiness and vigor. Your nursery can suggest possibilities for your soil and exposure. With just a little care you'll have grape leaves for stuffing and a shady bower for sitting in all summer long — and with a little more care, a mouth-watering crop for juice, jelly, and eating fresh off the vine in September.

Zones 5 to 6 / Native, Oriental, and European / Clinging vine

Wisteria floribunda (Japanese wisteria): This magnificent flowering vine makes a potent statement throughout the year. Its twining, twisted trunks are picturesque in winter; they grow very thick and gnarled in old age. Its leaves come out in late spring and are a bright yellowish-green. Its foot-long dangling clusters of purple flowers emerge about the same time as the leaves; they are breathtaking to see and almost overwhelmingly fragrant, although you should not count on them to bloom until the plant is around 7 years old. For best flowering, give wisteria full sun and a soil not too rich in nitrogen, but fertilize occasionally with phosphate. Since this is a fast-growing and eventually a very massive plant, give it a metal-pipe support or trellis: it can destroy wooden structures. It can also be trained (with support) to grow like a tree. Cultivars with different colored flowers include 'Alba' (white) and 'Rosea' (pink).

Zone 5 / Japan / Twining vine

FURTHER REFERENCE

The brief book list that follows includes some of my favorite standbys as well as books that are periodically updated to provide state-of-the-art information. All the works listed are widely available at bookstores, garden centers, and supply centers, or directly from their publishers. I do encourage you to seek advice from your local nurseryman or garden center; but if you have more questions than they have time to field, you may want to explore the literature.

The best all-around general garden encyclopedia:

Wyman, Donald. *Wyman's Gardening Encyclopedia*. Revised and Expanded Edition. New York: Macmillan, 1977.

Other encyclopedic works that you may want to consult:

Bush-Brown, James and Louise. *America's Garden Book*. Revised by the New York Botanical Garden. New York: Scribner's, 1980. I actually prefer the earlier editions, which are out of print (but available in libraries); but there is more up-to-date information in the recent one. I used to visit the Bush-Browns when I was in college, and they and their book were a wonderful inspiration.

Taylor, Norman, ed. *Taylor's Encyclopedia of Gardening*, Fourth edition. Boston: Houghton Mifflin, 1976.

Simon and Schuster's Step-by-Step Encyclopedia of Practical Gardening. Christopher Brickell, Editor-in-Chief. New York: Simon and Schuster, 1979–1981. Includes *Fruit*; *Gardening Techniques*; *Garden Pests and Diseases*; *Plant Propagation*; and *Lawns, Ground Cover & Weed Control*.

The best sources for specific topics in gardening, design, and construction are series of handbooks to which new titles are frequently added:

Brooklyn Botanic Garden Record/Plants & Gardens. Quarterly publication of Brooklyn Botanic Garden, Brooklyn, N.Y. 11225. Scores of these compact, inexpensive, largely black-and-white booklets are in print, ranging from soils and mulches to trees and shrubs to small-space gardens to garden structures to specialties like roses and bonsai. Catalogue available from BBG.

Time-Life Encyclopedia of Gardening. Alexandria, Va.: Time-Life Books, numerous dates. Over thirty titles on every aspect of landscape gardening from ground covers to design.

Ortho Books (San Francisco, Cal. 94119), a division of Chevron Chemical Company, puts out colorful paperback guides. Among the many titles available are *Award-Winning Small-Space Gardens*; *Do-It-Yourself Garden Construction Know-How*; *All About Fertilizers, Soils & Water*; *All About Growing Fruits and Berries*; *All About Roses*; and *Gardening with Color*.

Sunset Magazine has a book series (published by Lane Publishing Co., Menlo Park, Cal. 94025) that includes *Azaleas, Rhododendrons, Camellias*; *Lawns & Ground Covers*; *Gardening in Containers*; *How to Grow Roses*; *Pruning Handbook*; *How to Build Fences & Gates*; *Sunset Ideas for Patios & Decks*; *Bonsai*; and *Swimming Pools*.

U.S. Government Printing Office (Washington, D.C. 20402) offers a huge variety of inexpensive publications. The two best Subject Bibliographies (catalogues) in the landscaping area are SB-301, *Gardening*; and SB-041, *The Home*. You'll find helpful titles on construction, pest control, cultivation of all kinds of plants, choosing ornamental and fruiting trees and shrubs, attracting birds, and a host of other topics.

It goes without saying that your gardening library should include:

Crockett, James Underwood. *Crockett's Flower Garden*. Boston: Little, Brown, 1981.

———. *Crockett's Victory Garden*. Boston: Little, Brown, 1977.

For general reading and inspiration:

Jekyll, Gertrude. *Wood and Garden. Wall and Water Gardens. Color Schemes for the Flower Garden. The Home and the Garden. Roses*. Topsfield, Mass.: Merrimac Book Service/Antique Collectors Club, reissued 1982–1984. These are classics, written at the turn of the century and now reprinted. Gertrude Jekyll's style is endearing and her artistry and botanical expertise are unexcelled.

For the garden design connoisseur with the utmost patience:

Hubbard, Henry V. and Kimball, Theodora. *An Introduction to the Study of Landscape Design*. Revised Edition. Boston: Hubbard Educational Trust, 1959. The first book of required reading I encountered in my training, and still one of my favorites.

ZONE MAP

The hardiness zones mapped by the U.S. Department of Agriculture (USDA), shown here, are the ones you are most likely to encounter in gardening books and plantsmen's catalogues. (Some sources list plant hardiness according to the slightly different system of the Arnold Arboretum of Harvard University; just be aware of which set of zones you are working with.) The annual minimum temperature ranges of the USDA zones are listed here. These ranges are approximate and subject to many exceptions, however, as are the demarcations between zones.

Not represented on this map are the average dates of first and last frost for different areas. These vary widely from year to year. They also differ from one place to another, even within a single neighborhood. Some very general indications of spring and fall planting seasons for lawns, trees, and shrubs appear on page 72; but for your particular piece of land, you'll do best to rely on your own experience and that of knowledgeable neighbors.

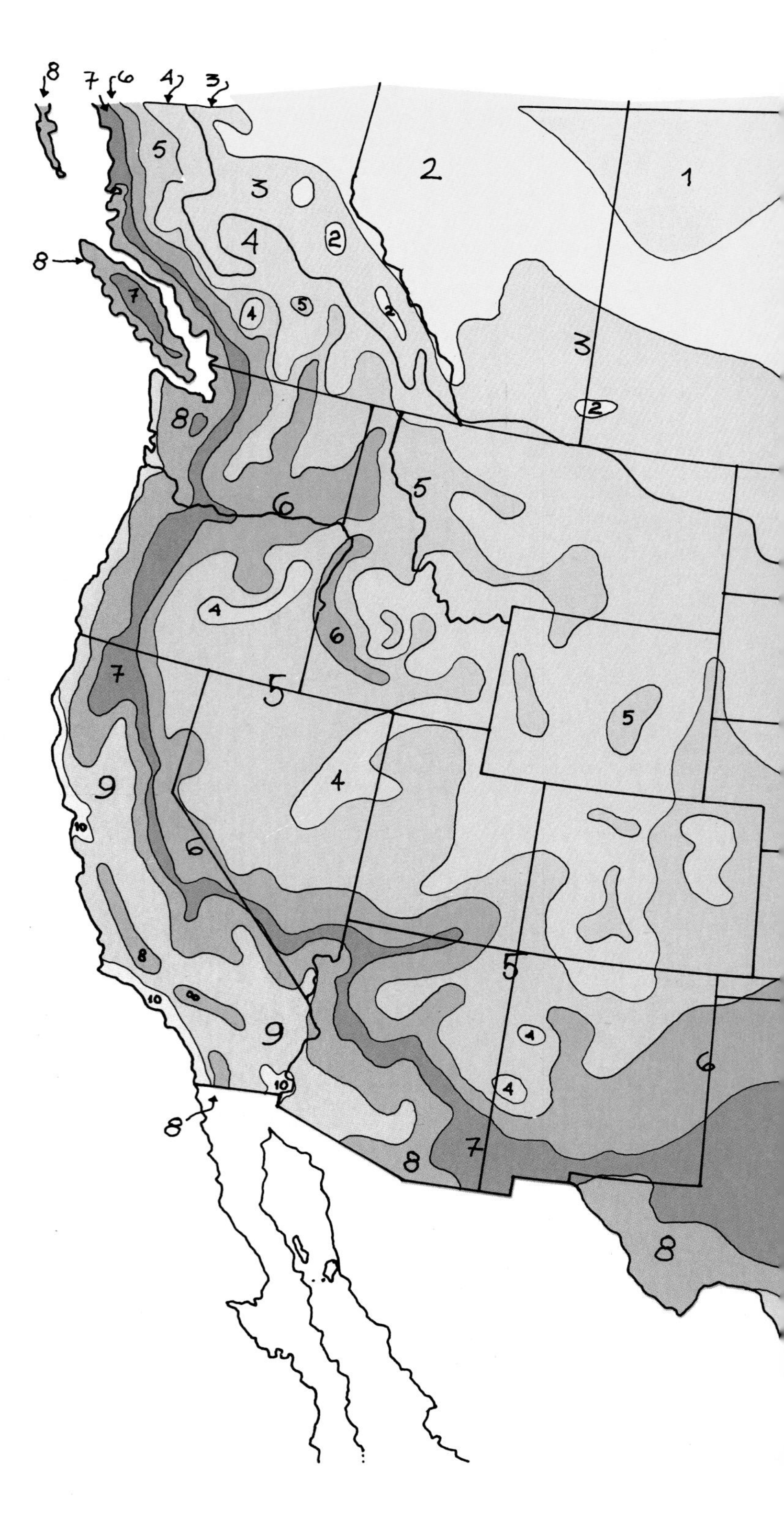

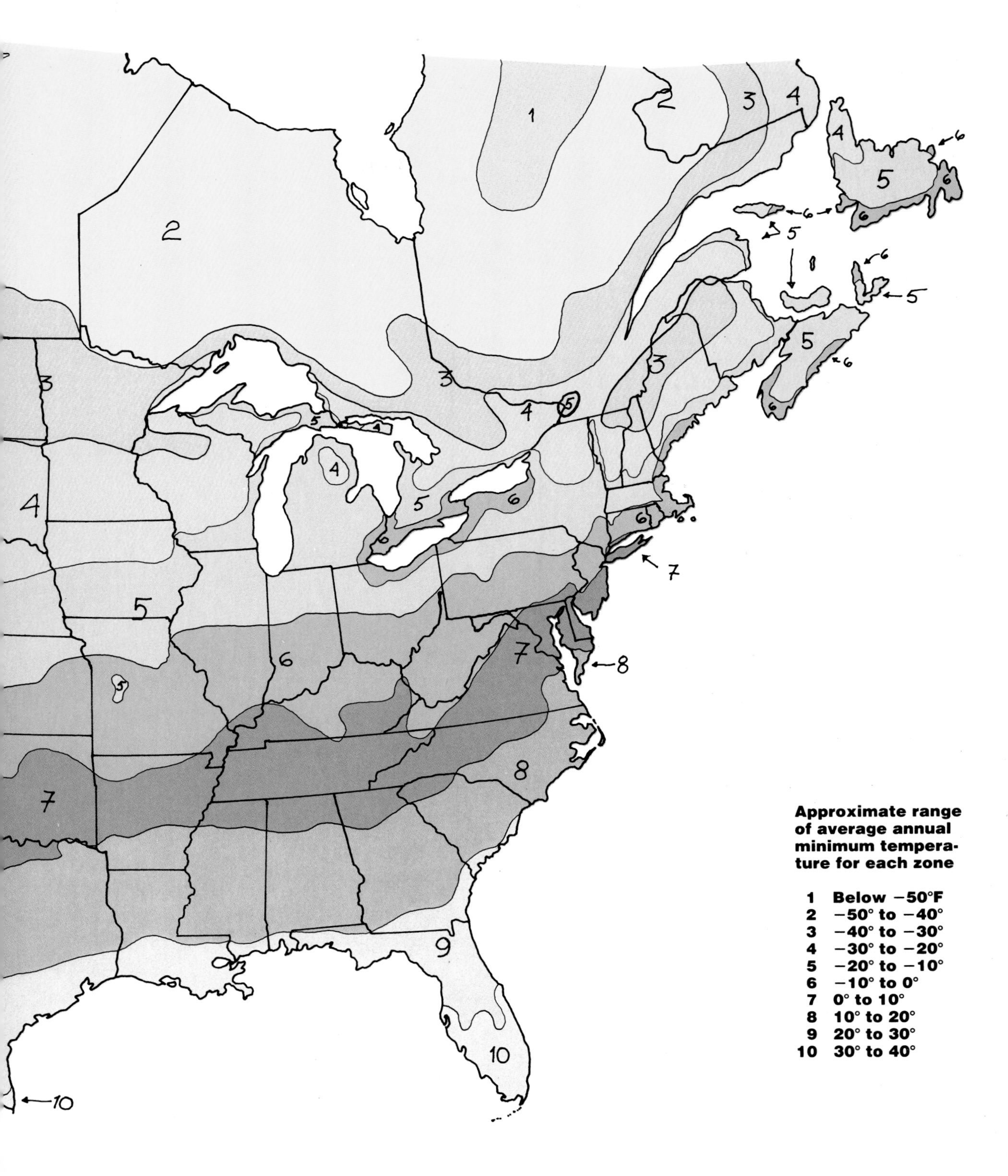
Approximate range of average annual minimum temperature for each zone
1 Below −50°F
2 −50° to −40°
3 −40° to −30°
4 −30° to −20°
5 −20° to −10°
6 −10° to 0°
7 0° to 10°
8 10° to 20°
9 20° to 30°
10 30° to 40°

INDEX

Numbers in italics indicate an illustration or photograph of the subject. Boldface numbers indicate the complete plant description in Part III.

C

CREDITS

Photographers

All photos in this book are by David M. Stone, except as follows:

Masao Kinoshita, pages 212–213.

Michael Lutch, title page, page 170.

Russell Morash, pages 91, 204 (left).

Christopher Pullman, pages 34, 61, 253.

James Radabaugh, page 200.

Bill Schwob, page 67.

Thomas Wirth, pages 12, 18, 21, 23, 28 (bottom left and right), 29 (top), 30, 31, 43, 50, 80–81, 82, 88, 89, 93, 96–97, 98, 107, 110, 119, 120 (top right), 136–137, 140 (right), 141, 144, 156–157, 161, 162 (top), 170 (bottom), 171 (right), 176–177, 179 (bottom), 183, 184 (left), 185, 187 (left), 189, 196–197, 203, 205 (right), 208, 223, 226–227, 230 (right), 248, 252 (left), 262–263, 267, 275 (top right), 276, 278–279, 283, 284, 289, 292, 298, 302.

Wesley Wirth, page 205 (left).

Landscape Architects

J. Walter Brain, pages 140 (left), 147.

Harriett W. Long, page 208.

Alice Page Pickman, pages 90 (left), 271, 280.

Michael Van Valkenburgh, page 219.

David Engel, pages 29 (top), 82.

Organizations

Helpful with various phases of preparation of the book have been:

F. Diehl & Son

MacDowell Company

The New England Wildflower Society

Seaward Inn

Weston Nurseries

The Grower's Market, Inc.